Ready® Classroom Mathematics

Grade 2 • Volume 2

Curriculum Associates

NOT FOR RESALE

978-1-4957-8035-6

North Billerica, MA 01862

5 6 7 8 9 10 11 12 13 14 15 21 20

BTS20

Contents

UNIT 1

Numbers Within 20
Addition, Subtraction, and Data

UNIT 2

Numbers Within 100
Addition, Subtraction, Time, and Money

UNIT 3

Numbers Within 1,000

Place Value, Addition, and Subtraction

UNIT 4

Length

Measurement, Addition and Subtraction, and Line Plots

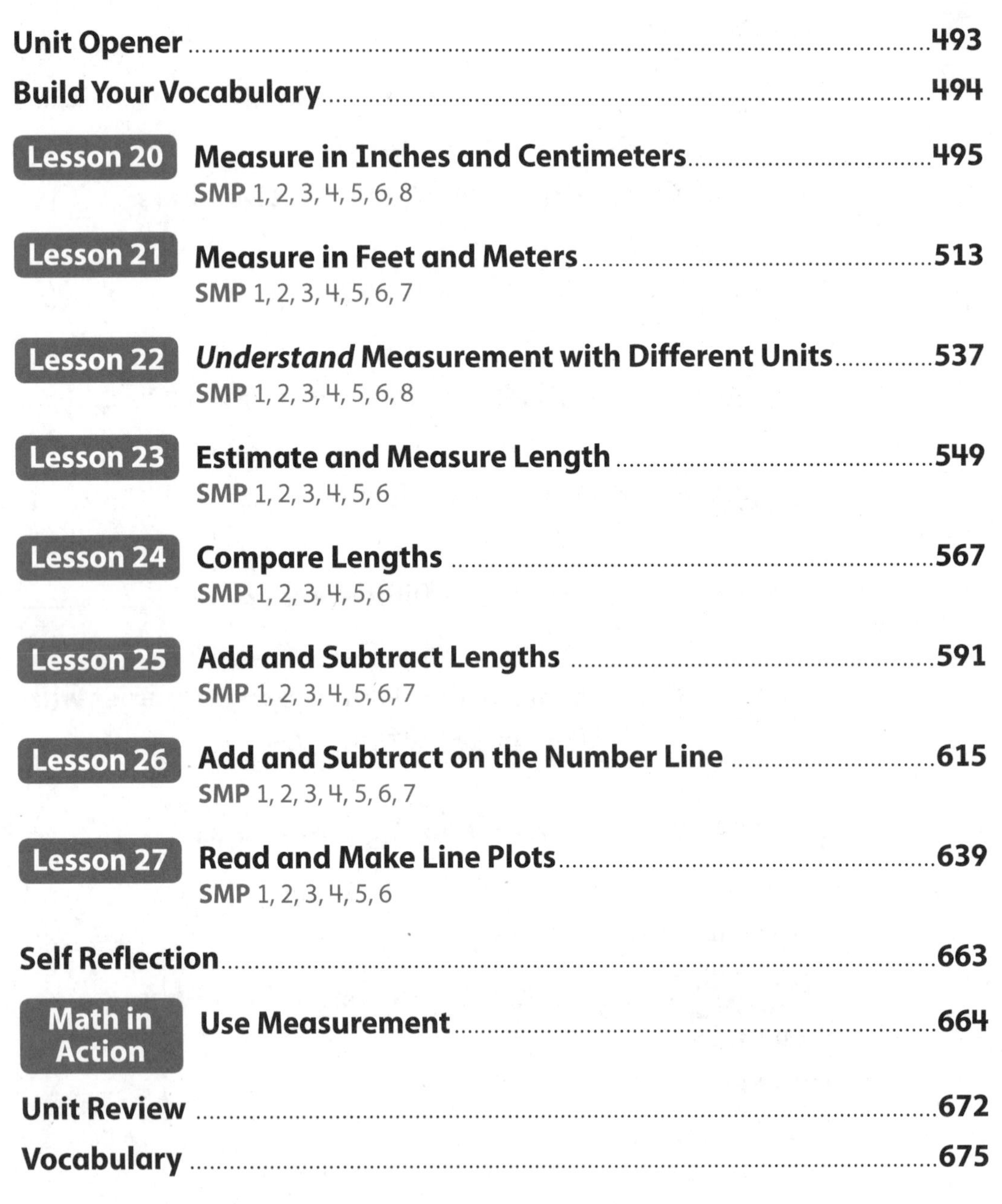

UNIT 5

Shapes and Arrays

Partitioning and Tiling Shapes, Arrays, Evens and Odds

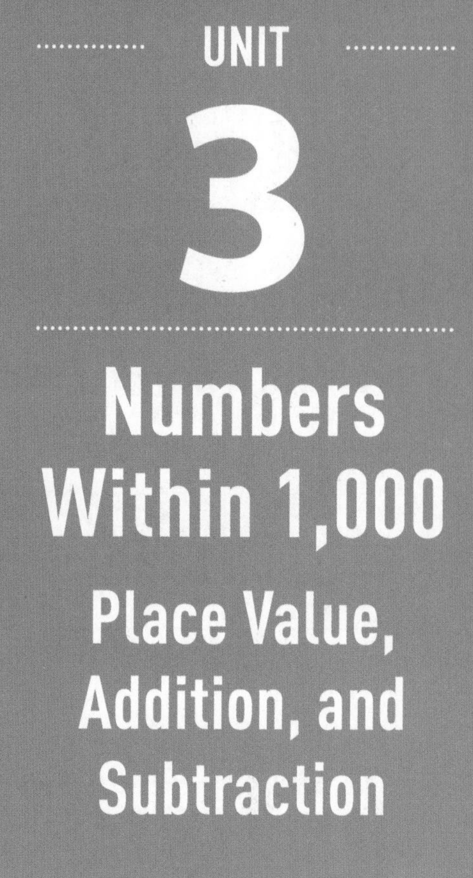

UNIT

3

Numbers Within 1,000

Place Value, Addition, and Subtraction

SELF CHECK

Before starting this unit, check off the skills you know below. As you complete each lesson, see how many more skills you can check off!

I can . . .	Before	After
Build three-digit numbers in different ways.	☐	☐
Read and write three-digit numbers.	☐	☐
Compare three-digit numbers.	☐	☐
Add 10 or 100 to a number.	☐	☐
Add three-digit numbers.	☐	☐
Subtract three-digit numbers.	☐	☐
Use different strategies to add and subtract three-digit numbers.	☐	☐
Add more than 2 two-digit numbers.	☐	☐

UNIT 3

Build Your Vocabulary

REVIEW

column
greater than (>)
less than (<)
place value

Math Vocabulary

Work with a partner to compare tens and ones.

Tens	Ones

Compare tens

.... tens is .... than .... tens

.... tens ○ .... tens

Tens	Ones

Compare ones

.... ones is .... than .... ones

.... ones ○ .... ones

Academic Vocabulary

Put a check next to the academic words you know. Then use the words to complete the sentences.

☐ apply ☐ include ☐ argument ☐ method

1. The crafts we made .... many types of materials such as paper, glue, and fabric.

2. Even though I used a different .... , I got the same answer.

3. I .... addition strategies when counting money.

4. I can make an .... in math and defend my answer by showing my work.

Understand Three-Digit Numbers

LESSON 12

Dear Family,

This week your child is exploring three-digit numbers.

The first three-digit number is 100. It is the same as 100 ones, 10 tens, or 1 hundred.

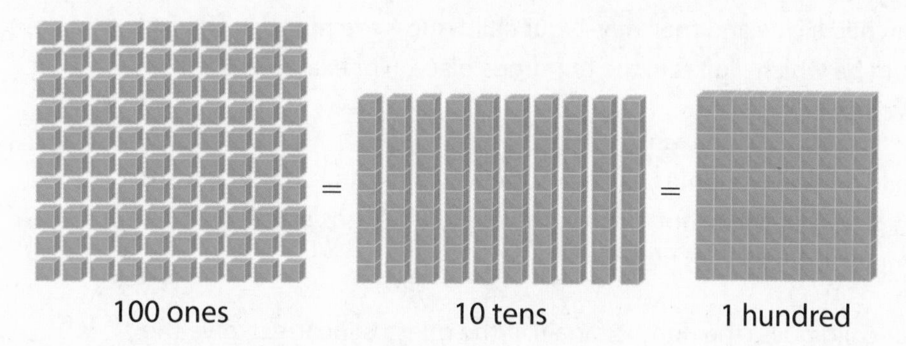

Three-digit numbers have a **hundreds** place, a tens place, and a ones place. A chart can show the **place value** of the digits.

	Hundreds	Tens	Ones
387	3	8	7

The hundreds place tells how many hundreds are in the number, the tens place tells how many tens, and the ones place tells how many ones.

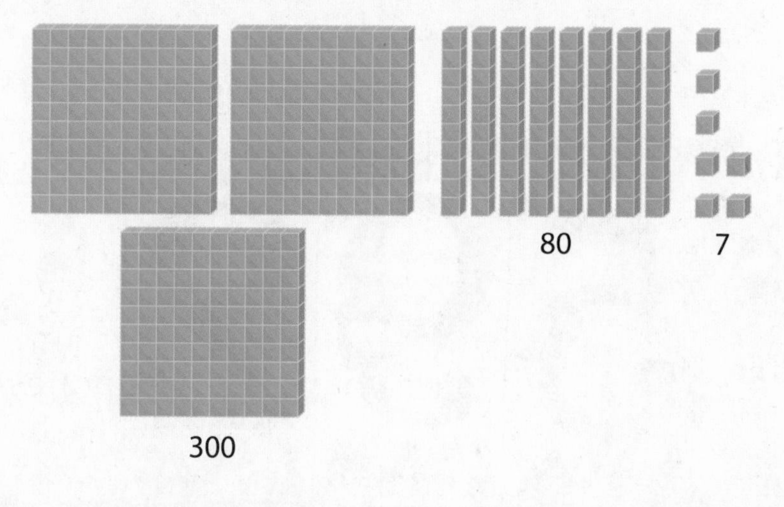

Invite your child to explain what he or she knows about three-digit numbers by doing the following activity together.

ACTIVITY HUNDREDS

Do this activity with your child to understand three-digit numbers.

Play the Guess My Number game.

- Think of a three-digit number. (For example, 592)
- Give your child a clue and then have your child guess the number. The first clue should be which digit is in the hundreds place. (For example: *5 is in the hundreds place.*)
- If your child guesses your number, he or she wins the game. If the guess is incorrect, give your child another clue, the digit in the tens place. (For example: *9 is in the tens place.*)
- Have your child guess the number again. If the guess is incorrect, give the final clue, the digit in the ones place. (For example: *2 is in the ones place.*)
- Encourage your child to use a place-value chart to keep track of the clues and write the number.

Hundreds	Tens	Ones
5	9	2

- Play the game again and have your child pick the number and give the clues.

Explore Three-Digit Numbers

What is one hundred?

Learning Targets

- 100 can be thought of as a bundle of ten tens – called a "hundred."
- The numbers 100, 200, 300, 400, 500, 600, 700, 800, 900 refer to one, two, three four, five, six, seven, eight, or nine hundreds (and 0 tens and 0 ones).

SMP 1, 2, 3, 4, 5, 6, 7

MODEL IT

Fill in the blanks below.

1. Show 90 in different ways.

90 is .... ones. 90 is .... tens.

2. Show 100 in different ways.

100 is .... ones. 100 is .... tens.

100 is .... hundred.

DISCUSS IT

- How are the ways of showing 100 different? How are they the same? Do you and your partner agree?
- I think counting to 100 by tens is easier than counting by ones because . . .

MODEL IT

Fill in the blanks below.

3 Look at the blocks below.

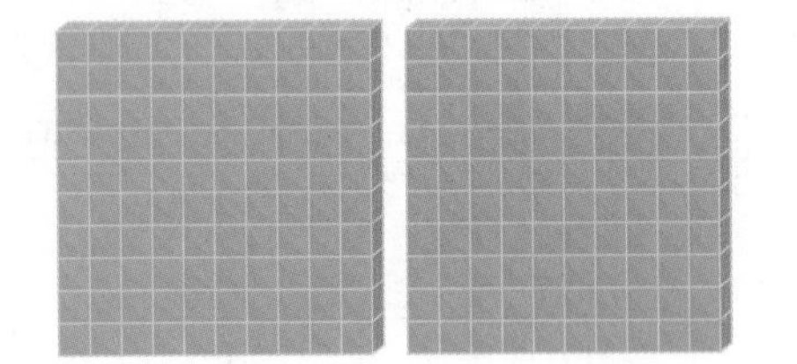

The blocks show .... **hundreds**.

4 Think about ways to show 200 using **place value**.

0 hundreds + 0 tens + ... ones

0 hundreds + ... tens + 0 ones

.... hundreds + 0 tens + 0 ones

5 REFLECT

Explain how you know that 19 tens is less than 200.

....

....

....

....

DISCUSS IT

- How did you and your partner decide how many ones, tens, and hundreds would complete the statements?
- I think 20 tens and 2 hundreds are different because . . .
- I think 20 tens and 2 hundreds are similar because . . .

Name: ____________________

Prepare for Exploring Three-Digit Numbers

1. Think about what you know about three-digit numbers. Fill in each box. Use words, numbers, and pictures. Show as many ideas as you can.

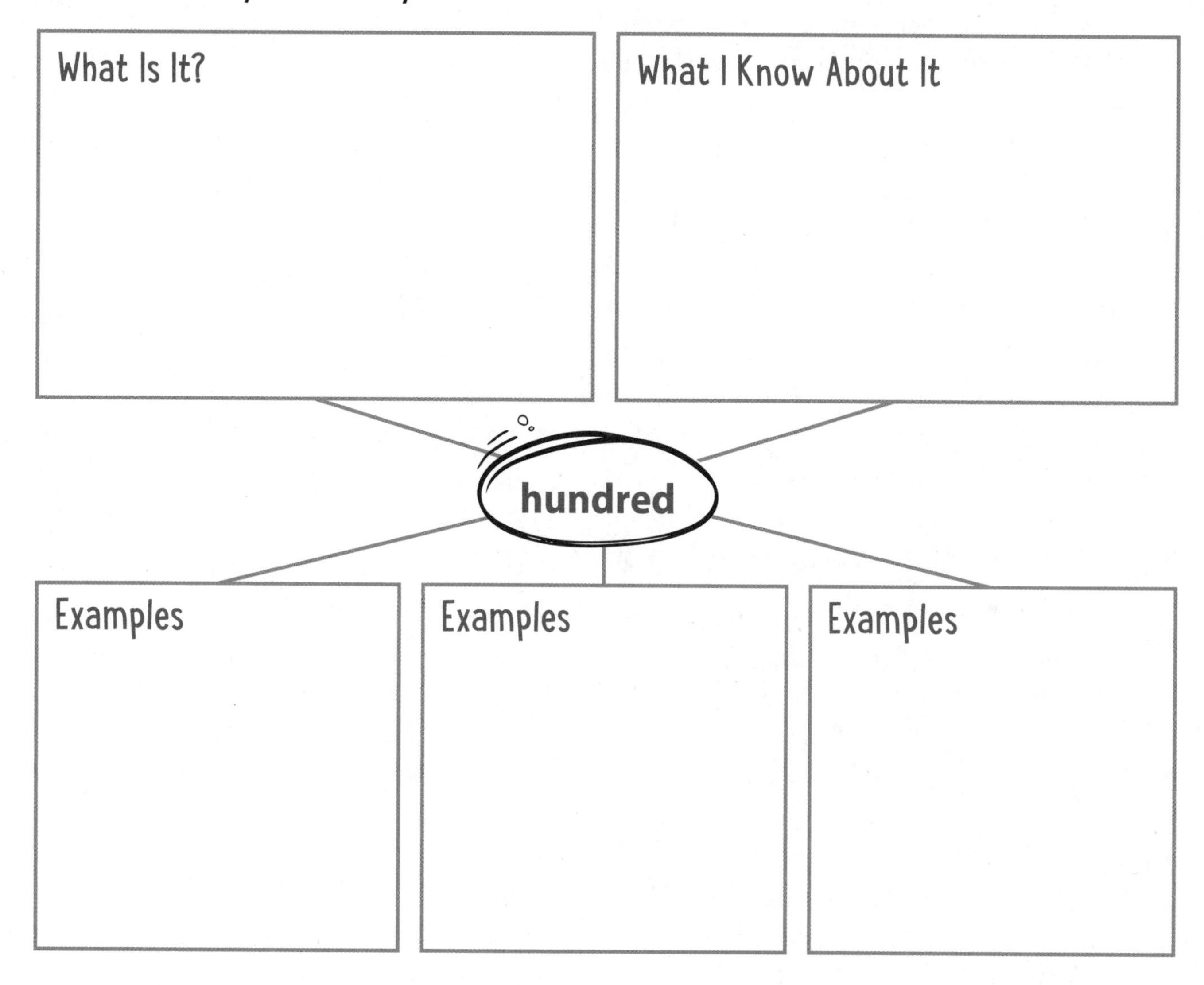

2. What do the zeros represent in 100?

Solve.

 Fill in the blank below.

The blocks show ______ hundreds.

4 Think about ways to show 300.

0 hundreds + 0 tens + ______ ones

0 hundreds + ______ tens + 0 ones

______ hundreds + 0 tens + 0 ones

5 What do the zeros represent in 300?

____

____

____

____

Develop Understanding of Three-Digit Numbers

MODEL IT: BASE-TEN BLOCKS

Try these four problems.

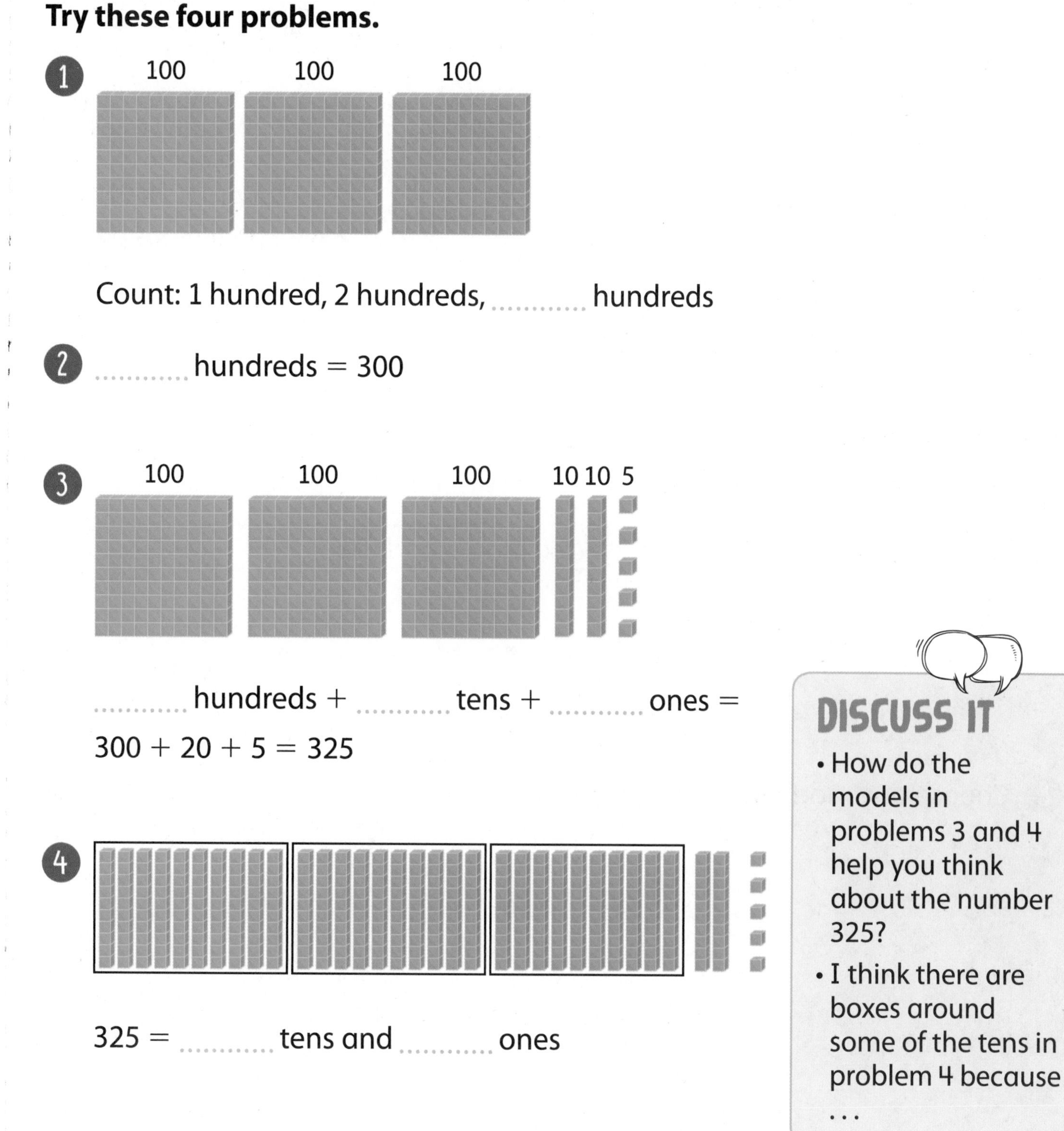

1. Count: 1 hundred, 2 hundreds, ... hundreds

2. .... hundreds = 300

3. .... hundreds + ... tens + ... ones =
   300 + 20 + 5 = 325

4. 325 = ... tens and .... ones

DISCUSS IT

- How do the models in problems 3 and 4 help you think about the number 325?
- I think there are boxes around some of the tens in problem 4 because . . .

MODEL IT: PLACE-VALUE CHART

Write hundreds, tens, and ones in a place-value chart.

5 3 hundreds + 0 tens + 0 ones

Hundreds	Tens	Ones

 3 hundreds + 2 tens + 5 ones

Hundreds	Tens	Ones

DISCUSS IT

- How did you know how many ones to show in the chart for problem 6?
- I think zeros are sometimes used in a place-value chart because . . .

CONNECT IT

Complete the problems below.

 What is the same about the base-ten blocks and the place-value chart for 325?

 Choose any model you like to show 606.

Name: ____________________

Practice Thinking About Three-Digit Numbers

Study how the Example shows counting hundreds, tens, and ones. Then solve problems 1–6.

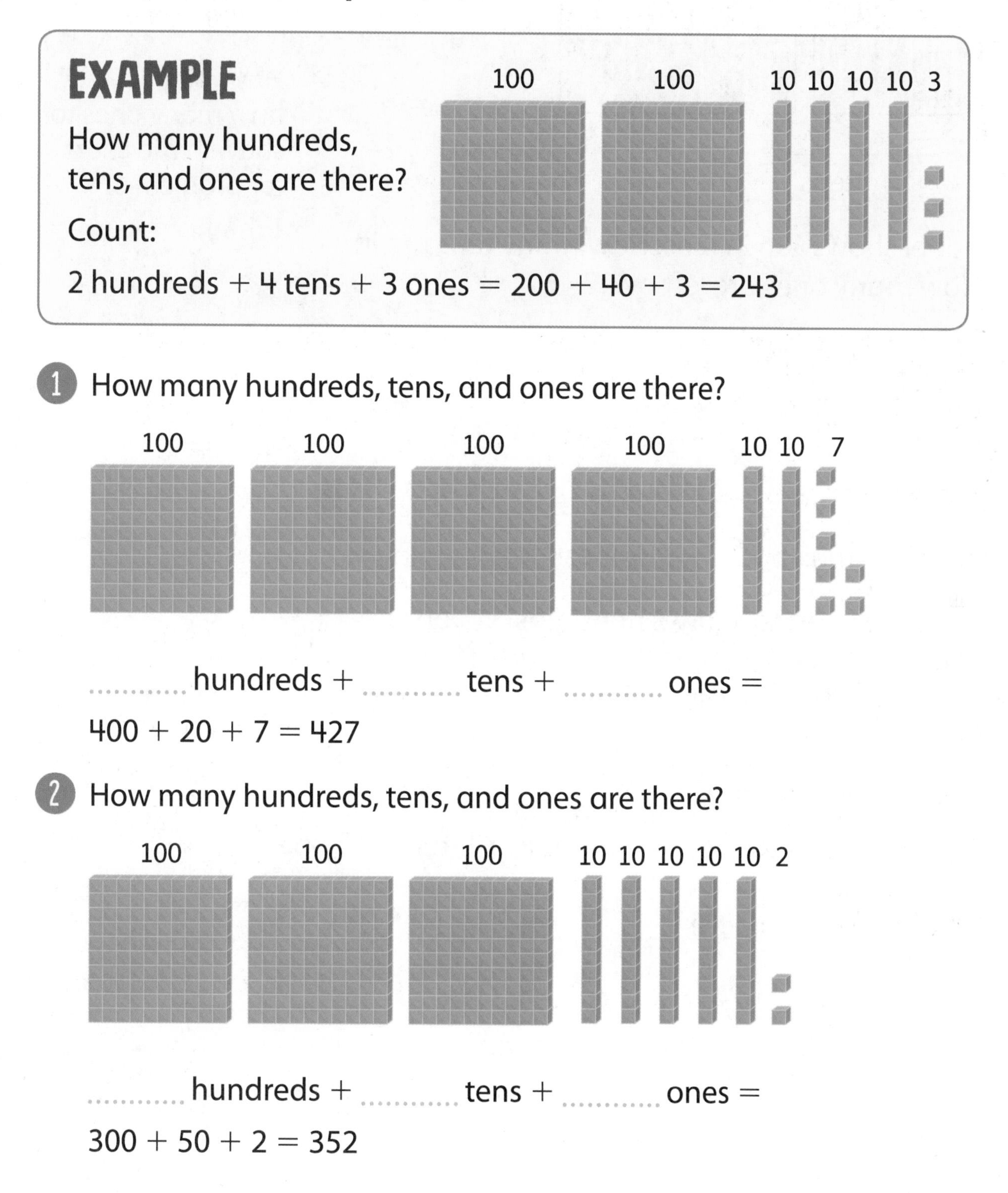

EXAMPLE

How many hundreds, tens, and ones are there?

Count:

2 hundreds + 4 tens + 3 ones = 200 + 40 + 3 = 243

1 How many hundreds, tens, and ones are there?

.... hundreds + ... tens + ... ones =

400 + 20 + 7 = 427

2 How many hundreds, tens, and ones are there?

.... hundreds + ... tens + ... ones =

300 + 50 + 2 = 352

3. This model shows 200 in tens. How many tens are in 200?

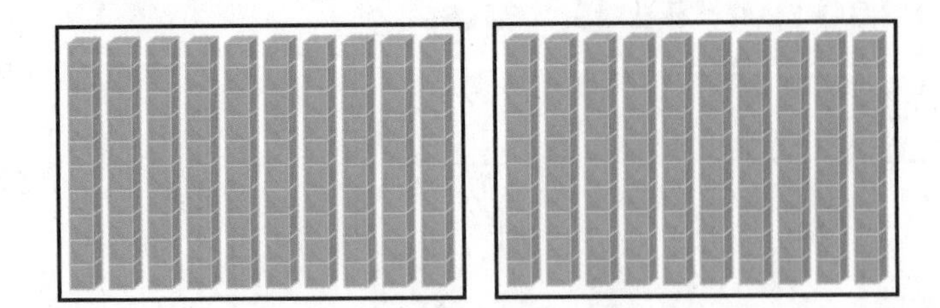

200 = ... tens

4. This model shows 136 in tens. How many tens are in 136? How many ones are left over?

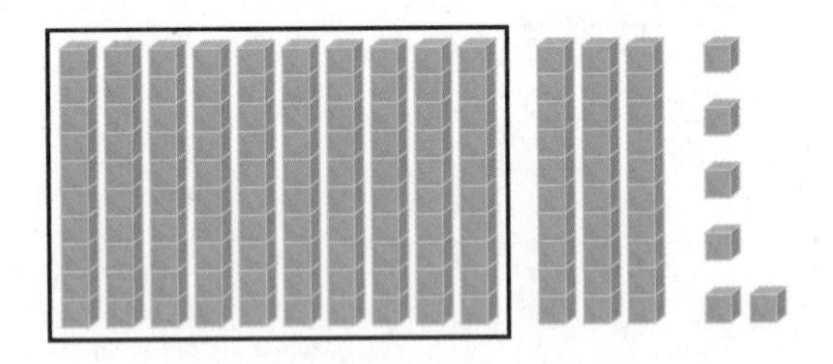

136 = ... tens and .... ones

5. Complete the chart to show 7 hundreds + 5 ones.

Hundreds	Tens	Ones
	0	5

6. Complete the chart to show 9 hundreds + 4 tens + 8 ones.

Hundreds	Tens	Ones

Refine Ideas about Three-Digit Numbers

APPLY IT

Complete these problems on your own.

1 EVALUATE

Lana does this homework problem.
What does she do wrong?

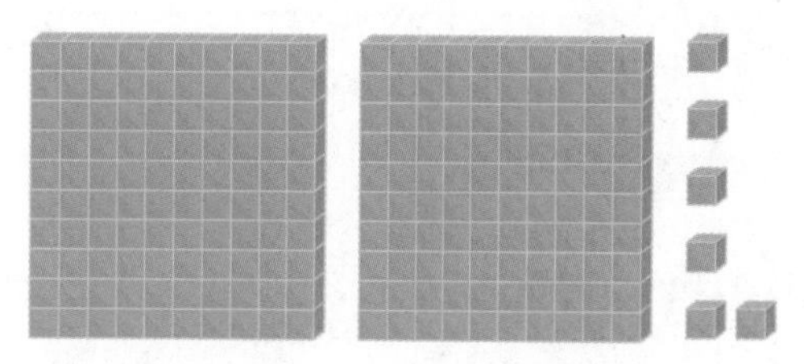

2 hundreds + 6 ones = 26

2 ANALYZE

Sam and Lev write 572.
Explain what each person does.

Sam: 572 = 57 tens + 2 ones

Lev: 572 = 5 hundreds + 7 tens + 2 ones

3 IDENTIFY

Fill in the blanks to show 900 in different ways.

900 = ... tens

900 = ... ones

PAIR/SHARE
Discuss your solutions for these three problems with a partner.

Use what you have learned to complete problem 4.

4 Nate puts his coins in stacks of ten. He has 12 stacks of coins with 4 coins left over.

Part A Draw a picture to show Nate's coins.

Part B How many coins does Nate have? Write the answer in two different ways.

5 MATH JOURNAL

Sasha uses base-ten blocks to show the number 700. If she uses only hundreds flats, how many will she use? Explain how you know.

Read and Write Three-Digit Numbers

Dear Family,

This week your child is learning to read and write three-digit numbers.

A digit is any one of the symbols we use to write numbers: 0, 1, 2, 3, 4, 5, 6, 7, 8, and 9. So, a three-digit number is a number such as 153 or 201 or 999.

All numbers can be represented in different ways. These different ways each show something about what the number means.

You can write the number 279 in many different ways.

- You can write it in **expanded form**: 200 + 70 + 9.
- You can use words: two hundred seventy-nine.
- You can use a model or chart:

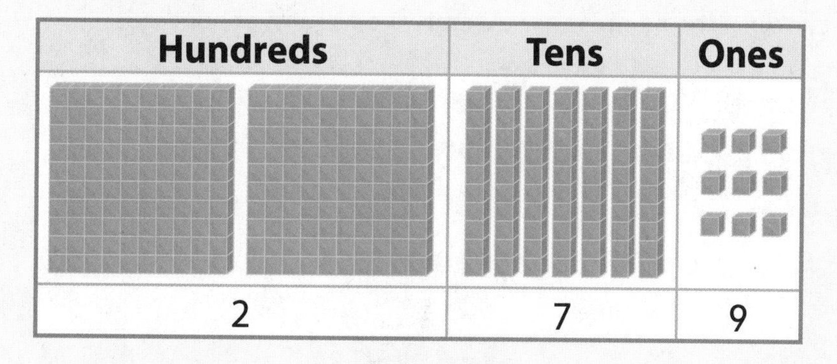

Invite your child to share what he or she knows about three-digit numbers by doing the following activity together.

ACTIVITY THREE-DIGIT NUMBERS

Do this activity with your child to read and write three-digit numbers.

- Give your child several three-digit numbers from your everyday life.
  For example:
  - Our neighbor's dog weighs 112 pounds.
  - A book about cars has 437 pages.
  - The monthly rent is 875 dollars.
  - Your cousins live 268 miles away.

- Have your child write each number as a numeral and as a sum of hundreds, tens, and ones. For example, 279 is a numeral, and it can be written as 200 + 70 + 9.

- Then let your child make up several three-digit numbers for you to write in both formats.

- Ask your child to check your work.

- Make up a short story together that includes several three-digit numbers. Each of you can write the numbers as numerals and as sums of hundreds, tens, and ones and check each other's work.

Explore Reading and Writing Three-Digit Numbers

Learning Target

- Read and write numbers to 1000 using base-ten numerals, number names, and expanded form.

SMP 1, 2, 3, 4, 5, 6, 7, 8

You know how to read and write two-digit numbers. Use what you know to try to solve the problem below.

Jan buys 200 blue balloons, 70 white balloons, and 5 green balloons. How many balloons does Jan buy?

TRY IT

Math Toolkit

- base-ten blocks
- hundreds place-value charts
- 200 charts
- open number lines

DISCUSS IT

Ask your partner: Do you agree with me? Why or why not?

Tell your partner: I agree with you about . . . because . . .

CONNECT IT

1 LOOK BACK

How many balloons does Jan buy? ....

2 LOOK AHEAD

a. The digits 0, 1, 2, 3, 4, 5, 6, 7, 8, and 9 make up all numbers. The digit's place in a number tells its value. The same digit can have different values. Write the value of each 4 in this number.

Hundreds	Tens	Ones
4	4	4
↓	↓	↓ ....

b. The number can be written using only digits as ....

c. The number can be written in **expanded form**. Complete the expanded form.

444 = ... + 40 + ...

d. The number can be written as words. Complete.

four hundred ....

3 REFLECT

Gabe says the number in the place-value chart is 400404. Explain what Gabe's mistake is.

....

....

Name: ______________________________

Prepare for Reading and Writing Three-Digit Numbers

1. Think about what you know about three-digit numbers. Fill in each box. Use words, numbers, and pictures. Show as many ideas as you can.

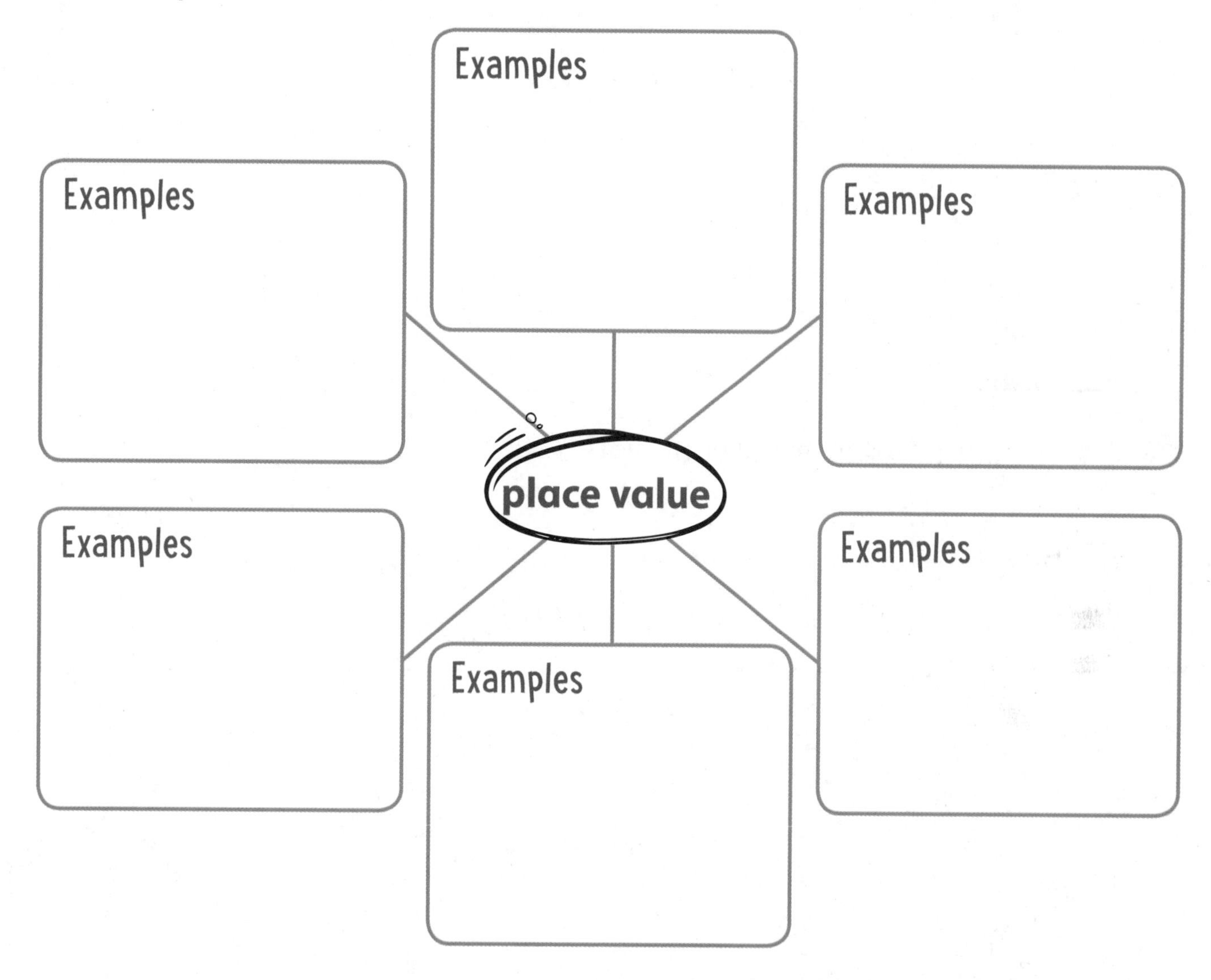

2. Bernadette writes this number as 200507. What is Bernadette's mistake?

Hundreds	Tens	Ones
2	5	7

 Solve the problem. Show your work.

Pavel buys 300 green party hats, 90 purple party hats, and 7 red party hats. How many party hats does Pavel buy?

Solution ....

4 Check your answer. Show your work.

Develop Finding the Value of Three-Digit Numbers

Read and try to solve the problem below.

Amir plays a board game that uses play money. He wins 1 tens bill, 2 hundreds bills and 3 ones bills. What is the total value of the bills Amir wins?

TRY IT

Math Toolkit

- base-ten blocks
- play money bills
- hundreds place-value charts
- 200 charts
- open number lines

DISCUSS IT

Ask your partner: Can you explain that again?

Tell your partner: The strategy I used to find the answer was . . .

Explore different ways to understand finding the value of three-digit numbers.

Amir plays a board game that uses play money. He wins 1 tens bill, 2 hundreds bills, and 3 ones bills. What is the total value of the bills Amir wins?

PICTURE IT

You can use play money to model the problem.

PICTURE IT

You can make a quick drawing to show hundreds, tens, and ones.

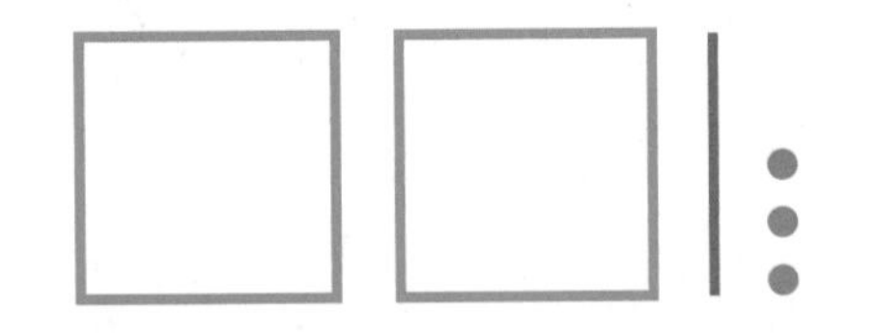

MODEL IT

You can show hundreds, tens, and ones in a chart.

Hundreds	Tens	Ones
2	1	3

CONNECT IT

Now you will use the problem from the previous page to help you find the value of three-digit numbers.

1. Look at the models on the previous page. How many hundreds, tens, and ones are there?

   .... hundreds .... ten .... ones

2. What is the value of the hundreds bills? .... dollars

   What is the value of the tens bill? .... dollars

   What is the value of the ones bills? .... dollars

3. Write an equation to find the total value of all the bills.

   .... + ... + ... = ... dollars

4. Amir wins 2 more tens bills. Tell how to write the new total value of Amir's play money.

5. ## REFLECT

   Look back at your **Try It**, strategies by classmates, and **Picture Its** and **Model It**. Which models or strategies do you like best for finding the value of three-digit numbers? Explain.

   ....

   ....

   ....

APPLY IT

Use what you just learned to solve these problems.

6 What is another way to show each number? Draw lines to connect each number to its expanded form.

392 329 239

300 + 20 + 9 200 + 30 + 9 300 + 90 + 2

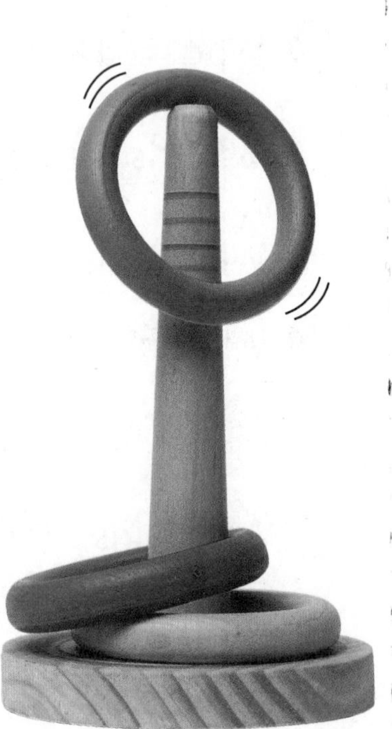

7 Tia is playing a ring toss game to win tokens. She wins 3 hundreds tokens, 4 tens tokens, and 7 ones tokens. What is another way to write the total value of the tokens Tia wins? Show your work.

Solution ....

8 When does the digit 8 mean eighty? When does the digit 8 mean eight hundred? When does the digit 8 mean just eight?

Practice Finding the Value of Three-Digit Numbers

Study the Example showing three-digit numbers in different ways. Then solve problems 1–6.

EXAMPLE

In a game, Jan pays money to the bank. She pays 2 hundreds bills, 4 tens bills, and 5 ones bills. What is the total value of the bills Jan pays?

Make a quick drawing.

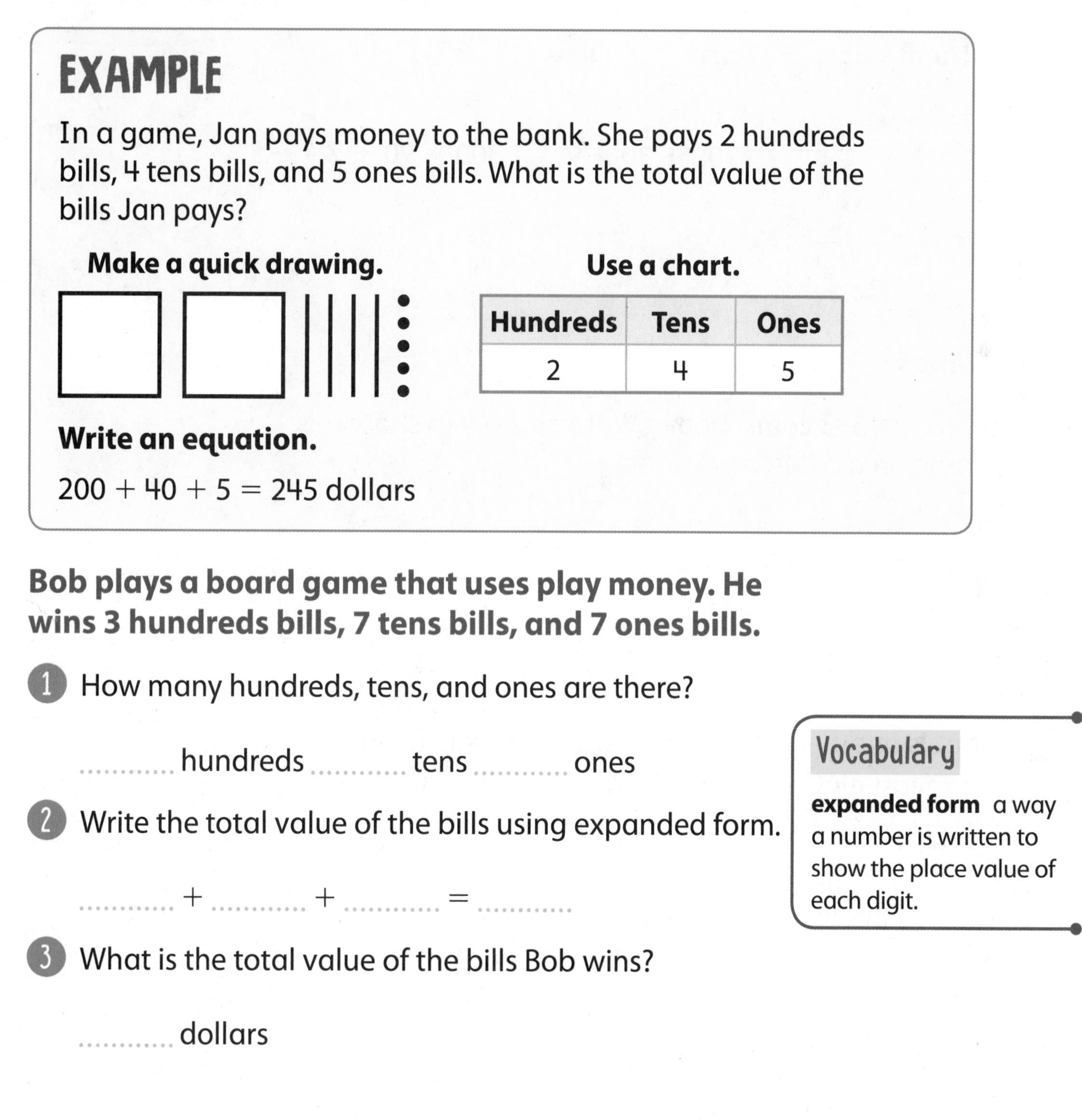

Use a chart.

Hundreds	Tens	Ones
2	4	5

Write an equation.

200 + 40 + 5 = 245 dollars

Bob plays a board game that uses play money. He wins 3 hundreds bills, 7 tens bills, and 7 ones bills.

1. How many hundreds, tens, and ones are there?

   .... hundreds .... tens .... ones

2. Write the total value of the bills using expanded form.

   .... + ... + ... = ...

3. What is the total value of the bills Bob wins?

   .... dollars

Vocabulary

expanded form a way a number is written to show the place value of each digit.

4 Ali plays a board game that uses play money. He wins 8 hundreds bills and 6 ones bills. What is the total value of the bills Ali wins? Fill in the chart and then write the answer. Show your work.

Hundreds	Tens	Ones

Solution ....

5 Audra has 533 comic books. Write or draw to show this number in a different way.

6 What is another way to show each number? Draw lines to connect each number to its expanded form.

784 | 874 | 748

$800 + 70 + 4$ | $700 + 80 + 4$ | $700 + 40 + 8$

Develop Writing Three-Digit Numbers

Read and try to solve the problem below.

Ryan has a collection of 284 shells. What is another way to write 284 using numbers? What is another way to write 284 using words?

TRY IT

Math Toolkit
- base-ten blocks
- hundreds place-value charts
- 200 charts
- open number lines

DISCUSS IT

Ask your partner: How did you get started?

Tell your partner: A model I used was . . . It helped me . . .

Explore different ways to understand writing three-digit numbers.

Ryan has a collection of 284 shells. What is another way to write 284 using numbers? What is another way to write 284 using words?

PICTURE IT

You can use base-ten blocks to show hundreds, tens, and ones. Then write the number in expanded form and in words.

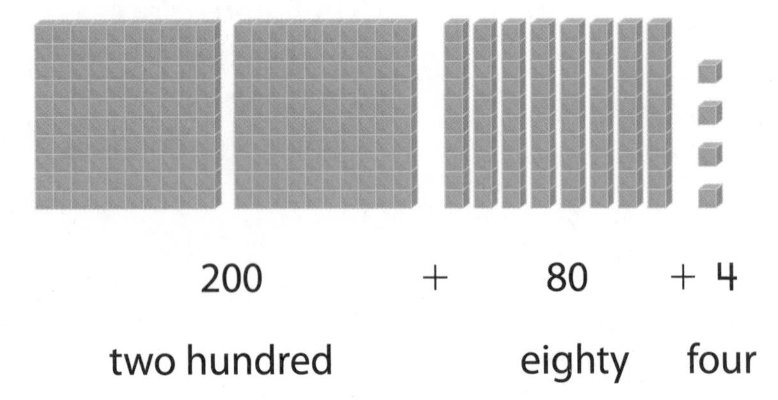

200 + 80 + 4

two hundred eighty four

MODEL IT

You can show hundreds, tens, and ones in a chart. Then write the values in numbers and words.

Hundreds	Tens	Ones
2	8	4

2 hundreds + 8 tens + 4 ones

two hundred + eighty + four

CONNECT IT

Now you will use the problem from the previous page to help you understand how to write three-digit numbers in different ways.

 Write the number of Ryan's shells using only digits.

Ryan has .... shells.

2 Look at **Picture It** on the previous page. Write 284 using words.

3 Look at **Model It**.

a. How many hundreds, tens, and ones are there?

.... hundreds .... tens .... ones

b. Write the number in expanded form to show the total number of shells as an equation.

.... + ... + ... = 284

4 **REFLECT**

Look back at your **Try It**, strategies by classmates, and **Picture It** and **Model It**. Which models or strategies do you like best for writing three-digit numbers? Explain.

....

....

....

....

APPLY IT

Use what you just learned to solve these problems.

5 There are 361 fish in the large tank at the aquarium. How do you write 361 in word form? Show your work.

Solution ....

6 Ella makes one hundred eighteen friendship bracelets. How would Ella write that number in expanded form? Show your work.

Solution ....

7 How do you write the number shown in the chart using words?

Hundreds	Tens	Ones
5	7	0

Ⓐ five seven zero

Ⓑ fifty-seven

Ⓒ five hundred seventeen

Ⓓ five hundred seventy

Practice Writing Three-Digit Numbers

Study the Example showing how to write a three-digit number in different ways. Then solve problems 1–6.

EXAMPLE

In a video game, Eduardo scores 753 points.

Write this number three different ways.

Using only digits: 753

Using expanded form: 700 + 50 + 3

Using words:

seven hundred + fifty + three =
seven hundred fifty-three

Use the chart below for problems 1–3.

Hundreds	Tens	Ones
3	2	2

1 Write the number using only digits. ....

2 Write the number in expanded form.

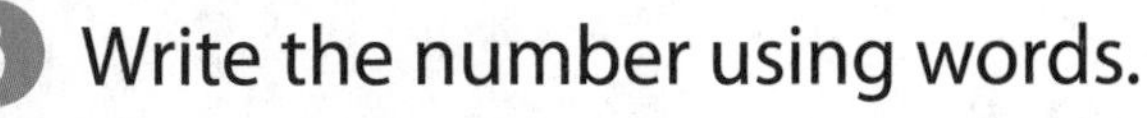

.... + ... + ...

3 Write the number using words.

4 There are 225 building bricks in a box.

How would you write 225 in expanded form?

Fill in the chart and then write the answer.

Hundreds	Tens	Ones

Solution ....

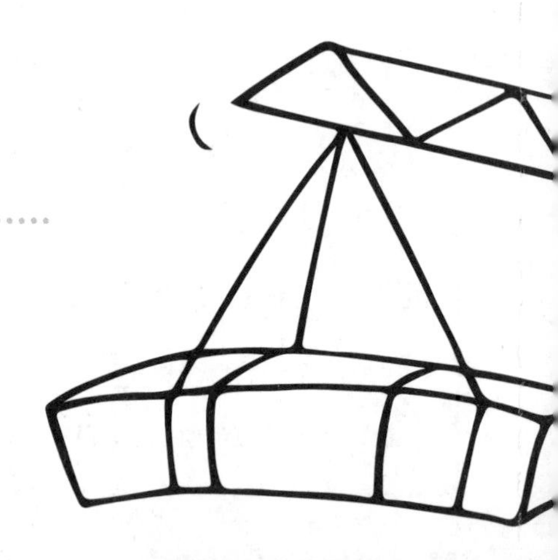

5 Helen counts her crayons. She writes the number as 700 + 3.

Write the number using only digits.

Solution ....

Write the number using only words.

Solution ....

6 What are other ways to show each number?

Look at each number shown using only digits. Draw a line to the expanded form and to the words for each number.

500 + 60 + 1	**651**	six hundred fifteen
600 + 10 + 5	**615**	five hundred sixty-one
600 + 50 + 1	**561**	six hundred fifty-one

Refine Reading and Writing Three-Digit Numbers

Complete the Example below. Then solve problems 1–3.

EXAMPLE

Mrs. Cole writes this number on a check.

five hundred ninety-four

How do you write this number using only digits?

You can show the number in a chart.

Hundreds	Tens	Ones
5	9	4

↓ ↓ ↓

five hundred ninety-four

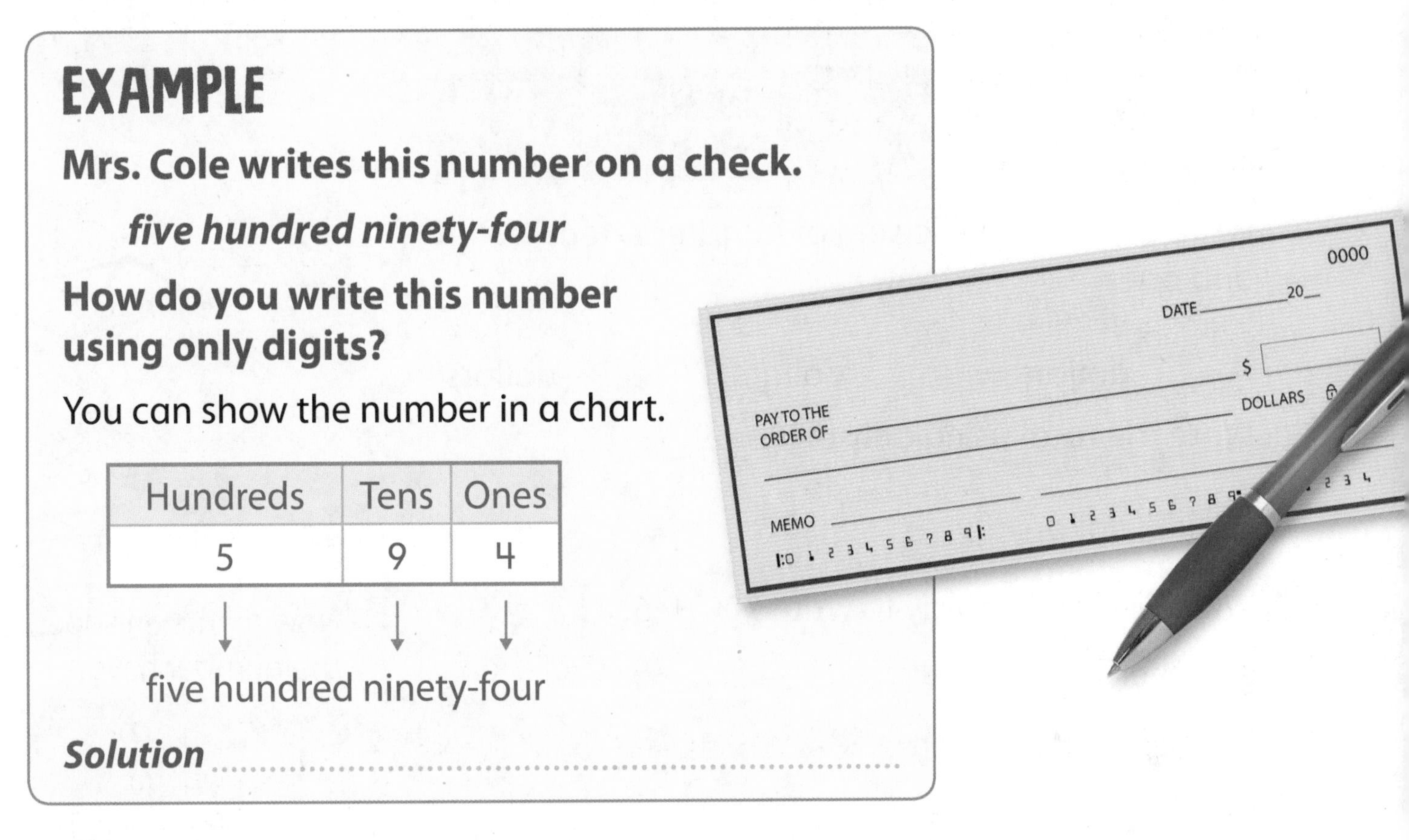

Solution ....

APPLY IT

1 Pat writes these clues about a three-digit number.

- The hundreds digit is 1 more than 8.
- The tens digit has a value of 40.
- The number has 2 ones.

What is the number? Show your work.

How many digits are in the number?

Solution ....

 Jim is playing a board game. This is his play money.

What is the value of each kind of bill in the problem?

Write the total as the sum of hundreds, tens, and ones.

.... dollars + ... dollars + ... dollars

Write the total using only digits.

.... dollars

3 Which is another way to write 700 + 6?

How many tens does the number have?

Ⓐ seventy-six

Ⓑ six hundred seven

Ⓒ seven hundred six

Ⓓ seven hundred sixty

Zoey chose Ⓐ as the answer. How did Zoey get her answer?

Name: ______________________________

Practice Reading and Writing Three-Digit Numbers

1. Which number is the same as $800 + 30$?

   Ⓐ 803

   Ⓑ 83

   Ⓒ 830

   Ⓓ 308

> Can you use a chart to help you?

2. Bev writes clues about a three-digit number.

   - The number has 5 hundreds.
   - The tens digit is 1 less than 9.
   - The ones digit is greater than the tens digit.

   What is the number?

   Ⓐ 589

   Ⓑ 598

   Ⓒ 959

   Ⓓ 590

> In a three-digit number, where is the tens digit?

3. Which are true about the number 720?

   Ⓐ It equals 72 tens.

   Ⓑ It is $700 + 2$.

   Ⓒ It has 7 hundreds and 2 tens.

   Ⓓ It is $700 + 20$.

   Ⓔ It is seventy-two.

   Ⓕ It is seven hundred twenty.

> How many hundreds, tens, and ones are in 720?

4. Here are clues about a three-digit number.
   - The hundreds digit has a value of 300.
   - The tens digit is 1 less than 2.
   - The ones digit is the same as the hundreds digit.

   Write the number in words. Show your work.

Can you write an equation to help you?

Solution ....

5. What is another way to show 4 hundreds and 3 tens? Circle the correct answer.

How can you show 3 tens?

Ⓐ 43

Ⓑ 400 + 3

Ⓒ 403

Ⓓ 400 + 30

Zack chose Ⓓ. How did Zack get his answer?

Refine Reading and Writing Three-Digit Numbers

APPLY IT

Solve the problems.

1 Which are other ways to show 2 hundreds and 5 ones?

Ⓐ 200 + 5

Ⓑ 25

Ⓒ 200 + 50

Ⓓ 205

Ⓔ 20 + 5

2 What does the model show? Fill in the chart and the blanks.

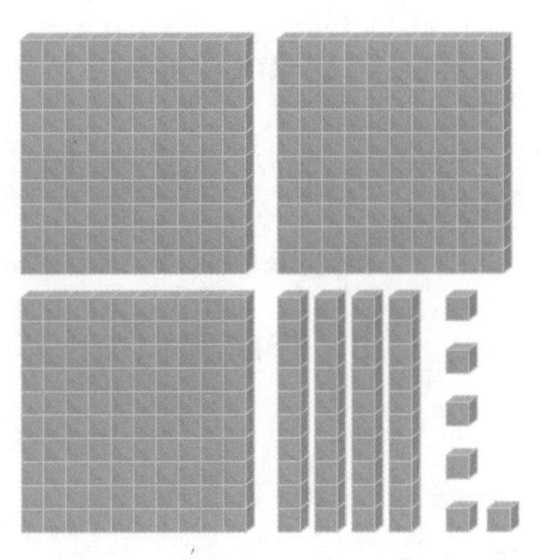

Hundreds	Tens	Ones

expanded form: .... + ... + ...

digits only: ....

3 A bear at the zoo weighs 360 pounds. Which are true about this number?

Ⓐ It is 300 + 6.

Ⓑ It is three hundred sixty.

Ⓒ It is 300 + 60.

Ⓓ It has 3 hundreds and 6 tens.

Ⓔ It is three hundred sixteen.

4 Write each number in expanded form.

275: ....

527: ....

5 Look at problem 4. Why do the 2, 5, and 7 have a different value in each number? Explain.

6 MATH JOURNAL

Here are clues about a three-digit number.

- The number has seven hundreds.
- The tens digit has a value of 30.
- The ones digit is less than any other digit in the number.

What could the number be? Explain.

SELF CHECK Go back to the Unit 3 Opener and see what you can check off.

Compare Three-Digit Numbers

Dear Family,

This week your child is learning how to compare three-digit numbers.

Your child might see a problem like this: *Mr. Perez drives 232 miles. Mr. Lee drives 213 miles. Who drives more miles?*

You can model both numbers using quick drawings.

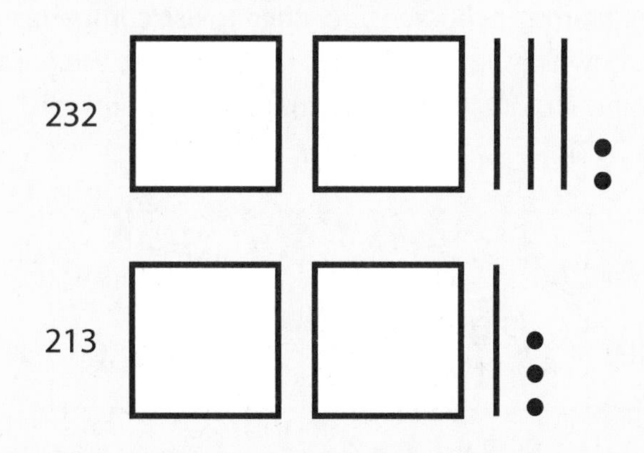

You can see that both models show 2 hundreds with 2 squares. But the top model shows 3 tens (with 3 lines), and the bottom model shows only 1 ten (with 1 line). So, the top model shows more. You don't have to compare ones, because there are already more tens in the top model.

The model shows that 232 is greater than 213, which we write with a **greater than symbol (>)** as 232 > 213. So, we know that Mr. Perez drives more miles. We could also use the **less than symbol (<)** and write 213 < 232.

Invite your child to share what he or she knows about comparing three-digit numbers by doing the following activity together.

ACTIVITY COMPARING THREE-DIGIT NUMBERS

Do this activity with your child to compare three-digit numbers.

Materials food or other items with (three-digit) weights listed on their labels (such as cans of fruit, boxes of dry cereal, or boxes of crackers), paper, pencil

- With your child, choose two items that seem to be about the same size. Write down the number of ounces and the number of grams inside, as shown on the label for each item.
- Ask your child to compare the number of ounces. Then have your child compare the number of grams. Encourage your child to use comparison words and symbols as shown in the table below. (For example: The number of grams for Cracker Brand A is greater than the number of grams for Cracker Brand B. 425 > 397)

<	>	=
is less than	is greater than	is equal to

Cracker Brand A

Cracker Brand B

Explore Comparing Three-Digit Numbers

Learning Target

- Compare two three-digit numbers based on meanings of the hundreds, tens, and ones digits, using >, =, and < symbols to record the results of comparisons.

SMP 1, 2, 3, 4, 5, 6, 7

You have learned how to compare two-digit numbers. Use what you know to try to solve the problem below.

Kim and Jon toss beanbags at a target. Who can make the greater number using the digits their beanbags land on?

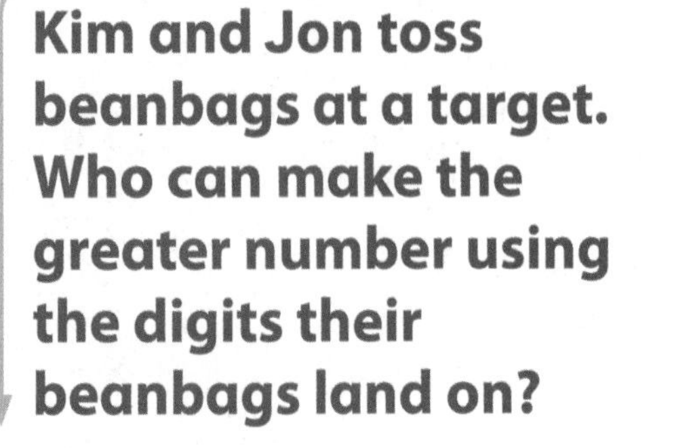

TRY IT

Math Toolkit

- base-ten blocks
- hundreds place-value charts
- blank number lines
- hundred charts

DISCUSS IT

Ask your partner: How did you get started?

Tell your partner: I started by . . .

CONNECT IT

1 LOOK BACK

Who can make the greater number? ....

2 LOOK AHEAD

Start with the greatest place value when you compare numbers.

A place-value chart can help you compare numbers.

Hundreds	Tens	Ones
0	8	9
1	5	2

a. Compare the hundreds to complete this sentence.

.... hundred is greater than .... hundreds.

You can use $=$, $<$ **(less than symbol)**, and $>$ **(greater than symbol)** to compare numbers.

The symbol points toward the lesser number. It opens toward the greater number.

b. Write 152 and 89 in the correct spaces below.

.... $<$ .... $>$ ....

3 REFLECT

Is a three-digit number always greater than a two-digit number? Explain.

....

....

Prepare for Comparing Three-Digit Numbers

1. Think about what you know about comparing numbers. Fill in each box. Use words, numbers, and pictures. Show as many ideas as you can.

Symbol	In My Own Words	Example
$<$		
$>$		
$=$		

2. Compare 14 and 18 using the $>$ symbol. Then compare 14 and 18 using the $<$ symbol.

3 Solve the problem. Show your work.

Victor rolls three number cubes. Sabra rolls two number cubes. Who can make the greater number using the digits they roll?

Solution ....

 Check your answer. Show your work.

Develop Ways to Compare Three-Digit Numbers

Read and try to solve the problem below.

There is a contest at the school fair. Students guess how many jelly beans are in a jar. Bart guesses 352 and Diego guesses 328. Which number is less?

TRY IT

Math Toolkit
- base-ten blocks
- hundreds place-value charts
- blank number lines
- hundred charts

DISCUSS IT

Ask your partner: Why did you choose that strategy?

Tell your partner: A model I used was . . . It helped me . . .

Explore different ways to understand comparing three-digit numbers.

There is a contest at the school fair. Students guess how many jelly beans are in a jar. Bart guesses 352 and Diego guesses 328. Which number is less?

PICTURE IT

You can model the numbers with base-ten blocks.

MODEL IT

You can write the numbers as hundreds, tens, and ones.

352 = 3 hundreds + 5 tens + 2 ones

328 = 3 hundreds + 2 tens + 8 ones

CONNECT IT

Now you will use the problem from the previous page to help you understand how to compare three-digit numbers.

 Look at **Picture It** and **Model It** on the previous page. Can you use the numbers in the hundreds place to decide which number is greater? Why or why not?

2 Now compare the tens. Which number has more tens?

3 Complete the comparison of 352 and 328.

.... $<$ ....

4 Bart says $2 < 8$, so $352 < 328$. Is Bart correct? Explain.

 REFLECT

Look back at your **Try It**, strategies by classmates, and **Picture It** and **Model It**. Which models or strategies do you like best for comparing three-digit numbers? Explain.

....

....

....

APPLY IT

Use what you just learned to solve these problems.

6 Compare 761 and 716 using $<$ or $>$. Explain why your comparison is true.

 Write two ways to compare 487 and 478.

8 Luz is building a city out of plastic blocks. She uses 238 blocks for the school and 283 blocks for the fire station. She compares the two values: $238 > 283$. Explain the mistake Luz makes and write a correct comparison using $<$ or $>$.

Practice Comparing Three-Digit Numbers

Study the Example showing how to compare three-digit numbers. Then solve problems 1–8.

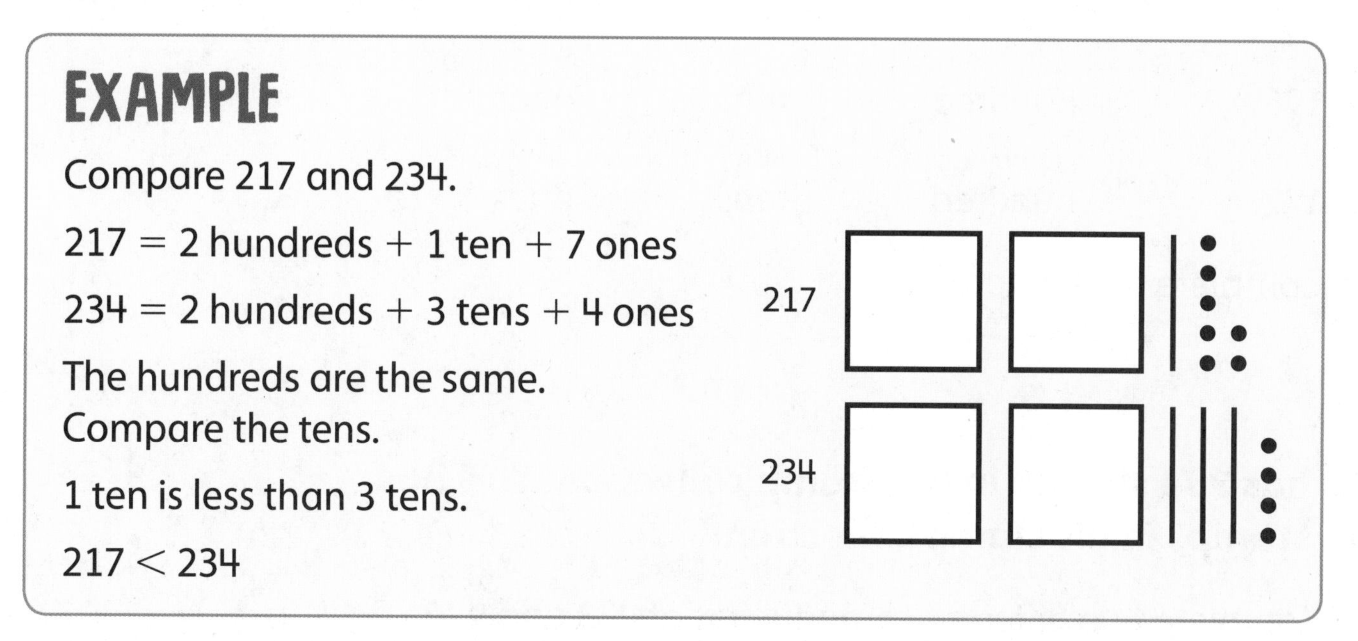

EXAMPLE

Compare 217 and 234.

217 = 2 hundreds + 1 ten + 7 ones

234 = 2 hundreds + 3 tens + 4 ones

The hundreds are the same.
Compare the tens.

1 ten is less than 3 tens.

$217 < 234$

Cam has 482 marbles. Joe has 439 marbles.

1. How many hundreds, tens, and ones are in each number?

   482 = ... hundreds .... tens .... ones

   439 = ... hundreds .... tens .... ones

2. The hundreds are the same. Compare the tens.

   .... tens is greater than .... tens.

3. Complete the comparison. .... $>$ ....

4. Use the same numbers as problem 3.
   Write a different comparison.

Vince and Rina guess how many paper clips are in a box. Vince guesses 195, and Rina guesses 172.

5. How many hundreds, tens, and ones are in each number?

195 = ... hundred .... tens .... ones

172 = ... hundred .... tens .... ones

6. Complete the comparison.

.... $<$ ....

Mel has 938 stamps in her stamp collection. Yuri has 926 stamps in his stamp collection.

7. Complete two different comparisons of 938 and 926.

.... $<$ .... and .... $>$ ....

8. Explain why your comparisons in problem 7 are true.

Develop More Ways to Compare Three-Digit Numbers

Read and try to solve the problem below.

These two paintings are in the school art contest. Which painting has more votes?

Painting A: 467 votes

Painting B: 463 votes

TRY IT

Math Toolkit

- base-ten blocks
- hundreds place-value charts
- blank number lines
- hundred charts

DISCUSS IT

Ask your partner: Do you agree with me? Why or why not?

Tell your partner: I do not understand how . . .

Explore more ways to understand comparing three-digit numbers.

These two paintings are in the school art contest. Which painting has more votes?

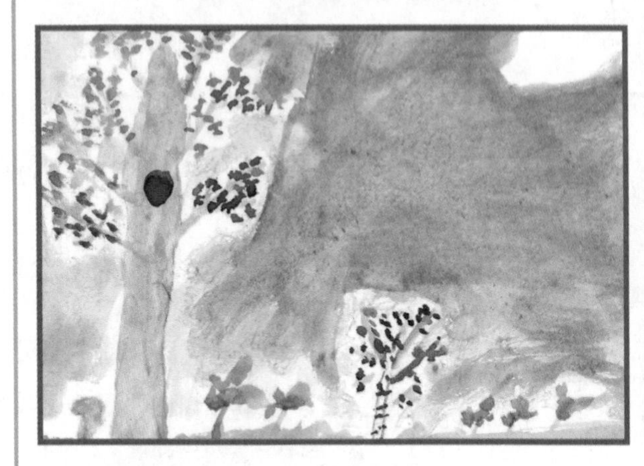

Painting A: 467 votes

Painting B: 463 votes

PICTURE IT

You can show the numbers in a quick drawing.

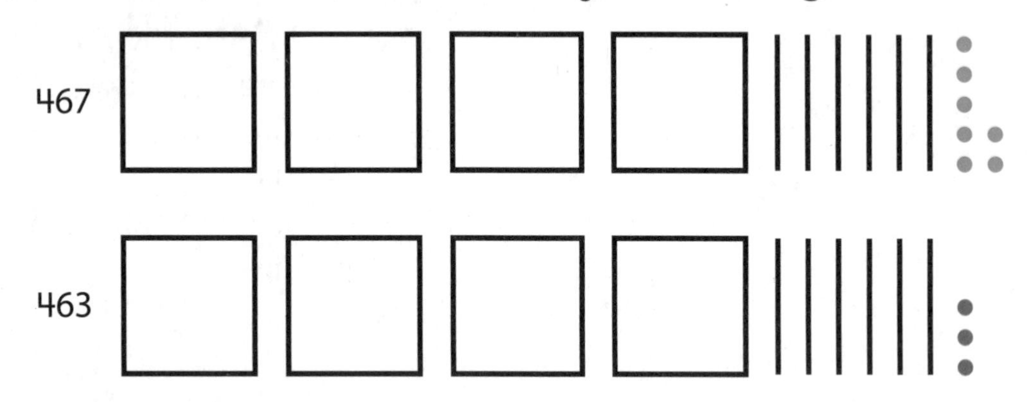

MODEL IT

You can model the numbers in a chart.

Hundreds	Tens	Ones
4	6	7
4	6	3

CONNECT IT

Now you will use the problem from the previous page to help you understand more ways to compare three-digit numbers.

1 Which place do you need to look at to compare the numbers of votes? Why?

2 Complete two different comparisons of 467 and 463.

.... > .... < ....

3 Why can 467 and 463 be compared two ways?

4 Which painting has more votes? How do you know?

5 REFLECT

Look back at your **Try It**, strategies by classmates, and **Picture It** and **Model It**. Which models or strategies do you like best for comparing three-digit numbers in different ways? Explain.

....

....

APPLY IT

Use what you just learned to solve these problems.

6 Write $>$ or $<$ to compare each pair of numbers.

a. 264 ◯ 462 **b.** 372 ◯ 379 **c.** 954 ◯ 950

d. 876 ◯ 867 **e.** 718 ◯ 788 **f.** 653 ◯ 553

7 Write two different ways to compare 772 and 774 using $<$ and $>$. Show your work.

Solution ....

8 Hope and Sara are collecting pennies. Hope has 189 pennies. Sara has 186 pennies. Which comparisons are correct?

Ⓐ $189 < 186$

Ⓑ $186 < 189$

Ⓒ $189 > 186$

Ⓓ $186 > 189$

Ⓔ $186 = 189$

Practice Comparing Three-Digit Numbers

Study the Example showing how to compare three-digit numbers. Then solve problems 1–8.

EXAMPLE

Compare 528 and 523.

The hundreds are the same.
The tens are the same.
Compare the ones.

8 ones is greater than 3 ones.

$528 > 523$ and $523 < 528$

Hundreds	Tens	Ones
5	2	8
5	2	3

Ned and Vera are playing a game. Ned has 142 points, and Vera has 147 points.

 Write the numbers in the chart.

Hundreds	Tens	Ones

2 Complete the comparison of 142 and 147.

.... $>$ ....

3 Which place did you have to look at to compare 142 and 147? Why?

4 Complete two different comparisons of 824 and 829.

.... > .... and .... < ....

5 Complete two different comparisons of 353 and 351.

.... > .... and .... < ....

6 Complete two different comparisons of 675 and 629.

.... > .... and .... < ....

7 Write $>$, $<$, or $=$ to compare each pair of numbers.

a. 465 ◯ 467 **b.** 392 ◯ 392

c. 885 ◯ 882 **d.** 214 ◯ 312

e. 691 ◯ 691 **f.** 484 ◯ 394

8 Han plays three games. Which game has the greatest score? Which game has the least score? Tell how you know.

Game 1: 328
Game 2: 289
Game 3: 325

Refine Comparing Three-Digit Numbers

Complete the Example below. Then solve problems 1–3.

EXAMPLE

Yen packs 250 oranges in a box. Gia packs 25 bags of oranges with 10 oranges in each bag. Who packs more oranges?

Look at how you can find the number of oranges Gia packs.

25 bags with 10 in each bag = 25 tens

25 tens = 250

250 oranges in a box = 250

Solution ....

APPLY IT

1 Write the number of hundreds and tens for each score in the table. Circle the names of the two players with the greatest scores.

Player	Score	Hundreds	Tens
Eden	92		
Sarita	233		
Paul	213		
Chen	236		

Remember to look at the hundreds place first.

2 Bella rides her bike 122 miles. Ariel rides her bike 126 miles. Who rides fewer miles? Show your work.

Are you looking for the lesser or greater number?

Solution ....

3 Jill and Iman each write a three-digit number.

Jill's number: 305

Iman's number: 3 hundreds 5 tens

Which correctly compares Jill's and Iman's numbers?

Ⓐ $305 < 305$

Ⓑ $305 > 350$

Ⓒ $350 > 305$

Ⓓ $350 < 305$

Dan chose Ⓑ as the answer. How did Dan get his answer?

What number is the same as 3 hundreds 5 tens?

Name: ______________________

Practice Comparing Three-Digit Numbers

1. In one week, Glen reads for 317 minutes. Fran reads for 372 minutes. Who reads for more minutes? Tell how you know. Show your work.

Are you looking for the lesser or greater number?

Solution ....

2. Choose *True* or *False* to tell if the comparison is correct.

	True	False
$131 < 119$	Ⓐ	Ⓑ
$605 = 650$	Ⓒ	Ⓓ
$454 > 451$	Ⓔ	Ⓕ
$709 < 722$	Ⓖ	Ⓗ

Which place value should you compare first?

3. Marcy has 237 stickers. Then she gives some stickers away. How many stickers could Marcy have now?

Ⓐ 239

Ⓑ 198

Ⓒ 229

Ⓓ 323

Ⓔ 237

Ⓕ 207

Does Marcy have more than or fewer than 237 stickers now?

4. Which comparison is true?

Ⓐ 420 < 4 hundreds 3 ones

Ⓑ 370 > 407

Ⓒ 6 hundreds 4 tens < 640

Ⓓ 919 < 991

Deb chose Ⓐ. How did Deb get her answer?

You can rewrite the numbers that are shown as tens and ones.

5. Use the digits 5, 2, and 9 to make the least three-digit number that you can. Explain how you find your answer.

5 2 9

I think I will choose the digit for the hundreds place first.

6. Use the digits from problem 5 to make the greatest three-digit number that you can. Write your number below.

Which is the greatest digit?

....

Refine Comparing Three-Digit Numbers

APPLY IT

Solve the problems.

1. Which comparisons are true?

   Ⓐ $431 > 427$

   Ⓑ $540 <$ 5 hundreds 4 ones

   Ⓒ $727 < 772$

   Ⓓ 9 hundreds 6 tens < 906

   Ⓔ $538 > 540$

2. Phil has 248 trading cards. Sean has more trading cards than Phil. How many cards could Sean have?

   Ⓐ 239

   Ⓑ 228

   Ⓒ 260

   Ⓓ 252

   Ⓔ 246

3. Choose *True* or *False* to tell if the comparison is correct.

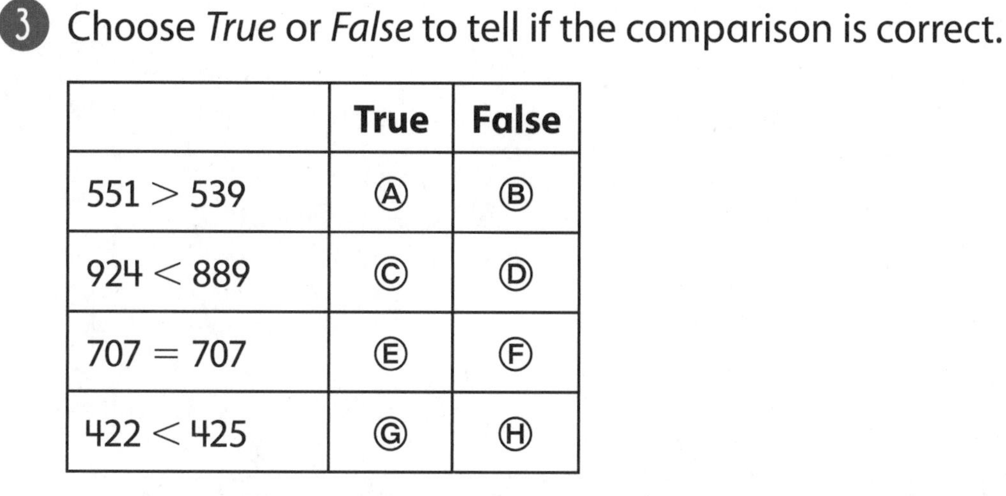

	True	False
$551 > 539$	Ⓐ	Ⓑ
$924 < 889$	Ⓒ	Ⓓ
$707 = 707$	Ⓔ	Ⓕ
$422 < 425$	Ⓖ	Ⓗ

4 Use the numbers below to make true comparisons. Use each number only once.

.... > 386 38 tens $=$ .... < 384

5 Josh uses the digits below to make the least number he can. He writes 184. Is this the least number Josh can make? Explain.

4 1 8

MATH JOURNAL

Write two different three-digit numbers. Then write two different comparisons of your numbers, using $<$ and $>$. Explain how you know your comparisons are correct.

☑ **SELF CHECK** Go back to the Unit 3 Opener and see what you can check off.

Mental Addition and Subtraction

LESSON 15

Dear Family,

This week your child is learning to count by fives, tens, and hundreds. He or she also is learning to add and subtract 10 or 100 mentally.

Your child will count forward and backward by fives and tens. For example:

Count forward by fives:	105, 110, 115, 120, 125, 130
Count backward by fives:	180, 175, 170, 165, 160, 155
Count forward by tens:	270, 280, 290, 300, 310, 320
Count forward by hundreds:	135, 235, 335, 435, 535, 635

Your child also will add 10 and 100 to a three-digit number and subtract 10 and 100 from a three-digit number. For example:

$534 - 100 = ?$ $819 + 100 = ?$ $682 - 10 = ?$ $265 + 10 = ?$

As your child solves these different types of problems, he or she will identify number patterns. For example, he or she will see that the hundreds digit, or first digit of a three-digit number, will go up or down by 1 when 100 is added or subtracted.

$534 - 100 = 434$ $819 + 100 = 919$

He or she will see that the tens digit, or middle digit of a three-digit number, will go up or down by 1 when 10 is added or subtracted.

$682 - 10 = 672$ $265 + 10 = 275$

Invite your child to share what he or she knows about adding and subtracting 10 and 100 by doing the following activity together.

ACTIVITY ADDING AND SUBTRACTING 10 AND 100

Do this activity with your child to practice mental addition and subtraction.

Materials pen and paper, scissors (optional)

- Help your child to make word problem cards, by cutting out the prompts below or writing the prompts on index cards.
- Ask your child to write a three-digit number between 100 and 900 and choose one category card and one addition or subtraction card.
- Then help your child to write a word problem using the number, the category card, and the addition or subtraction card. For example, if your child chooses *Flowers* and *Subtract 10*, he or she might say: *382 flowers are growing in the garden. I picked 10 of them. How many flowers are in the garden now?*
- Ask your child to solve the word problem.
- With your child, write and solve word problems with the remaining cards. He or she should write a different three-digit number for each word problem.

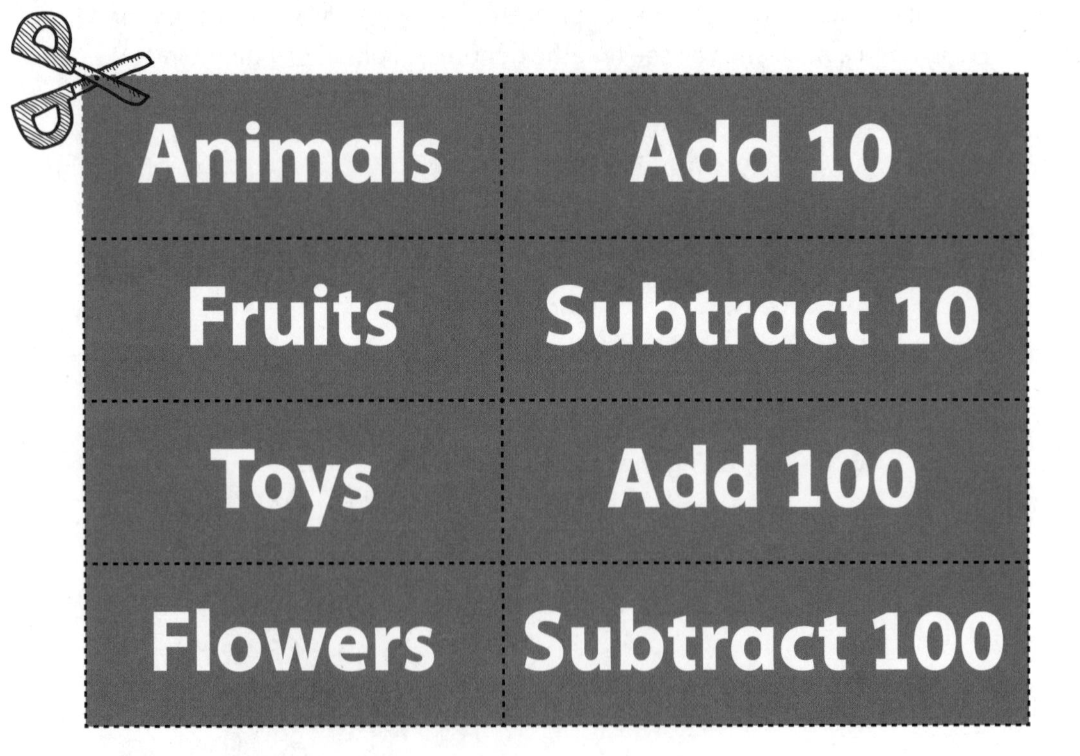

- Ask your child: *What patterns do you notice when you add and subtract 10? When you add and subtract 100?*

Explore Mental Addition and Subtraction

Learning Targets

- Count within 1000; skip-count by 5s, 10s, and 100s.
- Mentally add 10 or 100 to a given number 100–900, and mentally subtract 10 or 100 from a given number 100–900.

SMP 1, 2, 3, 4, 5, 6, 7, 8

You know how to compare three-digit numbers. Now you will learn to skip-count and add and subtract in your head with three-digit numbers. Use what you know to try to solve the problem below.

Amy is counting the pencils at the school store by fives. She has counted 45 so far. What are the next 6 numbers Amy says?

TRY IT

Math Toolkit

- connecting cubes
- hundred charts
- open number lines

DISCUSS IT

Ask your partner: Can you explain that again?

Tell your partner: At first, I thought . . .

CONNECT IT

1 LOOK BACK

What are the next 6 numbers Amy says?

............, ..., ..., ..., ..., ...

2 LOOK AHEAD

You can skip-count by other numbers, too. You can skip count forward and you can skip-count backward.

a. This pattern shows skip-counting forward by tens. The tens digit changes each time.

Write the missing numbers.

130, 140, 150, ..., ..., ...

b. This pattern shows skip-counting backward by hundreds. The hundreds digit changes each time.

Write the missing numbers.

700, 600, 500, ..., ..., ...

3 REFLECT

What would be the next number in the skip-counting backward by hundreds pattern above? How do you know?

....

....

....

Prepare for Mental Addition and Subtraction

1. Think about what you know about skip-counting. Fill in each box. Use words, numbers, and pictures. Show as many ideas as you can.

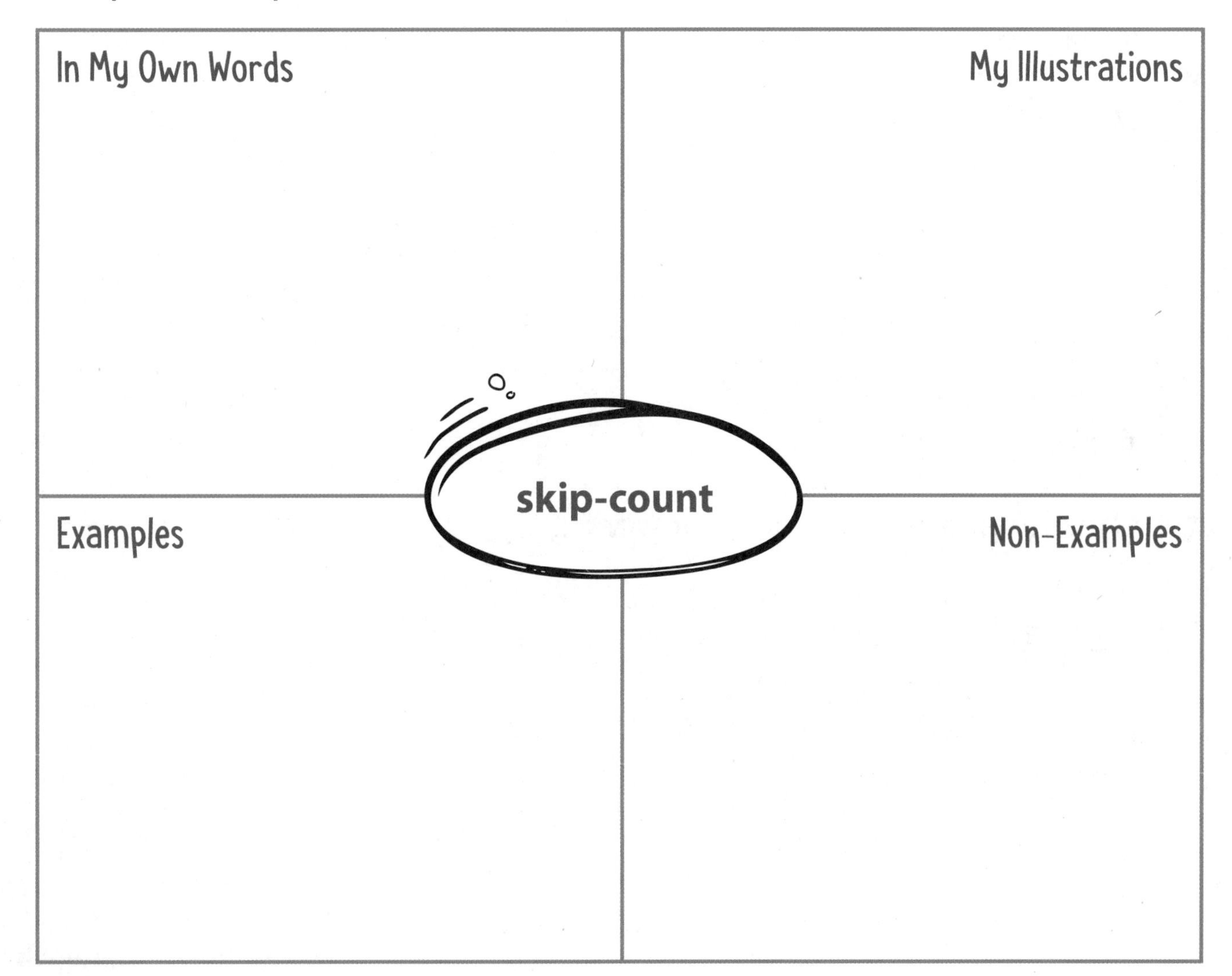

2. Carmen is trying to skip-count by fives. She counts 5, 15, 25, 35, 45, 55, and so on. Explain Carmen's mistake.

3 Solve the problem. Show your work.

Remy is counting the notebooks at the school store by tens. He has counted 120 so far. What are the next 5 numbers Remy says?

Solution ....

4 Check your answer. Show your work.

Develop Skip-Counting by Fives, Tens, and Hundreds

Read and try to solve the problem below.

Luis is skip-counting by tens. He starts at 235. What are the next 6 numbers Luis writes?

235 ? ? ? ? ? ?

TRY IT

Math Toolkit

- base-ten blocks
- 200 number charts
- hundreds place-value charts
- open number lines

DISCUSS IT

Ask your partner: Why did you choose that strategy?

Tell your partner: The strategy I used to find the answer was . . .

Explore different ways to understand skip-counting by fives, tens, and hundreds.

Luis is skip-counting by tens. He starts at 235. What are the next 6 numbers Luis writes?

MODEL IT

You can use an open number line.

Start at 235. Skip-count by tens.

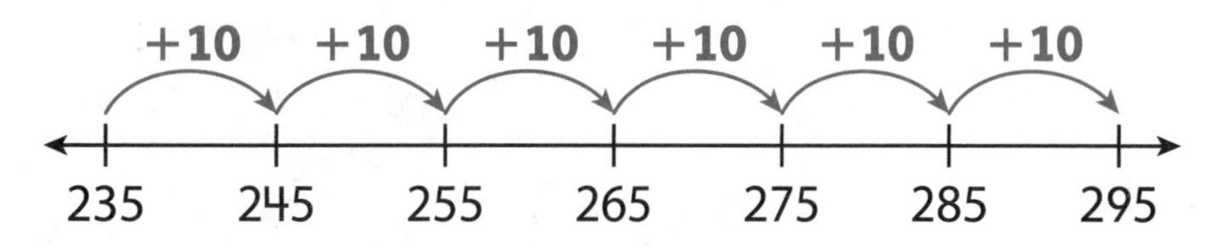

MODEL IT

You can use a number chart.

Circle **235**.

Then count 10 numbers to the right of 235. When you reach the end of a row, go to the next row. Circle the number where you stop counting.

Continue skip-counting by tens **5** more times.

201	202	203	204	205	206	207	208	209	210
211	212	213	214	215	216	217	218	219	220
221	222	223	224	225	226	227	228	229	230
231	232	233	234	235	236	237	238	239	240
241	242	243	244	245	246	247	248	249	250
251	252	253	254	255	256	257	258	259	260
261	262	263	264	265	266	267	268	269	270
271	272	273	274	275	276	277	278	279	280
281	282	283	284	285	286	287	288	289	290
291	292	293	294	295	296	297	298	299	300

CONNECT IT

Now you will use the problem from the previous page to help you understand how to skip-count.

 Look back at the **Model Its** on the previous page. Complete these equations.

235 + 10 = ...   245 + 10 = ...

255 + 10 = ...   265 + 10 = ...

2. Which digits stayed the same? Which changed?

3. Write the missing numbers to show how to skip-count from 235 by fives instead of tens.

240, 245, 250, ..., ..., ...

4. Write the missing numbers to skip-count by hundreds.

335, 435, 535, ..., ..., ...

5. ## REFLECT

Look back at your **Try It**, strategies by classmates, and **Model Its**. Which models or strategies do you like best for skip-counting? Explain.

....

....

....

APPLY IT

Use what you just learned to solve these problems.

6 Complete the forward and backward skip-counting patterns.

a. 821, 831, 841, ..., ..., ...

b. 349, 449, 549, ..., ..., ...

c. 920, 915, 910, ..., ..., ...

d. 783, 773, ..., ..., 743, ..., ...

7 Sadie says when she starts skip-counting forward by tens from 590, both the tens digit and the hundreds digit change. Is Sadie correct? Explain.

8 Which numbers go in the squares on this number line?

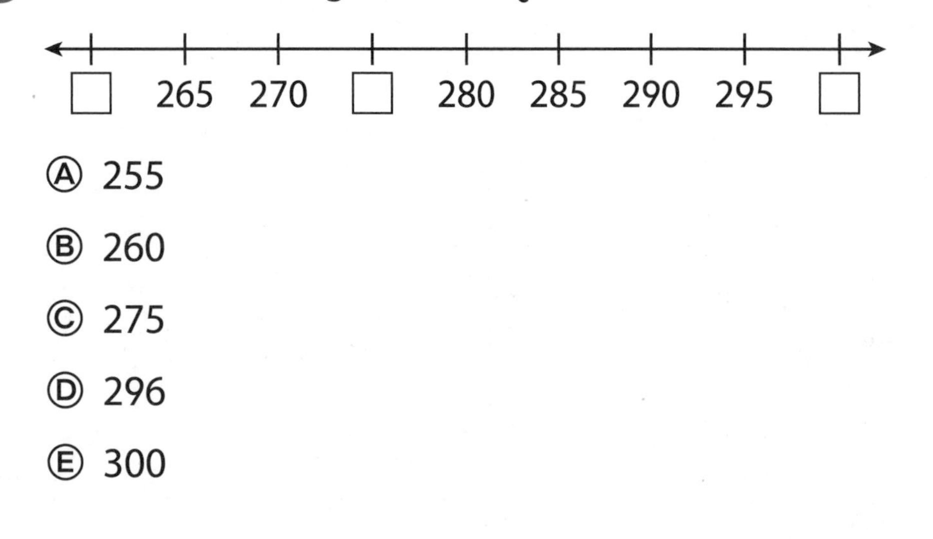

Ⓐ 255

Ⓑ 260

Ⓒ 275

Ⓓ 296

Ⓔ 300

Practice Skip-Counting by Fives, Tens, and Hundreds

Study the Example showing one way to use skip-counting by tens. Then solve problems 1–5.

EXAMPLE

Skip-count by tens from 128. What are the next 7 numbers?

You can use a number line to skip-count by tens.
Start at 128. Count by tens.

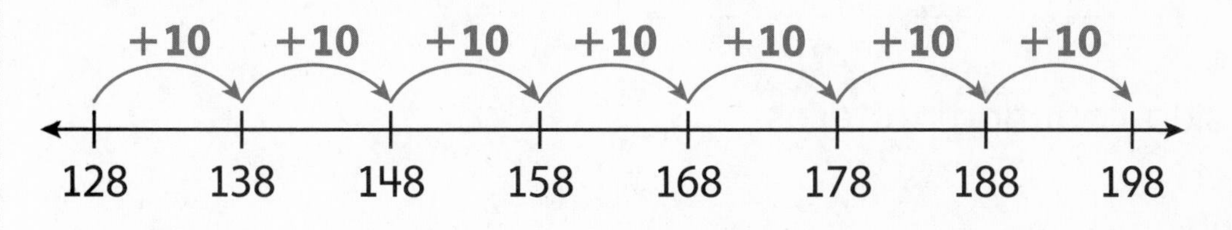

The next 7 numbers are 138, 148, 158, 168, 178, 188, and 198.

Skip-count by fives from 140. What are the next 5 numbers?

1. Use the open number line to solve the problem.

2. What are the next 5 numbers?

Jamal uses this number chart to skip-count by tens. Shade the next 3 numbers.

61	62	63	64	65	66	67	68	69	70
71	72	73	74	75	76	77	78	79	80
81	82	83	84	85	86	87	88	89	90
91	92	93	94	95	96	97	98	99	100
101	102	103	104	105	106	107	108	109	110
111	112	113	114	115	116	117	118	119	120

4. Complete the skip-counting patterns.

a. 460, 560, 660, ..., ..., ...

b. 310, 305, 300, ..., ..., ...

5. Does each group of numbers show skip-counting by fives, either forward or backward? Choose *Yes* or *No*.

	Yes	**No**
105, 110, 115, 120, 125, 130	Ⓐ	Ⓑ
355, 365, 375, 385, 395, 405	Ⓒ	Ⓓ
915, 925, 935, 945, 955, 965	Ⓔ	Ⓕ
285, 280, 275, 270, 265, 260	Ⓖ	Ⓗ

Develop Adding and Subtracting 10 and 100

Read and try to solve the problem below.

A class has 432 sheets of paper. They get 100 more for an art project. How many sheets of paper do they have now?

TRY IT

Math Toolkit

- connecting cubes
- base-ten blocks
- hundreds place-value mats
- open number lines
- three-digit number cards

DISCUSS IT

Ask your partner: Do you agree with me? Why or why not?

Tell your partner: I disagree with this part because . . .

Explore different ways to understand adding and subtracting 10 and 100.

A class has 432 sheets of paper. They get 100 more for an art project. How many sheets of paper do they have now?

PICTURE IT

You can draw a picture to show the number of sheets of paper.

432 is **4 hundreds** and 32 more.

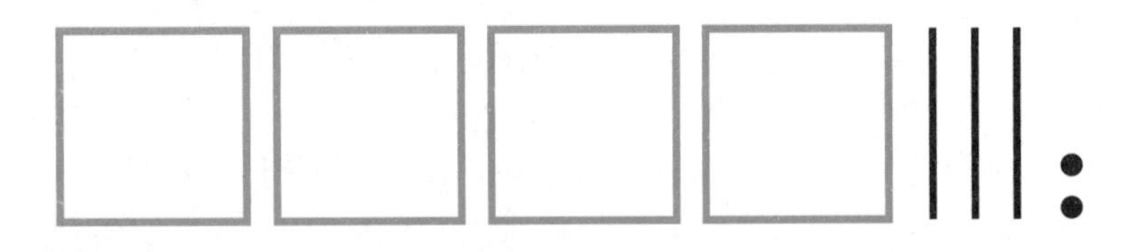

Adding 100 makes **5 hundreds** and 32 more.

MODEL IT

You can use facts you know.

432 and 100 more is **4**32 + **1**00.

You know **4** + **1** = 5.

So, you know **4** hundreds + **1** hundred = 5 hundreds.

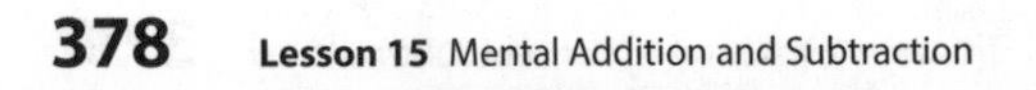

CONNECT IT

Now you will use the problem from the previous page to help you understand how to add and subtract 10 and 100.

1 Look at **Model It** on the previous page. How is adding hundreds like adding ones?

2 How many sheets of paper does the class have now?

....

3 Look at your answer for problem 1. How would adding and subtracting tens be like adding and subtracting ones?

4 REFLECT

Look back at your **Try It**, strategies by classmates, and **Picture It** and **Model It**. Which models or strategies do you like best for adding or subtracting 10 and 100? Explain.

....

....

....

APPLY IT

Use what you just learned to solve these problems.

5. A store has 893 granola bars. It sells 100 bars. How many granola bars does the store have now? Show your work.

Solution ....

6. Add or subtract 10 or 100.

a. $539 + 10 =$ ....

$704 + 100 =$ ....

$699 + 10 =$ ....

b. $675 - 100 =$ ....

$226 - 100 =$ ....

$491 - 10 =$ ....

7. What is $288 - 10$?

Ⓐ 188

Ⓑ 278

Ⓒ 287

Ⓓ 298

Name: ____________________

Practice Adding and Subtracting 10 and 100

Study the Example showing one way to add 100. Then solve problems 1–6.

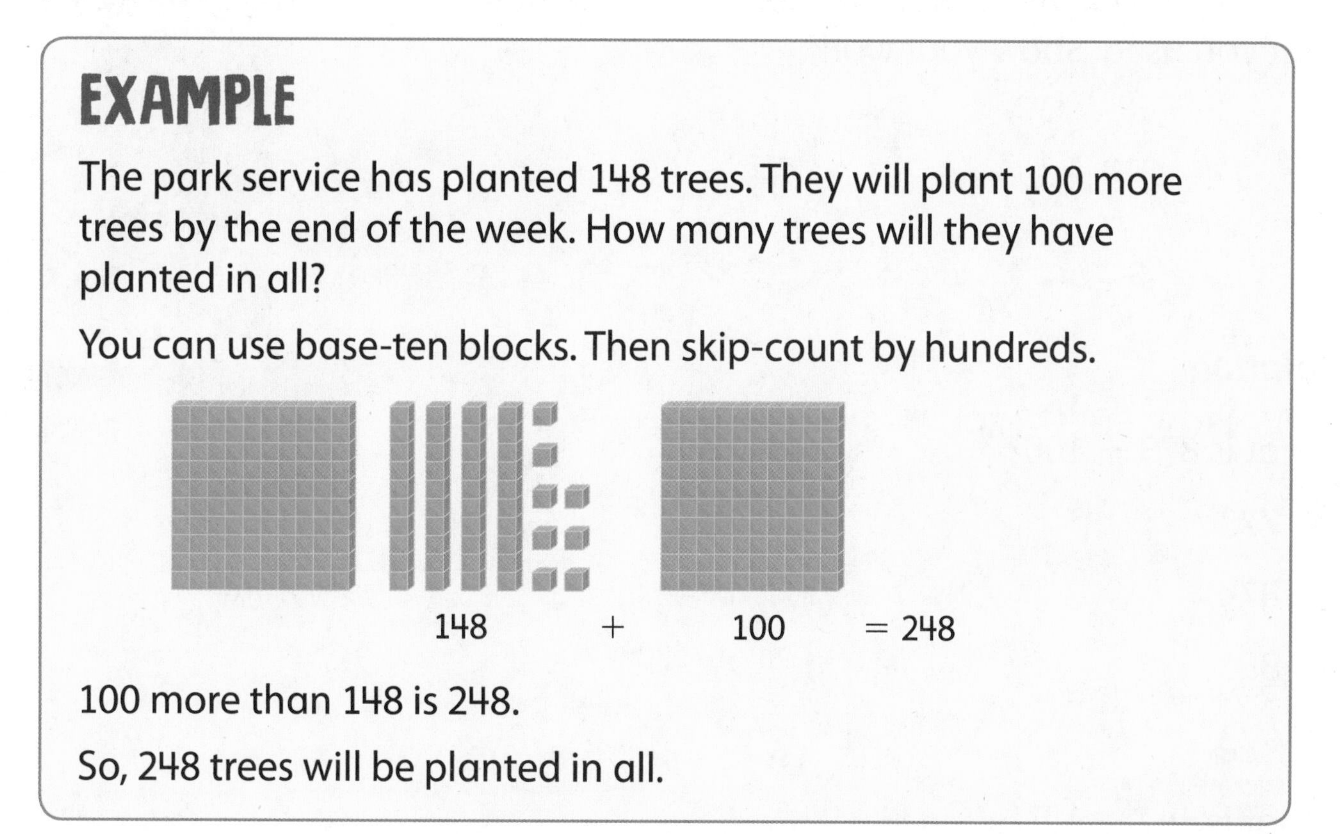

EXAMPLE

The park service has planted 148 trees. They will plant 100 more trees by the end of the week. How many trees will they have planted in all?

You can use base-ten blocks. Then skip-count by hundreds.

148 + 100 = 248

100 more than 148 is 248.

So, 248 trees will be planted in all.

Tim scores 318 points in a game. He plays another level and scores 10 more points. How many points does Tim score in all?

1. Draw base-ten blocks for 318 in one color. Then use a different color to draw more base-ten blocks to show how many points Tim scores in all.

2. How many points does Tim score in all? ....

3. Kevin has 452 stamps in his collection. Then he gives his sister 100 stamps. How many stamps does Kevin have now?

Solve the problem above. Then explain the strategy that you used. Show your work.

Solution ....

4. What is 873 + 100?

Ⓐ 773

Ⓑ 874

Ⓒ 883

Ⓓ 973

5. What is 547 − 10?

Ⓐ 557

Ⓑ 537

Ⓒ 527

Ⓓ 447

6. What is 10 + 865?

Ⓐ 765

Ⓑ 855

Ⓒ 875

Ⓓ 965

Refine Using Mental Addition and Subtraction

APPLY IT

Solve the problems.

1. Teresa has a box of raisins. She eats 10 of them. Now there are 190 raisins in the box. How many raisins were in the box at the start?

   Ⓐ 90

   Ⓑ 180

   Ⓒ 200

   Ⓓ 290

2. Carlos counts aloud and says these numbers. What number is Carlos skip-counting by?

   284, 384, 484, 584, 684, 784, 884

   Ⓐ twos

   Ⓑ fives

   Ⓒ tens

   Ⓓ hundreds

3. Which sets of numbers show skip-counting forward or backward by fives?

   Ⓐ 590, 595, 600, 605, 610, 615

   Ⓑ 845, 855, 865, 875, 885, 895

   Ⓒ 80, 75, 70, 65, 60, 55

   Ⓓ 390, 395, 400, 405, 410, 415

   Ⓔ 455, 555, 655, 755, 855, 955

 Ellen counts 349 stickers. Joseph counts 100 more stickers than Ellen.

How many stickers does Joseph count? Explain how you know.

 Which shows skip-counting by tens?

Ⓐ 210, 310, 410, 510, 610, 710

Ⓑ 829, 839, 849, 859, 869, 879

Ⓒ 440, 445, 450, 455, 460, 465

Ⓓ 320, 430, 540, 650, 760, 870

 What is 998 − 100? ....

7 MATH JOURNAL

Explain how skip-counting forward by tens and adding tens are alike.

☑ SELF CHECK Go back to the Unit 3 Opener and see what you can check off.

Add Three-Digit Numbers

LESSON 16

Dear Family,

This week your child is learning different strategies to add three-digit numbers.

Here are some ways he or she might find the sum 237 + 345.

- Add hundreds, tens, and ones using expanded form.

$$\begin{array}{rcl} 237 & \longrightarrow & 200 + 30 + 7 \\ +\ 345 & \longrightarrow & 300 + 40 + 5 \\ \hline & & \mathbf{500 + 70 + 12 = 582} \end{array}$$

- Break numbers into hundreds, tens, and ones.

$$\begin{array}{rcl} 237 & \longrightarrow & \text{2 hundreds} + \text{3 tens} + \text{7 ones} \\ +\ 345 & \longrightarrow & \text{3 hundreds} + \text{4 tens} + \text{5 ones} \\ \hline & & \textbf{5 hundreds + 7 tens + 12 ones = 582} \end{array}$$

- Add ones, then tens, then hundreds. Combine the sums.

$$\begin{array}{rl} 237 & \\ +\ 345 & \\ \hline 12 & \longleftarrow 7 + 5 \\ 70 & \longleftarrow 30 + 40 \\ +\ 500 & \longleftarrow 200 + 300 \\ \hline \mathbf{582} & \end{array}$$

500 + 70 + 12, 5 hundreds + 7 tens + 12 ones, and **582** are all ways to express the same value.

237 + 345 = 582

Invite your child to share what he or she knows about adding three-digit numbers by doing the following activity together.

ACTIVITY ADDING THREE-DIGIT NUMBERS

Do this activity with your child to practice adding three-digit numbers.

- Have your child choose and write a three-digit number from the numbers below. (*Example:* Your child picks 385.)
- Write the other number with the matching shape and color below your child's number. Write a plus sign to show addition. (*Example:* You write "+ 114.")
- Ask your child if he or she thinks the sum of the two numbers will be greater than or less than 500. (*Example:* Your child says it will be less than 500.)
- Have your child add the two numbers to check his or her answer. (*Example:* 385 + 114 = 499.) Ask your child whether his or her prediction about being greater or less than 500 was correct.
- Repeat the process with other numbers.

Explore Adding Hundreds, Tens, and Ones

You already know about hundreds, tens, and ones. Now you will use strategies to add three-digit numbers. Use what you know to try to solve the problem below.

There are 214 fish in the giant tank at an aquarium. There are 131 other sea animals in the tank. How many animals live in the giant tank?

Learning Target

- Add and subtract within 1000, using concrete models or drawings and strategies based on place value, properties of operations, and/or the relationship between addition and subtraction; relate the strategy to a written method. Understand that in adding or subtracting three digit numbers, one adds or subtracts hundreds and hundreds, tens and tens, ones and ones; and sometimes it is necessary to compose or decompose tens or hundreds.

SMP 1, 2, 3, 4, 5, 6, 7

TRY IT

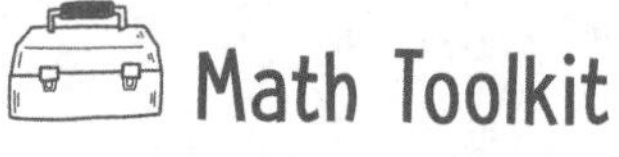

- connecting cubes
- counters
- base-ten blocks
- number charts
- open number lines

Ask your partner:

How did you get started?

Tell your partner:

A model I used was . . . It helped me . . .

CONNECT IT

1 LOOK BACK

How many animals live in the giant tank?

....

2 LOOK AHEAD

You can also show jumps on an open number line to add three-digit numbers.
What is 248 + 143? Write the missing numbers on the open number line to find the sum.

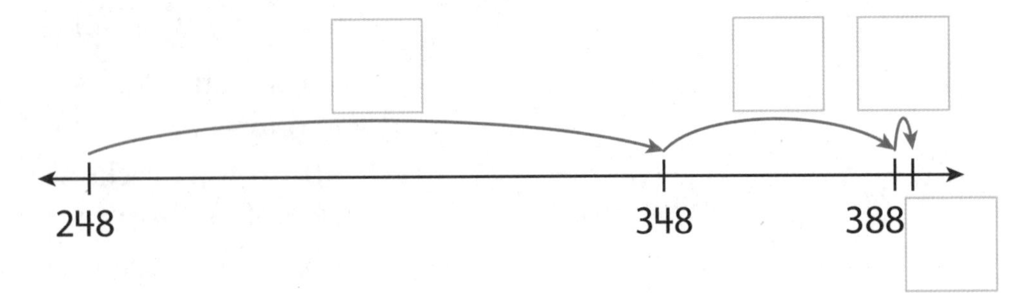

3 REFLECT

Do you always have to add hundreds, then tens, then ones? Why or why not?

....

....

....

....

Name: ____________________

Prepare for Adding Hundreds, Tens, and Ones

1. Think about what you know about adding numbers. Fill in each box. Use words, numbers, and pictures. Show as many ideas as you can.

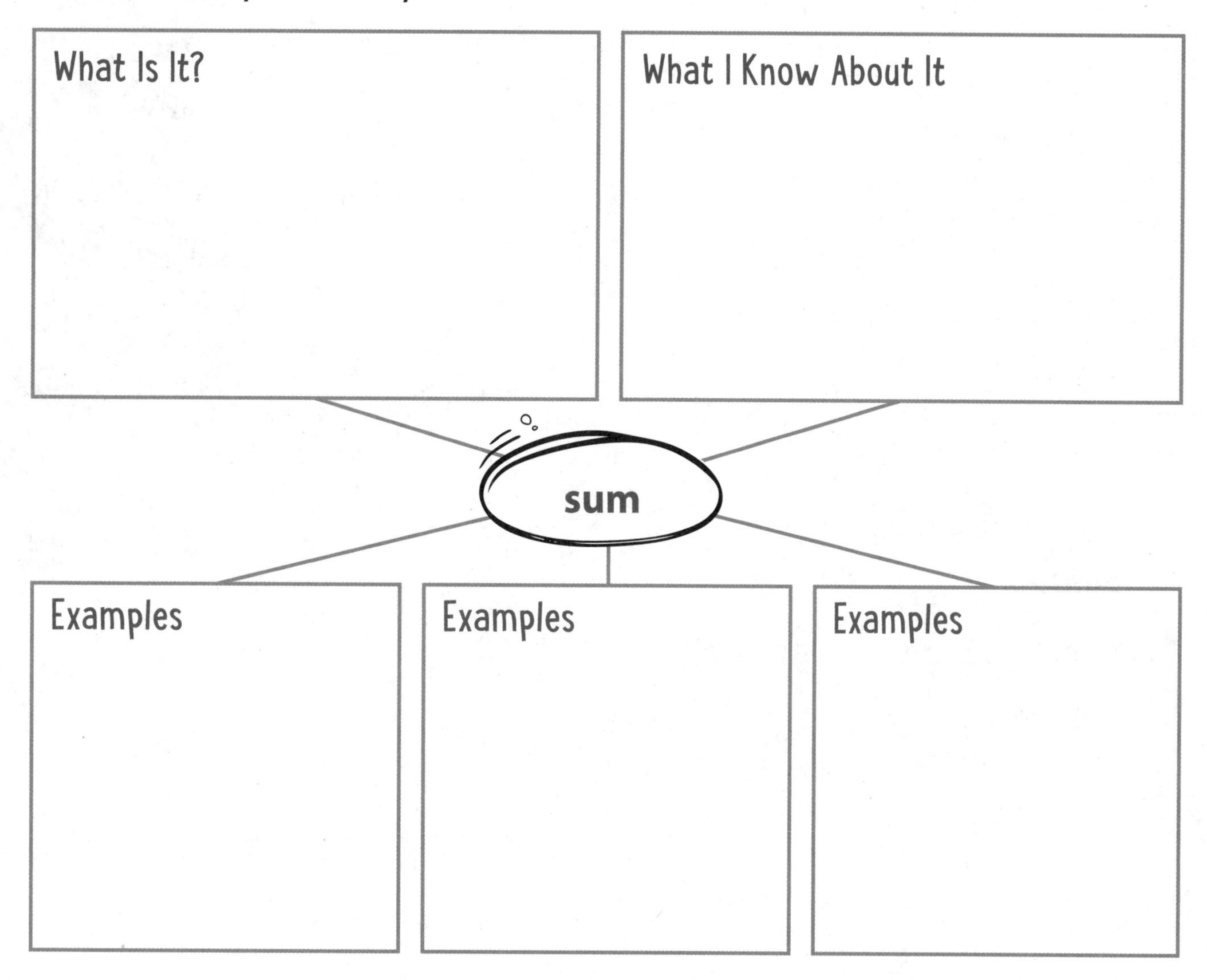

2. Sasha has 263 silver paper clips and 124 gold paper clips. He will find $263 + 124$ to find out how many paper clips he has in all. Explain how you would find the sum $263 + 124$.

3 Solve the problem. Show your work.

There are 236 animals that live in the first part of a zoo. There are 152 animals that live in the second part of the zoo. How many animals live in both parts?

Solution ....

4 Check your answer. Show your work.

Develop Adding and Regrouping Ones

Read and try to solve the problem below.

There are 254 adults and 328 children helping to clean up their city. How many people are helping to clean up the city?

TRY IT

Math Toolkit
- connecting cubes
- base-ten blocks
- number charts
- hundreds place-value mats
- open number lines

DISCUSS IT

Ask your partner: Why did you choose that strategy?

Tell your partner: I knew . . . so I . . .

Explore different ways to understand adding three-digit numbers.

There are 254 adults and 328 children helping to clean up their city. How many people are helping to clean up the city?

PICTURE IT

You can show the numbers in a quick drawing.

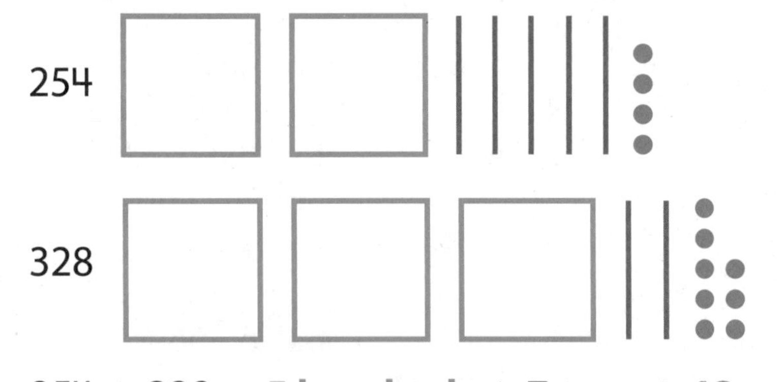

254 + 328 = **5 hundreds** + **7 tens** + **12 ones**

MODEL IT

You can show jumps on an open number line.

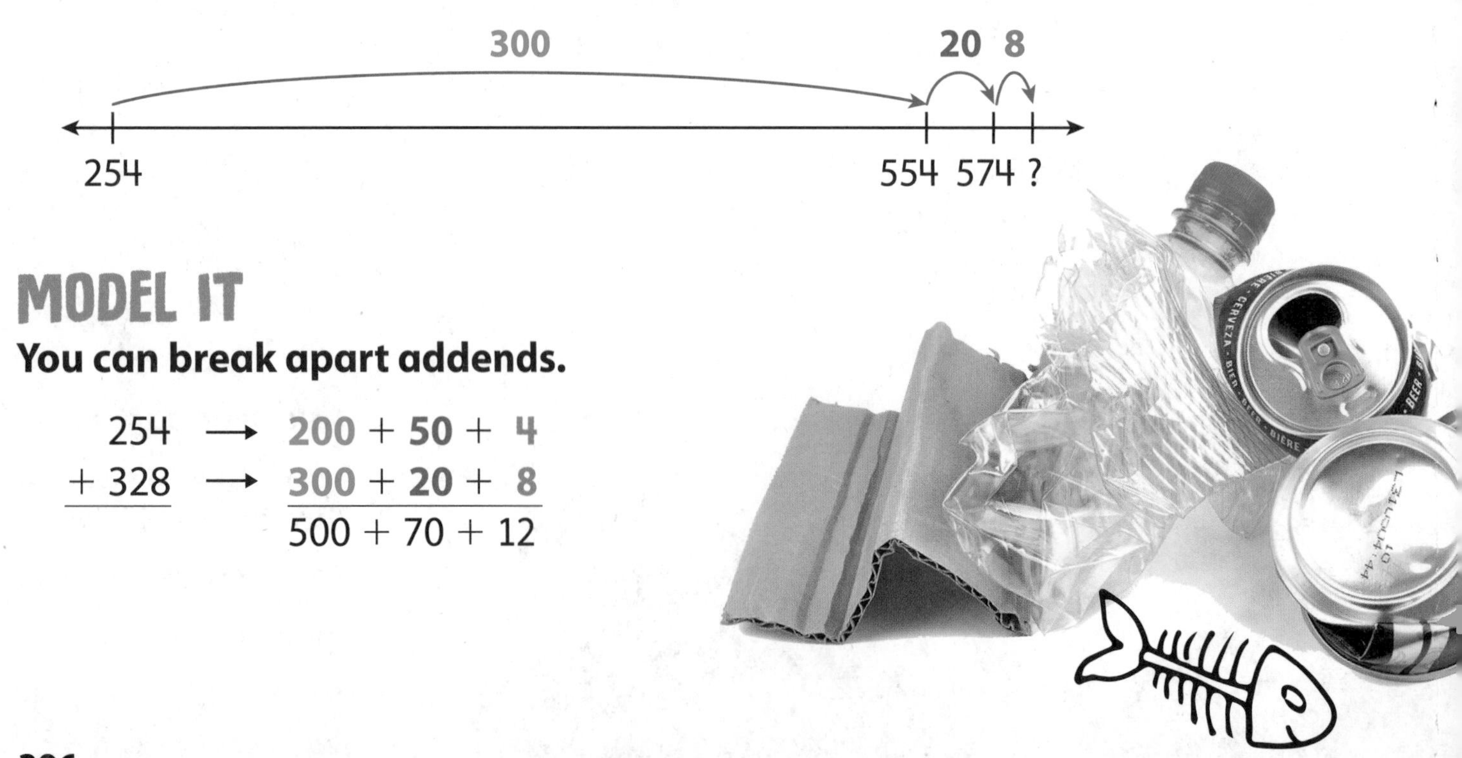

MODEL IT

You can break apart addends.

254	→	**200 + 50 + 4**
+ 328	→	**300 + 20 + 8**
		500 + 70 + 12

CONNECT IT

Now you will use the problem from the previous page to help you understand how to add three-digit numbers.

 Look at **Picture It**. How do you write 12 ones as tens and ones?

12 ones = ... ten + ... ones

2 Look at the second **Model It**. What is the total number of tens in 70 + 12? Explain.

3 How many people are helping to clean the city? Show how to find the sum.

 REFLECT

Look back at your **Try It**, strategies by classmates, and **Picture It** and **Model Its**. Which models or strategies do you like best for adding three-digit numbers? Explain.

....

....

....

APPLY IT

Use what you just learned to solve these problems.

5 Find the sum. Show your work.

$$\begin{array}{r} 526 \\ +\ 235 \\ \hline \end{array}$$

6 Find the sum. Show your work.

$167 + 426$

 Juanita's family is on vacation. They drive 258 miles one day and 209 miles the next day. Which shows one way to find how many miles they drive on both days?

Ⓐ $200 + 58 + 9$

Ⓑ $200 + 200 + 8 + 9$

Ⓒ $400 + 5 + 8 + 9$

Ⓓ $400 + 50 + 17$

Practice Adding and Regrouping Ones

Study the Example showing two ways to add three-digit numbers. Then solve problems 1–7.

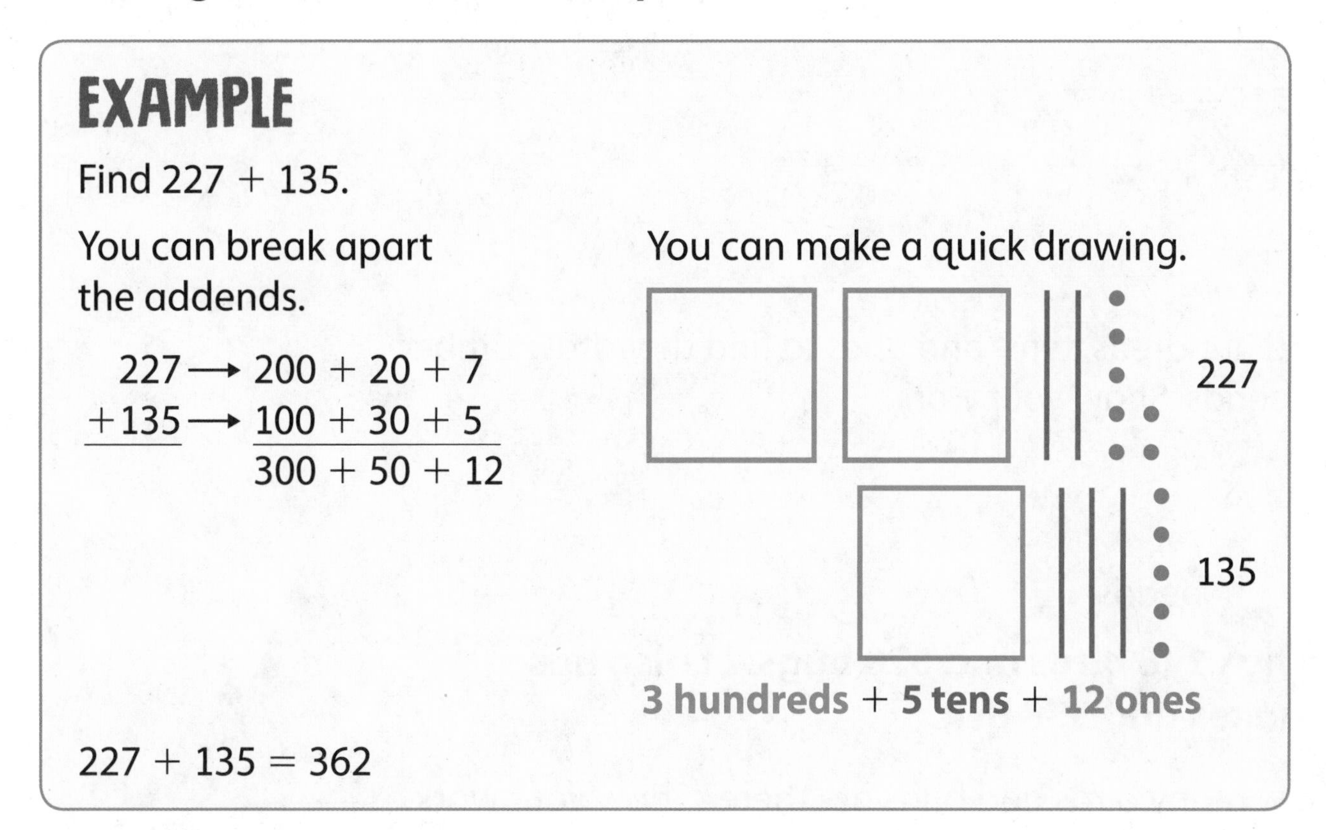

There are 416 oak trees and 238 pine trees in the park.

1. Fill in the boxes to help you find the total number of trees.

   416 → 400 + 10 + 6
   + 238 → 200 + 30 + 8

   ☐ + ☐ + 14

2. 14 ones = ... ten + ... ones

3. How many trees are there altogether? .... trees

Paul has 547 beads. Amy has 219 beads.

4. Fill in the boxes to help you find the total number of beads.

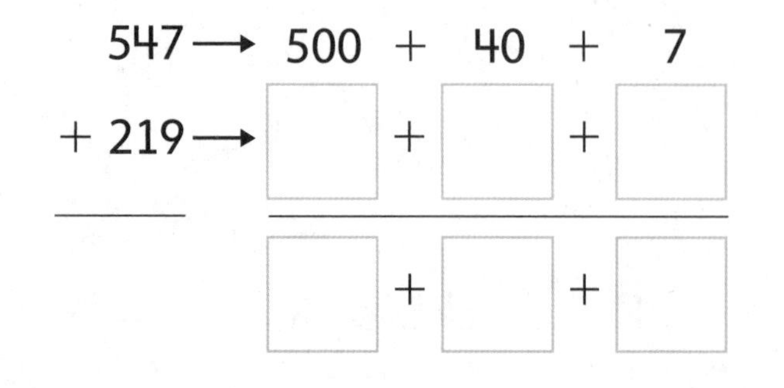

5. Add hundreds, tens, and ones to find the total number of beads. Show your work.

.... beads

A zoo has 146 birds and 628 bugs. It also has 258 snakes and 338 fish.

6. How many birds and bugs are there? Show your work.

$$\begin{array}{r} 146 \\ +\ 628 \\ \hline \end{array}$$

Solution ....

7. How many snakes and fish are there? Show your work.

258 + 338

Solution ....

Develop Adding and Regrouping Tens

Read and try to solve the problem below.

There are 476 rocks and 148 minerals in a museum display. What is the total number of rocks and minerals in the display?

TRY IT

Math Toolkit
- connecting cubes
- base-ten blocks
- number charts
- hundreds place-value mats
- open number lines

DISCUSS IT

Ask your partner: Do you agree with me? Why or why not?

Tell your partner: The strategy I used to find the answer was. . .

Explore more different ways to understand adding three-digit numbers.

There are 476 rocks and 148 minerals in a museum display. What is the total number of rocks and minerals in the display?

MODEL IT

You can show each number as hundreds, tens, and ones.

476	→	4 hundreds + 7 tens + 6 ones
+ 148	→	1 hundred + 4 tens + 8 ones
		5 hundreds + 11 tens + 14 ones

MODEL IT

You can add hundreds, then tens, then ones.

476		
+ 148		
500	→	400 + 100
110	→	70 + 40
14	→	6 + 8

500 + 110 + 14

MODEL IT

You can add ones, then tens, then hundreds.

476		
+ 148		
14	→	6 + 8
110	→	70 + 40
500	→	400 + 100

14 + 110 + 500

CONNECT IT

Now you will use the problem from the previous page to help you understand another way to add.

1 Write the number of ones, tens, and hundreds.

14 = ... ones   110 = ... tens   500 = ... hundreds

2 You can regroup when you have 10 or more ones or 10 or more tens.

Regroup.

Fill in the blanks.

$$\begin{array}{r} 476 \\ +\ 148 \\ \hline 14 \\ 110 \\ 500 \end{array}$$

14 → .... ten and 4 ones

110 → .... hundred and .... ten

500 → 5 hundreds

3 Look at problem 2. Write the total number of ones, tens, and hundreds after regrouping.

.... ones + ... tens + ... hundreds

4 Why should you get the same total when you use different strategies to find 476 + 148?

5 ## REFLECT

Look back at your **Try It**, strategies by classmates, and **Model Its**. Which models or strategies do you like best for adding three-digit numbers? Explain.

....

....

....

APPLY IT

Use what you just learned to solve these problems.

6 What is 649 + 184? Show your work.

Solution ....

7 Find the sum. Show your work.

$$\begin{array}{r} 427 \\ +\ 297 \\ \hline \end{array}$$

Solution ....

8 Explain how you would find the sum 375 + 545.

Practice Adding and Regrouping Tens

Study the Example showing how to add hundreds, tens, and ones. Then solve problems 1–5.

EXAMPLE

Find 346 + 487.

You can add hundreds, then tens, then ones.

```
  346
+ 487
  700 → 300 + 400
  120 → 40 + 80
   13 → 6 + 7
```

700 + 120 + 13 = 833

You can add ones, then tens, then hundreds.

```
  346
+ 487
   13 → 6 + 7
  120 → 40 + 80
  700 → 300 + 400
```

13 + 120 + 700 = 833

Mina's class collects 368 cans to recycle. Willa's class collects 254 cans.

1. Fill in the boxes to show how you can add hundreds, then tens, then ones.

```
  368
+ 254
  [  ]
  110
  [  ]
```

2. How many cans do the classes collect altogether? Fill in the blanks.

………… + 110 + ………… = …………

 Show how to find 579 + 358.

 Show how you can add 157 and 296.

5 Find the greatest possible sum by using two of the numbers from the box below. Then find the least possible sum. Tell how you solved the problem.

268	275	242	259

Refine Adding Three-Digit Numbers

Complete the Example below. Then solve problems 1–3.

EXAMPLE

There are 146 firefighters and 158 police officers marching in a parade. What is the total number of firefighters and police officers marching in the parade?

You can show your work on an open number line.

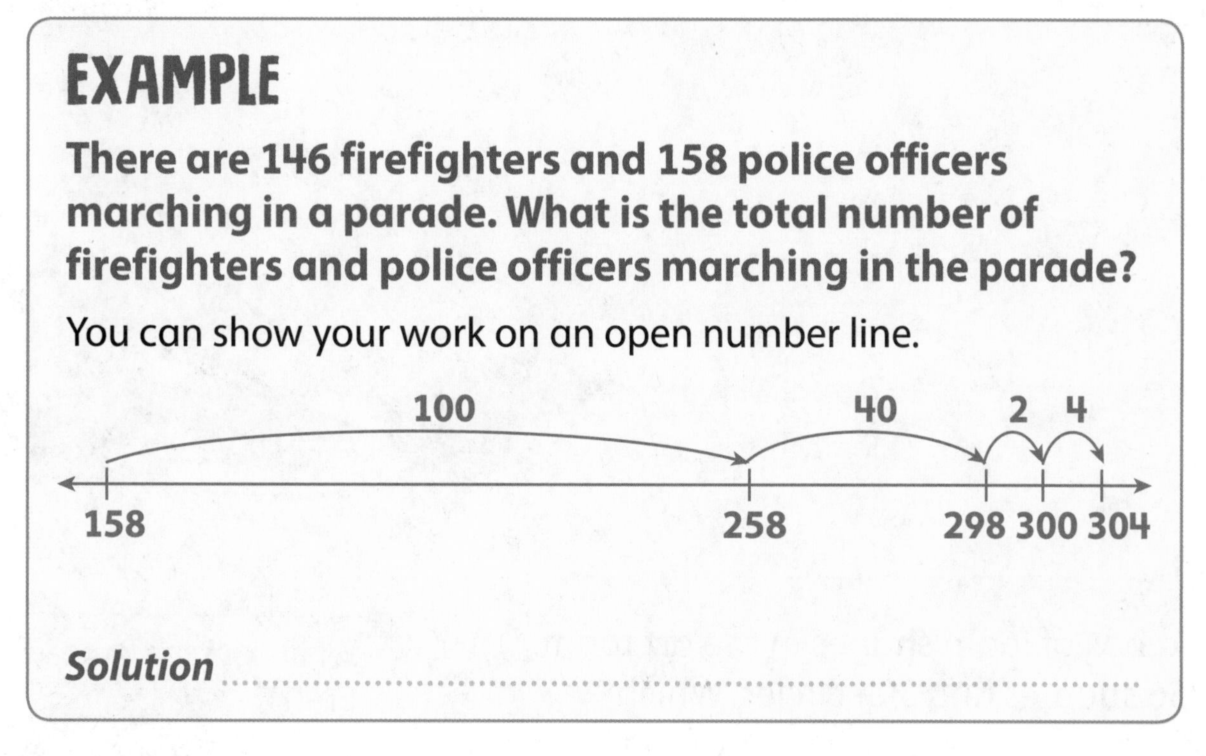

Solution ....

APPLY IT

1 A basketball team sells 379 tickets before game day. Another 136 tickets are sold at the door. How many tickets are sold in all? Show your work.

How many hundreds, tens, and ones does each number have?

Solution ....

 Ms. Stone's students work in the school garden. They plant 267 beet plants and 278 onion plants. What is the total number of plants? Show your work.

Remember: you can add in any order.

Solution ....

3 There is a box of foam shapes in the art room. It has 356 squares and 304 circles. Which addition problem shows how many foam shapes there are in all?

What does the 0 mean in 304?

Ⓐ 600 + 5 + 10

Ⓑ 600 + 50 + 10

Ⓒ 600 + 90 + 6

Ⓓ 300 + 50 + 6

Dean chose Ⓐ as the answer. How did Dean get his answer?

Name: ______________________

Practice Adding Three-Digit Numbers

1. Charlie has 378 play coins. Ting has 147. How many coins do Charlie and Ting have in all? Show your work.

Will you add hundreds or ones first?

Solution ....

2. A flower store sells 285 roses in the morning and 260 roses in the afternoon. Which addition problem shows how many roses the store sells in all?

How many hundreds, tens, and ones does each number have?

Ⓐ 200 + 140 + 50

Ⓑ 200 + 140 + 5

Ⓒ 400 + 140 + 5

Ⓓ 400 + 140 + 50

Lance chose Ⓑ. How did Lance get his answer?

3 Find 426 + 315. Write the missing numbers on the open number line below.

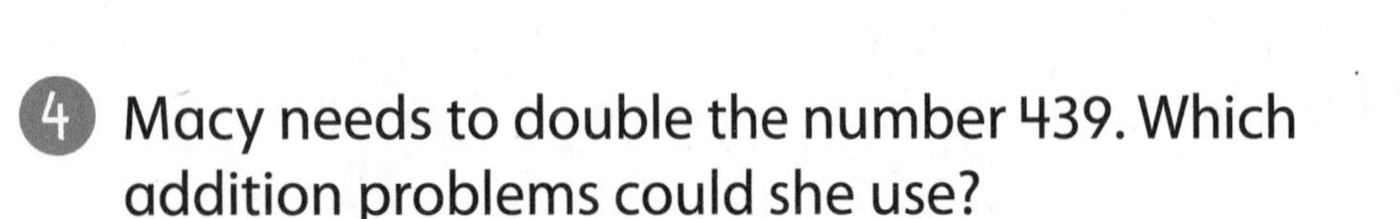

What number do you add to 426 to get 726?

4 Macy needs to double the number 439. Which addition problems could she use?

Ⓐ 18 + 60 + 800

Ⓑ 400 + 60 + 18

Ⓒ 800 + 60 + 10 + 8

Ⓓ 800 + 60 + 90

What are the two numbers in the addition problem?

5 Elsa writes 500 + 70 + 6. What two three-digit numbers could she be adding?

Ⓐ 371 + 275

Ⓑ 145 + 421

Ⓒ 403 + 273

Ⓓ 252 + 324

How many hundreds do you need?

Refine Adding Three-Digit Numbers

APPLY IT

Solve the problems.

1. Which are ways to show 203 + 160?

Ⓐ 300 + 60 + 3

Ⓑ 300 + 90

Ⓒ 200 + 100 + 60 + 3

Ⓓ 3 + 60 + 300

Ⓔ 3 + 6 + 100 + 200

2. Jane writes 700 + 90 + 9 to add two three-digit numbers. Which sum could she be finding?

Ⓐ 354 + 455

Ⓑ 396 + 313

Ⓒ 521 + 278

Ⓓ 590 + 290

3. Find 563 + 127. Fill in the chart. Then complete the equation.

Hundreds	Tens	Ones

.... hundreds + ... tens + ... ones = ...

4 Write the missing numbers on the open number line. Then write the addition equation that the number line shows.

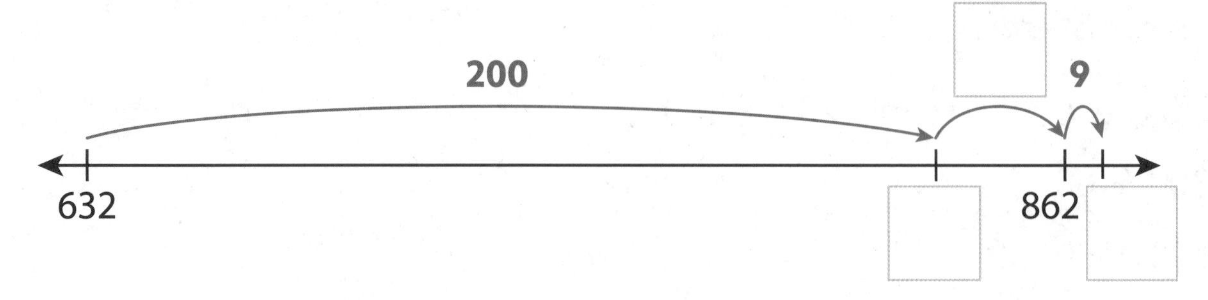

.... + ... = ...

5 Carmen has 172 photos of her family. She also has 153 photos of friends. She has 3 photo albums.

Album A holds 225 photos. Album B holds 275 photos. Album C holds 375 photos.

Which photo album will hold all of her pictures? Show your work.

6 MATH JOURNAL

Write your own problem about the photo albums described above. Then solve your problem.

SELF CHECK Go back to the Unit 3 Opener and see what you can check off.

Subtract Three-Digit Numbers

LESSON 17

Dear Family,

This week your child is learning to subtract three-digit numbers using place value.

For example, your child might be asked to find 352 − 139.

The number 352 can be represented by a quick drawing of hundreds, tens, and ones.

There are not enough ones to subtract the 9 ones in 139. Regroup a ten in 352 to get more ones.

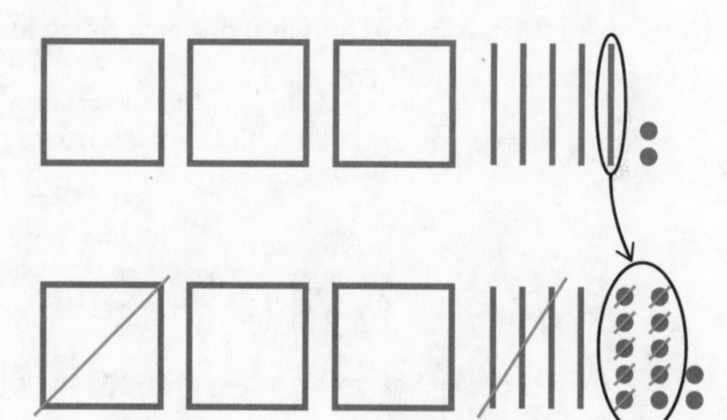

Now, subtract 139 by crossing out 1 hundred, 3 tens, and 9 ones.

Count the number of hundreds, tens, and ones remaining: 2 hundreds + 1 ten + 3 ones = 213.

352 − 139 = 213

As another example, your child might be asked to find 647 − 481.

Compare the digits in each place.

647 = 6 hundreds + 4 tens + 7 ones
481 = 4 hundreds + 8 tens + 1 one
6 > 4   4 < 8   7 > 1

There are not enough tens to subtract the 8 tens in 481. Regroup a hundred to get more tens.

$$\begin{array}{r} \overset{500}{\cancel{600}} + \overset{140}{\cancel{40}} + 7 \\ -\ 400 + 80 + 1 \\ \hline 100 + 60 + 6 \end{array}$$

647 − 481 = 166

Invite your child to share what he or she knows about subtracting three-digit numbers by doing the following activity together.

ACTIVITY SUBTRACTING THREE-DIGIT NUMBERS

Do this activity with your child to subtract three-digit numbers.

- Talk with your child about a purchase you made where you compared prices of similar items or services. Examples include clothing or sports equipment, or appliance or car repairs.
- Compare items and prices shown on the catalog pages below, noting the pages show two stores that sell the same appliances, but not for the same prices.
- Have your child choose an item from one of the catalog pages and compare its cost with the same item from the other catalog page.
- Ask your child at which store the item costs less. Help your child use subtraction to compare the two prices and find out how much less the item costs at one store compared to another.
- Take turns, so that you and your child each compare prices for several appliances.

Washing machine... $699
Dryer.................. $597
Refrigerator.......... $548
Oven $471
Microwave............. $209

Main Street Home Store

Sale

Washing machine... $659
Dryer.................. $564
Refrigerator.......... $589
Oven $482
Microwave............. $205

Explore Subtracting Hundreds, Tens, and Ones

You know how to subtract two-digit numbers. Now you will learn to use place value to subtract three-digit numbers. Use what you know to try to solve the problem below.

Holly has 368 pet pal cards. Dara has 243 cards. How many more cards does Holly have than Dara?

Learning Target

- Add and subtract within 1000, using concrete models or drawings and strategies based on place value, properties of operations, and/or the relationship between addition and subtraction; relate the strategy to a written method. Understand that in adding or subtracting three digit numbers, one adds or subtracts hundreds and hundreds, tens and tens, ones and ones; and sometimes it is necessary to compose or decompose tens or hundreds.

SMP 1, 2, 3, 4, 5, 6, 7

TRY IT

Math Toolkit

- connecting cubes
- base-ten blocks
- hundred charts
- hundreds place-value mats
- open number lines

DISCUSS IT

Ask your partner:

Why did you choose that strategy?

Tell your partner:

I started by . . .

CONNECT IT

1 LOOK BACK

How many more cards does Holly have than Dara?

....

2 LOOK AHEAD

Sometimes you have to regroup to subtract three-digit numbers.

a. Write <, >, or = to compare hundreds, tens, and ones.

368	=	300	+	60	+	8
249	=	200	+	40	+	9

3 ◯ 2 6 ◯ 4 8 ◯ 9

b. Complete the sentence. There are not enough

.... in 368 to subtract 249 without regrouping.

c. Show how to write 368 a different way to show more ones.

368 = 3 hundreds + 5 tens + ... ones.

3 REFLECT

How can you tell when you need to regroup to subtract?

....

....

....

....

Prepare for Subtracting Hundreds, Tens, and Ones

1. Think about what you know about subtracting numbers. Fill in each box. Use words, numbers, and pictures. Show as many ideas as you can.

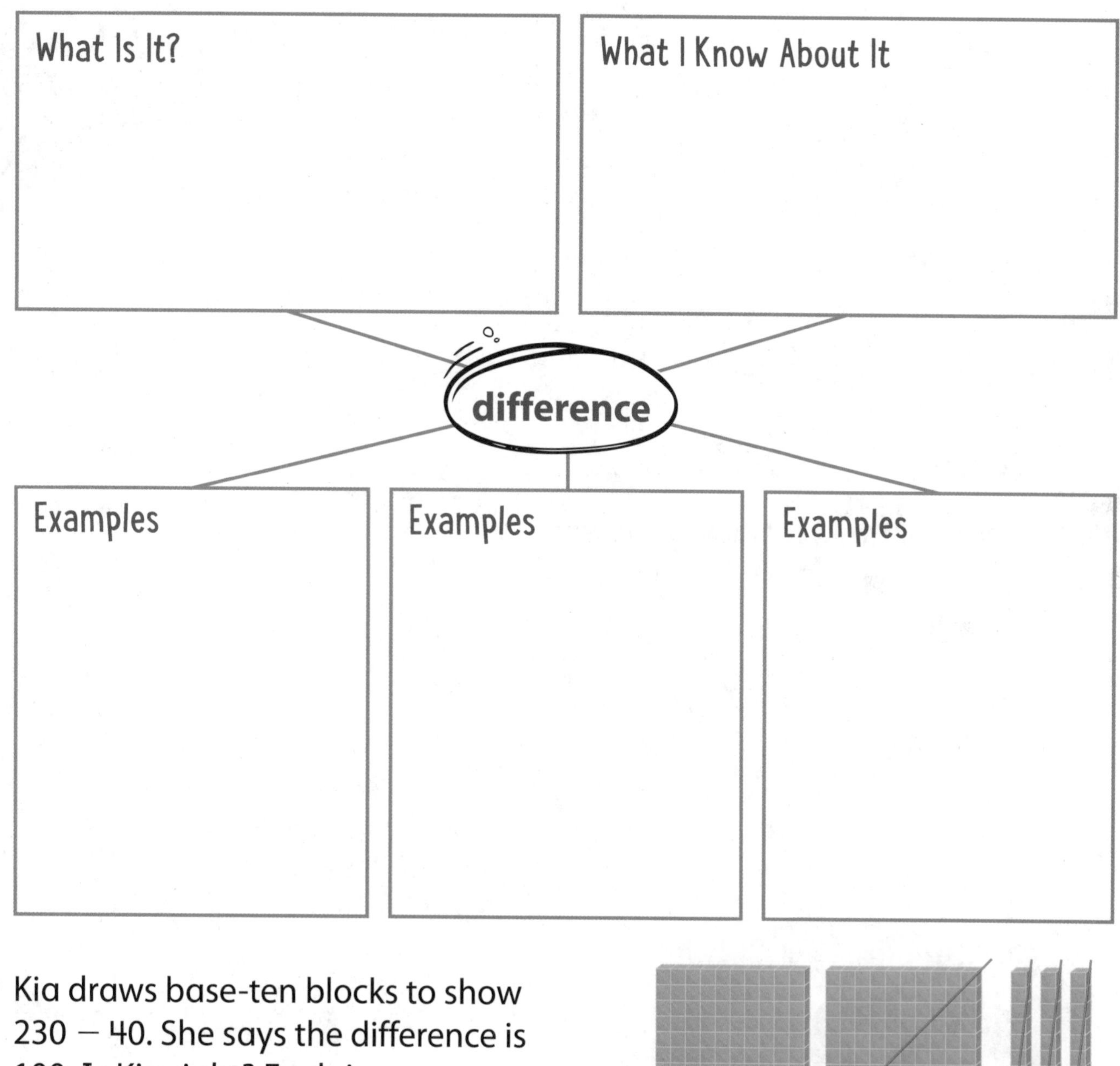

2. Kia draws base-ten blocks to show 230 − 40. She says the difference is 100. Is Kia right? Explain.

 Solve the problem. Show your work.

Lionel has 379 stickers. 258 of them are animal stickers. The rest are flower stickers. How many flower stickers does Lionel have?

Solution ....

4 Check your answer. Show your work.

Develop Regrouping Tens to Ones

Read and try to solve the problem below.

There are 450 campers at Camp Cody. One day, 218 campers do art projects. The rest do sports. How many campers do sports that day?

TRY IT

Math Toolkit
- base-ten blocks
- hundred charts
- hundreds place-value mats
- open number lines

DISCUSS IT

Ask your partner:

How did you get started?

Tell your partner:

The strategy I used to find the answer was . . .

Explore different ways to understand subtracting three-digit numbers.

There are 450 campers at Camp Cody. One day, 218 campers do art projects. The rest do sports. How many campers do sports that day?

PICTURE IT

You can make a quick drawing.

Show 450.

Regroup 1 ten as 10 ones.
Then take away 218.

MODEL IT

You can subtract hundreds, tens, and ones.

Think: 218 = **200** + **10** + **8**

$$\begin{array}{r} 450 \\ -\ 200 \\ \hline 250 \\ -\ 10 \\ \hline 240 \\ -\ 8 \\ \hline ? \end{array}$$

MODEL IT

You can break apart the numbers.

Look at the ones: **0** < **8**.
Regroup **1 ten** as **10 ones**.
Then subtract.

$$\begin{array}{rcl} & & \quad\ \ 40 + 10 \\ 450 & \rightarrow & 400 + \cancel{50} + \cancel{0} \\ -\ 218 & \rightarrow & 200 + 10 + 8 \\ \hline & & 200 + 30 + 2 \end{array}$$

CONNECT IT

Now you will use the problem from the previous page to help you understand how to subtract three-digit numbers.

1. Look at **Picture It**. Why do you need to regroup 1 ten as 10 ones?

2. How many campers do sports? ....

3. Look at the first **Model It**. How is the way the problem is solved like the way shown in the second **Model It**? How is it different?

4. REFLECT

Look back at your **Try It**, strategies by classmates, and **Picture It** and **Model Its**. Which models or strategies do you like best for subtracting three-digit numbers? Explain.

....

....

....

....

APPLY IT

Use what you just learned to solve these problems.

5 Jim has 572 stamps. Leo has 347 stamps. How many more stamps does Jim have than Leo? Show your work.

Solution ....

6 Find the difference. Show your work.

473 − 235

Solution ....

Rita and Jose are playing a game. Rita has 224 points. Jose has 330 points. Explain how you would find how many more points Jose has than Rita.

Practice Regrouping Tens to Ones

Study the Example showing one way to subtract three-digit numbers. Then solve problems 1–6.

EXAMPLE

Find 874 − 235.

Look at the ones: 4 ones < 5 ones.
Regroup a ten in 874 as 10 ones.

$$
\begin{array}{rcl}
 & & \phantom{800 + {}}60 + 14 \\
874 & \longrightarrow & 800 + \cancel{70} + \cancel{4} \\
-\ 235 & \longrightarrow & -\ 200 + 30 + 5 \\
\hline
 & & 600 + 30 + 9 = 639
\end{array}
$$

874 − 235 = 639

There are 546 students at Lincoln School. On Mondays, 327 students have art class. The rest have music class.

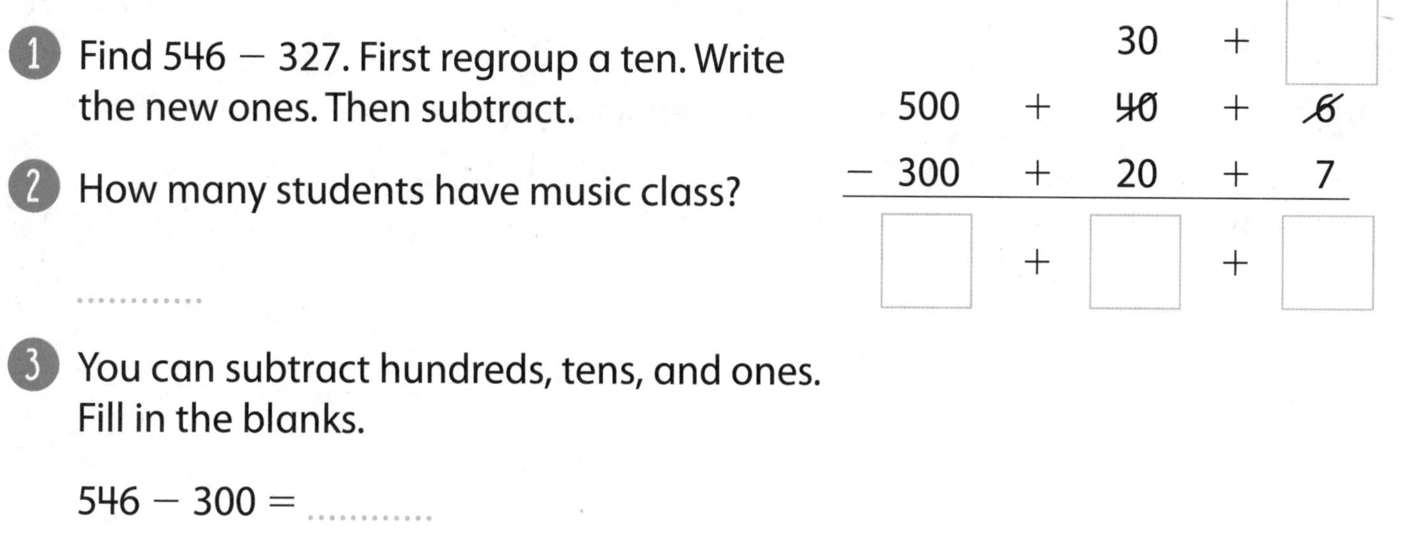

1. Find 546 − 327. First regroup a ten. Write the new ones. Then subtract.

$$
\begin{array}{rcrcr}
 & & 30 & + & \square \\
500 & + & \cancel{40} & + & \cancel{6} \\
-\ 300 & + & 20 & + & 7 \\
\hline
\square & + & \square & + & \square
\end{array}
$$

2. How many students have music class?

....

3. You can subtract hundreds, tens, and ones. Fill in the blanks.

546 − 300 = ...

246 − 20 = ...

226 − 7 = ...

 472 people see the school play. On Saturday, 248 people see the play. The rest see it on Sunday. How many people see the play on Sunday? Show your work.

Solution ....

5 Find the difference 220 − 117. Show your work.

Solution ....

6 Blake has 583 stickers. Sasha has 324 fewer stickers than Blake. How many stickers do they have in all? Show your work.

Solution ....

Develop Regrouping Hundreds to Tens

Read and try to solve the problem below.

At Brown School, there are 327 girls and 276 boys. How many more girls are there than boys?

TRY IT

Math Toolkit

- connecting cubes
- base-ten blocks
- hundred charts
- hundreds place-value mats
- open number lines

DISCUSS IT

Ask your partner: Can you explain that again?

Tell your partner: I agree with you about . . . because . . .

Explore more different ways to understand subtracting three-digit numbers.

At Brown School, there are 327 girls and 276 boys. How many more girls are there than boys?

PICTURE IT

You can use base-ten blocks to subtract.

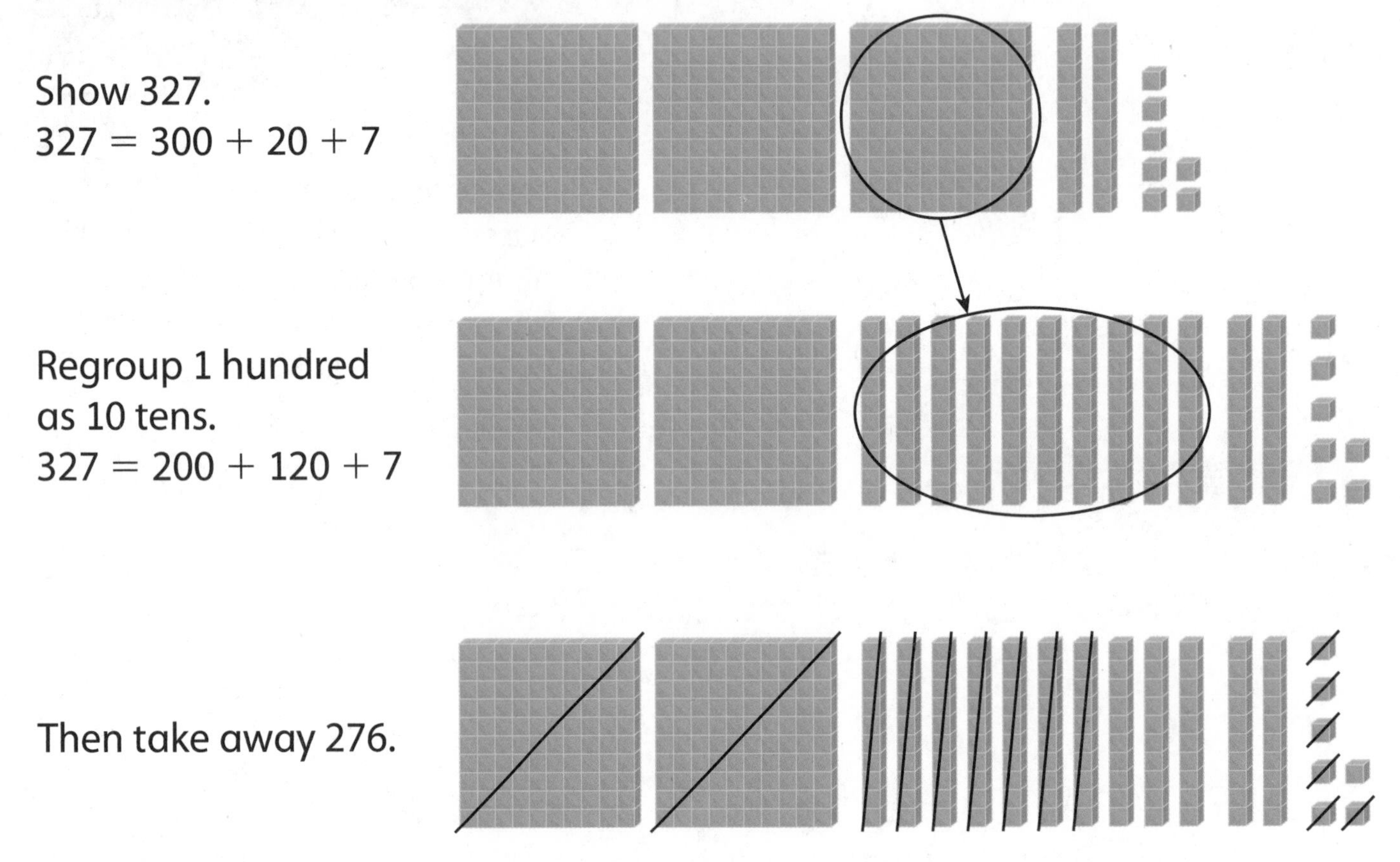

MODEL IT

You can use an open number line.

Think of subtraction as addition: 276 + ? = 327.

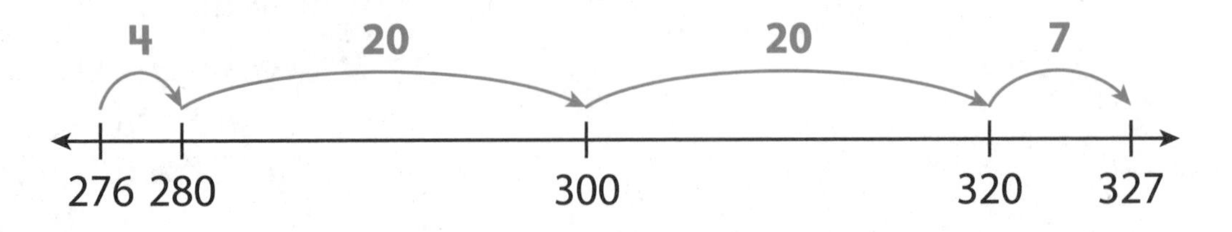

CONNECT IT

Now you will use the problem from the previous page to understand how to subtract three-digit numbers.

1. Compare the digits in each place in 327 and 276. Do you need to regroup to show more tens or more ones? Explain.

   ....

2. Fill in the blanks to regroup a hundred to show more tens in 327.

   $327 = 300 +$ .... $+ 7$

   $327 = 200 +$ .... $+ 20 + 7$

   $327 = 200 +$ .... $+ 7$

3. How many hundreds, tens, and ones are there after you regroup? Fill in the boxes. Then subtract 276.

4. How many more girls are there than boys?

   ....

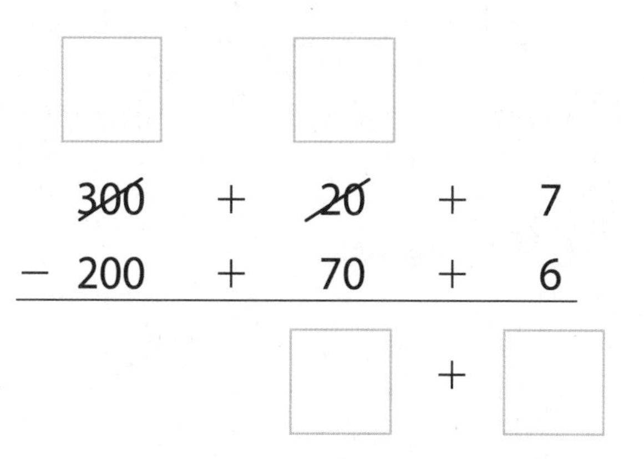

5. ## REFLECT

   Look back at your **Try It**, strategies by classmates, and **Picture It** and **Model It**. Which models or strategies do you like best for subtracting three-digit numbers? Explain.

   ....

   ....

   ....

APPLY IT

Use what you just learned to solve these problems.

6 At Taylor School, students go to school for 180 days. They have already been in school for 136 days. How many school days are left? Show your work.

Solution ....

7 What is 636 − 353? Show your work.

Solution ....

8 Find 319 − 225.

Ⓐ 94

Ⓑ 96

Ⓒ 104

Ⓓ 106

Practice Regrouping Hundreds to Tens

Study the Example showing how to regroup to subtract three-digit numbers. Then solve problems 1–7.

EXAMPLE

Find 517 − 362.

Look at the tens: 1 ten < 6 tens.

Regroup a hundred in 517.

500 + 10 + 7 =
400 + 100 + 10 + 7 =
400 + 100 + 10 + 7 =
400 + 110 + 7

$$\begin{array}{rcr} 517 & \longrightarrow & \overset{400}{\cancel{500}} + \overset{110}{\cancel{10}} + 7 \\ -\ 362 & \longrightarrow & -\ 300 + 60 + 2 \\ \hline & & 100 + 50 + 5 = 155 \end{array}$$

517 − 362 = 155

Jodi's book has 428 pages. She has read 275 pages. Her father asks her how many pages she has left.

1. Compare the digits in each place. Write <, >, or = in each circle.

4 hundreds	+	2 tens	+	8 ones
2 hundreds	+	7 tens	+	5 ones
4 ◯ 2		2 ◯ 7		8 ◯ 5

2. Show how to regroup a hundred.

400 + 20 + 8 =

300 + ... + 20 + 8 =

300 + ... + 8

3. Fill in the problem to show the regrouping. Then subtract.

$$\begin{array}{rcccc} \square & & \square & & \\ \cancel{400} & + & \cancel{20} & + & 8 \\ -\ 200 & + & 70 & + & 5 \\ \hline \square & + & \square & + & \square = \square \end{array}$$

4 Fill in the boxes to show how you can add up to find 215 − 153.

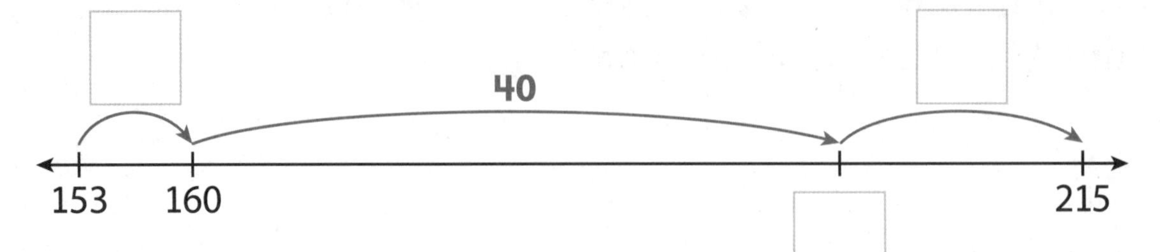

5 How do you use the numbers above the open number line in problem 4 to find 215 − 153?

6 Ken has 449 paper clips. There are 379 small paper clips. The rest are large. How many large paper clips are there? Show your work.

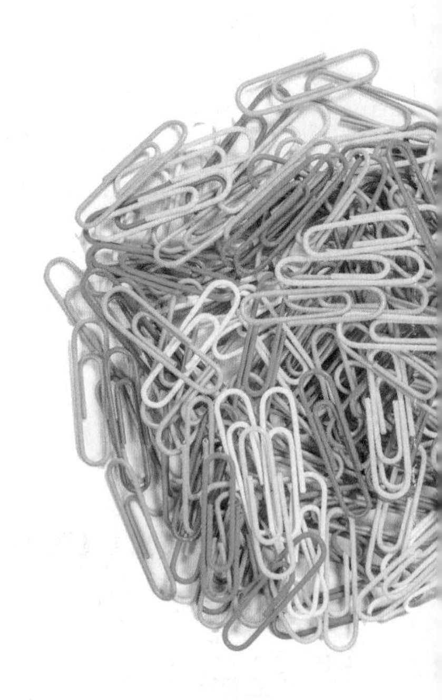

Solution ....

7 Tim shows his work to answer a subtraction problem. Tell how to find an equation to represent the problem Tim starts with, and its answer.

Tim's Work:
863 + 7 = 870
870 + 30 = 900
900 + 55 = 955

Refine Subtracting Three-Digit Numbers

Complete the Example below. Then solve problems 1–3.

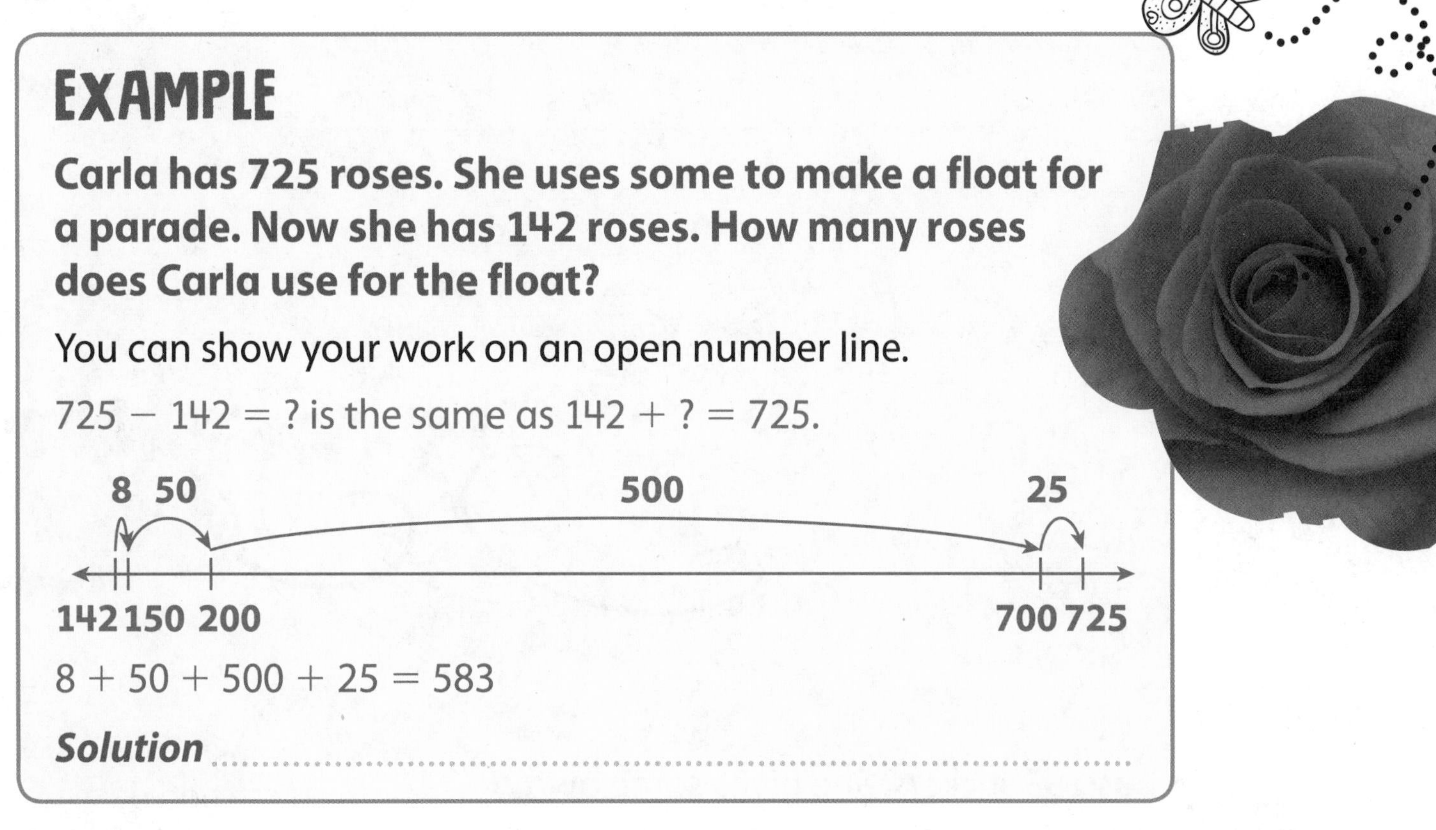

EXAMPLE

Carla has 725 roses. She uses some to make a float for a parade. Now she has 142 roses. How many roses does Carla use for the float?

You can show your work on an open number line.

725 − 142 = ? is the same as 142 + ? = 725.

8 + 50 + 500 + 25 = 583

Solution ....

APPLY IT

1 Gus has 872 pennies. He gives 725 pennies to the pet shelter. How many pennies does Gus have left? Show your work.

Do you need to regroup? If so, how?

Solution ....

2 Students need to paint 525 pumpkins for the fair. They have painted 193 so far. How many pumpkins are left to paint? Show your work.

How could you add up to find the answer?

Solution ....

3 Ms. Diaz has 185 stickers. She gives some away. Now she has 139 stickers. How many stickers does Ms. Diaz give away?

You can add or subtract to find the answer.

Ⓐ 46

Ⓑ 54

Ⓒ 56

Ⓓ 146

Ria chose Ⓓ as the answer. How did Ria get her answer?

Practice Subtracting Three-Digit Numbers

1 Fill in the boxes to find 826 − 635.

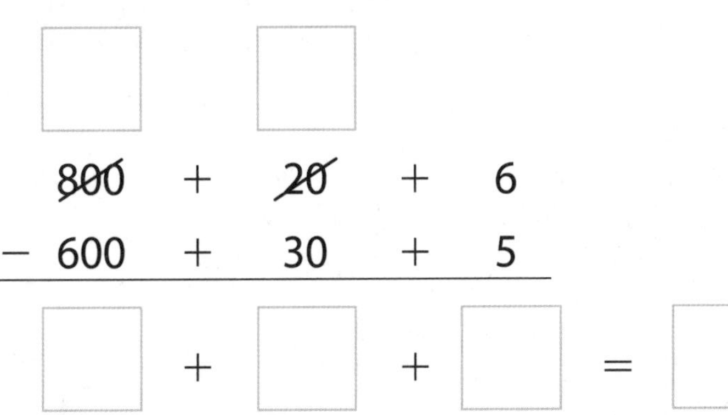

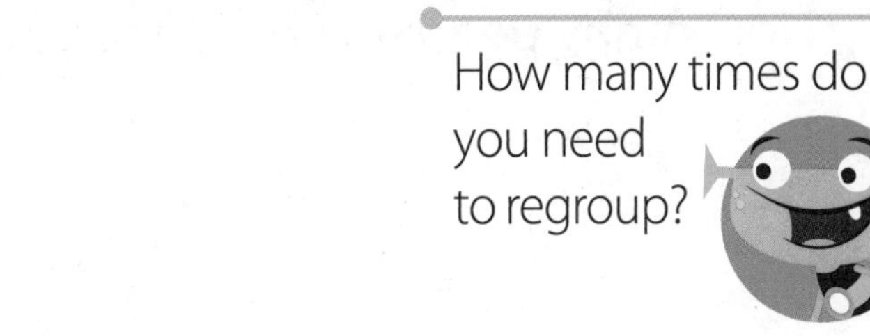

2 Sally has 237 marbles. Gina has 184 marbles. How many more marbles does Sally have than Gina?

Ⓐ 157

Ⓑ 153

Ⓒ 87

Ⓓ 53

How could you add up to find the answer?

3 For each subtraction problem, tell if you need to regroup tens to subtract. Then tell if you need to regroup hundreds to subtract. Write *Yes* or *No* for each problem.

I can compare ones digits to see if I need to regroup tens.

	Regroup Tens?	Regroup Hundreds?
643 − 225		
812 − 511		
574 − 346		
709 − 488		

4 There are 951 people in a parade. There are 728 people marching. The rest ride on floats. How many people ride on floats? Show your work.

You can add up or subtract hundreds, tens, and ones.

Solution ....

5 Mr. Grant has 357 plums. He sells some. Now he has 219 plums. How many plums does Mr. Grant sell?

How many hundreds, tens, and ones are in each number?

Ⓐ 38

Ⓑ 147

Ⓒ 148

Ⓓ 138

Matt chose Ⓒ. How did Matt get his answer?

Refine Subtracting Three-Digit Numbers

APPLY IT

Solve the problems.

1. For each subtraction problem, tell if you need to regroup tens to subtract. Then tell if you need to regroup hundreds to subtract. Write *Yes* or *No* for each problem.

	Regroup Tens?	Regroup Hundreds?
927 − 845		
673 − 581		
392 − 270		
557 − 148		

2. Fill in the boxes to find 574 − 335.

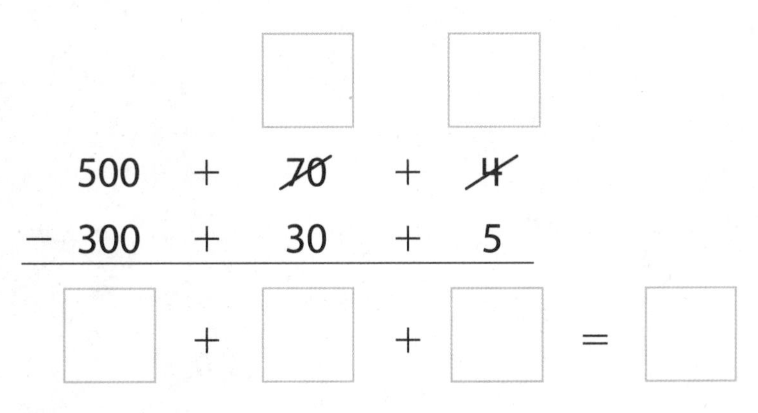

3. Kali has some shells. She finds 132 more. Now she has 215 shells. How many shells did Kali have to begin with?

Ⓐ 83
Ⓑ 123
Ⓒ 183
Ⓓ 347

4 Two classes are trying to earn 750 points to earn a pizza party. Which class has more points? How many more points? Show your work.

Class	Points
A	585
B	617

Solution ....

5 Look at problem 4. Ben says Class B needs 143 more points to earn a pizza party. Is Ben correct? Explain.

6 MATH JOURNAL

Explain what strategy you would use to find 529 − 285. Why do you like this strategy?

SELF CHECK Go back to the Unit 3 Opener and see what you can check off.

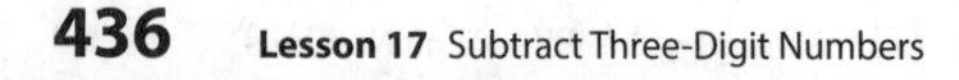

Use Addition and Subtraction Strategies with Three-Digit Numbers

Dear Family,

This week your child is learning strategies for adding and subtracting three-digit numbers.

Previously, your child learned to use place value to add and subtract three-digit numbers. In this lesson, your child will use both addition and subtraction strategies to solve many different types of problems.

Here are some ways that your child might find 600 − 238.

- Subtract hundreds, tens, and ones.

  238 = 200 + 30 + 8
  First, subtract **200**.
  Then subtract **30**.
  Last, subtract **8**.

$$\begin{array}{r} 600 \\ -\,200 \\ \hline 400 \\ -\,30 \\ \hline 370 \\ -\,8 \\ \hline 362 \end{array}$$

- Use an open number line.
  You can change the subtraction problem into a missing addend addition problem. To find 600 − 238, you can find 238 + ? = 600.

  Start at **238**.
  Add **2** to reach 240.
  Then add **60** to reach 300.
  Then add **300** to reach 600.

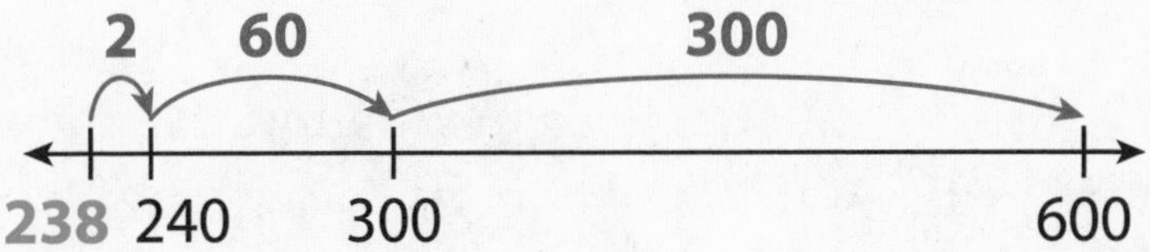

  You added on **2 + 60 + 300**, or **362**.

Your answer to 600 − 238 is 362 using either strategy.

Invite your child to share what he or she knows about adding and subtracting three-digit numbers by doing the following activity together.

ACTIVITY USING ADDITION AND SUBTRACTION STRATEGIES WITH THREE-DIGIT NUMBERS

Do this activity with your child to use addition and subtraction strategies with three-digit numbers.

- Ask your child to choose and write a three-digit number from below.
- Add the number on the matching shape and color as your child's number. Have your child check the sum.
- Ask your child to use those same two numbers and subtract the lesser number from the greater number. Have your child explain the strategy he or she used to find the answer.
- Switch roles and repeat so that you and your child take turns doing either the addition or the subtraction of the two numbers with matching colors.
- Ask your child what his or her favorite strategy is for adding three-digit numbers. Ask what his or her favorite strategy is for subtracting three-digit numbers.

Explore Using Addition and Subtraction Strategies with Three-Digit Numbers

You know how to add and subtract three-digit numbers. Use what you know to try to solve the problem below.

Ms. Mendez's class has 243 storybooks. Then the class gets some new storybooks. Now the class has 372 storybooks. How many new storybooks does Ms. Mendez's class get?

Learning Target

- Add and subtract within 1000, using concrete models or drawings and strategies based on place value, properties of operations, and/or the relationship between addition and subtraction; relate the strategy to a written method. Understand that in adding or subtracting three digit numbers, one adds or subtracts hundreds and hundreds, tens and tens, ones and ones; and sometimes it is necessary to compose or decompose tens or hundreds.

SMP 1, 2, 3, 4, 5, 6, 7

TRY IT

Math Toolkit

- base-ten blocks
- hundreds place-value mats
- number charts
- open number lines

DISCUSS IT

Ask your partner: How did you get started?

Tell your partner: I started by . . .

CONNECT IT

1 LOOK BACK

How many new storybooks does Ms. Mendez's class get?

Solution ....

2 LOOK AHEAD

Mr. Lumell's class gets 300 new storybooks. How many more new storybooks does Mr. Lumell's class get than Ms. Mendez's class?

a. Write an equation that you could use to solve the problem. ....

b. How many hundreds, tens, and ones will be subtracted from 300?

.... hundred .... tens .... ones

c. How many more new storybooks does Mr. Lumell's class get than Ms. Mendez's class? ....

3 REFLECT

How could you count up to find $300 - 129$?

....

....

....

....

Name: ____________________

Prepare for Using Strategies to Add and Subtract Three-Digit Numbers

1. Think about what you know about adding and subtracting. Fill in each box. Use words, numbers, and pictures. Show as many ideas as you can.

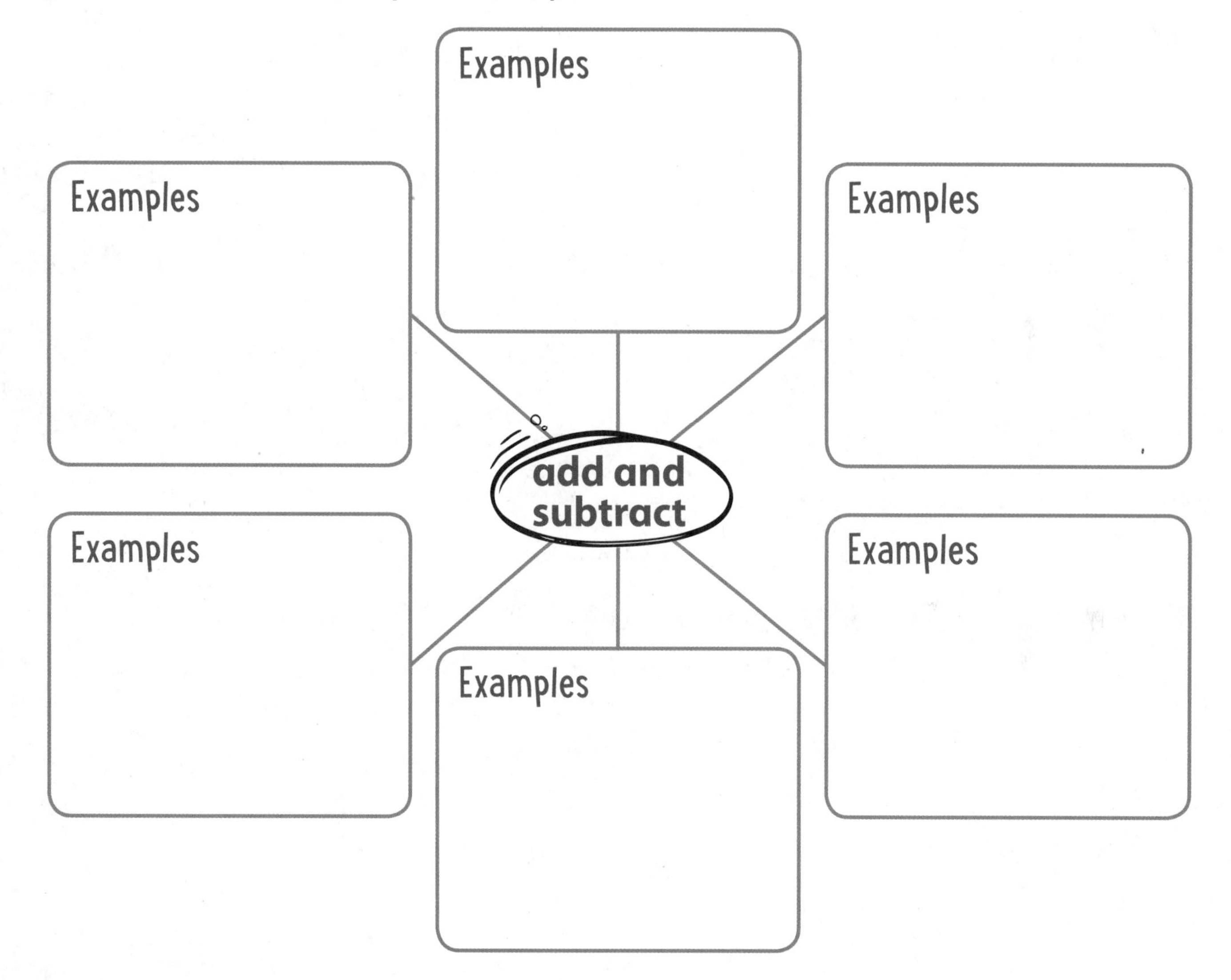

2. Shen has 200 pennies. Diana has 137 pennies. Write addition and subtraction equations that can be solved to find how many more pennies Shen has than Diana.

.... + ... = ... − .... = ...

3 Solve the problem. Show your work.

Lakeview Elementary School has 238 coloring books. Then the school gets some new coloring books. Now the school has 357 coloring books. How many new coloring books does the school get?

Solution ....

4 Check your answer. Show your work.

Develop Using Addition Strategies with Three-Digit Numbers

Read and try to solve the problem below.

Janelle has 263 pennies and 137 nickels in her piggy bank. How many pennies and nickels in all does she have in her piggy bank?

TRY IT

Math Toolkit

- connecting cubes
- base-ten blocks
- hundreds place-value mats
- number charts
- open number lines

DISCUSS IT

Ask your partner: Why did you choose that strategy?

Tell your partner: The strategy I used to find the answer was . . .

Explore different ways to understand addition strategies with three-digit numbers.

Janelle has 263 pennies and 137 nickels in her piggy bank. How many pennies and nickels in all does she have in her piggy bank?

MODEL IT

You can use a place-value chart.

Write the numbers in the chart.
Regroup ones and tens.

	Hundreds	Tens	Ones
	2	6	3
	+ 1	3	7
Add hundreds, add tens, add ones. →	3	9	10
Regroup 10 ones as 1 ten. →	3	10	0
Regroup 10 tens as 1 hundred. →	?	?	?

MODEL IT

You can use an open number line.

Start at 263. Add the ones, tens, and hundreds in 137.

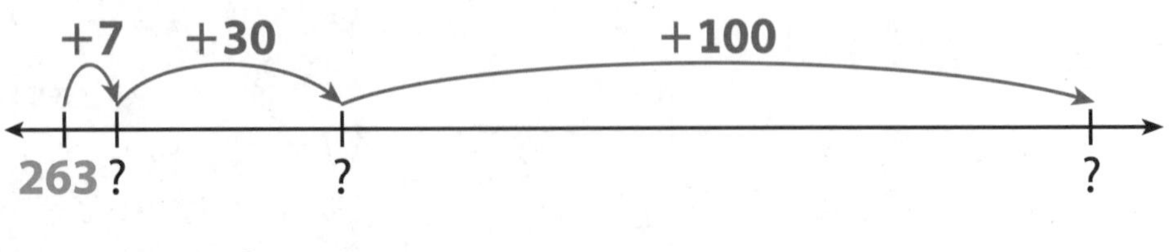

$263 + 137 = ?$

CONNECT IT

Now you will use the problem from the previous page to help you understand how to use addition strategies with three-digit numbers.

1 Look at the first **Model It** on the previous page.

How many hundreds, tens, and ones should be in the last row of the place-value chart?

.... hundreds .... tens .... ones

2 What number does the last row show? ....

3 Look at the second **Model It** on the previous page.

What is 263 + 7? ....

What is 270 + 30? ....

What is 300 + 100? ....

4 Janelle has .... pennies and nickels in all.

5 REFLECT

Look back at your **Try It**, strategies by classmates, and **Model Its**. Which models or strategies do you like best for adding three-digit numbers? Explain.

....

....

....

APPLY IT

Use what you just learned to solve these problems.

6 Grace has 412 pictures on her phone. Lennie has 251 pictures on his phone. How many more pictures does Lennie need to have the same number as Grace? Show your work.

Solution ....

7 What is 524 + 278? Show your work.

Solution ....

8 Which addition problems could you use to find 481 + 295?

Ⓐ 600 + 170 + 6

Ⓑ 700 + 17 + 6

Ⓒ 600 + 70 + 6

Ⓓ 6 ones + 7 tens + 6 hundreds

Ⓔ 6 + 70 + 700

Ⓕ 6 hundreds + 17 tens + 6 ones

Name: ____________________

Practice Addition Strategies with Three-Digit Numbers

Study the Example showing one way to add three-digit numbers. Then solve problems 1–6.

EXAMPLE

At Elm School, 176 students are in the first grade, and 139 students are in the second grade. How many students are in both grades?

Find 176 + 139.

You can break apart the addends.

$$\begin{array}{rl} 176 \longrightarrow & 100 + 70 + 6 \\ +\ 139 \longrightarrow & 100 + 30 + 9 \\ \hline & 200 + 100 + 15 = 300 + 15 = 315 \end{array}$$

So, there are 315 students in both grades.

Luis saves $285. Then he saves $152 more. How much money does Luis save?

1. Break apart the numbers. Find the total.

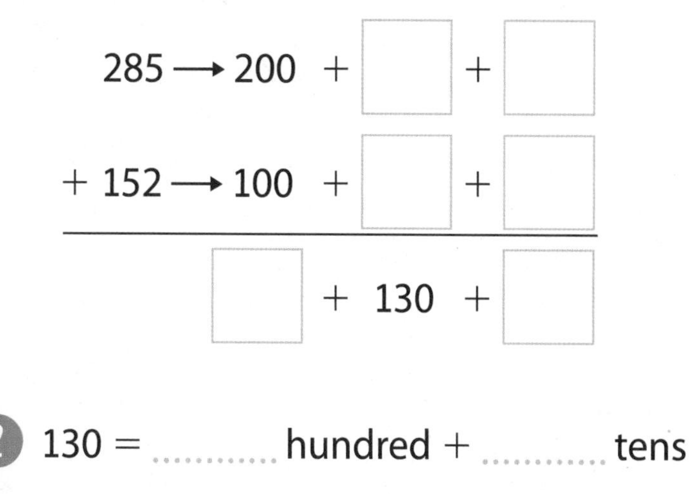

2. 130 = ... hundred + ... tens

3. How much money does Luis save? $ ....

4 On Monday, Kim's family starts driving on their vacation. On Tuesday, they drive 258 miles. Kim's family drives 484 miles during both days. How many miles do they drive on Monday? Show your work.

Solution ....

5 Use two different ways to solve this equation. Show your work.

247 + ? = 673

Solution ....

6 What is 518 + 384?

Ⓐ 902 Ⓑ 892 Ⓒ 872 Ⓓ 802

Develop Using Subtraction Strategies with Three-Digit Numbers

Read and try to solve the problem below.

A class has 500 tickets to sell for the Fun Fair. Some tickets are sold during the first week. After the first week, the class has 278 tickets left. How many tickets does the class sell during the first week?

TRY IT

Math Toolkit

- connecting cubes
- base-ten blocks
- hundreds place-value mats
- number charts
- open number lines

DISCUSS IT

Ask your partner: Do you agree with me? Why or why not?

Tell your partner: I disagree with this part because . . .

Explore different ways to understand subtraction strategies for three-digit numbers.

A class has 500 tickets to sell for the Fun Fair. Some tickets are sold during the first week. After the first week, the class has 278 tickets left. How many tickets does the class sell during the first week?

MODEL IT

You can subtract hundreds, tens, and ones.

Think: 278 = **200** + **70** + **8**

$$\begin{array}{r} 500 \\ -\ 200 \\ \hline 300 \\ -\ 70 \\ \hline 230 \\ -\ 8 \\ \hline ? \end{array}$$

MODEL IT

You can use addition to subtract.

500 − ? = 278 is the same as 278 + ? = 500.

Start with 278 and add 200 to get to 478.

Then add 20 to get to 498.

Then add 2 to get to 500.

200 + 20 + 2 = ?

CONNECT IT

Now you will use the problem from the previous page to help you understand how to use subtraction strategies for three-digit numbers.

1. Look at the first **Model It** on the previous page.

   How many hundreds, tens, and ones were subtracted from 500?

   .... hundreds .... tens .... ones

2. What is the difference after subtracting $230 - 8$?

   ....

3. Look at the second **Model It** on the previous page.

   What is $200 + 20 + 2$? ....

4. Why are your answers the same for problems 2 and 3?

5. ## REFLECT

   Look back at your **Try It**, strategies by classmates, and **Model Its**. Which models or strategies do you like best for subtracting three-digit numbers? Explain.

   ....

   ....

   ....

APPLY IT

Use what you just learned to solve these problems.

6 There are 700 seats. There are people sitting in 463 seats. The rest of the seats are empty. How many seats are empty?

Use two different strategies to solve this problem. Show your work.

Solution 

7 What is the unknown number in this equation?

$? - 524 = 257$

....

 Solve the subtraction problem. Then explain how you would use addition to check your answer.

$$\begin{array}{r} 809 \\ -\ 395 \\ \hline \square \end{array}$$

Name: ______________________________

Practice Using Subtraction Strategies with Three-Digit Numbers

Study the Example showing one way to subtract three-digit numbers. Then solve problems 1–5.

EXAMPLE

Grant School has 408 students. 146 of the students play an instrument. The rest of the students do not play an instrument. How many students do not play an instrument?

Find $408 - 146$.

Look at the tens: 0 tens $<$ 4 tens.

Regroup a hundred in 408 as 10 tens.

$$408 \rightarrow 300 + 100 + 8$$
$$-\ 146 \rightarrow 100 + 40 + 6$$
$$200 + 60 + 2 = 262$$

So, 262 students do not play an instrument.

Max scores 372 points in a computer game. Abby scores 481 points in the same game. How many fewer points does Max score than Abby?

1. Find $481 - 372$. First regroup 1 ten as 10 ones in 481. Then subtract.

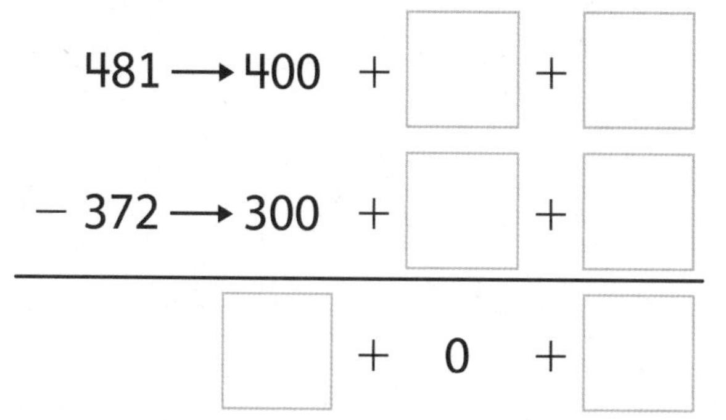

2. How many fewer points does Max score than Abby? ....

3 Which equations could you use to check if this subtraction equation is correct?

$473 - 187 = 286$

Ⓐ $286 + 187 = 473$

Ⓑ $286 + 286 = 572$

Ⓒ $187 + 286 = 473$

Ⓓ $473 - 286 = 187$

Ⓔ $473 + 286 = 759$

Ⓕ $759 - 286 = 473$

4 Show two different ways that you could use a number line to find $604 - 398$.

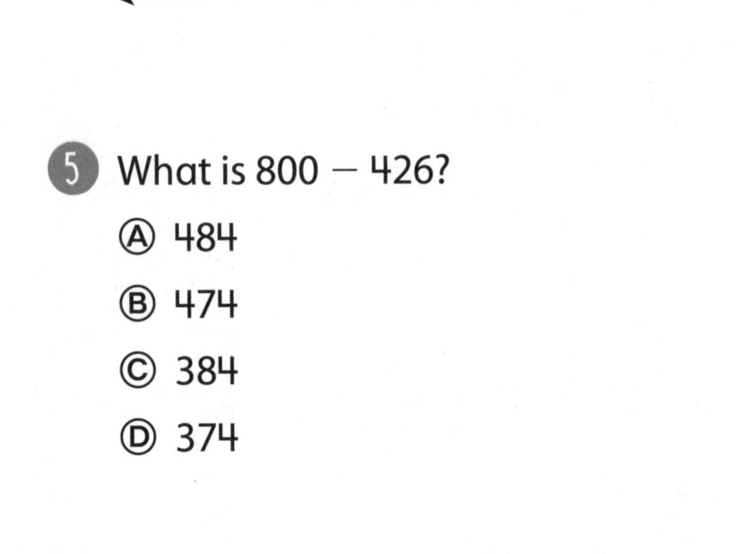

5 What is $800 - 426$?

Ⓐ 484

Ⓑ 474

Ⓒ 384

Ⓓ 374

Refine Using Addition and Subtraction Strategies with Three-Digit Numbers

Complete the Example below. Then solve problems 1–3.

EXAMPLE

Two numbers have a sum of 300. What could the two numbers be? Write addition equations to show three possible pairs of numbers.

You can use any two numbers that have a sum of 300.

$100 + 200 = 300$
$300 = 150 + 150$
$124 + 176 = 300$

Solution ....

....

APPLY IT

1 Tina has 250 shapes. Some are triangles, and the rest are circles. How many of each shape could Tina have? Complete three different equations to show the number of each shape Tina could have.

How are the missing numbers in each equation related to 250?

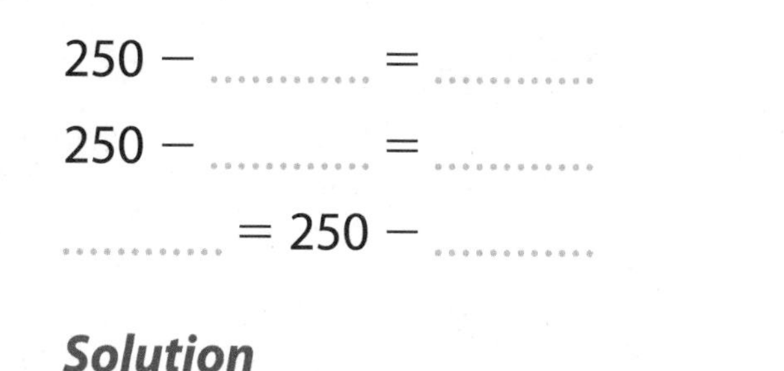

250 − .... = ...

250 − .... = ...

.... = 250 − ....

Solution ....

....

 A store has 328 bags of peanuts and 519 bags of walnuts for sale. How many bags of peanuts and walnuts does the store have in all? Show your work.

What are some strategies you could use to solve this problem?

Solution ....

3 Devon builds a toy car with 436 pieces. Gus builds a toy car with 219 fewer pieces than Devon. How many pieces does Gus use?

Ⓐ 217

Ⓑ 227

Ⓒ 645

Ⓓ 655

Nadia chose Ⓑ as an answer. How did Nadia get her answer?

If Gus's car has fewer pieces than Devon's car, whose car has more pieces?

Name: ________________________________

Practice Addition and Subtraction Strategies with Three-Digit Numbers

1 Tammy has 400 stamps. She has 225 more stamps than Dave has. How many stamps does Dave have?

Solve the problem using addition. Then solve the problem using subtraction. Show your work.

Will your answer be the same whether you use addition or subtraction to solve the problem?

Solution ....

2 Tell if you can use the equations to solve the problem below. Choose *Yes* or *No* for each equation.

$? - 382 = 417$

	Yes	No
$417 - ? = 382$	Ⓐ	Ⓑ
$382 + 417 = ?$	Ⓒ	Ⓓ
$417 - 382 = ?$	Ⓔ	Ⓕ
$417 + 382 = ?$	Ⓖ	Ⓗ

How are the numbers in each equation related?

3 Kevin and Caitlin solve the same subtraction problem. How can you use addition to check their answers?

Kevin	Caitlin
700	700
− 354	− 354
446	346

What addition problems can you solve to check these answers?

4 In problem 3, whose answer is correct? Whose answer is incorrect? How do you know?

Could both answers be correct?

5 A flower store has 355 roses. There are 180 white roses. The rest are red. Which equations could you use to find how many roses are red?

Ⓐ $355 - ? = 180$

Ⓑ $180 + 355 = ?$

Ⓒ $? + 180 = 355$

Ⓓ $? - 355 = 180$

Ⓔ $355 - 180 = ?$

Ⓕ $180 + ? = 355$

Darius chose Ⓑ as the answer. How did Darius get his answer?

Is there more than one answer for this problem?

Refine Using Addition and Subtraction Strategies with Three-Digit Numbers

APPLY IT

Solve the problems.

1 Mrs. Cruz takes some money to the store. She spends \$235 on a small TV. When she leaves the store, she has \$457. How much money does Mrs. Cruz take to the store?

Ⓐ \$212 Ⓑ \$222 Ⓒ \$682 Ⓓ \$692

2 There are 250 adults watching a parade. The rest of the people watching are children. There are 569 people watching the parade in all. How many children are watching the parade?

Choose *Yes* or *No* to tell if each equation could be used to solve the problem.

	Yes	No
$250 + ? = 569$	Ⓐ	Ⓑ
$250 + 569 = ?$	Ⓒ	Ⓓ
$569 = ? + 250$	Ⓔ	Ⓕ
$569 - 250 = ?$	Ⓖ	Ⓗ

3 Juan solves this subtraction problem. Explain how Juan could use addition to find out if his subtraction is correct.

$$\begin{array}{r} 900 \\ -\ 289 \\ \hline 601 \end{array}$$

4 Debbie has 253 buttons in a jar. Then she puts more buttons in the jar. Now she has 462 buttons in the jar. How many more buttons does Debbie put in the jar?

Which could you use to solve this problem?

Ⓐ 253 + 462 = ?

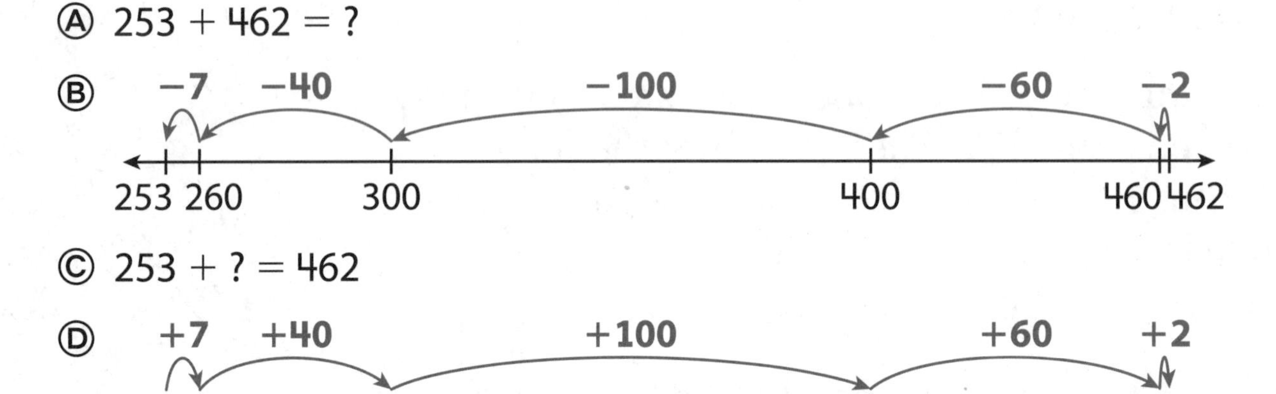

Ⓕ ? = 253 + 462

5 In problem 4, Marcus chose Ⓐ as the answer. How did Marcus get his answer?

6 MATH JOURNAL

Choose any number between 701 and 799. Tell how you could subtract your number from 900.

☑ SELF CHECK Go back to the Unit 3 Opener and see what you can check off.

Add Several Two-Digit Numbers

LESSON 19

Dear Family,

This week your child is learning different ways to add three or four two-digit numbers.

Here are some ways he or she might add 18 + 34 + 22 + 26.

- One way is to break each number into tens and ones and then add pairs of numbers.

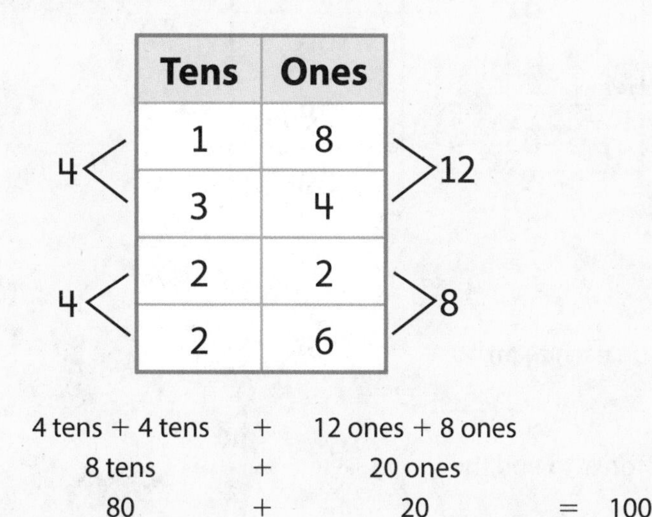

Tens	Ones
1	8
3	4
2	2
2	6

4 tens + 4 tens	+	12 ones + 8 ones		
8 tens	+	20 ones		
80	+	20	=	100

So, 18 + 34 + 22 + 26 = 100.

- Another way is to add two numbers at a time. If you can find pairs of numbers with ones digits that make a ten, add those first.

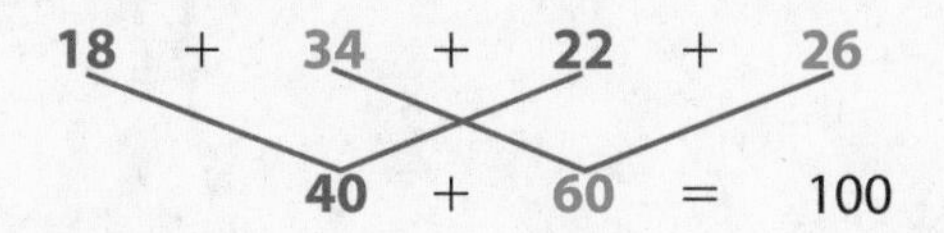

So, 18 + 34 + 22 + 26 = 100.

Invite your child to share what he or she knows about adding three or more two-digit numbers by doing the following activity together.

ACTIVITY ADDING TWO-DIGIT NUMBERS

Do this activity with your child to explore adding several two-digit numbers.

- Work with your child to solve the following problem.
  A school is holding a math team competition. Each team has four students. The team score is the sum of the four students' scores. Which team won the competition?

Tigers
35
68
42
55

Lions
67
88
41
39

Bears
56
62
44
63

Hawks
35
90
28
60

- Ask your child to add the four scores on each team. (See totals below.)
- Work with your child to compare the totals to find the winner.
- Ask your child to make up a new team. Ask your child what scores he or she could give each student on the new team in order to win the competition.

Answers: Tigers: 200; Lions: 235; Bears: 225; Hawks: 213

Explore Adding Several Two-Digit Numbers

Learning Target

- Add up to four two-digit numbers using strategies based on place value and properties of operations.

SMP 1, 2, 3, 4, 5, 6, 8

You have learned how to add two-digit numbers. Use what you know to try to solve the problem below.

Gia follows directions to find a secret code for a treasure hunt.

- **Start at the oak tree. Take 36 steps toward the fence.**
- **Turn right. Take 28 steps.**
- **Turn left. Take 42 steps.**
- **The total number of steps is the secret code.**

What is the secret code?

TRY IT

Math Toolkit

- base-ten blocks
- connecting cubes
- number bonds
- bar models
- open number lines

DISCUSS IT

Ask your partner: How did you get started?

Tell your partner: I knew . . . so I . . .

CONNECT IT

1 LOOK BACK

How did you find the total of all three numbers?

2 LOOK AHEAD

There are many ways to add three numbers. Sometimes there are two numbers with ones digits that make a ten or two numbers that make a hundred. It can help to add those two numbers first. Then add the third number.

$75 + 55 + 25 = ?$

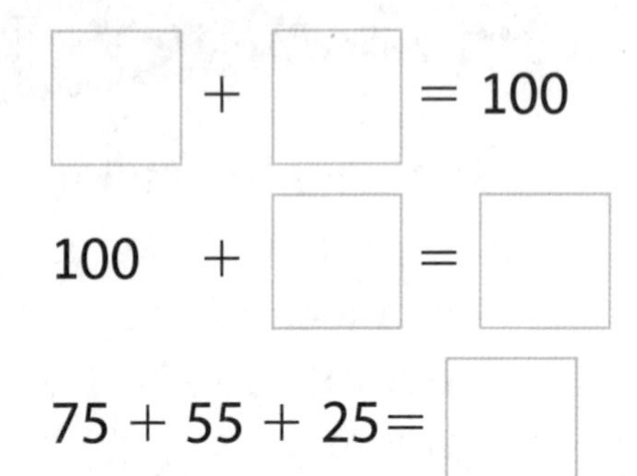

3 REFLECT

How can changing the order that you add three numbers help to find the sum?

Prepare for Adding Several Two-Digit Numbers

1 Think about what you know about breaking apart numbers. Fill in each box. Use words, numbers, and pictures. Show as many ideas as you can.

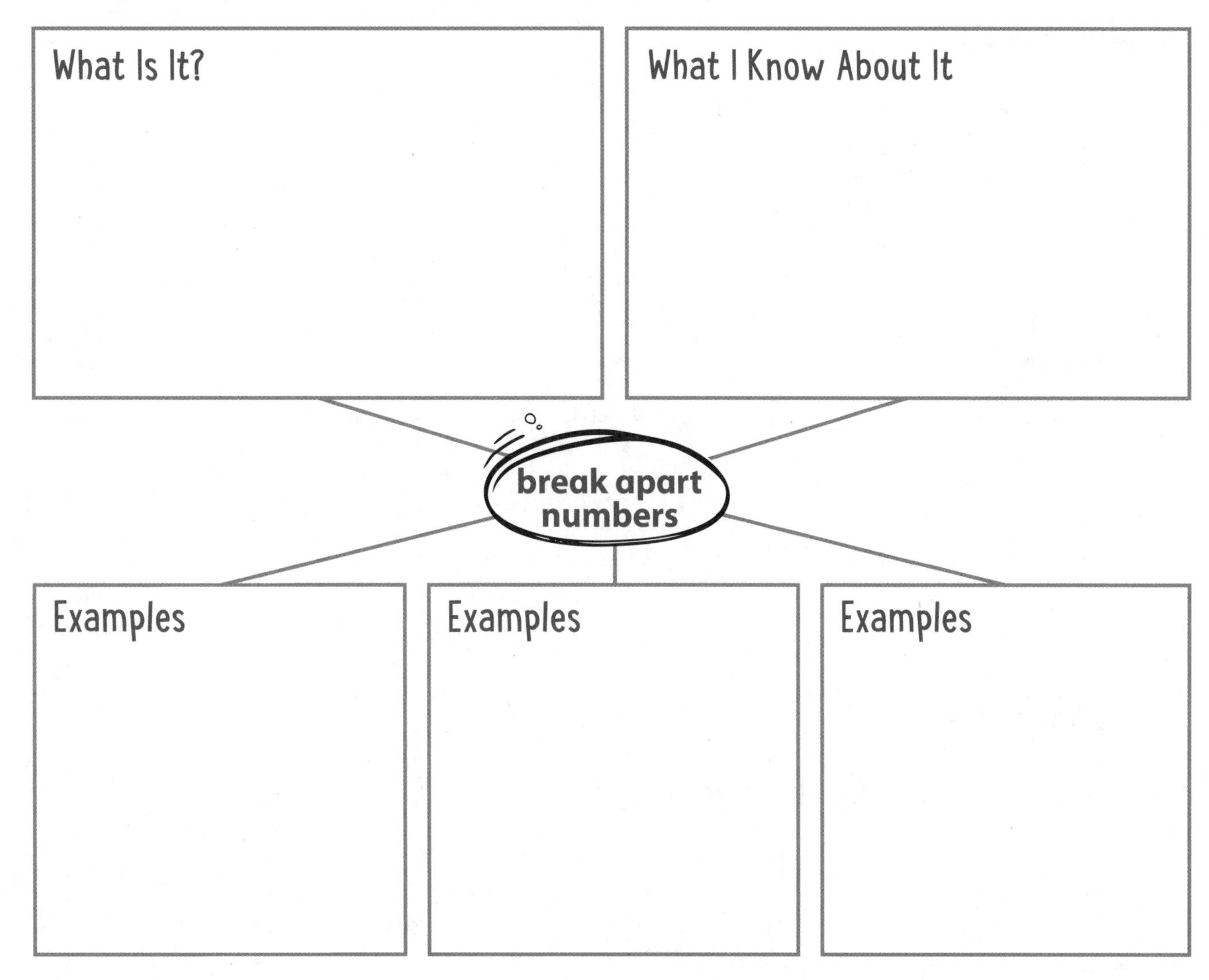

2 How could you break apart numbers to find 34 + 12 + 45?

3 Solve the problem. Show your work.

Jean walks on a path. The first part of the path is 38 steps long. The second part is 23 steps long. The third part is 47 steps long. How many steps does Jean walk?

Solution

4 Check your answer. Show your work.

Develop Adding Four Two-Digit Numbers

Read and try to solve the problem below.

Ray and Cho fill water balloons for a game. Ray fills 16 red balloons and 41 white balloons. Cho fills 22 red balloons and 39 white balloons. How many balloons do they fill in all?

TRY IT

Math Toolkit

- base-ten blocks
- connecting cubes
- number bonds
- bar models
- open number lines

DISCUSS IT

Ask your partner: Do you agree with me? Why or why not?

Tell your partner: The strategy I used to find the answer was . . .

Explore different ways to understand adding four two-digit numbers.

Ray and Cho fill water balloons for a game. Ray fills 16 red balloons and 41 white balloons. Cho fills 22 red balloons and 39 white balloons. How many balloons do they fill in all?

MODEL IT

You can break the numbers into tens and ones.

Break each number into tens and ones.
Then add pairs of numbers.

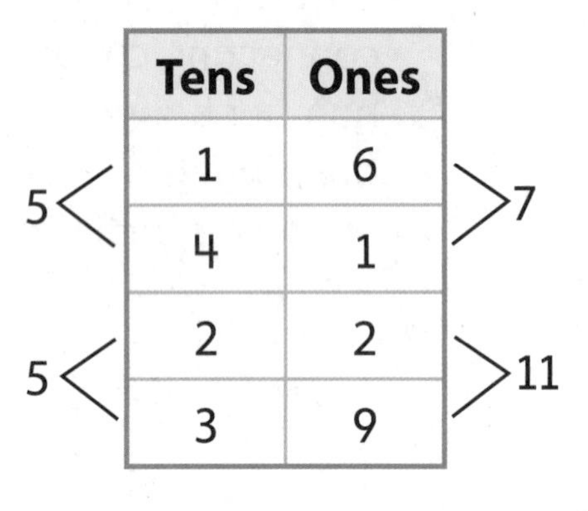

Tens	Ones
1	6
4	1
2	2
3	9

5 + 5 tens   7 + 11 ones

MODEL IT

You can add two numbers at a time.

Look for numbers with digits in the ones place that make a ten. Add those numbers first.

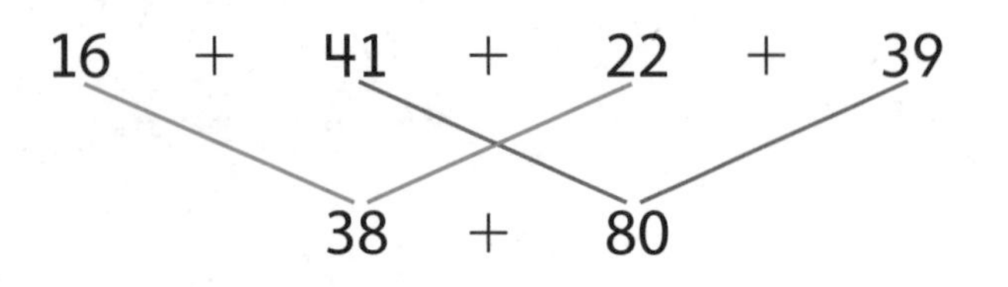

CONNECT IT

Now you will use the problem from the previous page to help you understand how to add four two-digit numbers.

 Look at the first **Model It**. Fill in the blanks to find the total number of balloons.

.... tens + ... ones = ...

2 The paper shows how Ella adds the numbers. How is this like adding in the first **Model It**?

10 +	6
40 +	1
20 +	2
30 +	9
100 +	18

3 Look at the second **Model It**. Why are 41 and 39 grouped together?

4 Complete the work in the second **Model It** to find the number of balloons Ray and Cho fill in all.

 REFLECT

Look back at your **Try It**, strategies by classmates, and **Model Its**. Which models or strategies do you like best for adding four two-digit numbers? Explain.

....

....

....

....

APPLY IT

Use what you just learned to solve these problems.

6 Yuri's bowling scores are 45, 62, 68, and 55. What is the total of Yuri's four scores? Show your work.

Solution ....

7 Sarah, Diego, Don, and Shari each have money in their pockets. Sarah has 25¢, Diego has 19¢, Don has 35¢, and Shari has 11¢. How much money do they have in total? Show your work.

Solution ....

8 Amber plays soccer for 65 minutes on Monday and 46 minutes on Tuesday. She plays for 53 minutes on Thursday and 35 minutes on Friday. How many minutes does Amber spend playing soccer in all? Show your work.

Solution ....

Name: ______________________

Practice Adding Four Two-Digit Numbers

Study the Example showing different ways to add four two-digit numbers. Then solve problems 1–7.

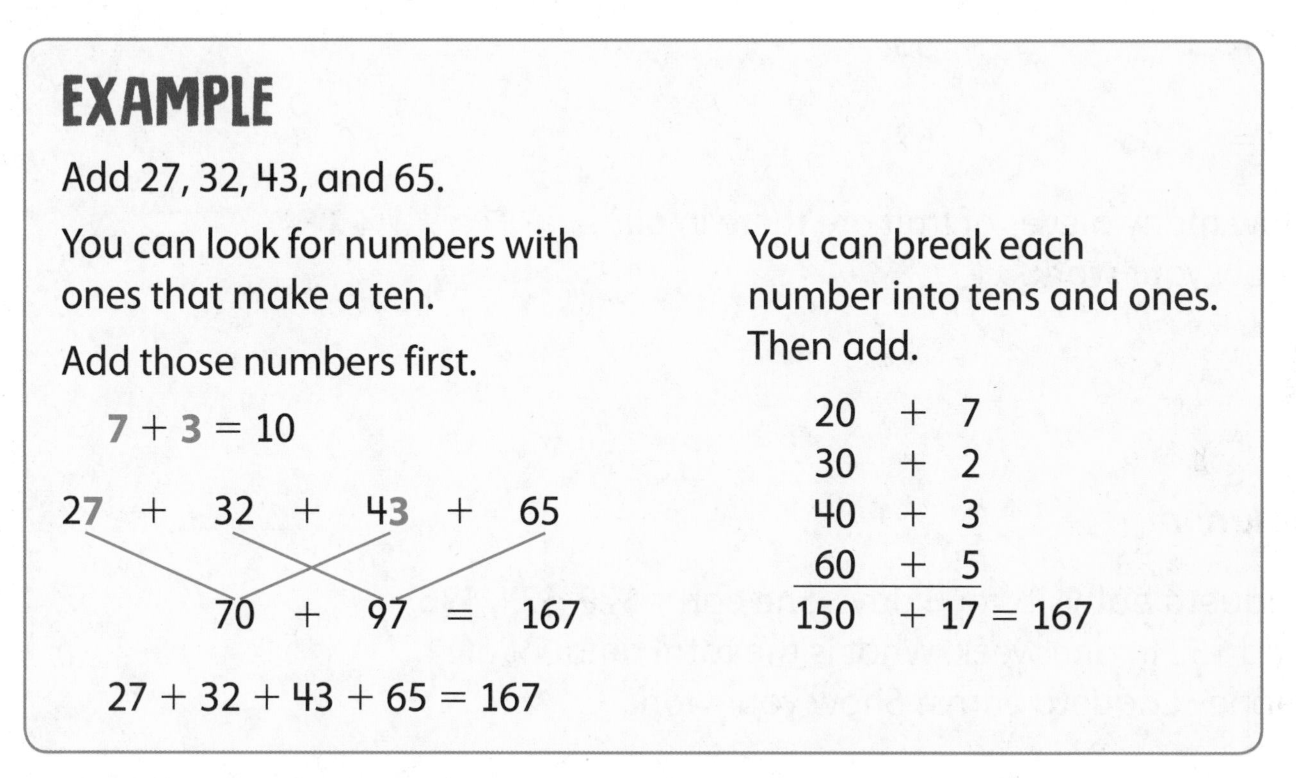

EXAMPLE

Add 27, 32, 43, and 65.

You can look for numbers with ones that make a ten.

Add those numbers first.

$7 + 3 = 10$

$27 + 32 + 43 + 65$

$70 + 97 = 167$

$27 + 32 + 43 + 65 = 167$

You can break each number into tens and ones. Then add.

$20 + 7$
$30 + 2$
$40 + 3$
$60 + 5$

$150 + 17 = 167$

Mr. Dell runs four times in a week. He runs for 25, 27, 28, and 32 minutes.

1. Which two numbers have ones that make a ten? Add those first. $28 +$ .... $= 60$

2. Add the other two numbers. $25 + 27 =$ ....

3. Show how to find the total minutes Mr. Dell runs.

There are 47 apples and 49 pears for sale. There are also 53 peaches and 62 plums.

4 Break each number into tens and ones.

47 = ... + ...   53 = ... + ...

49 = ... + ...   62 = ... + ...

5 How many pieces of fruit are there in all? Show your work.

Solution ....

6 Laqueta babysits for 4 days. She earns \$29, \$34, \$36, and \$52 in one week. What is the total amount of money Laqueta earns? Show your work.

Solution ....

7 Dom has 21 red blocks and 24 blue blocks. He has 29 green blocks and 35 pink blocks. How many blocks does Dom have? Show your work.

Solution ....

Refine Adding Several Two-Digit Numbers

Complete the Example below. Then solve problems 1–3.

EXAMPLE

Mr. Carey's class takes a nature walk. The chart shows what they collect. How many objects do they collect in all?

Rocks	Pinecones	Feathers	Acorns
52	37	12	63

You can add two numbers at a time.

$37 + 63 = 100$

$52 + 12 = \underline{\ \ 64}$

164

Solution ....

APPLY IT

1 There are 28 fish and 23 turtles in the nature center. There are also 22 frogs and 25 snakes. What is the total number of animals? Show your work.

Do any ones digits make a ten?

Solution ....

2 It is race day at the city park. The chart shows how many people sign up for each race. What is the total number of people who sign up?

You can break the numbers into tens and ones.

1-Mile Race	Bike Race	Swim Race
66	49	37

Show your work.

Solution ....

3 Gita adds the number of cans in the school recycling bins. There are 28, 16, 32, and 2 cans. What is the total?

How many tens are in each number?

$28 + 16 + 32 + 2 = ?$

Ⓐ 68

Ⓑ 76

Ⓒ 78

Ⓓ 96

Jeff chose Ⓓ as the answer. How did Jeff get his answer?

Practice Adding Several Two-Digit Numbers

1. People from Rico's school help clean up the park. The chart shows how many people do each job. How many people clean up the park?

Rake Leaves	Plant Flowers	Paint Benches
42	49	18

Show your work.

Which two numbers will you add first?

Solution ....

2. Sid adds these numbers.

51 + 18 + 19 + 38

Which are ways Sid could correctly add the numbers?

Ⓐ 70 + 56

Ⓑ 80 + 39

Ⓒ 90 + 37

Ⓓ 100 + 26

Remember: you can add tens and then ones. Or you can add numbers with ones that make a ten

3 Pete is jumping rope. He does 38, 50, 22, and 29 jumps. How many jumps does he do in all?

Ⓐ 94 Ⓑ 114

Ⓒ 139 Ⓓ 179

Jess chose Ⓐ. How did Jess get her answer?

Do the ones in any two numbers make a ten?

4 Complete each equation using a number from the box at the right.

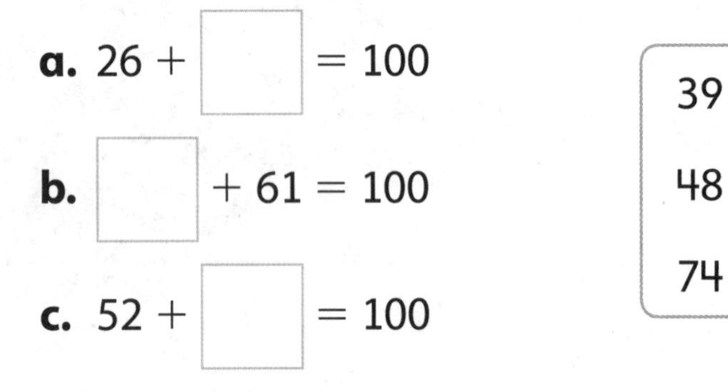

a. $26 + \square = 100$

b. $\square + 61 = 100$

c. $52 + \square = 100$

39
48
74

What are the tens and ones in each number?

5 Meg's garden has 31 daisies, 16 roses, 25 tulips, and 34 sunflowers. How many flowers are in Meg's garden? Show your work.

How many tens in all? How many ones?

Solution ....

Refine Adding Several Two-Digit Numbers

APPLY IT

Solve the problems.

1 Complete each equation using a number from the box at the right.

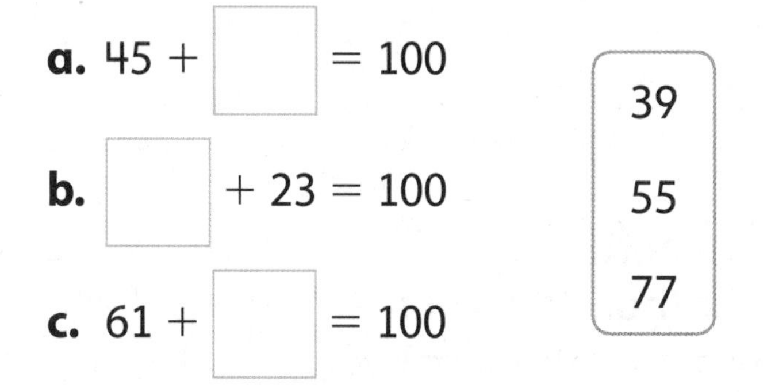

a. 45 + ☐ = 100

b. ☐ + 23 = 100

c. 61 + ☐ = 100

39
55
77

2 A train has four cars. The number of people in each car is 25, 18, 24, and 15. Which of the following are true?

Ⓐ The number of people in two of the cars add up to 40.

Ⓑ More than 90 people are on the train.

Ⓒ Fewer than 100 people are on the train.

Ⓓ There are 82 people on the train.

Ⓔ The number of people in two of the cars add up to 32.

3 Coach buys 3 bats that each cost $25 and one mitt that costs $32. How much does Coach spend?

Ⓐ $57

Ⓑ $82

Ⓒ $107

Ⓓ $117

Use these number cards for problems 4–5.

4 Pablo picks two cards with ones digits that make a ten. Which two cards does he pick? Explain.

5 Pablo loses the 29 card. Taj picks three of the cards that are left. His cards have a sum less than 100. What three cards does Taj pick? Show how to find the sum by adding tens and ones.

6 MATH JOURNAL

Mia and Jonah are finding the sum of $17 + 77 + 23$. Mia says she can first add two numbers with ones digits that make a ten. Jonah says he can first add two numbers that make a hundred.
Who is correct? Explain your answer.

SELF CHECK Go back to the Unit 3 Opener and see what you can check off.

UNIT 3

Self Reflection

In this unit you learned to . . .

Skill	Lesson
Build three-digit numbers in different ways.	12, 13
Read and write three-digit numbers.	12, 13
Compare three-digit numbers.	14
Add 10 or 100 to a number.	15
Add three-digit numbers.	16
Subtract three-digit numbers.	17
Use different strategies to add and subtract three-digit numbers.	16, 17, 18
Add more than 2 two-digit numbers.	19

Think about what you learned.

Use words, numbers, and drawings.

1 I am proud that I can . . .

2 I worked hardest to learn how to . . .

3 One thing I still need to work is . . .

Add, Subtract, and Compare Numbers

Study an Example Problem and Solution

SMP 1 Make sense of problems and persevere in solving them.

Read this problem about adding numbers.
Then look at Plory's solution to the problem.

Cookie Order

Sweet T is in the Bake Stars' kitchen.
He takes notes about a cookie order.

Cookie Order

- Make between 400 and 500 cookies.
- Make chocolate chip, peanut butter, and oatmeal cookies.
- Make the same number of each kind of cookie.

How many of each kind of cookie should the Bake Stars make? Show why your numbers work.

Show how Plory's solution matches the checklist.

☑ PROBLEM-SOLVING CHECKLIST

- ☐ Tell what is known.
- ☐ Tell what the problem is asking.
- ☐ Show all your work.
- ☐ Show that the solution works.

a. Circle something that is known.

b. Underline something that you need to find.

c. Draw a box around what you do to solve the problem.

d. Put a checkmark next to the part that shows the solution works.

PLORY'S SOLUTION

Hi, I'm Plory. Here's how I solved this problem.

- **I know** there are 3 kinds of cookies. The total is between 400 and 500 cookies.
- **I need to find** 3 numbers that have a sum between 400 and 500.

  Try 100: 100 + 100 + 100 = 300
  Try 200: 200 + 200 + 200 = 600

Using 100 makes too few cookies. Using 200 makes too many cookies.

- 150 is between 100 and 200.
- **I can make a quick drawing** to help me add.

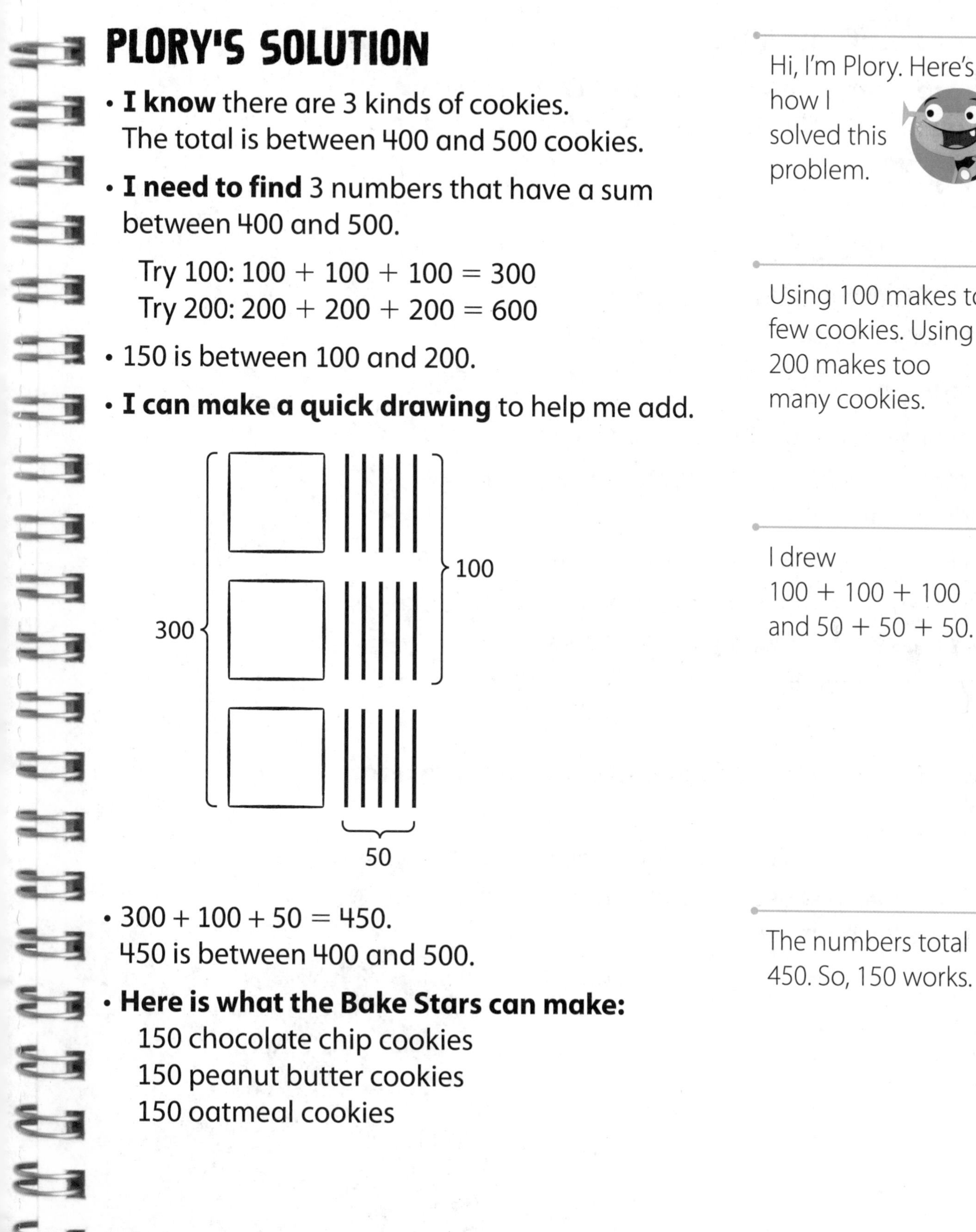

I drew 100 + 100 + 100 and 50 + 50 + 50.

- 300 + 100 + 50 = 450. 450 is between 400 and 500.

The numbers total 450. So, 150 works.

- **Here is what the Bake Stars can make:**
  150 chocolate chip cookies
  150 peanut butter cookies
  150 oatmeal cookies

Try Another Approach

There are many ways to solve problems. Think about how you might solve the Cookie Order problem in a different way.

Cookie Order

Sweet T is in the Bake Stars' kitchen.
He takes notes about a cookie order.

Cookie Order

- Make between 400 and 500 cookies.
- Make chocolate chip, peanut butter, and oatmeal cookies.
- Make the same number of each kind of cookie.

How many of each kind of cookie should the Bake Stars make? Show why your numbers work.

PLAN IT

Answer this question to help you start thinking about a plan.

Look at the numbers for each kind of cookie in Plory's solution. Could you use numbers greater than these? Less than these? Explain.

SOLVE IT

Find a different solution for the Cookie Order problem. Show all your work on a separate sheet of paper.

You may want to use the Problem-Solving Tips to get started.

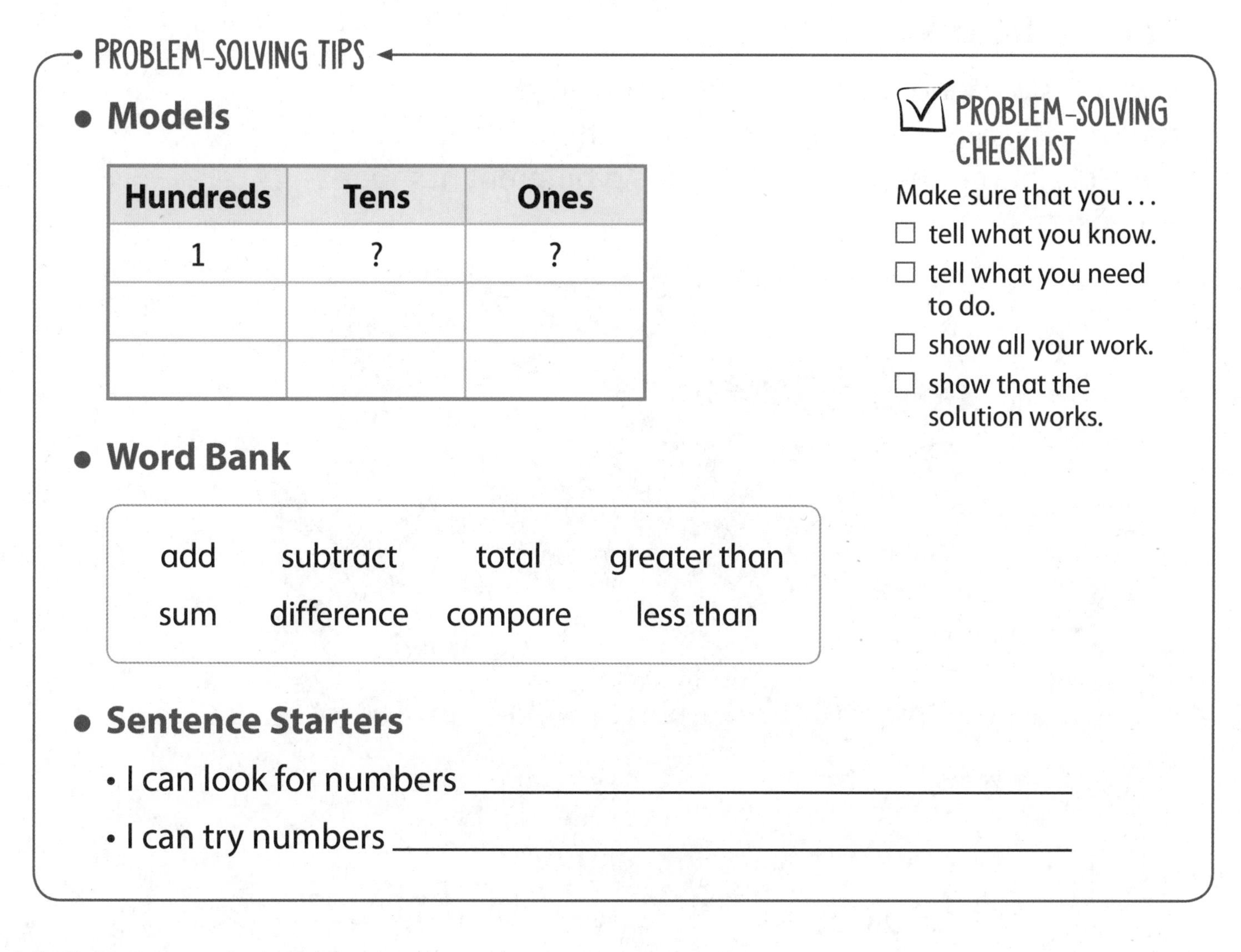

PROBLEM-SOLVING TIPS

- **Models**

Hundreds	Tens	Ones
1	?	?

- **Word Bank**

add	subtract	total	greater than
sum	difference	compare	less than

- **Sentence Starters**
  - I can look for numbers ______
  - I can try numbers ______

PROBLEM-SOLVING CHECKLIST

Make sure that you . . .

- ☐ tell what you know.
- ☐ tell what you need to do.
- ☐ show all your work.
- ☐ show that the solution works.

REFLECT

Use Mathematical Practices Talk about this question with a partner.

- **Reason with Numbers** How can the numbers in Plory's solution help you solve this problem?

Discuss Models and Strategies

Solve the problem on a separate sheet of paper. There are different ways you can solve it.

Cookie Boxes

Sweet T is packing an order of 145 chocolate chip cookies. The pictures below show the different-size boxes there are at the shop. Each box holds a different number of cookies.

How can Sweet T pack the cookies?

PLAN IT AND SOLVE IT

Find a solution to the Cookie Boxes problem.

Decide which boxes Sweet T should use to pack the cookies.

- Tell why you chose these boxes.
- Show that your answer works.

You may want to use the Problem-Solving Tips to get started.

PROBLEM-SOLVING TIPS

- **Questions**
  - Would I rather use fewer boxes or more boxes?
  - Do I want to make sure that every box I use is full?
- **Word Bank**

add	sum	total
hundred	tens	ones

- **Sentence Starters**
  - I can use ______________ boxes.
  - The box holds ______________________________
  - I used these boxes because ______________________________

PROBLEM-SOLVING CHECKLIST

Make sure that you . . .

- ☐ tell what you know.
- ☐ tell what you need to do.
- ☐ show all your work.
- ☐ show that the solution works.

REFLECT

Use Mathematical Practices Talk about this question with a partner.

- **Make an Argument** How can you explain the reason for the boxes that you chose?

Persevere On Your Own

Solve each problem on a separate sheet of paper.

Fruits and Vegetables

Sweet T likes to talk about numbers with the Bake Stars.

Here are some of the things he said about last month.

- We used more than 200 pounds of vegetables last month.
- We used less than 300 pounds of fruit last month.
- The total amount of fruit and vegetables we used was between 500 and 550 pounds.

How many pounds of fruit could the Bake Stars have used? How many pounds of vegetables?

SOLVE IT

Find the amount of fruit and vegetables that the Bake Stars could have used.

- Tell how many pounds of fruit they might have used.
- Tell how many pounds of vegetables they might have used.
- Show that the total weight is between 500 and 550 pounds.

REFLECT

Use Mathematical Practices Talk about this question with a partner.

- **Be Precise** How did you use words or symbols to show that your answer works?

Fruit Kabobs

One day, the Bake Stars make a mistake! They make 448 fruit kabobs for a customer. The customer only wants 248 fruit kabobs. Here is what they plan to do with the extra food.

- Donate some fruit kabobs to the youth center.
- Keep some fruit kabobs at the shop. Give them out for free to customers.

How many fruit kabobs should the Bake Stars donate? How many should they give out for free?

SOLVE IT

Decide what to do with the extra fruit kabobs.

- Tell how many to give to the youth center.
- Tell how many to keep at the shop.
- Explain why your numbers work.

REFLECT

Use Mathematical Practices Talk about this question with a partner.

- **Make Sense of Problems** What was the first thing that you did to solve this problem? Why?

Unit Review

Compare each pair of numbers. Choose $<$, $>$, or $=$ for each comparison.

	$<$	$>$	$=$
560 ◯ 5 hundreds 6 tens	Ⓐ	Ⓑ	Ⓒ
726 ◯ 729	Ⓓ	Ⓔ	Ⓕ
398 ◯ 389	Ⓖ	Ⓗ	Ⓘ
4 hundreds 2 tens ◯ 4 hundreds 21 ones	Ⓙ	Ⓚ	Ⓛ

2 Which are ways to show 517 + 386?
Choose all the correct answers.

Ⓐ 386 + 51 + 7

Ⓑ 500 + 300 + 10 + 80 + 7 + 6

Ⓒ 300 + 80 + 6 + 500 + 10 + 7

Ⓓ 800 + 90 + 13

Ⓔ 517 + 80 + 6

3 Diego has 138 stickers. Paige has 247 stickers.
How many more stickers does Paige have than Diego?
Show your work.

Paige has .... more stickers than Diego.

 Sarah collects rocks for four days and records the numbers in a chart.

Monday	Tuesday	Wednesday	Thursday
65	31	11	42

Sarah adds two numbers that make at least 100 first. Then, she finds the sum. How did Sarah get her answer? Explain your thinking.

....

....

....

....

5 Which is another way to show 5 hundreds and 7 tens?

Ⓐ 57

Ⓑ 500 + 7

Ⓒ 507

Ⓓ 500 + 70

6 Skip-count to complete the number pattern. Write your answers in the blanks.

445, ..., 435, ..., 425, ...

Performance Task

Answer the questions. Show all your work on separate paper.

Four students want to order tickets to play their favorite games at the school fair. They have to order some packs of 100, some sheets of 10, and some single tickets.

- The table below shows the total number of tickets each student wants.
- The limit for packs of 100 is 5 per student.

How many packs of 100, sheets of 10, and single tickets can the students order to get the total number of tickets they want? Fill in the table.

Name	Packs of 100	Sheets of 10	Single Tickets	Total
Lori				555
Penn				662
Maria				656
Antoine				593

Checklist

Did you . . .

- ☐ use place value correctly?
- ☐ check your answers?
- ☐ explain your answers with words and numbers?

REFLECT

Look for Structure How did you use what you know about place value to solve this problem?

Vocabulary

Draw or write to show examples for each term. Then draw or write to show other math words in the unit.

expanded form a way a number is written to show the place value of each digit. For example, $249 = 200 + 40 + 9$.

My Example

greater than symbol (>) a symbol used to compare two numbers when the first is greater than the second.

My Example

hundreds groups of 10 tens.

My Example

less than symbol (<) a symbol used to compare two numbers when the first is less than the second.

My Example

place value the value assigned to a digit based on its position in a number. For example, the 2 in 324 is in the tens place and has a value of 2 tens or 20.

My Example

My Word: ____________________

____

____

My Example

My Word: ____________

____

____

My Example

My Word: ____________

____

____

My Example

My Word: ____________

____

____

My Example

My Word: ____________

____

____

My Example

My Word: ____________

____

____

My Example

My Word: ____________

____

____

My Example

UNIT

4

Length

Measurement, Addition and Subtraction, and Line Plots

☑ SELF CHECK

Before starting this unit, check off the skills you know below. As you complete each lesson, see how many more skills you can check off!

I can . . .	Before	After
Use a ruler to measure the length of an object.	☐	☐
Choose the correct tool for measuring an object.	☐	☐
Measure the same object using different units.	☐	☐
Estimate the length of an object.	☐	☐
Compare lengths to tell which of two objects is longer and how much longer that object is.	☐	☐
Add and subtract lengths to solve problems.	☐	☐
Add and subtract lengths on a number line.	☐	☐
Measure lengths and show data on a line plot.	☐	☐

UNIT 4

Build Your Vocabulary

REVIEW

compare data
tally chart

Math Vocabulary

Work with a partner and use the review words to complete the sentences below.

Marker	Tally Marks
Blue	卌 卌 ||
Red	卌 |||
Yellow	卌 卌 卌

1 I can organize my data in

a ....

2 I use the tally marks to

show ....

3 A tally chart helps me .... the data. This tally chart helps me see that there are more yellow than blue markers.

Academic Vocabulary

Put a check next to the academic words you know. Then use the words to complete the sentences.

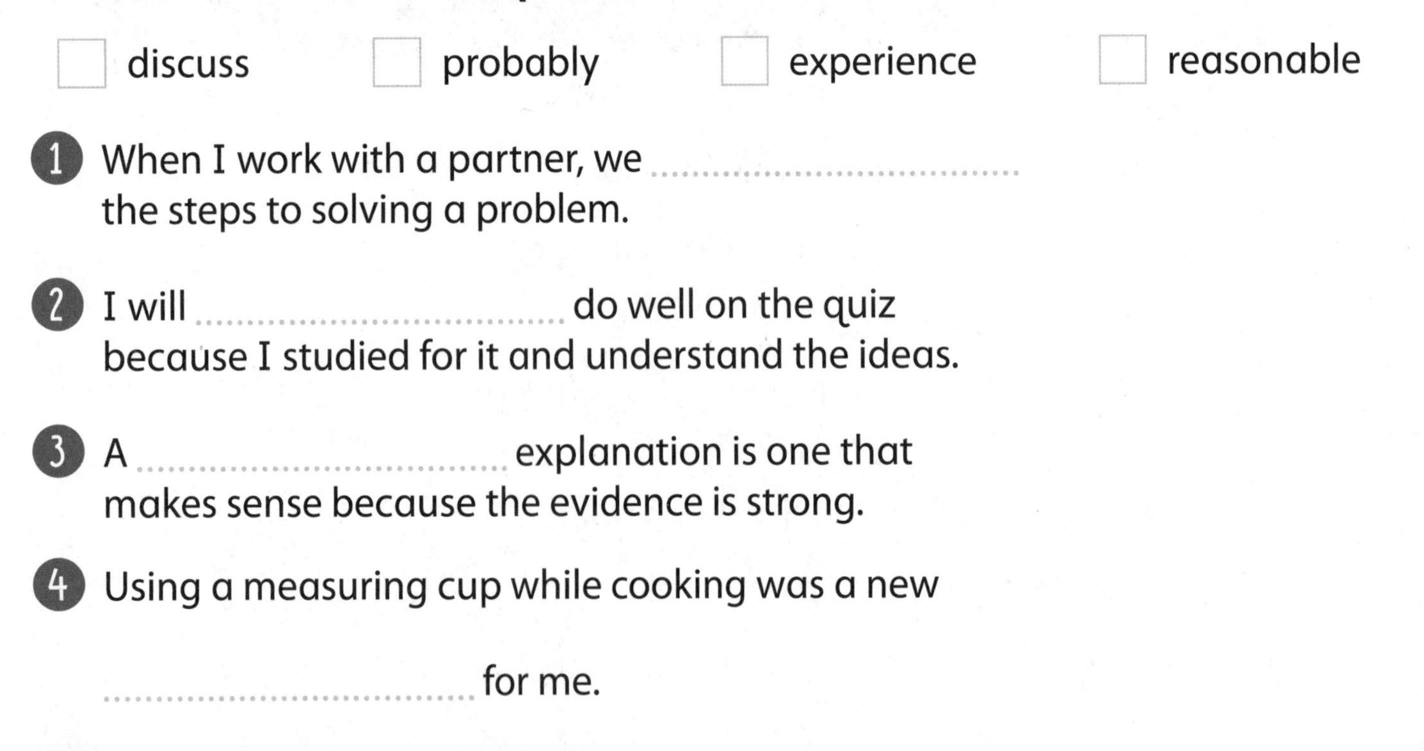

☐ discuss ☐ probably ☐ experience ☐ reasonable

1 When I work with a partner, we .... the steps to solving a problem.

2 I will .... do well on the quiz because I studied for it and understand the ideas.

3 A .... explanation is one that makes sense because the evidence is strong.

4 Using a measuring cup while cooking was a new

.... for me.

Measure in Inches and Centimeters

LESSON 20

Dear Family,

This week your child is learning about measuring in inches and centimeters.

Your child will encounter measurements throughout his or her life, and it is important that he or she understands standard units of measurement.

Standard units are used to make sure that a measurement unit is always the same size and so that all measurements are consistent. Inches and centimeters are two examples of standard units.

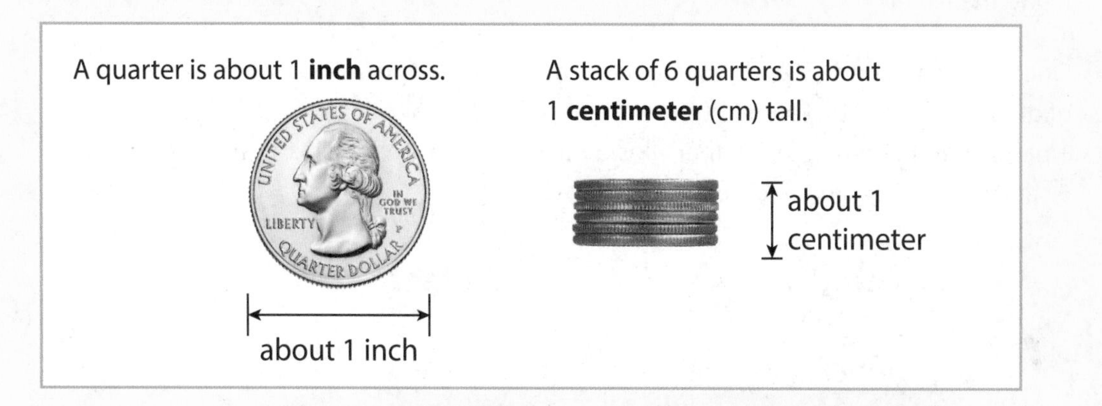

You can use a **ruler** to **measure lengths**. A ruler is a tool that measures using standard units. It is divided into equal parts, such as inches or centimeters.

This ruler shows inches on the top and centimeters on the bottom.

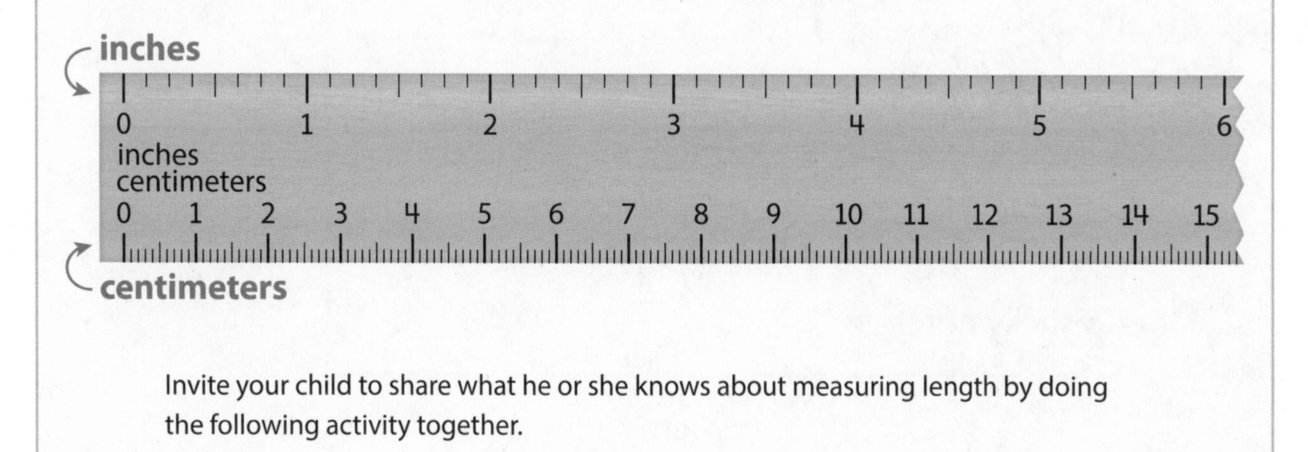

Invite your child to share what he or she knows about measuring length by doing the following activity together.

ACTIVITY EXPLORING LENGTH MEASUREMENT

Do this activity with your child to measure in nonstandard units.

Remind your child length can be measured by placing same-sized units alongside an object.

Materials paper clips, small sticky notes, or other small objects of the same length

- Review how to align the first measuring unit with the end of the object being measured.
- Measure several objects by lining up the nonstandard measuring units end to end with no gaps or overlaps from one end to the other end of the object being measured.
- Once your child understands how to use same-sized units to measure lengths of objects, go on a scavenger hunt for objects that are specific lengths: 1 paper clip, 1 sticky note, 3 paper clips, 3 sticky notes, 6 paper clips, and 6 sticky notes. Record the objects in the table.

Length	Object
1 paper clip	
1 sticky note	
3 paper clips	
3 sticky notes	
6 paper clips	
6 sticky notes	

Explore Measuring in Inches and Centimeters

Learning Target

- Measure the length of an object by selecting and using appropriate tools such as rulers, yardsticks, meter sticks, and measuring tapes.

SMP 1, 2, 3, 4, 5, 6, 8

You have learned how to find how long an object is. Use what you know to try to solve the problem below.

How long is this marker?

1 inch	1 inch	1 inch	1 inch	1 inch	1 inch	1 inch

TRY IT

Math Toolkit

- inch ruler
- measuring tape
- inch tiles
- number lines

DISCUSS IT

Ask your partner: Can you explain how you found how long the marker is?

Tell your partner: I started by . . .

CONNECT IT

1 LOOK BACK

How long is the marker? ....

2 LOOK AHEAD

You can **measure length** with inches or centimeters.

A quarter is about 1 **inch** across.

Your little finger is about 1 **centimeter** (cm) across.

A **ruler** is a tool used to measure length.

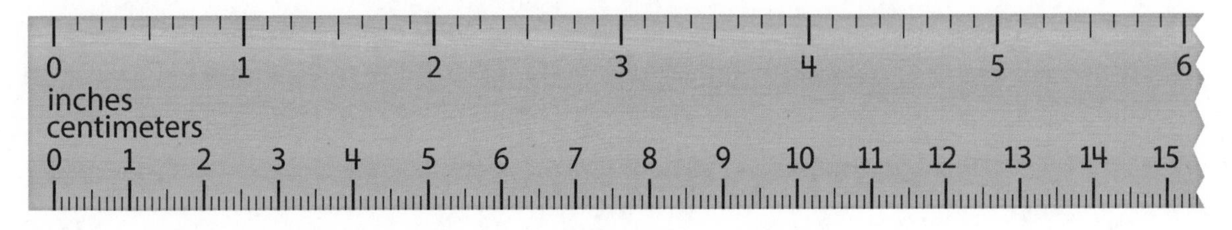

What units can you measure with this ruler?

3 REFLECT

Bruno says it is more useful to measure a shoelace with a ruler than with paper clips. Explain why.

....

....

Name: ______________________________

Prepare for Measuring in Inches and Centimeters

1. Think about what you know about measuring. Fill in each box. Use words, numbers, and pictures. Show as many ideas as you can.

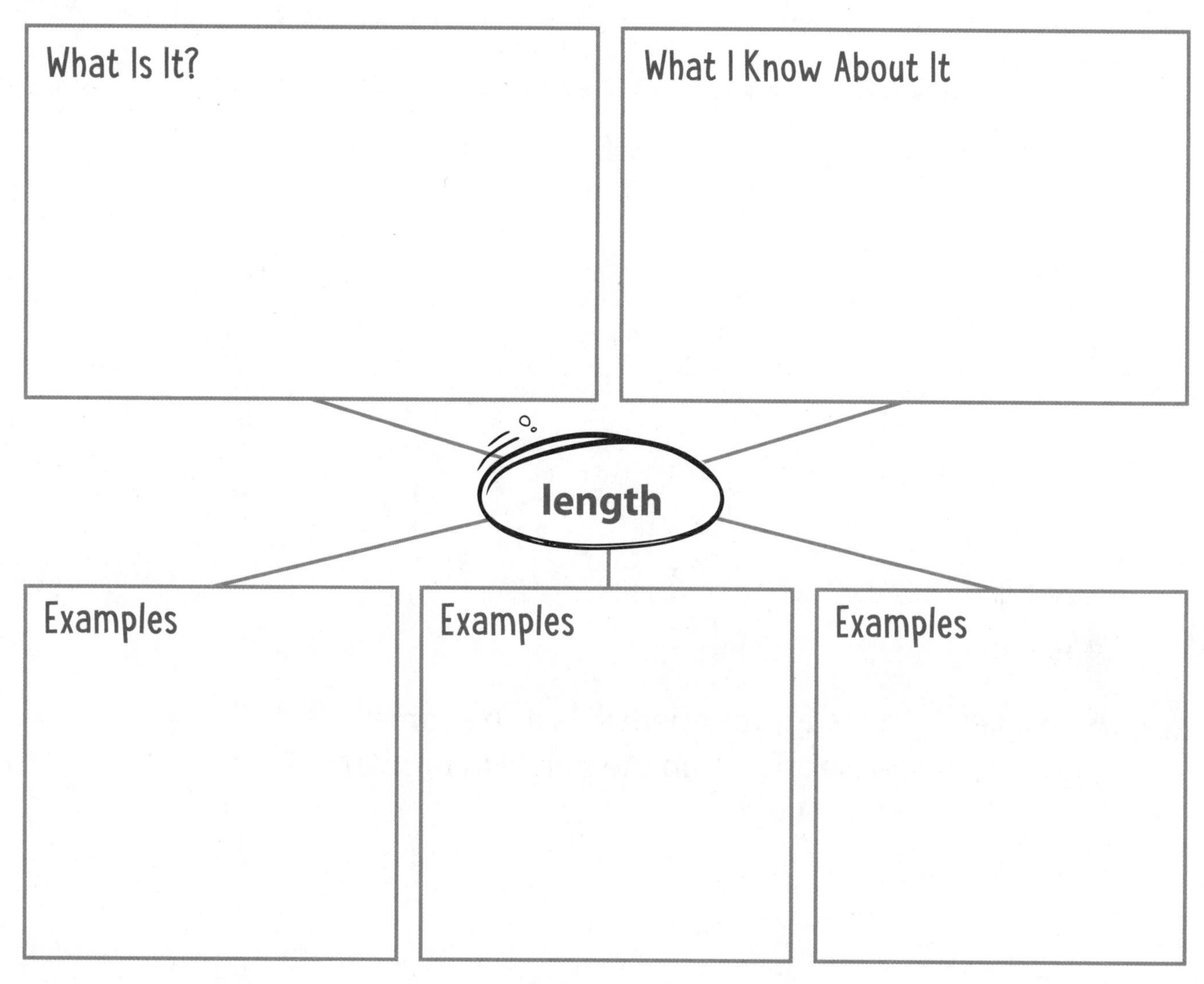

2. What is something you might want to measure the length of? Why?

 Solve the problem. Tell how you know.

What is the length of this pencil?

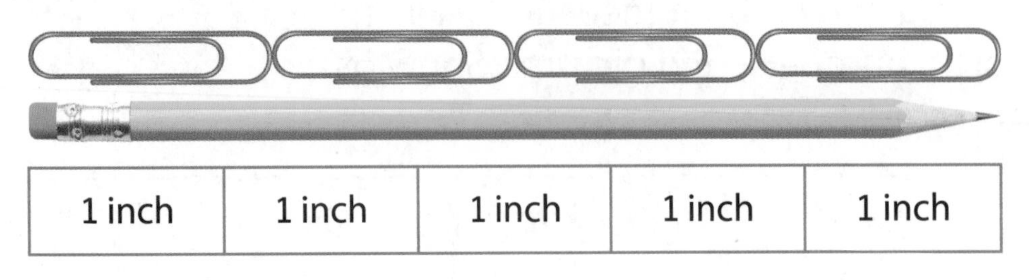

1 inch	1 inch	1 inch	1 inch	1 inch

Solution ....

4 Use a ruler to measure your pencil. Is it the same length, longer, or shorter than the pencil in problem 3?

Develop Measuring in Inches and Centimeters

Read and try to solve the problem below.

**Which piece of yarn is 11 centimeters long?
Which piece of yarn is 4 inches long?**

TRY IT

Math Toolkit
- inch ruler
- centimeter ruler
- inch tiles
- measuring tape

DISCUSS IT

Ask your partner: Do you agree with me? Why or why not?

Tell your partner: I agree with you about . . . because . . .

Explore different ways to understand measuring in inches and centimeters.

Which piece of yarn is 11 centimeters long?
Which piece of yarn is 4 inches long?

MODEL IT

You can measure the lengths with an inch ruler.

Line up the left end of the yarn with the 0 mark on the ruler.

0 1 2 3 4
inches

This ruler is not life-sized.

Look at the number on the ruler under the other end of the yarn.

MODEL IT

You can measure the lengths with a centimeter ruler.

Line up the left end of the yarn with the 0 mark on the ruler.

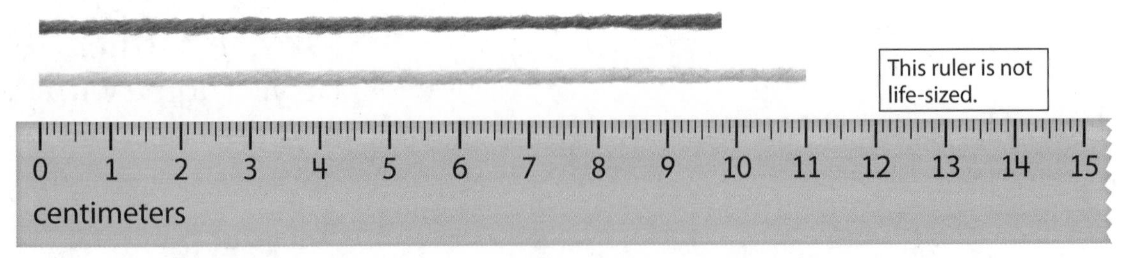

Look at the number on the ruler under the other end of the yarn.

CONNECT IT

Now you will use the problem from the previous page to help you understand how to measure using rulers.

 How do you know what units a ruler shows?

 Which color yarn is 4 inches long? ....

3 Which color yarn is 11 centimeters long? ....

4 How do you use a ruler to measure the length of the yarn in inches or centimeters?

REFLECT

Look back at your **Try It**, strategies by classmates, and **Model Its**. Which models or strategies do you like best for measuring in inches and centimeters? Explain.

....

....

....

....

APPLY IT

Use what you just learned to solve these problems.

6 Ty made the top ruler. Lynn made the bottom ruler.

Circle the ruler that is made correctly. Explain how you know.

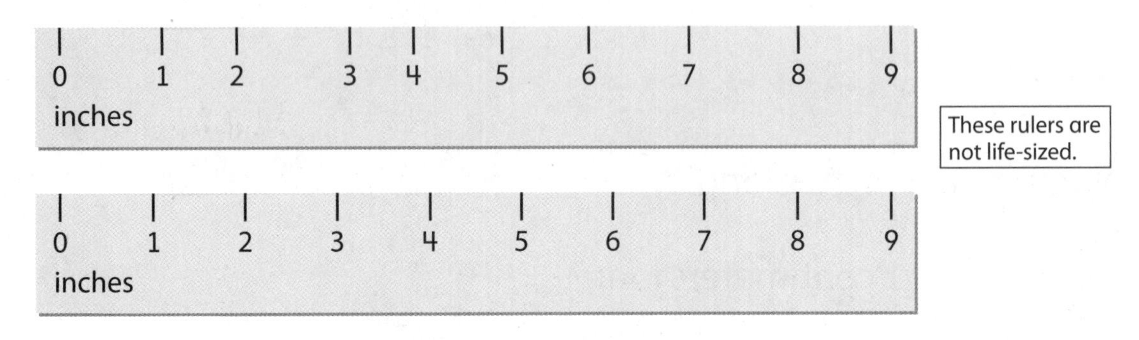

7 Use a ruler. How long is the paintbrush in inches?

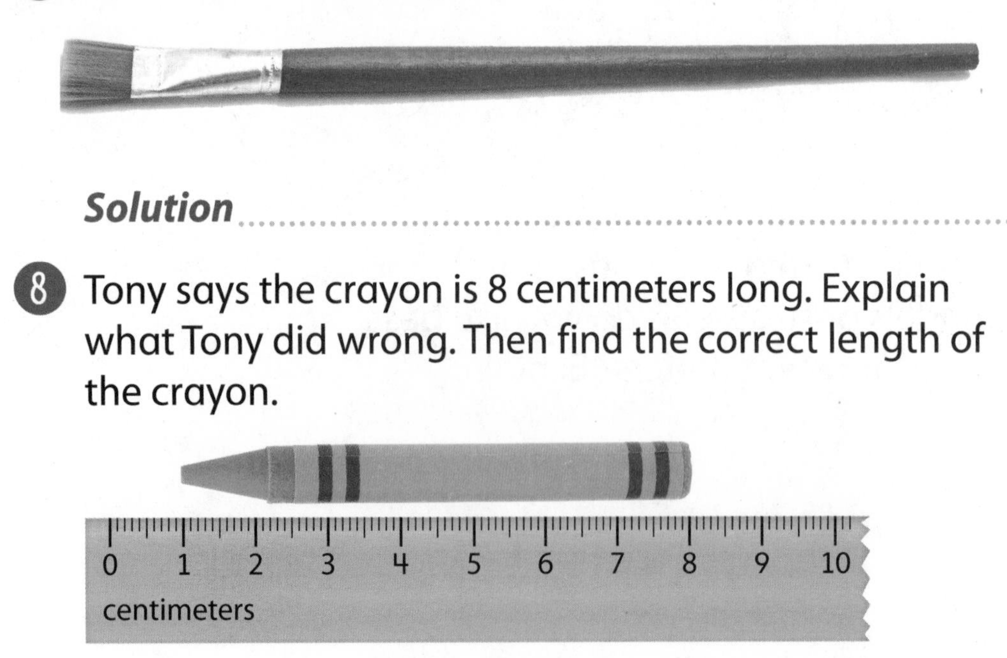

Solution ....

8 Tony says the crayon is 8 centimeters long. Explain what Tony did wrong. Then find the correct length of the crayon.

Name: ____________________

Practice Measuring in Inches and Centimeters

Study the Example showing how to measure with a ruler. Then solve problems 1–7.

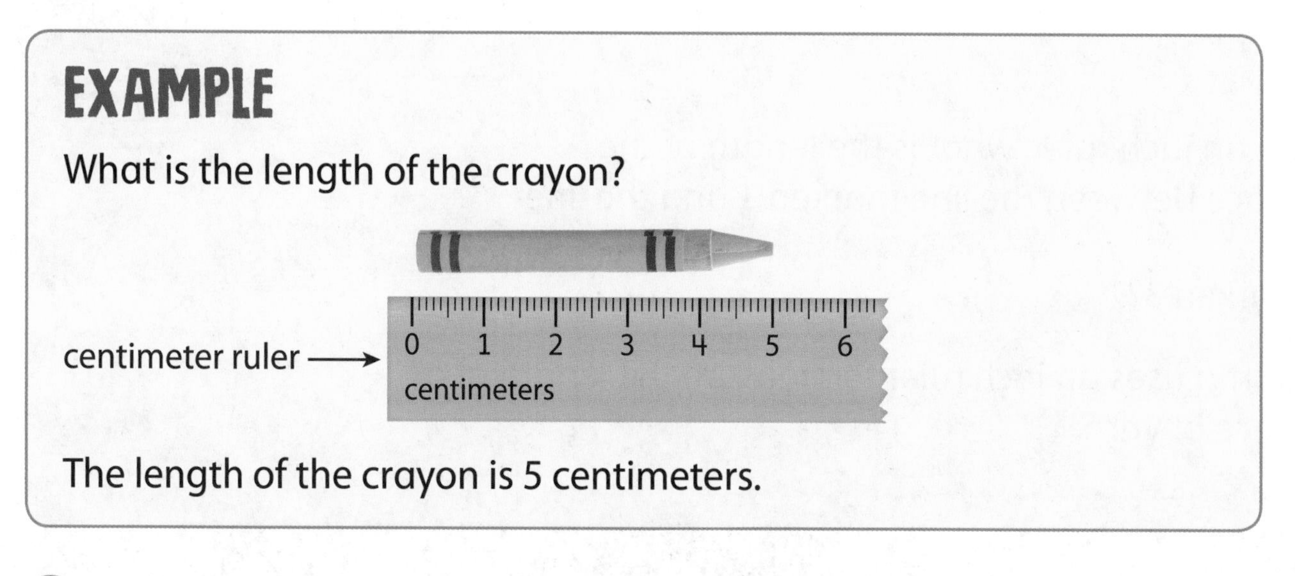

1. What do the numbers on a centimeter ruler represent?

2. When measuring with a ruler, where do you line up the left end of the object?

3. Use a ruler to measure the length of a piece of string in centimeters.

   What is the length of the string?

4 Al needs 8 inches of string for a project. How could he find the correct length of string?

5 On an inch ruler, what is the length of the space between the line marked 1 and the line marked 3? ....

6 Emma uses an inch ruler to measure the length of a piece of yarn.

0 1 2 3 4 5 6
inches

What is the length of the yarn? ....

7 Use a ruler to measure the length of the pencil below in inches.

What is the length of the pencil? ....

Refine Measuring in Inches and Centimeters

Complete the Example below. Then solve problems 1–3.

EXAMPLE

What is the length of the pretzel?

You can use a ruler.

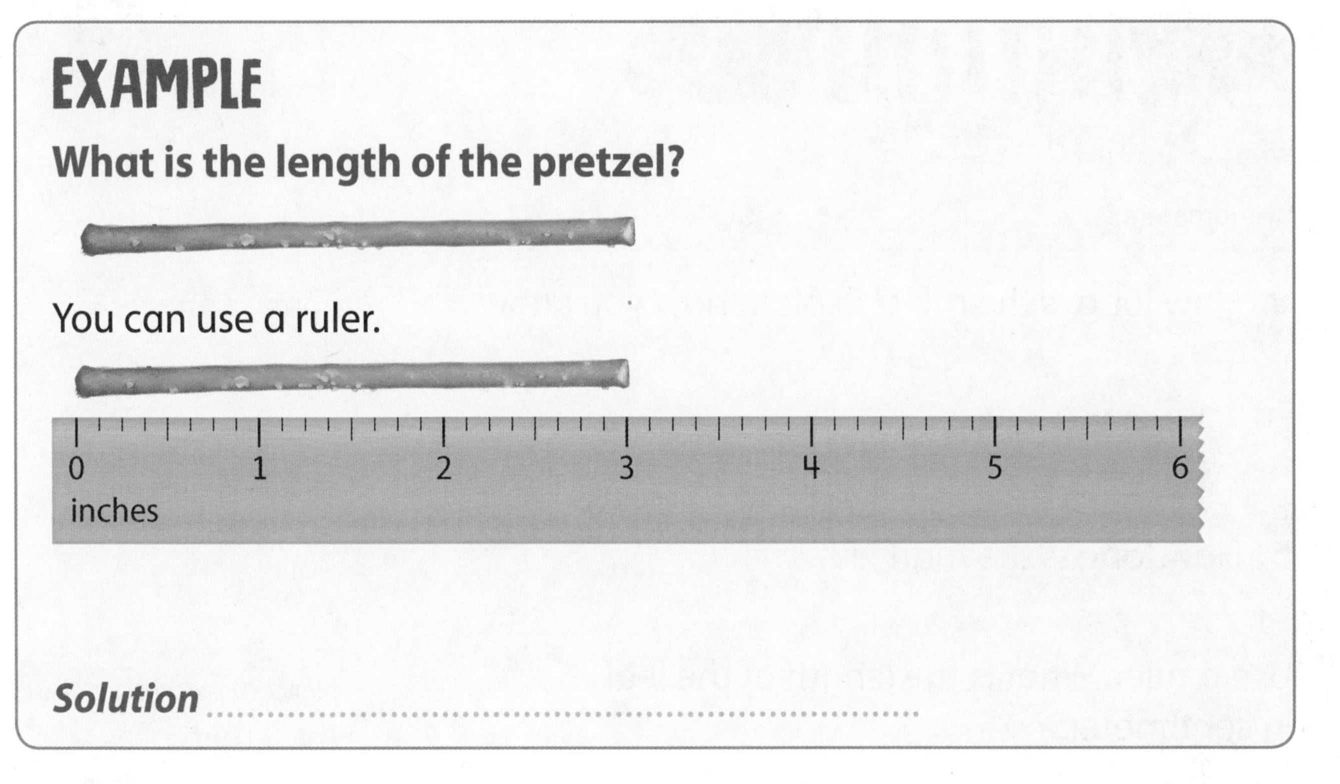

Solution ....

APPLY IT

1 Shannon uses one-inch tiles to measure the pretzel in the Example. How many tiles will she need to measure the pretzel? Explain how you know.

How are one-inch tiles and the ruler alike?

2 Bobby is making his own centimeter ruler. He marks centimeters on a piece of paper. Fill in the blanks to finish making the ruler.

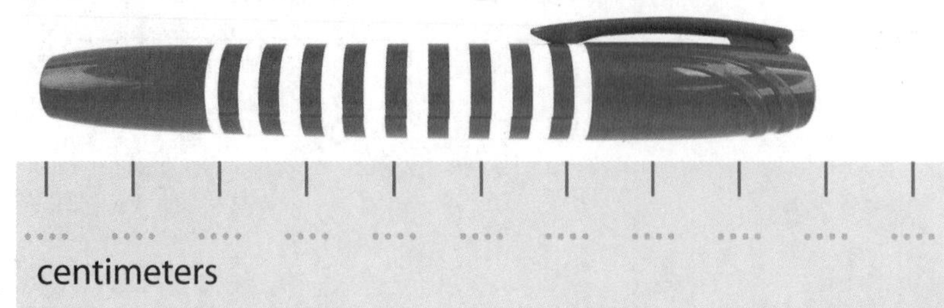

What should the first number on the ruler be?

a. How long is the ruler? Explain how you know.

b. How long is the marker?

3 Use a ruler. What is the length of the leaf in centimeters?

How do you measure the length of an object that is curved?

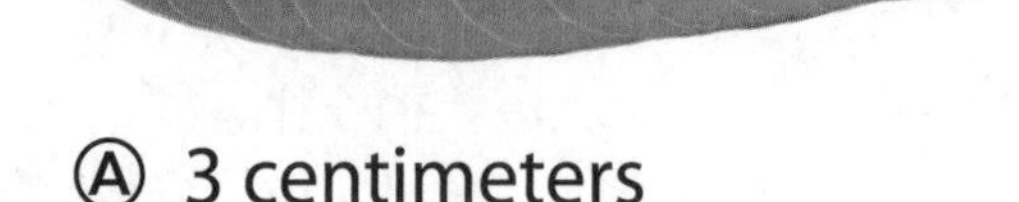

Ⓐ 3 centimeters

Ⓑ 4 centimeters

Ⓒ 6 centimeters

Ⓓ 8 centimeters

Tani chose D as the correct answer. How did Tani get her answer?

Name: ______________________________

Practice Measuring in Inches and Centimeters

1 Amber makes this centimeter ruler on a strip of paper.

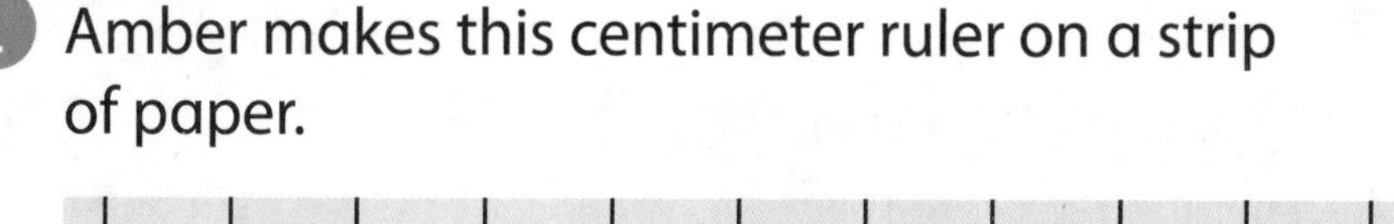

Amber says that her ruler is 11 centimeters long. Do you agree with Amber? Explain your answer.

What do the numbers on the ruler mean?

2 Jim wants to measure a piece of string. Which shows a correct way to measure the string?

How do you measure the length of objects with a ruler?

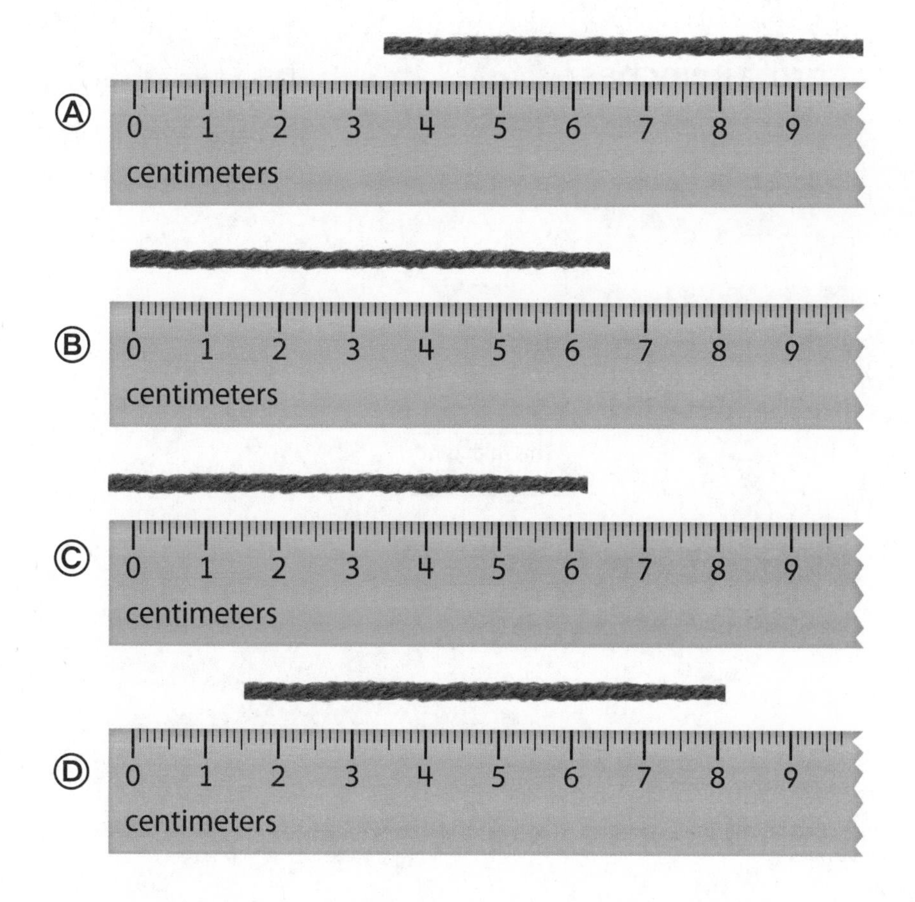

3 Tell if each measurement could be the length of the pencil. Choose *Yes* or *No*.

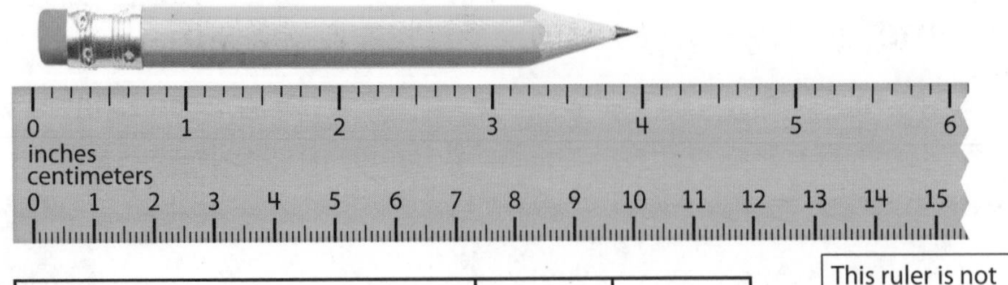

This ruler is not life-sized.

	Yes	No
4 inches	Ⓐ	Ⓑ
9 centimeters	Ⓒ	Ⓓ
5 inches	Ⓔ	Ⓕ
10 centimeters	Ⓖ	Ⓗ

How do you use the numbers on the ruler to find the length of the pencil?

4 What is the length of the carrot in inches?

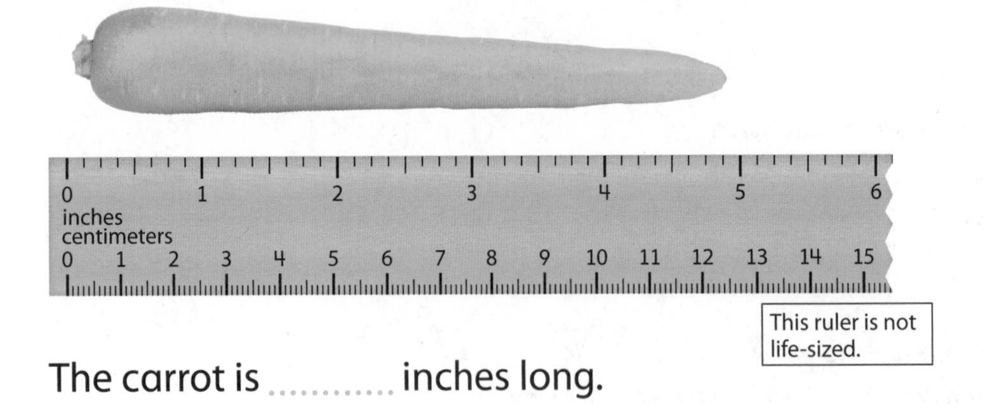

This ruler is not life-sized.

The carrot is .... inches long.

How does the ruler show the length in inches?

Refine Measuring in Inches and Centimeters

APPLY IT

Solve the problems.

Use a ruler. What is the length of the bracelet in inches?

The bracelet is .... inches long.

2 Use a ruler. What is the length of the piece of celery?

Ⓐ 9 centimeters

Ⓑ 10 centimeters

Ⓒ 11 centimeters

Ⓓ 12 centimeters

3 Suzie and Gary are measuring a piece of wood. Suzie's piece is 3 inches long. Gary's piece is 9 inches long. Whose piece of wood is longer?

4 Use a ruler. Which pencils are 6 centimeters long?

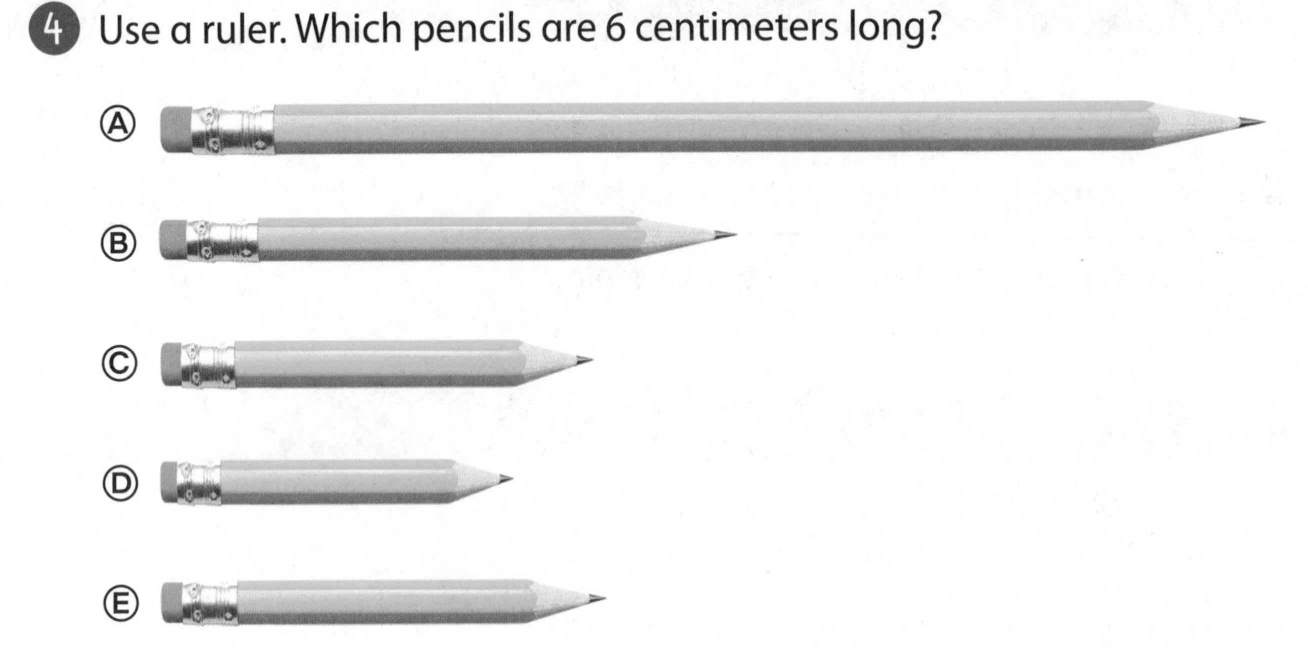

5 MATH JOURNAL

List the steps of measuring a toy car with a centimeter ruler. Imagine you are teaching someone who has never used a ruler.

☑ SELF CHECK Go back to the Unit 4 Opener and see what you can check off.

Measure in Feet and Meters

LESSON 21

Dear Family,

This week your child is learning how to use different measuring tools to measure the lengths of objects.

Your child will continue to use a ruler and will be introduced to other measuring tools, such as a yardstick, a meter stick, and a measuring tape.

- A standard ruler is marked in inches and centimeters. It shows 12 inches and 30 centimeters. A 12-inch ruler is equal to 1 **foot**.
- A **yardstick** is a measuring stick that is one **yard** long and shows 36 inches.
- A **meter stick** is a measuring stick that is 1 **meter** long and shows 100 centimeters.
- A **measuring tape** is a flexible measuring strip that shows inches and centimeters.

How long is this line to the nearest inch? You can use a ruler to measure the length.

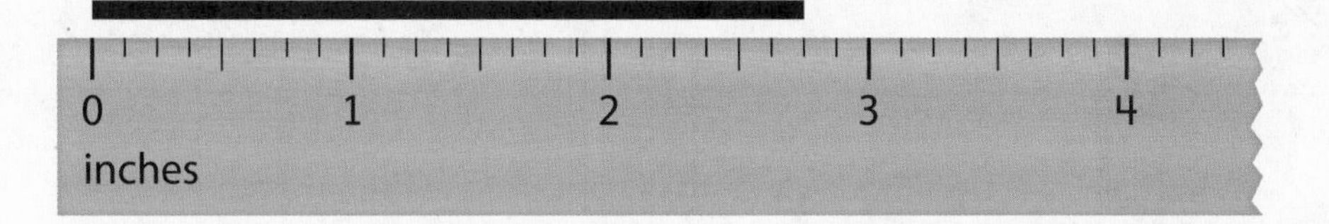

Line up the 0 with one end of the line. The other end of the line is between the 2 and the 3. It is closer to 3, so 3 is the nearest inch. The line is about 3 inches long.

Different tools may be easier to use when measuring different objects. For example, it is easier to measure a crayon with a ruler than with a yardstick, but it's easier to measure the length of the couch with a yardstick than a ruler.

Invite your child to share what he or she knows about measuring length by doing the following activity together.

ACTIVITY MEASURING

Do this activity with your child to explore measuring in feet and meters.

Materials measuring tool (ruler, yardstick, measuring tape), household objects

- Work with your child to practice measuring items around the house. Use whatever measuring tools you have available or cut out the centimeter ruler to the right. Measure in inches or centimeters, depending on the tool you are using. Measure all objects to the nearest inch or centimeter. Explain to your child that if the length of an object falls between two inch or centimeter measurements, he or she should pick the one that is closer to the length of the object.

- Ask your child to explain how he or she is measuring each item. Challenge your child to measure at least one object in each room of your home.

- Remind your child to include the units of measurement when he or she fills in the table. For example, write the length of a pen as 6 inches, not 6.

Object	Length

0 1 2 3 4 5 6 7 8 9 10 11 12 13 14 15 16 17 18
centimeters

Explore Measuring in Feet and Meters

Learning Target

- Measure the length of an object by selecting and using appropriate tools such as rulers, yardsticks, meter sticks, and measuring tapes.

SMP 1, 2, 3, 4, 5, 6, 7

You already know how to measure in inches and centimeters. Use what you know to try to solve the problem below.

Alex uses his scissors to cut out some shapes.

About how long are his scissors, measured in centimeters? How do you know?

TRY IT

Math Toolkit

- centimeter ruler
- measuring tape

DISCUSS IT

Ask your partner: Do you agree with me? Why or why not?

Tell your partner: I disagree with this part because . . .

CONNECT IT

1 LOOK BACK

About how long are the scissors?

2 LOOK AHEAD

Rulers often show both inches and centimeters. Many rulers show 12 inches. This is equal to 1 **foot**.

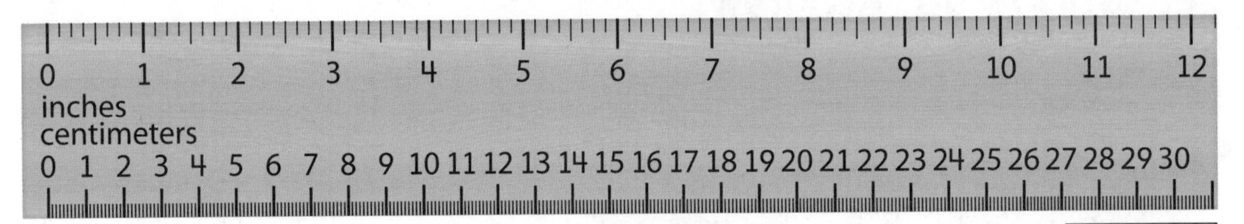

This ruler is not life-sized.

a. How many inches are on the ruler?

b. How many centimeters are on the ruler?

Some measuring tools are longer than a ruler.

- A **yardstick** shows 36 inches.
  There are 36 inches in a **yard**.
- A **meter stick** shows 100 centimeters.
  There are 100 centimeters in a **meter**.
- A **measuring tape** can show inches and centimeters.

3 REFLECT

How is a yardstick like an inch ruler? How is it different?

....

....

Name: ______________________

Prepare for Measuring in Feet and Meters

1 Think about what you know about measuring tools. Fill in each box. Use words, numbers, and pictures. Show as many ideas as you can.

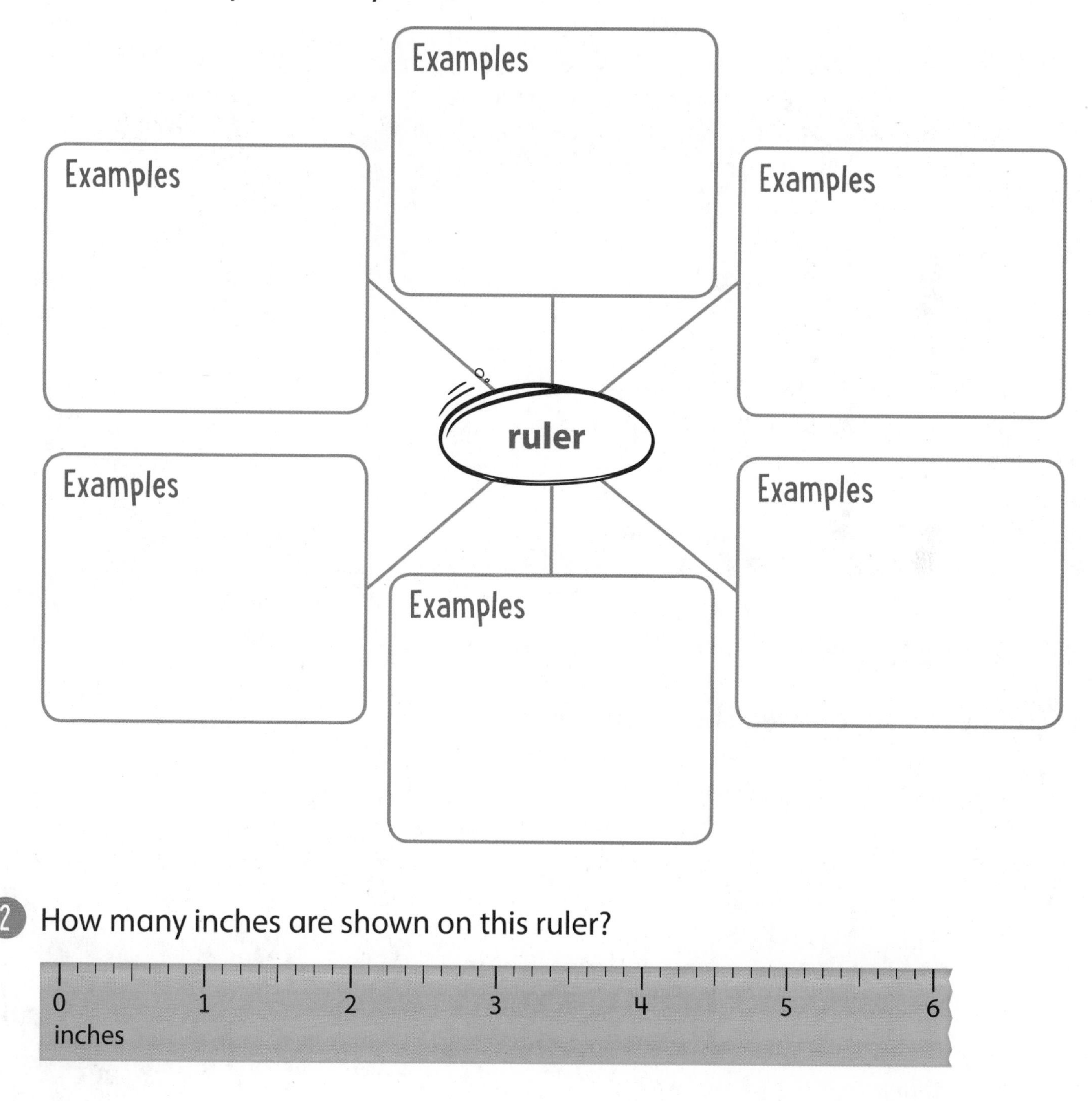

2 How many inches are shown on this ruler?

3 Solve the problem. Show your work.

Kalea has sharpened her pencil many times. What is the length of her pencil in centimeters? How do you know?

0 1 2 3 4 5 6 7 8 9 10 11 12 13 14 15
centimeters

Solution ....

4 Check your answer. Show your work.

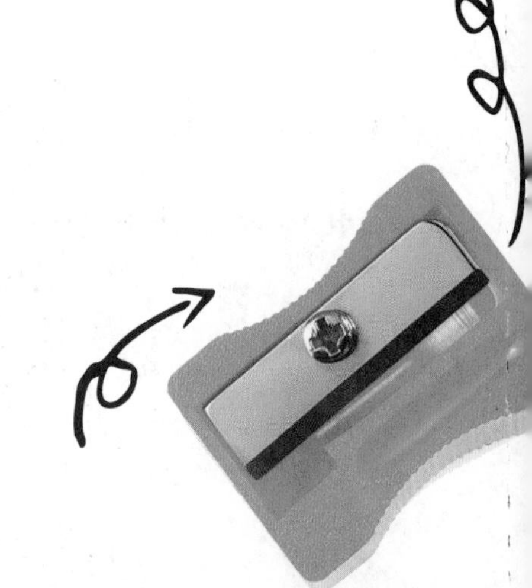

Develop Measuring in Inches and Feet

Read and try to solve the problem below.

Measure the length of your desk in feet.
About how long is your desk, measured in feet?

TRY IT

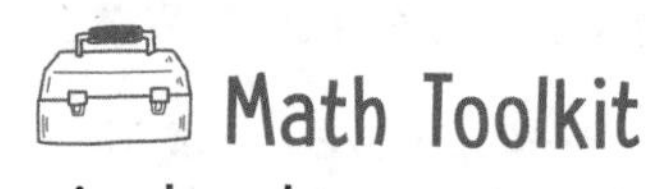

Math Toolkit
- inch ruler
- measuring tape
- yardstick

DISCUSS IT

Ask your partner: Why did you choose that strategy?

Tell your partner: The strategy I used to find the answer was . . .

Explore different ways to understand measuring in inches and feet.

Measure the length of your desk in feet.
About how long is your desk, measured in feet?

MEASURE IT

You can use a measuring tape to find the length.

Line up one edge of the desk with the 0 on a measuring tape. Find the number of feet closest to the other edge.

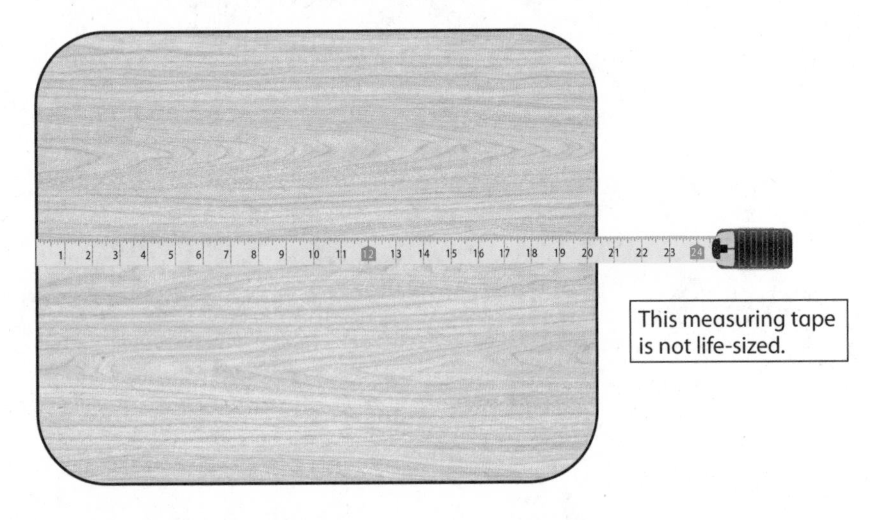

MEASURE IT

You can use two 12-inch rulers to find the length.

Line up one edge of the desk with the 0 on one of the rulers. Line up the 0 of the second ruler with the 12 of the first ruler.

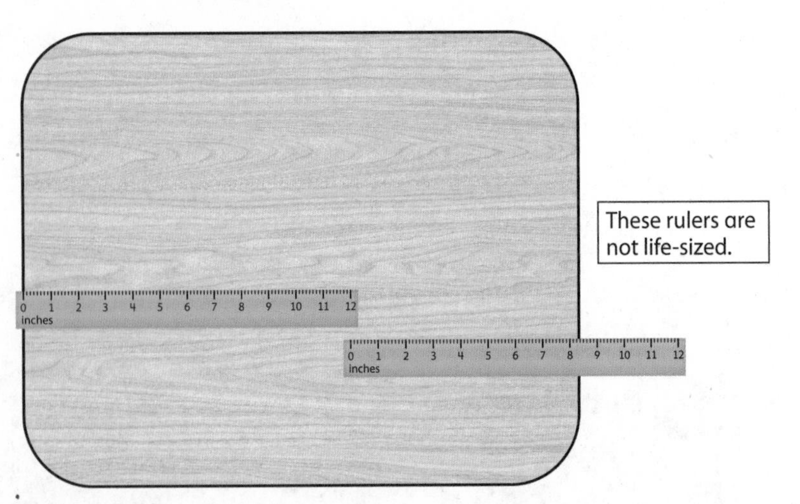

CONNECT IT

Now you will use the problem from the previous page to help you understand how to measure in feet.

1. Look at the second **Measure It**. Is the length of this desk closer to 1 foot or 2 feet? ....

2. Long objects can be measured with a yardstick.
   1 yard = 3 feet   1 yard = 36 inches

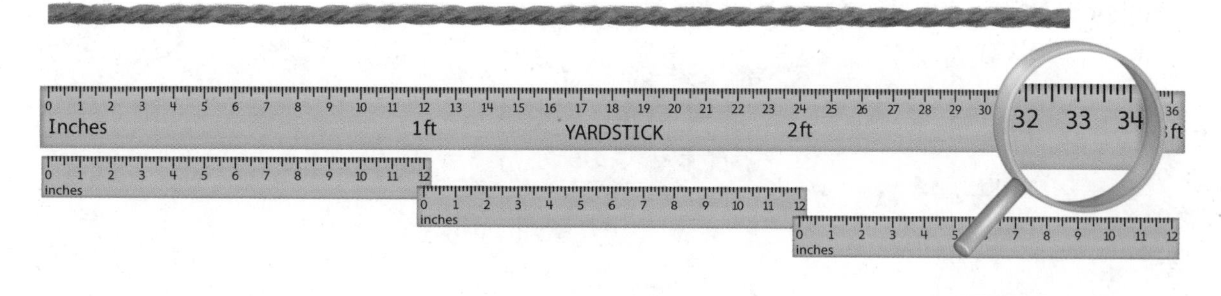

This yardstick and rulers are not life-sized.

What is the length of the rope to the:

a. nearest inch? .... inches

b. nearest foot? .... feet

c. nearest yard? .... yard

3. ## REFLECT

Look back at your **Try It**, strategies by classmates, and **Measure Its**. Which models or strategies do you like best for measuring the length of long objects? Explain.

....

....

APPLY IT

Use what you just learned to solve these problems.

4. Circle the objects that are easier to measure with an inch ruler. Underline the objects that are easier to measure with a yardstick.

a car a shoe a stamp

an envelope your classroom

5. Use a ruler. Measure the feather to the nearest inch.

The feather is about .... inches long.

Vivian measures her wagon. She says that it is about 2 feet long. Maddox says that it is about 3 feet long. Who is correct? Explain your answer.

Practice Measuring in Inches and Feet

Study the Example showing how to measure length with a yardstick. Then solve problems 1–4.

EXAMPLE

What is the length of the picture to the nearest foot?

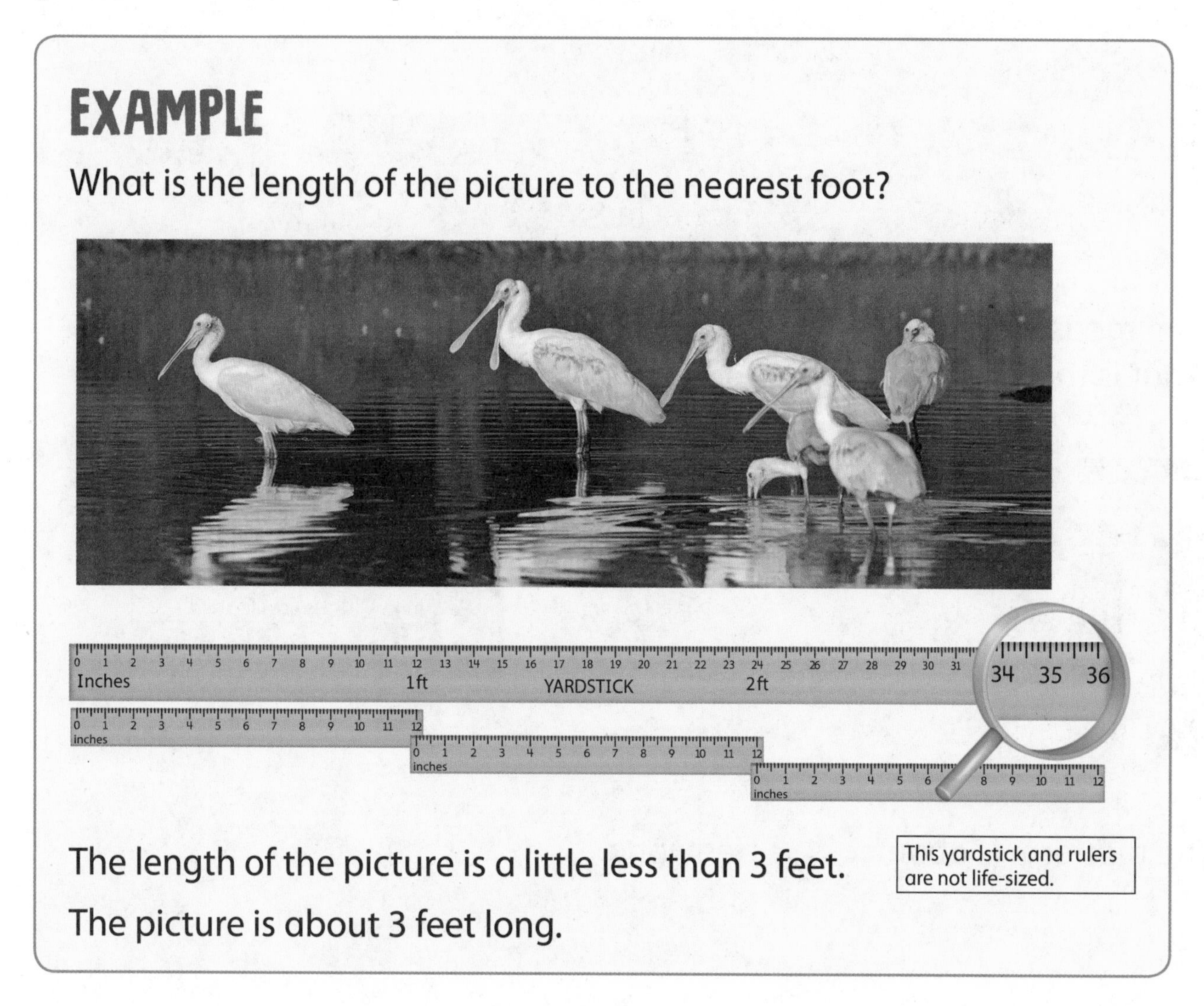

The length of the picture is a little less than 3 feet.

The picture is about 3 feet long.

1 In the above example, why is the picture described as about 3 feet and not about 2 feet?

 Marty measured this marker using an inch ruler. What is the length of the marker to the nearest inch?

.... inches

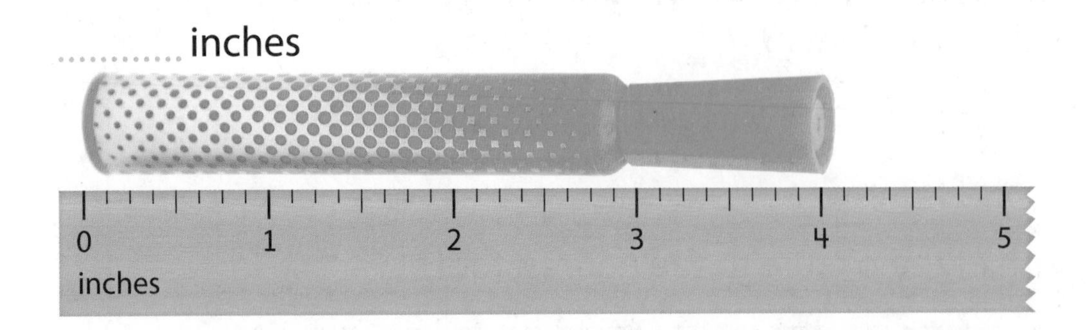

3 Sam measures a platform using a measuring tape. What is the length of the platform to the nearest foot?

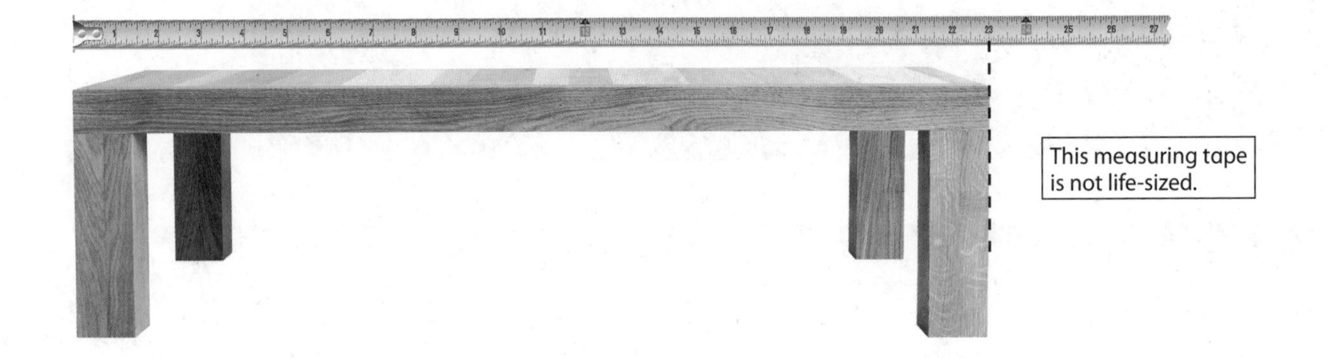

The platform is about .... feet long.

 In problem 3, about how long is the platform in inches? Explain how you found your answer.

Develop Measuring in Centimeters and Meters

Read and try to solve the problem below.

Look around your classroom. Choose a large object to measure, such as your teacher's desk, a rug, a whiteboard, or a bookshelf. Measure the length of the item you choose. How long is the item to the nearest centimeter?

TRY IT

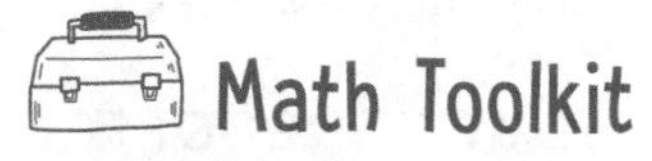

- centimeter ruler
- meter stick
- measuring tape
- number lines

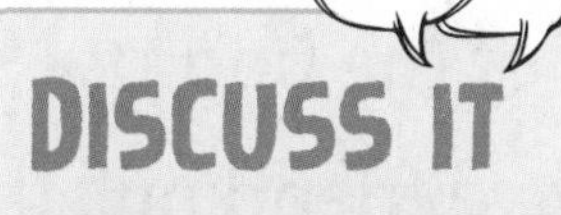

DISCUSS IT

Ask your partner: Can you explain that again?

Tell your partner: I am not sure how to find the answer because . . .

Explore different ways to understand measuring in centimeters and meters.

Look around your classroom. Choose a large object to measure, such as your teacher's desk, a rug, a whiteboard, or a bookshelf. Measure the length of the item you choose. How long is the item to the nearest centimeter?

MEASURE IT

You can use a meter stick to find the length.

Use your finger or marker to mark 100 centimeters, move the meter stick, and line up with 0 again. Repeat until you find the length.

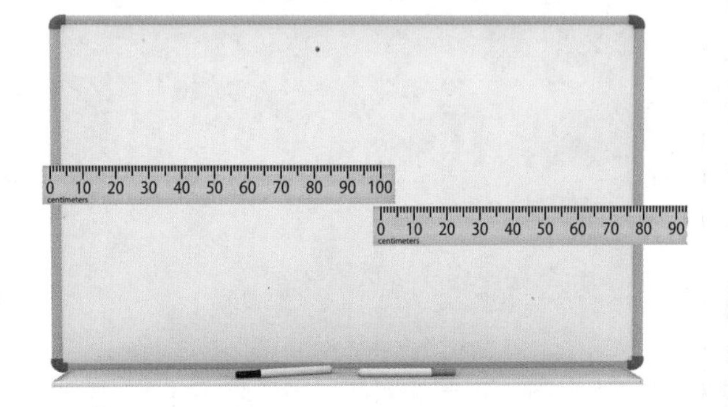

MEASURE IT

You can use a measuring tape to find the length.

Hold one end of the measuring tape at one end of the board.

Have a friend pull the measuring tape to the other end of the board.

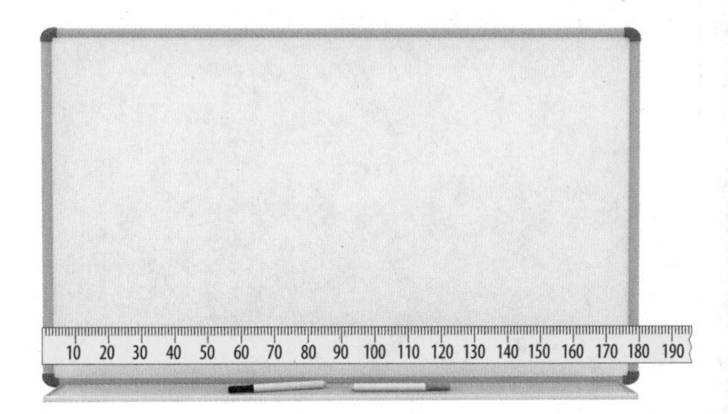

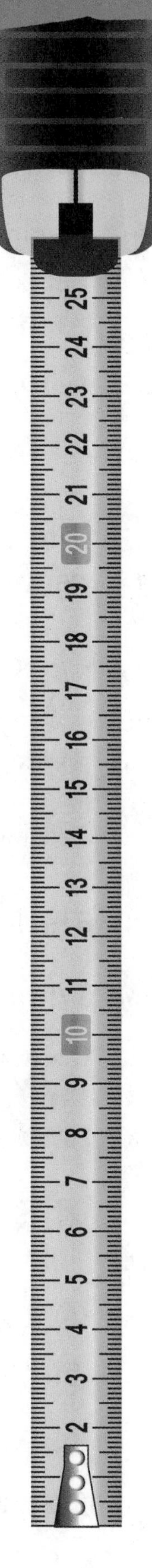

CONNECT IT

Now you will use the problem from the previous page to help you understand how to measure in centimeters and meters.

1 Look at the first **Measure It**. Why can you add 100 and 80 to find the total length of the whiteboard in centimeters?

2 Longer objects can be measured in meters.
1 meter is the same as 100 centimeters.
A meter stick is 1 meter long.
How long is the whiteboard to the nearest meter?

.... meters

3 Why could it be easier to measure a whiteboard with a measuring tape than with a meter stick?

4 REFLECT

Look back at your **Try It**, strategies by classmates, and **Measure Its**. Which models or strategies do you like best for measuring length of long objects? Explain.

....

....

APPLY IT

Use what you just learned to solve these problems.

5 Circle the objects that are easier to measure with a centimeter ruler. Underline the objects that are easier to measure with a meter stick.

a hot dog a jump rope a pencil

your height this book

6 What is the length of the key to the nearest centimeter?

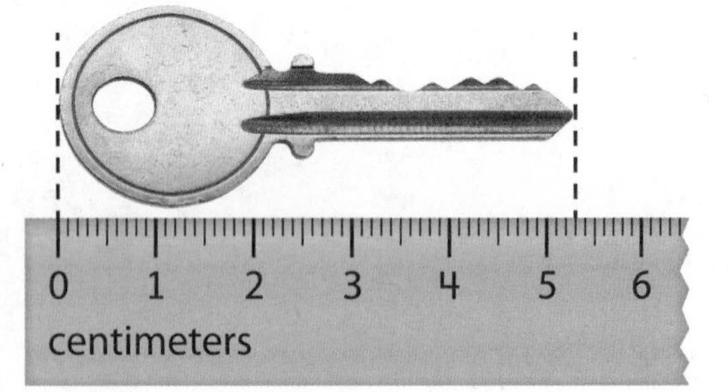

The key is about .... centimeters long.

7 What is the length of the ribbon to the nearest meter?

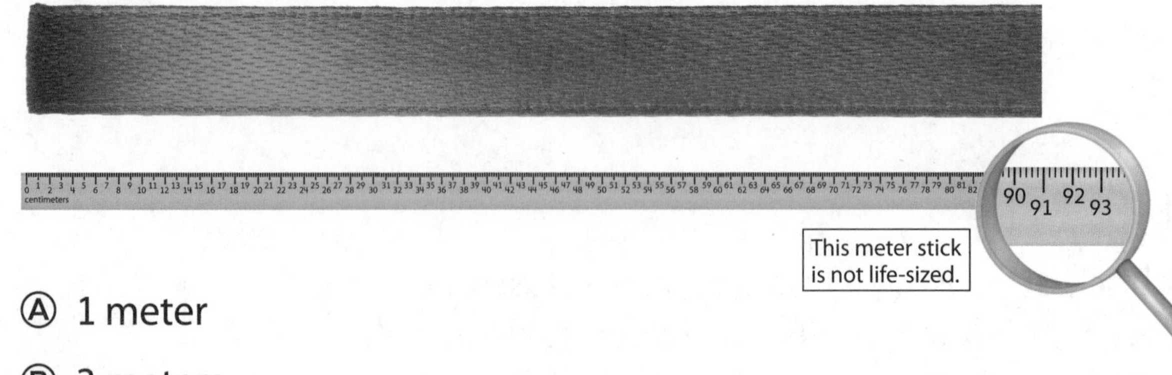

Ⓐ 1 meter

Ⓑ 3 meters

Ⓒ 90 meters

Ⓓ 100 meters

Practice Measuring in Centimeters and Meters

Study the Example showing ways to measure an object. Then solve problems 1–5.

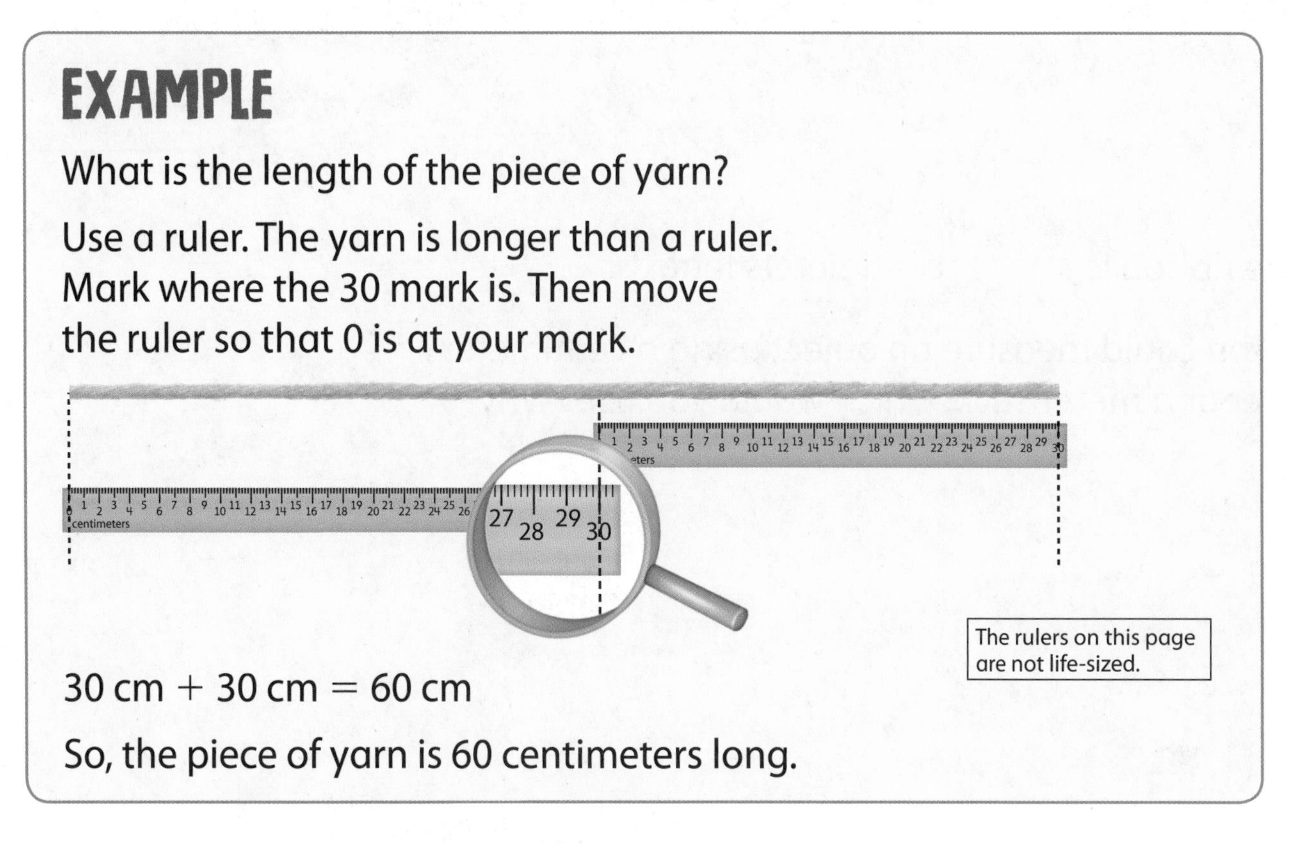

EXAMPLE

What is the length of the piece of yarn?

Use a ruler. The yarn is longer than a ruler. Mark where the 30 mark is. Then move the ruler so that 0 is at your mark.

The rulers on this page are not life-sized.

30 cm + 30 cm = 60 cm

So, the piece of yarn is 60 centimeters long.

What is the length of the string? Find the length of the string.

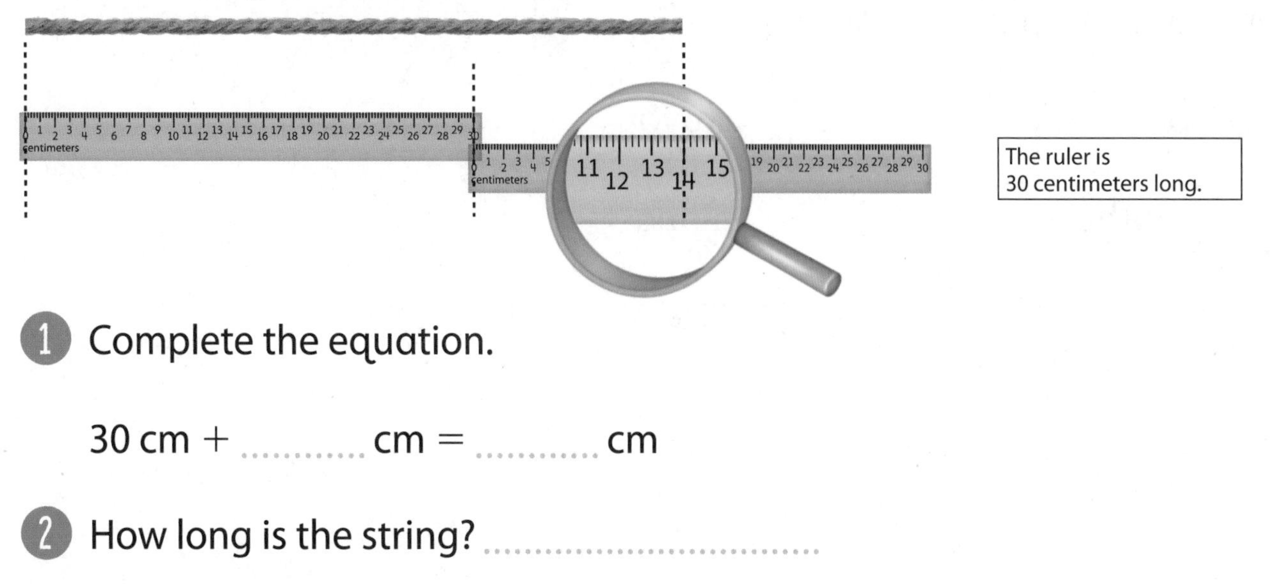

The ruler is 30 centimeters long.

1. Complete the equation.

   30 cm + ... cm = ... cm

2. How long is the string? ....

3 How long is the ribbon? Look at the meter stick.

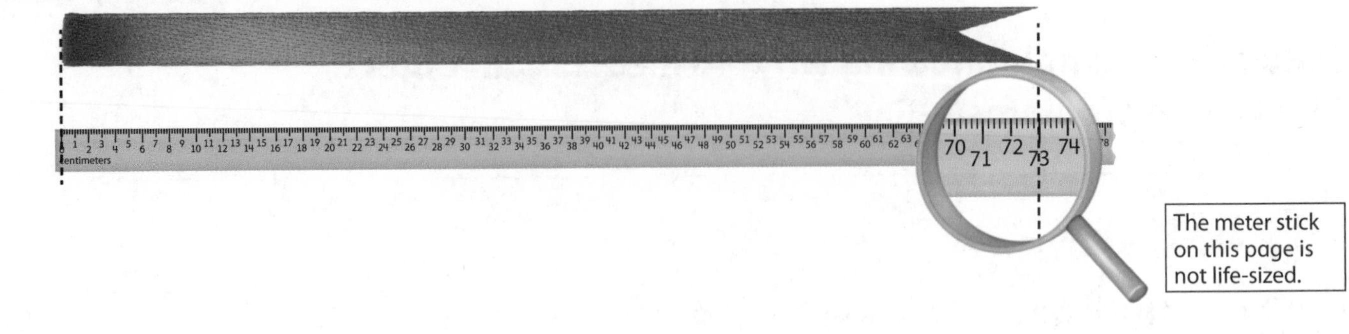

The meter stick on this page is not life-sized.

The ribbon is .... centimeters long.

4 If you could measure an object using a centimeter ruler or a meter stick, which would you use? Why?

5 Circle the objects that are easier to measure with a centimeter ruler. Underline the objects that are easier to measure with a meter stick.

picnic table	crayon
toothbrush	piano
sofa	slice of bread

Refine Measuring in Feet and Meters

Complete the Example below. Then solve problems 1–3.

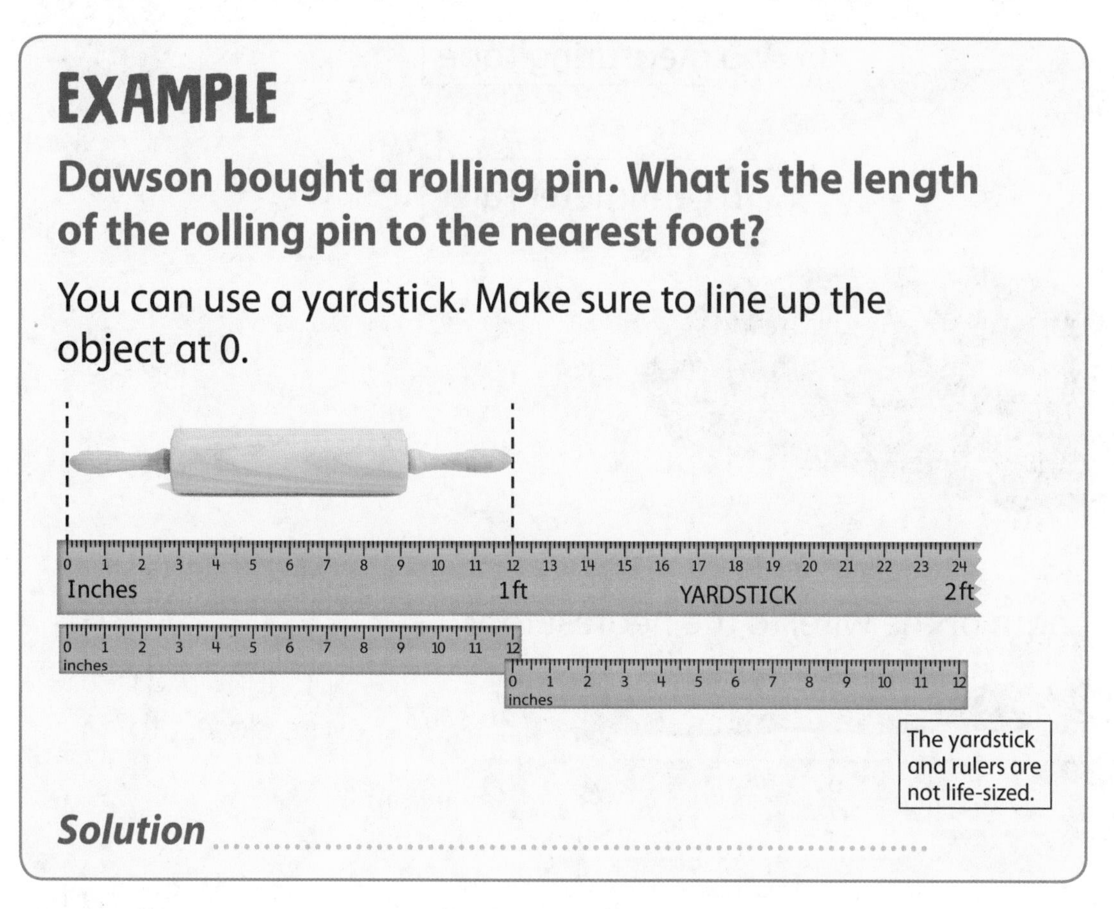

EXAMPLE

Dawson bought a rolling pin. What is the length of the rolling pin to the nearest foot?

You can use a yardstick. Make sure to line up the object at 0.

Solution ....

APPLY IT

1 Use a ruler. What is the length of the eraser to the nearest inch?

What kind of ruler should you use?

The eraser is .... inches long.

Think about the length of the actual objects. Draw lines to match each object with the best tool for measuring it.

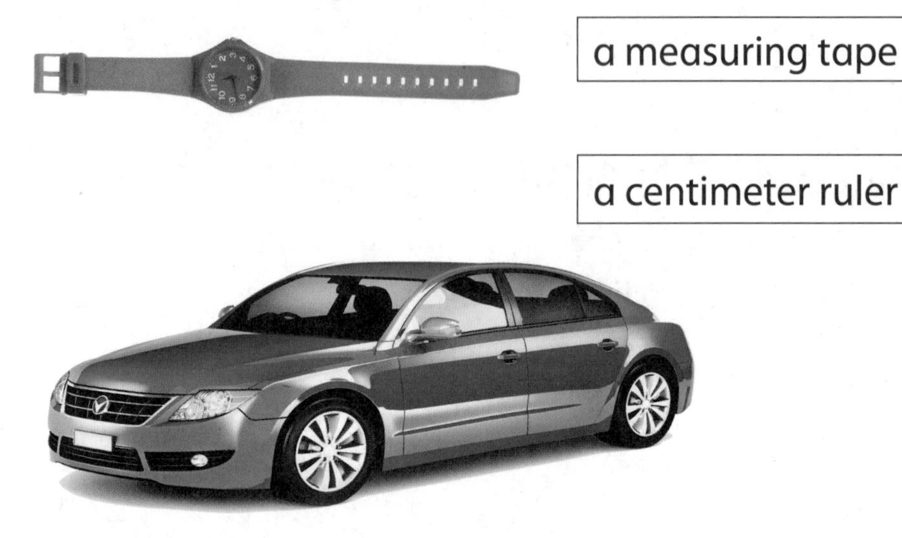

Which tool is used to measure very long objects?

3 What is the length of the wire, to the nearest foot?

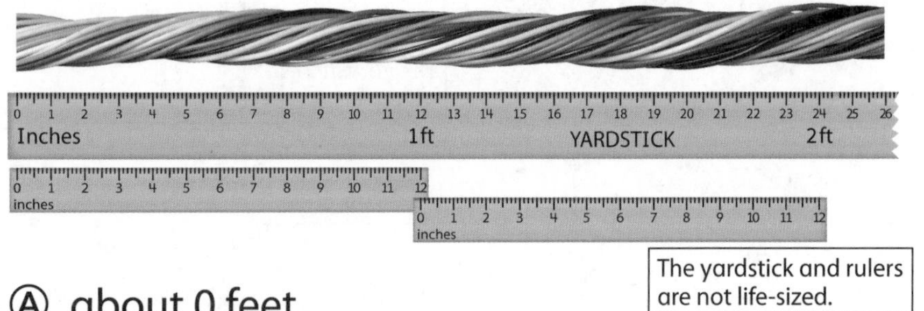

The yardstick and rulers are not life-sized.

Ⓐ about 0 feet

Ⓑ about 1 foot

Ⓒ about 2 feet

Ⓓ about 3 feet

Kyle chose Ⓓ as the answer. How did Kyle get his answer?

Which mark for feet is the right end of the wire closest to?

Practice Measuring in Feet and Meters

1 What is the length of the string?

Ⓐ 1 centimeter

Ⓑ 1 meter

Ⓒ 10 centimeters

Ⓓ 10 meters

What kind of ruler is being used to measure the string?

Glen chose Ⓐ. How did Glen get his answer?

2 Layla started drawing the line above the ruler. Finish drawing the line to make it 2 inches long.

Where on the ruler is the mark for 2 inches?

3 Circle the objects that are easier to measure with a centimeter ruler. Underline the objects that are easier to measure with a meter stick.

park bench stamp

paper clip sandbox

Is it easier to measure large or small objects with a ruler?

4 Which piece of yarn is about 4 centimeters long?

Ⓐ 0 1 2 3 4 centimeters

Ⓑ 0 1 2 3 4 centimeters

Ⓒ 0 1 2 3 4 centimeters

Ⓓ 0 1 2 3 4 centimeters

Where do you line up the left edge of the object you are measuring with a ruler?

5 Jed wants to measure the length of the classroom chalkboard in inches. Which tools could he use?

Ⓐ measuring tape

Ⓑ yardstick

Ⓒ meter stick

Ⓓ inch ruler

Ⓔ centimeter ruler

Which tools show inches?

Refine Measuring in Feet and Meters

APPLY IT

Solve the problems.

1 Leah wants to measure the length of her bike in feet. Which tools could she use?

Ⓐ 12-inch ruler

Ⓑ yardstick

Ⓒ meter stick

Ⓓ measuring tape

Ⓔ centimeter ruler

2 What is the length of the worm to the nearest inch?

Ⓐ 2 inches

Ⓑ 3 inches

Ⓒ 5 inches

Ⓓ 6 inches

3 Ruby measures each line to the nearest centimeter. She writes the length of each line after it. Did she measure correctly? Choose *Yes* or *No* for each length.

	Yes	No
———————— 5 cm	Ⓐ	Ⓑ
———— 3 cm	Ⓒ	Ⓓ
——— 2 cm	Ⓔ	Ⓕ
—————— 4 cm	Ⓖ	Ⓗ

4 Marcus says the length of the stick is 3 feet. What did Marcus do wrong?

1 ft
2 ft
3 ft

Ⓐ He measured in inches.

Ⓑ He used the wrong side of the ruler.

Ⓒ He didn't line up one end of the stick at 0.

Ⓓ He should have used an inch ruler.

5 What is the actual length of the stick in feet?

....

6 Brian wants to measure the length of his bed in meters. He says the best tool to use is a ruler. Do you agree? Why or why not?

7 MATH JOURNAL

Name two objects that have very different lengths. Describe what tool you would use to measure each object and explain why you chose that tool.

☑ SELF CHECK Go back to the Unit 4 Opener and see what you can check off.

Understand Measurement with Different Units

LESSON 22

Dear Family,

This week your child is exploring using different units to measure the length of an object.

An object can be measured using many different units of length, such as inches, feet, yards, centimeters, or meters.

0 1 2 3 4 5 6 7 8 9 10 11
centimeters

0 1 2 3 4
inches

The toy fire truck is 5 centimeters long.
The toy fire truck is about 2 inches long.

It takes fewer inches than centimeters to measure the fire truck. An inch is longer than a centimeter, so you need fewer of them to measure an object. A centimeter is shorter than an inch, so you need more of them to measure an object.

Invite your child to share what he or she knows about measuring length with different units by doing the following activity together.

ACTIVITY EXPLORING DIFFERENT UNITS

Do this activity with your child to understand measurement with different units.

Materials ruler, household objects

Play the following game with your child to help him or her see the results of measuring with longer or shorter units.

- Have your child pick an object to measure. Give your child a choice between measuring in inches, centimeters, feet, or yards.
- Choose one of the remaining units for yourself.
- Measure the object together, once for each unit. Measure to the nearest whole unit. Complete the table.
- Pick another object and repeat with new units for each player.
- For each object, ask your child to circle the player who used fewer units to measure the object.

Object 1		
	Player 1	**Player 2**
Unit		
Measurement		

Object 2		
	Player 1	**Player 2**
Unit		
Measurement		

Tell your child that you are going to measure the height of the refrigerator and that you are going to use centimeters. Ask your child which unit they would pick to use fewer units to measure the refrigerator. Test your child's answer by measuring with the chosen units.

Explore Measurement with Different Units

What happens when you measure the same object using different units?

Learning Target

- Measure the length of an object twice, using length units of different lengths for the two measurements; describe how the two measurements relate to the size of the unit chosen.

SMP 1, 2, 3, 4, 5, 6, 8

MODEL IT

Kim and Nadia measure the same piece of fabric. Fill in each blank.

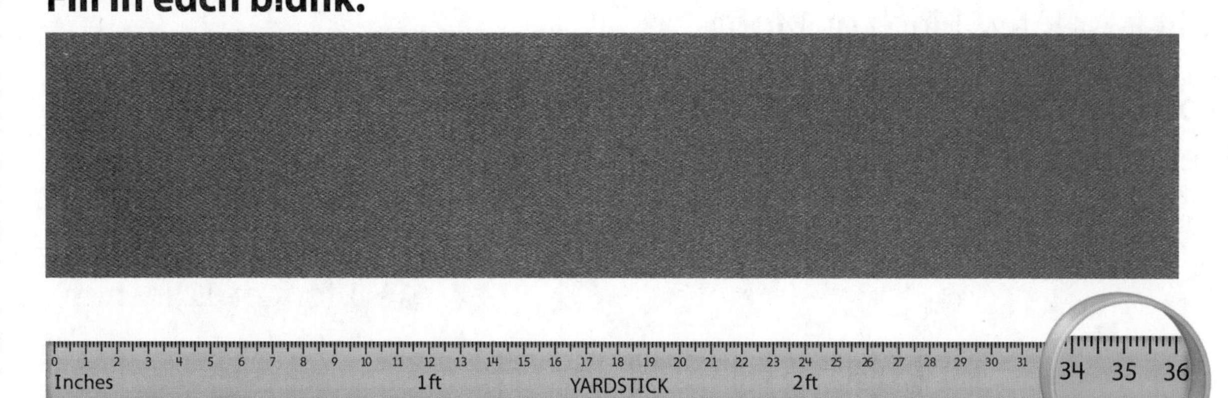

The yardstick and rulers are not life-sized.

1 Kim reads the length in inches.

How long is the fabric in inches? ....

2 Nadia reads the length in feet.

How long is the fabric in feet? ....

DISCUSS IT

- Compare Kim and Nadia's measurements. Are they the same?
- I think different units can be used to measure because . . .

MODEL IT

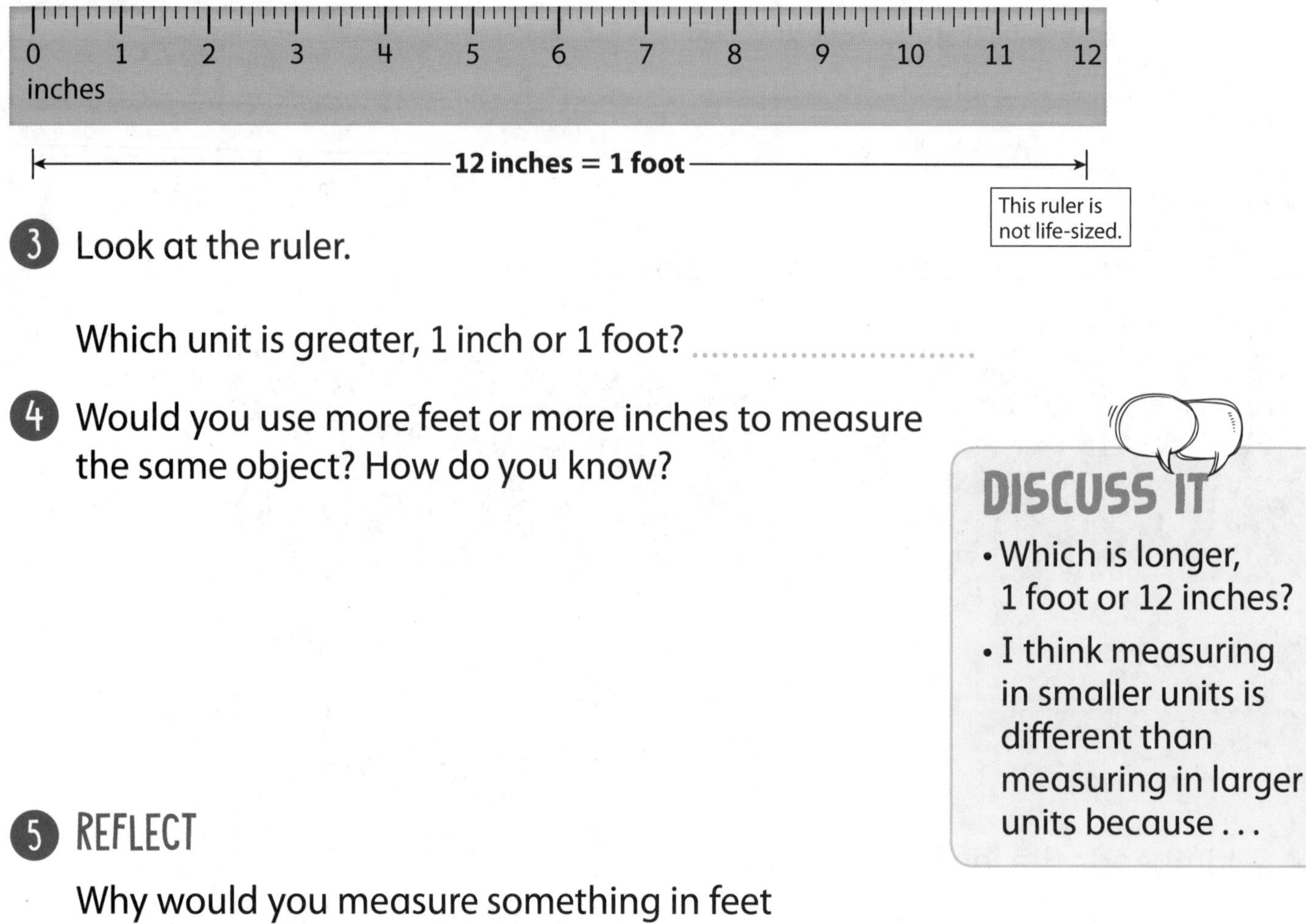

3 Look at the ruler.

Which unit is greater, 1 inch or 1 foot? ....

4 Would you use more feet or more inches to measure the same object? How do you know?

DISCUSS IT

- Which is longer, 1 foot or 12 inches?
- I think measuring in smaller units is different than measuring in larger units because . . .

5 REFLECT

Why would you measure something in feet instead of inches? Why would you measure something in inches instead of feet?

....

....

....

....

....

Name: ____________________

Prepare for Measuring with Different Units

1 Think about what you know about measuring length.
Fill in each box. Use words, numbers, and pictures.
Show as many ideas as you can.

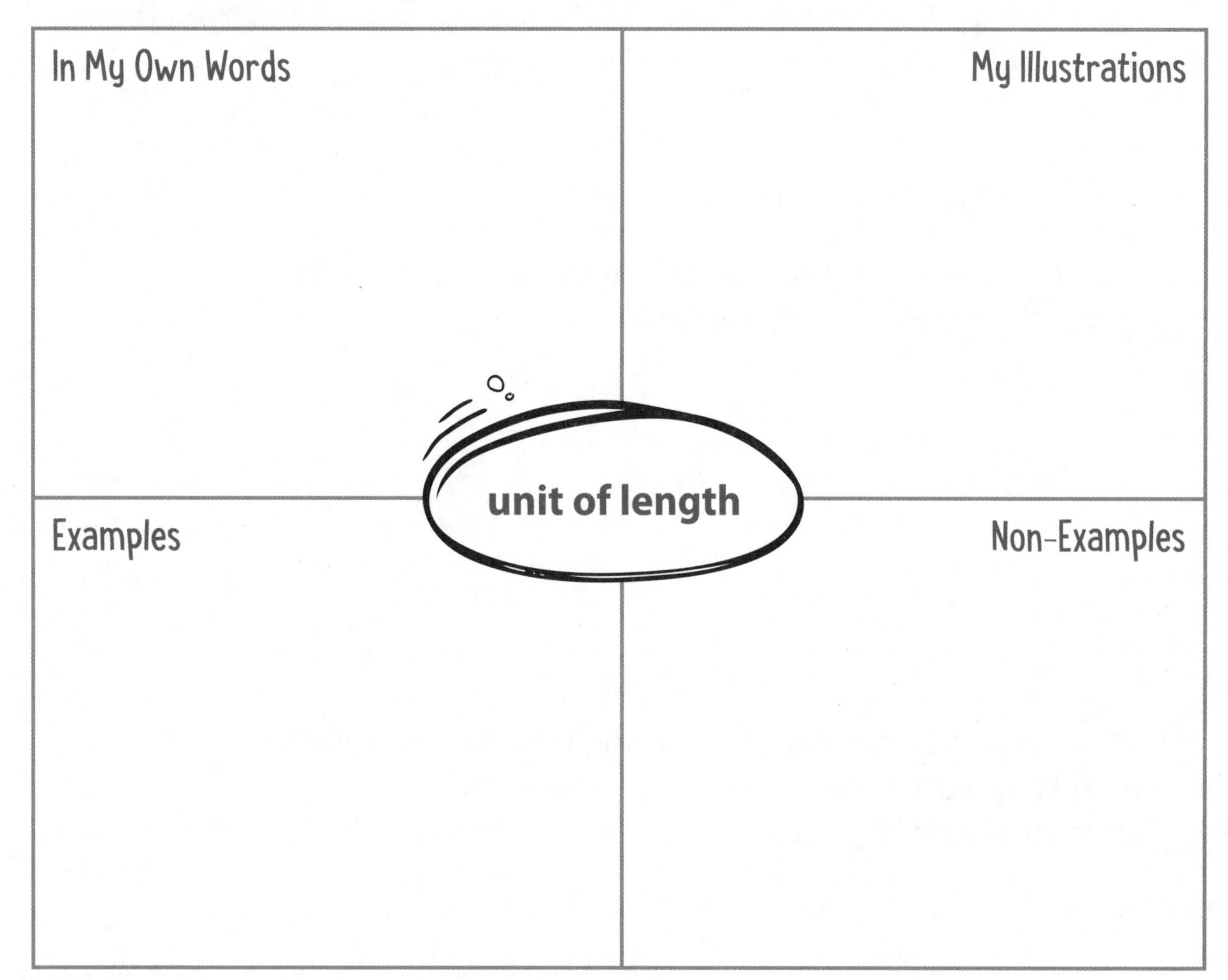

2 What is the unit of length on the ruler?

0 1 2 3 4 5 6 7 8 9 10 11 12 13 14 15
centimeters

The unit of length on the ruler is ....

Solve.

3. Look at the yardstick.

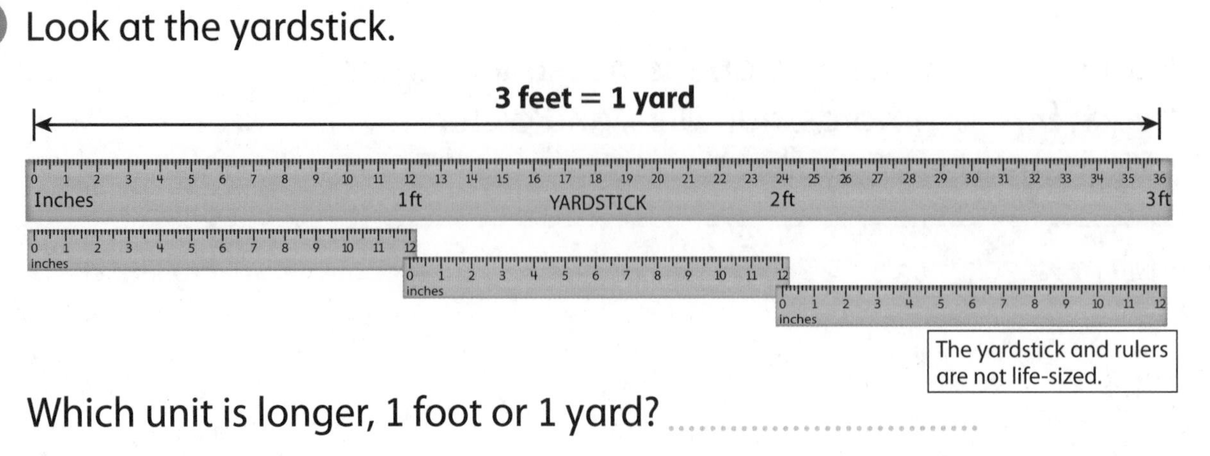

Which unit is longer, 1 foot or 1 yard? ....

4. Would you use more yards or more feet to measure the same object? How do you know?

5. Why would you measure something in yards instead of feet? Why would you measure something in feet instead of yards?

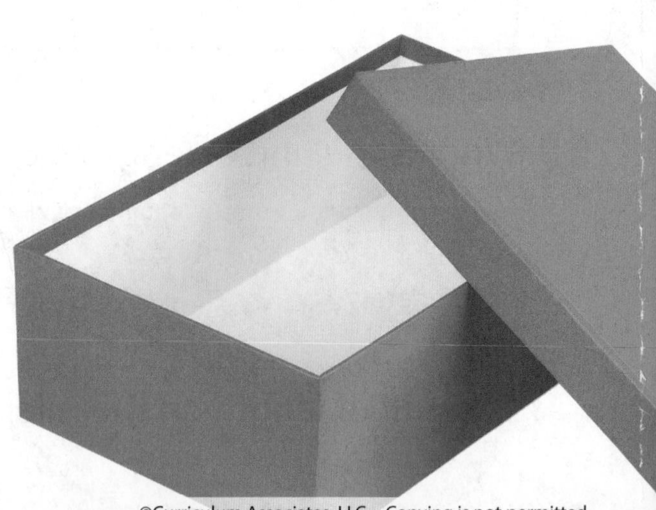

Develop Understanding of Different Units of Length

MODEL IT: MEASURE IN INCHES AND CENTIMETERS

Fill in each blank.

1. Use a ruler. Measure the length of the paper clip in inches and in centimeters.

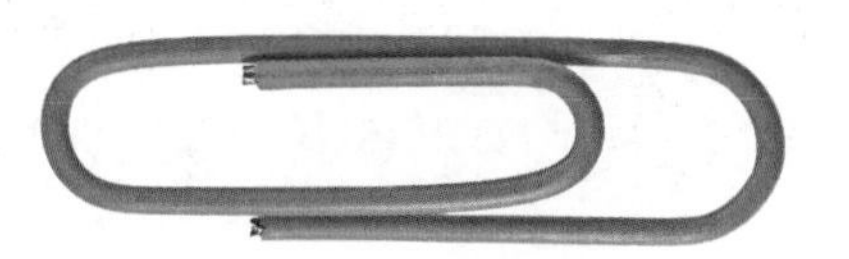

The paper clip is .... inches long.

The paper clip is about .... centimeters long.

2. Use a ruler. Measure the length of the leaf in inches and in centimeters.

The leaf is about .... inches long.

The leaf is .... centimeters long.

DISCUSS IT

- Can the length of an object be the same number of centimeters as inches?
- I think you should say whether a measurement is in centimeters or in inches because . . .

MODEL IT: COMPARE OTHER UNITS

DISCUSS IT

- Will it take fewer or more buttons than crayons to measure the length of your shoe?
- I think the eraser could be used for measuring when . . .

3

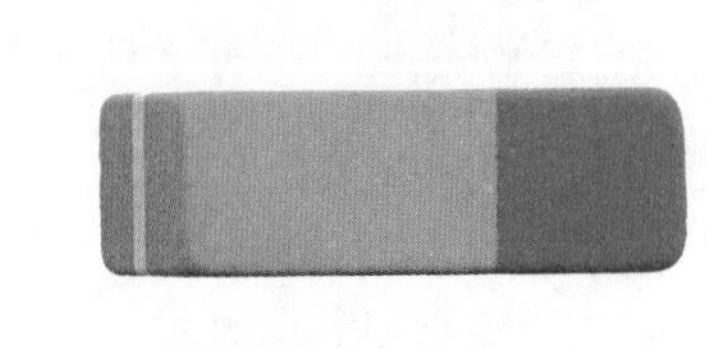

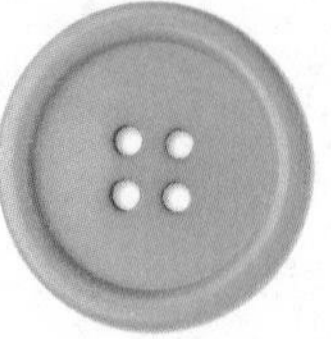

Circle the longer object.

Would it take fewer erasers or fewer buttons to measure the length of your pencil?

CONNECT IT

Complete the problems below.

4 If you measure the length of your math book, will it take more inches or more centimeters? Why?

5 Use a ruler. Measure the marker below in inches and in centimeters. Then circle the one you needed more of.

.... inches

.... centimeters

Name: ____________________

Practice Comparing Units of Measure

Study the Example showing how to measure an object in inches and centimeters. Then solve problems 1–8.

EXAMPLE

How long is the ribbon in centimeters and in inches?

It is 5 centimeters long.

It is about 2 inches long.

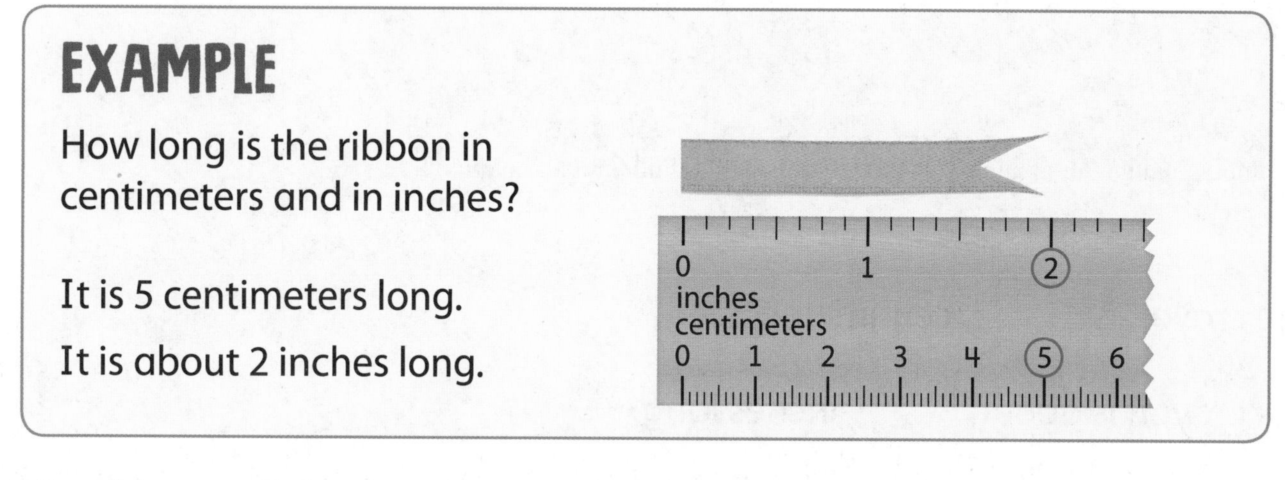

Use this pencil for problems 1 and 2.

1. The pencil is .... centimeters long.

2. The pencil is about .... inches long.

3. Does it take fewer centimeters or inches to measure the length of the pencil? Why?

Use this crayon for problems 4 and 5.

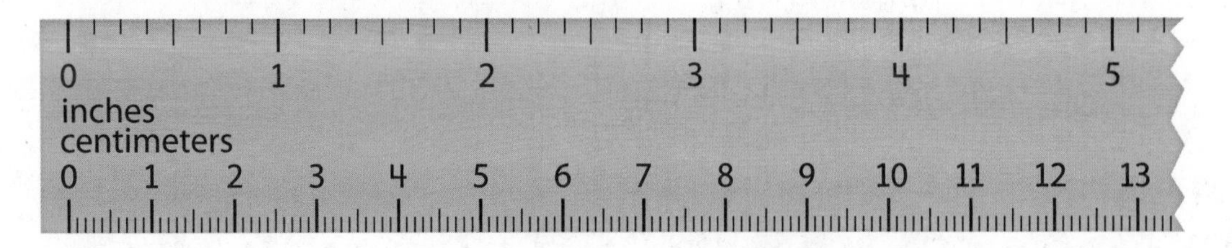

4 The crayon is .... centimeters long.

5 The crayon is about .... inches long.

6 Does it take more centimeters or inches to measure the length of the crayon? Why?

7 Would it take fewer centimeters or meters to measure the length of your school? ....

8 Would it take more feet or yards to measure the length of your street? ....

Refine Ideas About Measurement with Different Units

APPLY IT

Complete these problems on your own.

1 COMPARE

Eduardo's picnic table is 200 centimeters long. Eduardo also measures the picnic table in meters. Is the length of the picnic table fewer centimeters or fewer meters? Explain.

2 COMPARE

Joe's bedroom is 6 yards long. He also measures it in feet. Does Joe use more yards or more feet to measure the length of his bedroom? Explain.

3 EXPLAIN

Kit's red ribbon is 12 inches long. Her blue ribbon is 12 centimeters long. Kit says they are the same length. Do you agree? Explain.

PAIR/SHARE

Discuss your solutions for these three problems with a partner.

Use what you have learned to complete problem 4.

4 Eric measures the length of his model car.

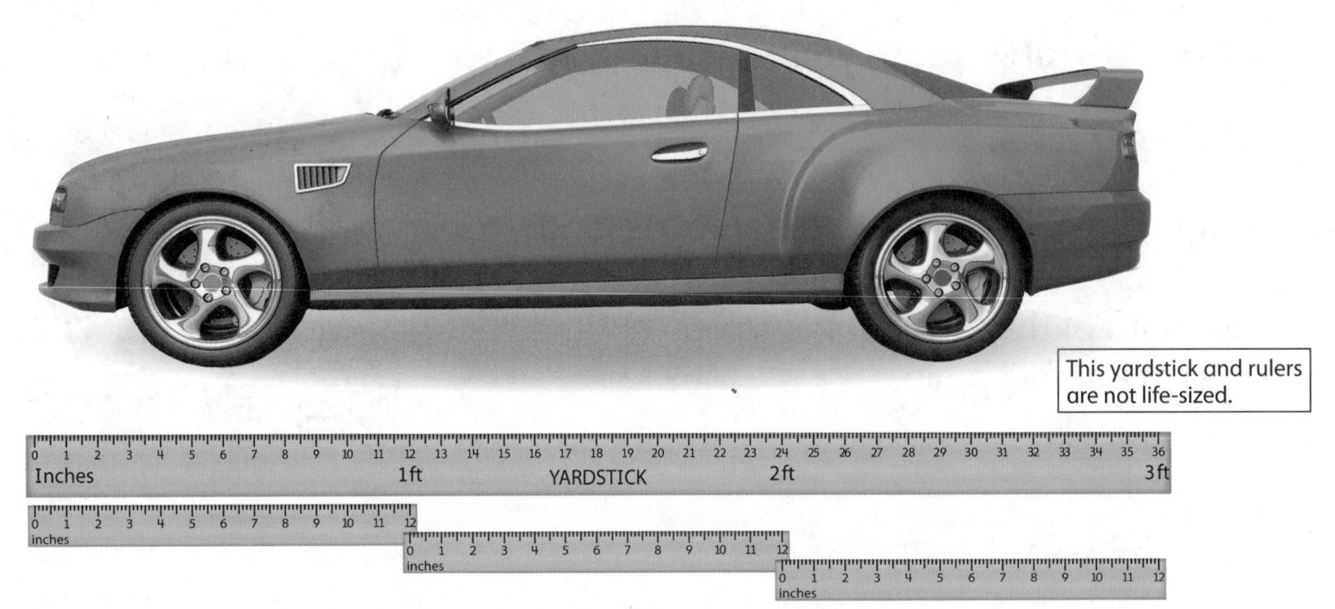

Part A What is the length of Eric's car in feet and in yards?

.... feet .... yard(s)

Part B Which units would you need the fewest of to measure the length of Eric's car? Circle the correct answer.

inches yards feet

5 MATH JOURNAL

Choose any two different units of measure. Then explain which of the units you would need fewer of to measure the height of a door.

Estimate and Measure Length

LESSON 23

Dear Family,

This week your child is learning about estimating lengths of objects using benchmark objects.

If you know the length of a common object, you can use that length to **estimate** the length of other objects.

Here are some helpful benchmarks you can use with your child to estimate length.

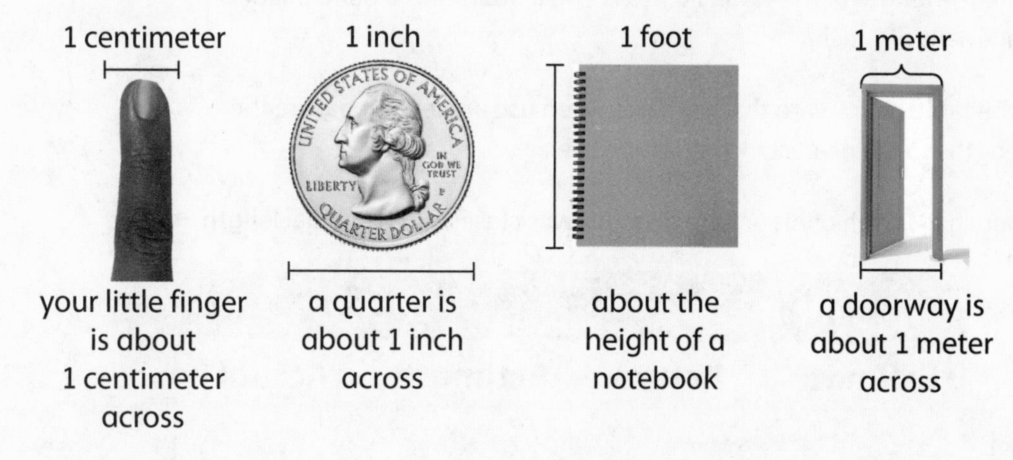

To estimate the length of this ribbon, your child might compare it to quarters and estimate that it would take 5 quarters to measure the ribbon. So, it is about 5 inches long.

Invite your child to share what he or she knows about estimating length by doing the following activity together.

ACTIVITY ESTIMATING LENGTH

Do this activity with your child to estimate and measure length.

Materials quarter, ruler, toys or household objects

- Have your child collect three of his or her favorite small toys.
- Work with your child to estimate the length of each toy in centimeters. Encourage your child to use his or her little finger as a benchmark measurement of 1 centimeter.
- Estimate the length of the toy in inches, using a quarter as a benchmark measurement of 1 inch.
- Fill in the table below with the estimates. Then use a ruler to measure the toys' lengths to the nearest inch or centimeter.
- Ask your child which of his or her estimates was closest to the actual length.

	Centimeters		Inches	
	Estimate	**Actual**	**Estimate**	**Actual**
Toy #1				
Toy #2				
Toy #3				

Keep an eye open for examples of benchmark lengths in your everyday life. Share these with your child. For example, the height of a tree might be a good example of 20 feet, and the length of a sidewalk square might be a good example of 1 meter.

Explore Estimating and Measuring Length

- Estimate lengths using units of inches, feet, centimeters, and meters.

SMP 1, 2, 3, 4, 5, 6

Previously, you used different units to measure length. Use what you know to try to solve the problem below.

A quarter is about 1 inch across, so it is a good estimate for 1 inch.

Ty wants to estimate the length of his toy car. What is a good estimate for its length in inches?

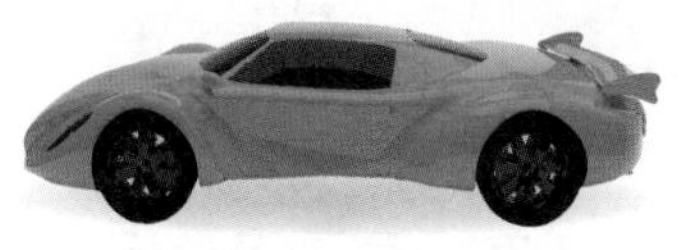

TRY IT

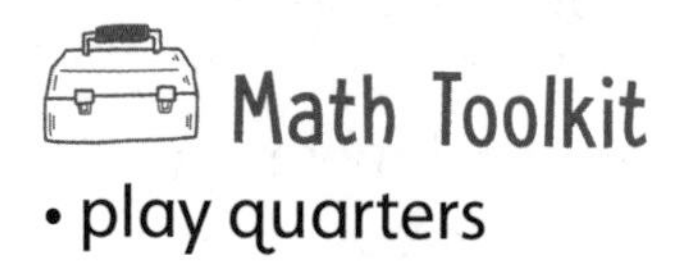

- play quarters

Ask your partner: How did you get started?

Tell your partner: At first, I thought . . .

CONNECT IT

1 LOOK BACK

What is a good **estimate** for the length of Ty's car? .... inches

2 LOOK AHEAD

You can use other objects to help you **estimate** lengths.

1 centimeter

your little finger is about 1 centimeter across

1 inch

a quarter is about 1 inch across

1 foot

about the length of a loaf of bread

1 meter

a door is about 1 meter across

Julia knows a marker is about 14 centimeters long. Is the length of the pencil case more or less than 14 centimeters? Explain how you know.

3 REFLECT

Hannah estimates that Julia's pencil case is 28 centimeters long. Is this a good estimate? Explain.

....

....

Name: ____________________

Prepare for Estimating and Measuring Length

1. Think about what you know about estimating. Fill in each box. Use words, numbers, and pictures. Show as many ideas as you can.

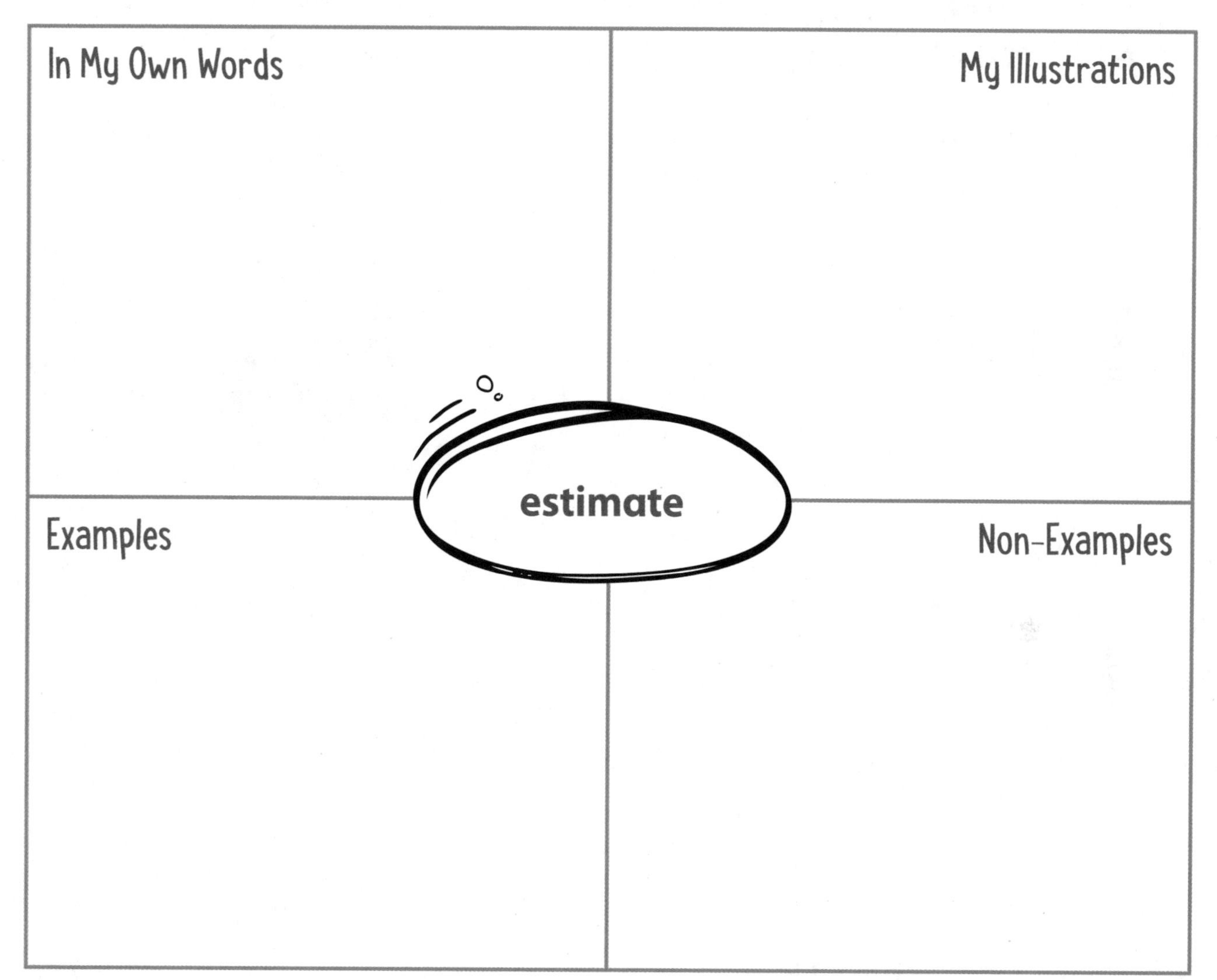

2. Balin knows the stapler is about 15 centimeters long. Is the length of the glasses more or less than 15 centimeters? Explain.

3 Solve the problem. Show your work.

Since a quarter is about 1 inch across, it is a good estimate for 1 inch.

Gena wants to estimate the length of the toy boat. What is a good estimate for its length in inches?

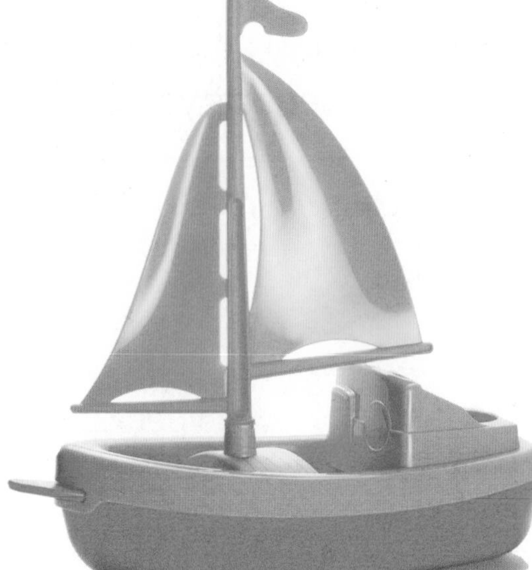

Solution ....

 Check your answer. Show your work.

Develop Using Different Units to Estimate Length

Read and try to solve the problem below.

1 centimeter is a good estimate for the distance across your little finger.

What is a good estimate for the length of this stamp?

TRY IT

Math Toolkit
- play quarters
- centimeter cubes

DISCUSS IT

Ask your partner: Why did you choose that strategy?

Tell your partner: I'm not sure how to find the answer because . . .

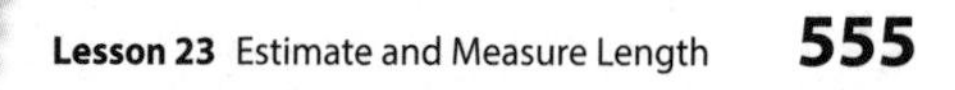

Explore different ways to understand estimating length.

1 centimeter is a good estimate for the distance across your little finger.

What is a good estimate for the length of this stamp?

PICTURE IT

You can use other objects you know to estimate lengths.

Think about the distance across the middle of the quarter and the length of the stamp.

Think about the distance across your little finger and the length of the stamp.

CONNECT IT

Now you will use the problem from the previous page to help you understand how to estimate length.

1. Look at **Picture It** on the previous page. What is a good estimate of the length of the stamp in inches?

   The stamp is about .... inch(es) long.

2. Look at **Picture It** on the previous page. What is a good estimate of the length of the stamp in centimeters?

   The stamp is about .... centimeter(s) long.

3. You can use a ruler to measure the length.

   What is the length of the stamp to the nearest

   centimeter? ....

4. ## REFLECT

   Look back at your **Try It**, strategies by classmates, and **Picture It**. Which models or strategies do you like best for estimating length? Explain.

   ....

   ....

   ....

APPLY IT

Use what you just learned to solve these problems.

Use the hair clip and ribbon to answer problems 5 and 6.

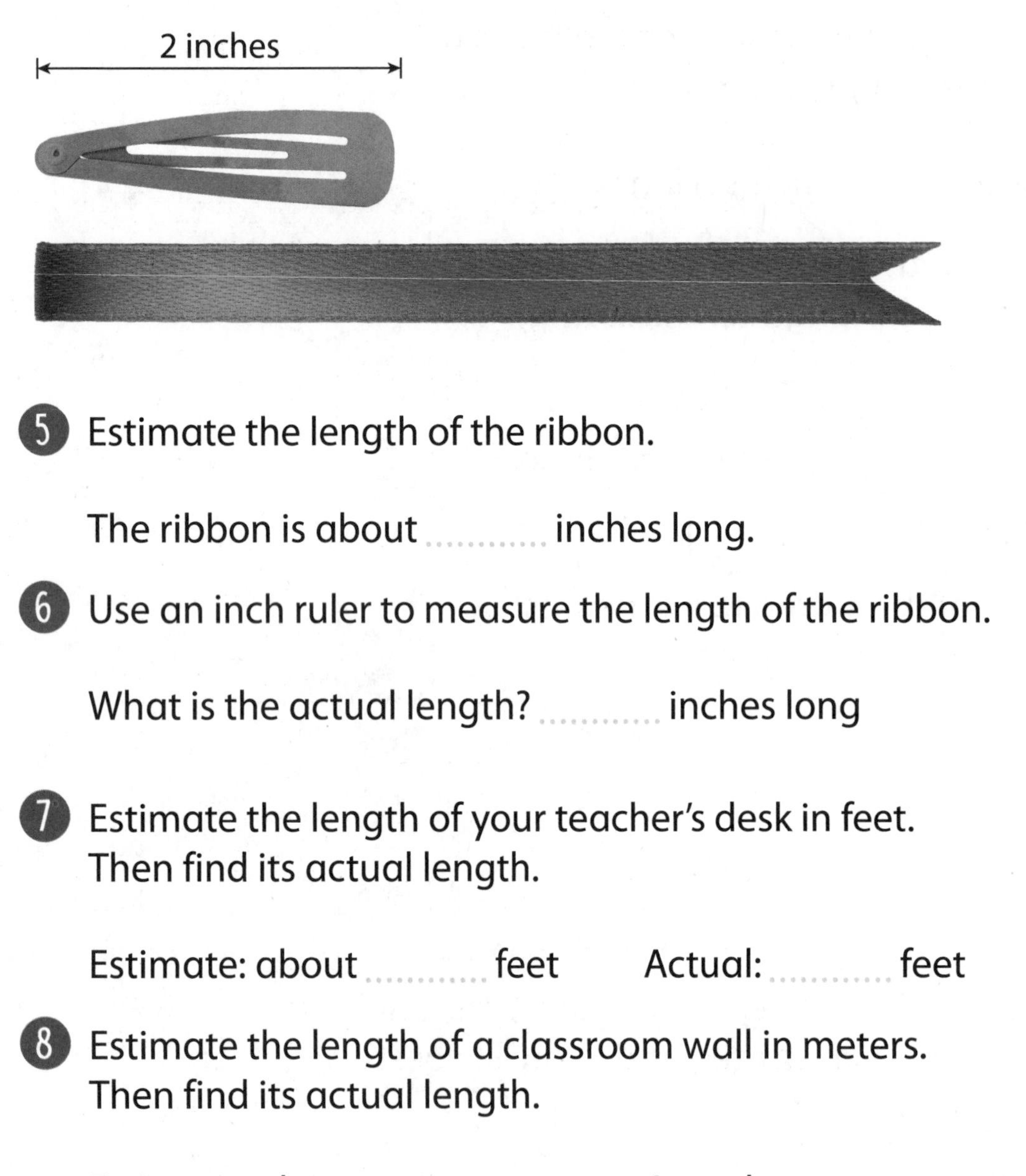

5 Estimate the length of the ribbon.

The ribbon is about .... inches long.

6 Use an inch ruler to measure the length of the ribbon.

What is the actual length? .... inches long

7 Estimate the length of your teacher's desk in feet. Then find its actual length.

Estimate: about .... feet Actual: .... feet

8 Estimate the length of a classroom wall in meters. Then find its actual length.

Estimate: about .... meters Actual: .... meters

Name: ______________________________

Practice Using Different Units to Estimate Length

Study the Example showing how to estimate length. Then solve problems 1–8.

EXAMPLE

Estimate the length of the yarn. Then find the actual length.

Use the paper clip to estimate the length of the yarn. It looks like about 2 paper clips would fit above the yarn. So, the estimate is about 6 centimeters.

Then use the ruler to measure the actual length of the yarn. So, the actual length is 5 centimeters.

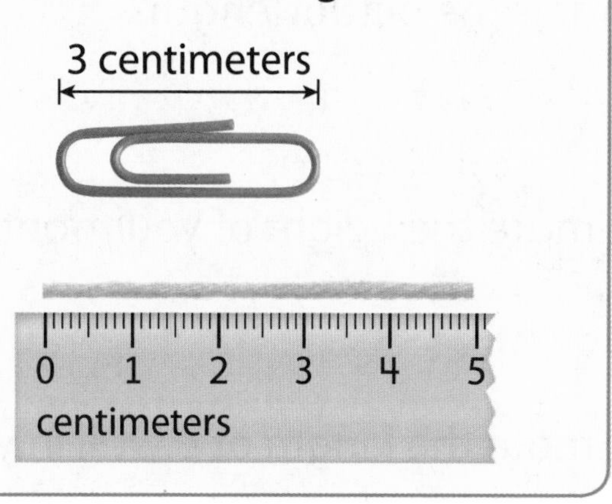

1. Use the eraser to estimate the length of the marker.

1 inch

The marker is about .... inches long.

2. Use a ruler to find the actual length of the marker.

What is the actual length? .... inches

Vocabulary

estimate (noun) a close guess made using mathematical thinking.

estimate (verb) to make a close guess based on mathematical thinking.

3 Use your little finger to estimate the length of the sticker.

The sticker is about .... centimeters long.

4 Use the centimeter ruler to measure the length of the sticker.

What is the actual length? .... centimeters

5 Estimate the height of your front door in feet.

.... feet

6 Estimate the length of a wall in your home in meters.

.... meters

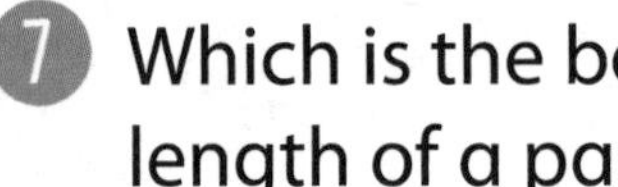

7 Which is the best estimate for the length of a park bench?

10 inches   24 feet   2 meters

8 Which is the best estimate for the length of a piano keyboard?

12 inches   5 feet   20 centimeters

Refine Estimating and Measuring Length

Complete the Example below. Then solve problems 1–3.

EXAMPLE

Which is the best estimate for the length of a seesaw?

30 inches 100 meters 4 meters

30 inches is between 2 and 3 feet.
100 meters is longer than a football field.
4 meters is the length of 4 meter sticks.
A seesaw is about as long as 4 meter sticks.
So, 4 meters is a good estimate for a seesaw.

Solution ....

APPLY IT

1. A sticky note is about 3 inches long. Use a sticky note to estimate the length of an object you see in your classroom.

   What did you measure? What is your estimate?

   Explain how you found your estimate.

How can you use a sticky note to estimate?

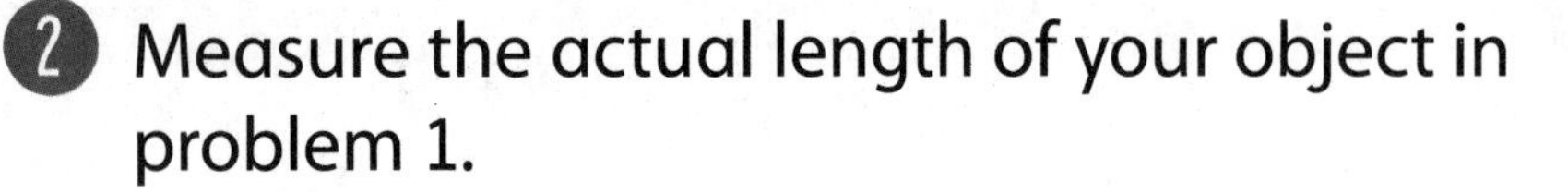

2 Measure the actual length of your object in problem 1.

What is the actual length of your object?

How does the actual length compare with your estimate?

How will you choose a tool to use for finding the actual length?

3 Which is the best estimate for the length of a car in the school parking lot?

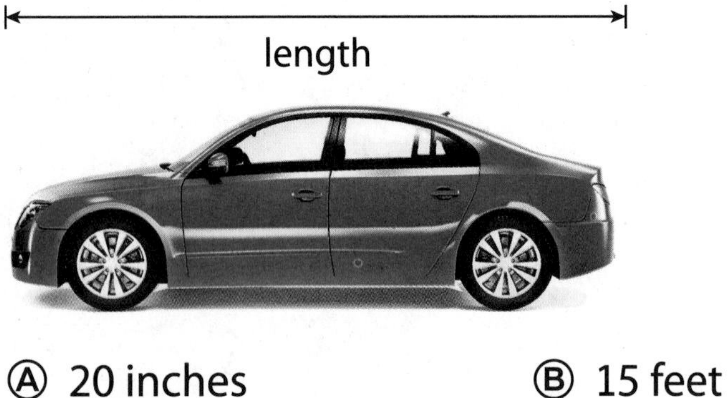

Ⓐ 20 inches

Ⓑ 15 feet

Ⓒ 50 meters

Ⓓ 100 centimeters

Kyle chose Ⓐ as an answer. How did Kyle get his answer?

How does each measurement compare to the length of an actual car?

Practice Estimating and Measuring Length

1. Use the paper clip to estimate the length of the string.

2 inches

The string is about .... inches long.

About how many paper clips would fit above the length of the string?

2. Use the ruler to find the actual length of the string in inches. Was your estimate in problem 1 a good estimate for the length of the string? Explain.

How can you use the ruler to find the actual length?

3. Pedro's science book is about a foot long. Which of these objects are about a foot long?

Ⓐ a sheet of notebook paper

Ⓑ a desk

Ⓒ a stamp

Ⓓ an egg carton

Ⓔ a finger

How many inches are equal to 1 foot?

Choose *Yes* or *No* to tell if each measurement is a good estimate for the length of a second-grader's shoe.

length

	Yes	No
8 inches	Ⓐ	Ⓑ
2 inches	Ⓒ	Ⓓ
20 centimeters	Ⓔ	Ⓕ
2 feet	Ⓖ	Ⓗ

Which units would be good to use for measuring the length of a shoe?

Which is the best estimate for the length of a dog?

length

Ⓐ 8 feet

Ⓑ 15 inches

Ⓒ 3 meters

Ⓓ 95 centimeters

How does each measurement compare to the length of a dog?

Refine Estimating and Measuring Length

APPLY IT

Solve the problems.

1 Estimate the length of your arm. Use centimeters, inches, feet, or meters to make your estimate. Explain how you made your estimate.

2 The length of a license plate is about a foot. Which of these objects have a length that is about a foot?

Ⓐ a house

Ⓑ a newspaper

Ⓒ a hand

Ⓓ a loaf of bread

Ⓔ a quarter

3 Choose *Yes* or *No* to tell if each measurement is a good estimate for the height of a door.

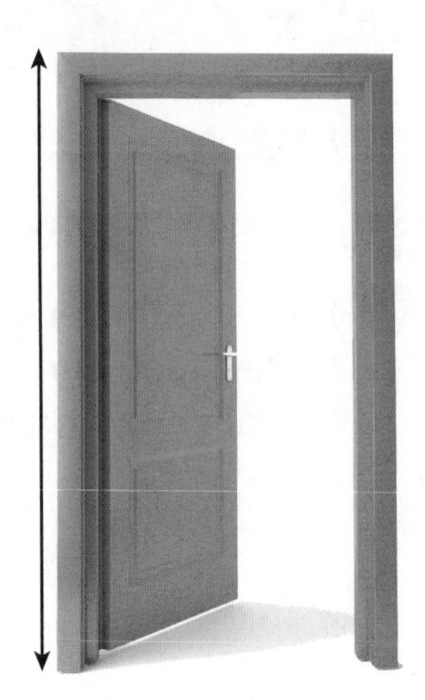

	Yes	No
10 inches	Ⓐ	Ⓑ
2 meters	Ⓒ	Ⓓ
20 centimeters	Ⓔ	Ⓕ
3 feet	Ⓖ	Ⓗ

4 What is the best estimate for the length of a desk?

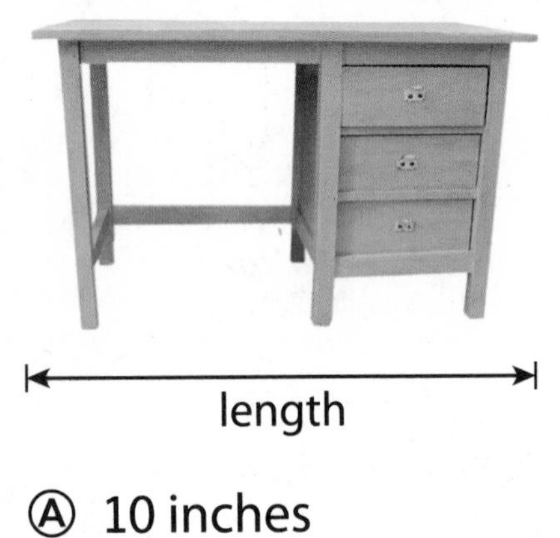

Ⓐ 10 inches
Ⓑ 20 centimeters
Ⓒ 3 meters
Ⓓ 3 feet

5 MATH JOURNAL

Explain why you might estimate a length rather than measuring it.

SELF CHECK Go back to the Unit 4 Opener and see what you can check off.

Compare Lengths

LESSON 24

Dear Family,

This week your child is learning to compare measurements and find the difference in lengths.

Your child might see a question like the one below.

Troy and Gus measure their pencils. How much longer is Gus's pencil?

Troy

The rulers on this page are not life-sized.

0 1 2 3 4 5
inches

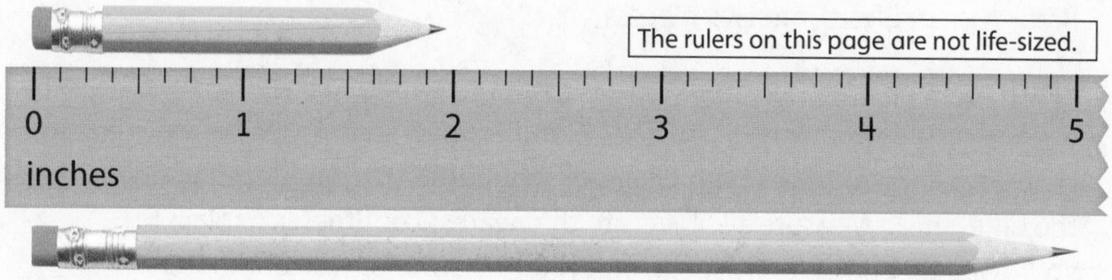

Gus

- One way to find how much longer one pencil is than the other is to find the difference between the lengths of the pencils.
  Gus's pencil is 5 inches long and Troy's is 2 inches long.
  Since $5 - 3 = 2$, you know Gus's pencil is 3 inches longer than Troy's pencil.

- Another way to find the difference is to simply measure the difference.

Gus

Troy

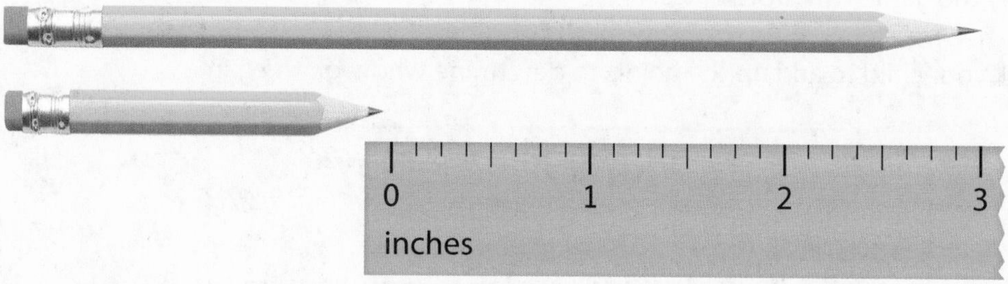

0 1 2 3
inches

The ends of the pencils are at the same point. The ruler is placed at the end of the shorter pencil.
Gus's pencil extends to the 3-inch line. Gus's pencil is 3 inches longer than Troy's pencil.

Invite your child to share what he or she knows about comparing lengths by doing the following activity together.

ACTIVITY COMPARING LENGTHS

Do this activity with your child to compare lengths.

Materials ruler, uncooked spaghetti (or strips of paper)

Play the following game with your child to practice comparing lengths.

- Hold one end of a piece of uncooked spaghetti and have your child hold the other end.
- Break the spaghetti into two pieces.
- Compare the lengths to determine who has the longer piece.
- Help your child measure both pieces of spaghetti in centimeters and find the difference. (Measure all objects to the nearest centimeter. Explain to your child that if the length of an object falls between two centimeter measurements, he or she should pick the one that is closer to the length of the object.)
- The person with the longer piece gets 1 point for each centimeter of difference. (So, a difference of 3 centimeters = 3 points.) Record the winner's points in the table.
- Play the game two more times.
- Ask your child to add up the points to determine who won the game.

	Player A	**Player B**
Game 1		
Game 2		
Game 3		
Total		

Explore Comparing Lengths

Previously, you have measured lengths of objects. Use what you know to try to solve the problem below.

Learning Target

- Measure to determine how much longer one object is than another, expressing the length difference in terms of a standard length unit.

SMP 1, 2, 3, 4, 5, 6

What is the difference between the length of the spoon and the length of the fork in centimeters?

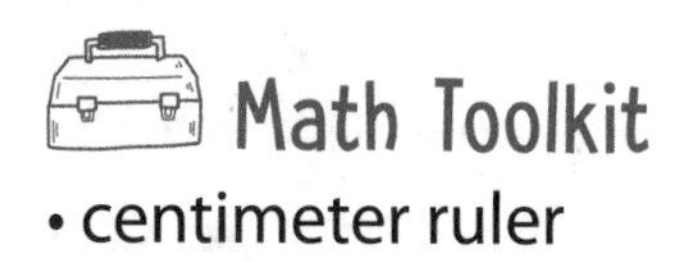

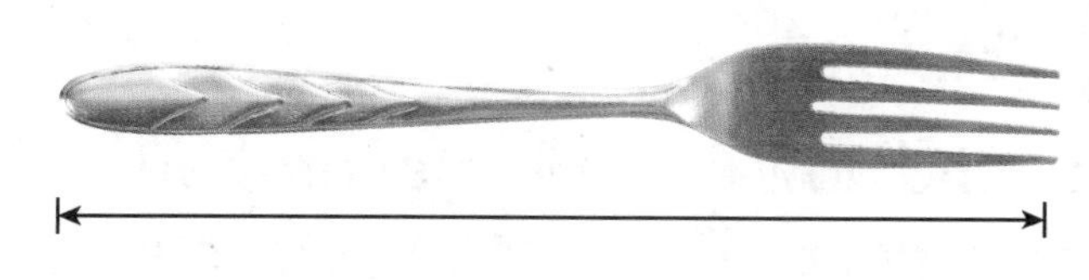

TRY IT

Math Toolkit

- centimeter ruler

DISCUSS IT

Ask your partner: Can you explain that again?

Tell your partner: I don't understand how . . .

CONNECT IT

1 LOOK BACK

Explain how to find the difference between the length of the spoon and the length of the fork in centimeters.

2 LOOK AHEAD

You can find how much longer or shorter one object is than the other by lining up the objects above a ruler. Then you can measure the difference.

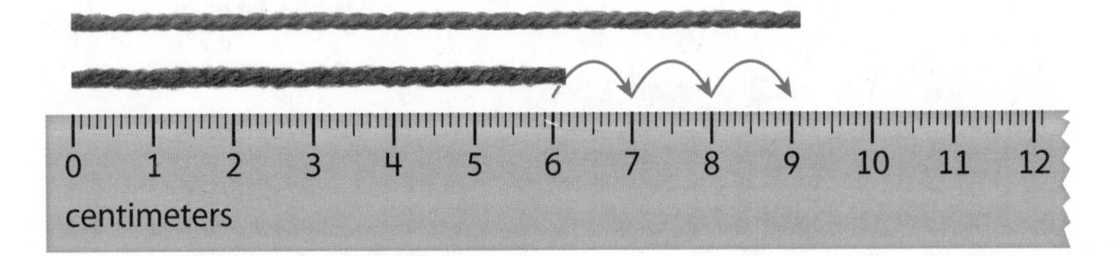

The .... piece of yarn is .... centimeters longer

than the .... piece of yarn.

3 REFLECT

How does measuring help you find the difference between two lengths?

....

....

....

Prepare for Comparing Lengths

1. Think about what you know about comparing lengths. Fill in each box. Use words, numbers, and pictures. Show as many ideas as you can.

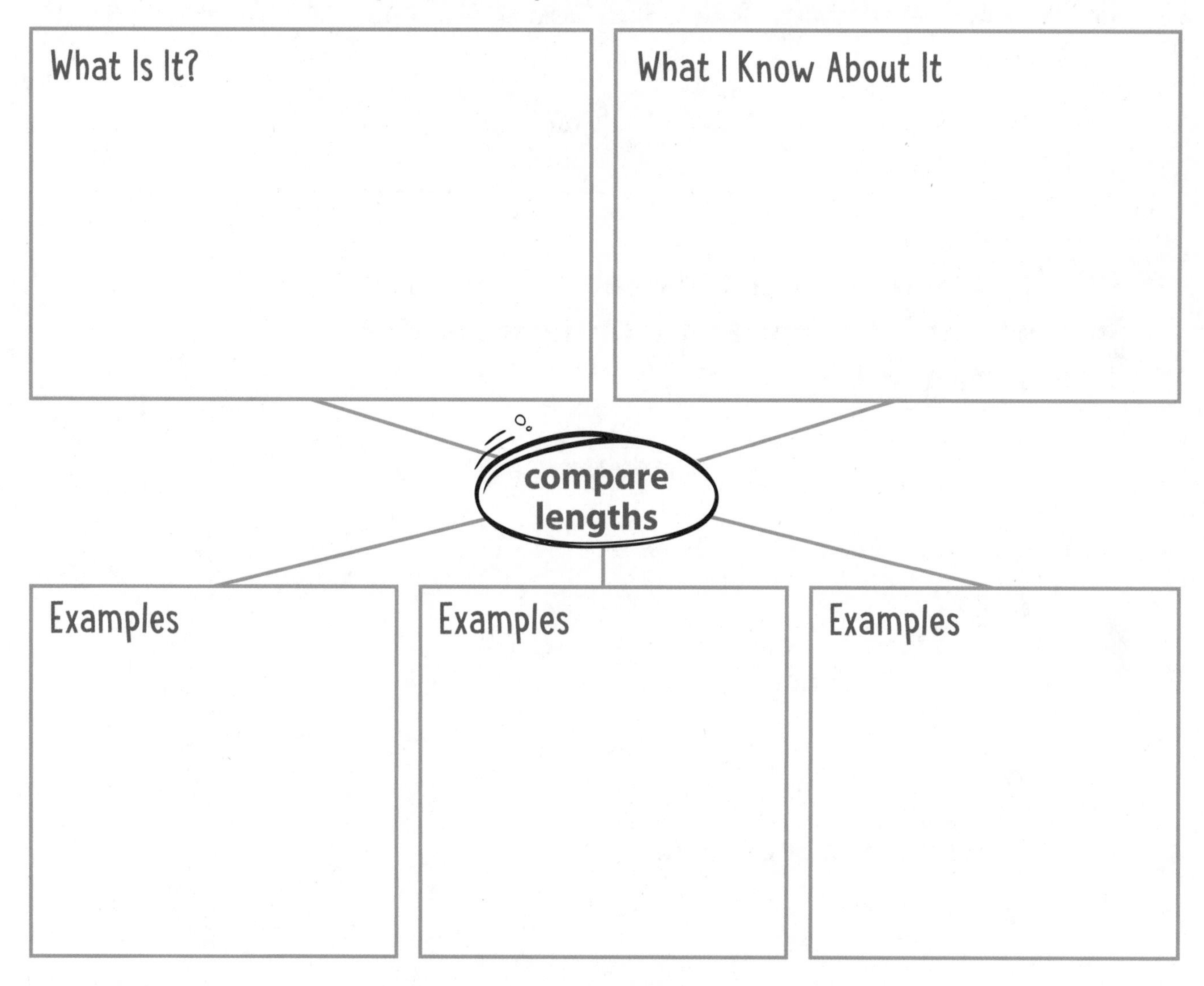

2. A pencil is 5 inches long. A crayon is 4 inches long. What is the difference between their lengths?

3 Solve the problem. Show your work.

Boone found this pencil and glue stick in his desk.

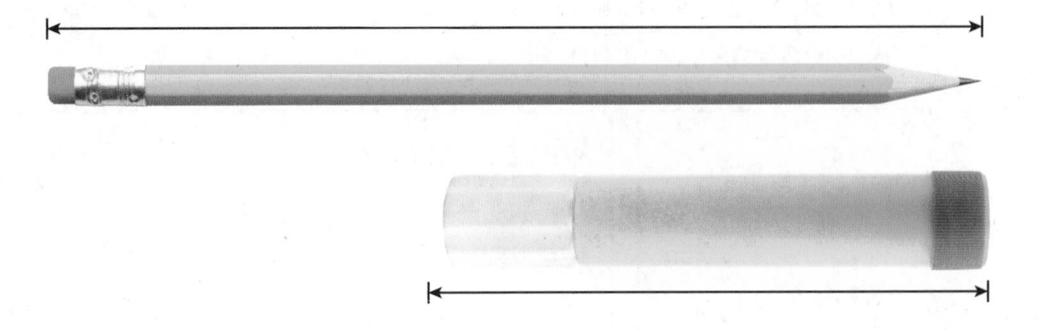

What is the difference between the length of the pencil and the length of the glue stick in centimeters?

Solution ....

4 Check your answer. Show your work.

Develop Finding Differences Between Lengths

Read and try to solve the problem below.

Nate and Jen each have a piece of tape.

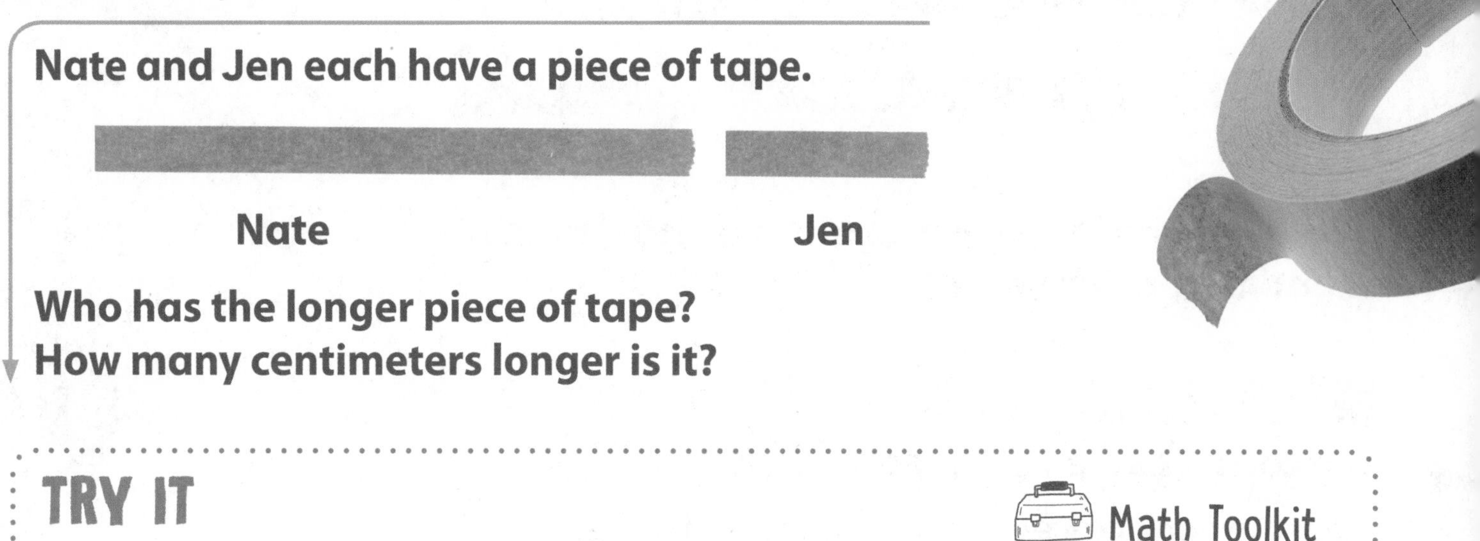

Who has the longer piece of tape?
How many centimeters longer is it?

TRY IT

Math Toolkit
- centimeter ruler

DISCUSS IT

Ask your partner: Why did you choose that strategy?

Tell your partner: The strategy I used to find the answer was . . .

Explore different ways to understand finding differences between lengths.

Nate and Jen each have a piece of tape.

Nate **Jen**

Who has the longer piece of tape? How many centimeters longer is it?

MEASURE IT

You can measure each piece of tape.

Measure each piece of tape using centimeters.

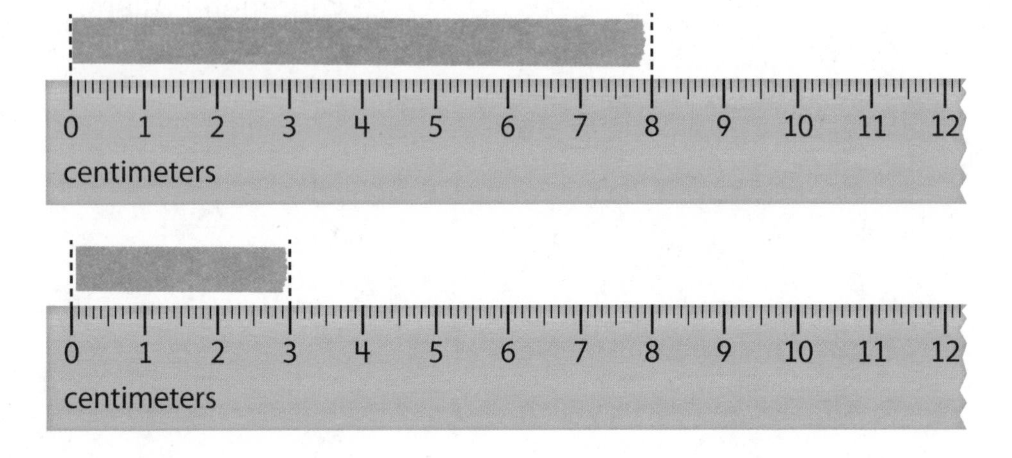

MODEL IT

You can make a bar model.

You can make a bar model to compare the lengths.

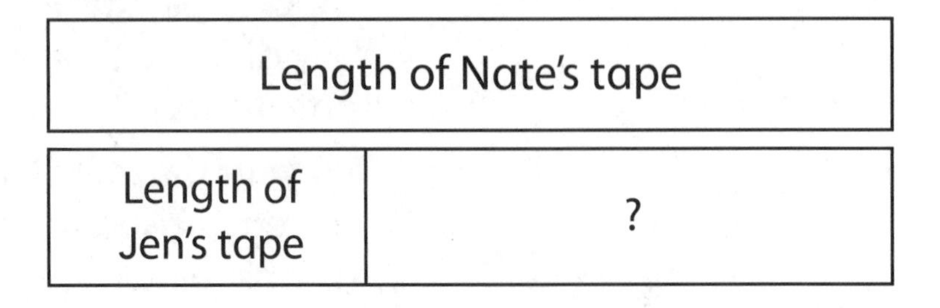

CONNECT IT

Now you will use the problem from the previous page to help you understand how to find differences between lengths.

1. Write the lengths in the bar model.

2. Who has the longer piece of tape? Explain how you know.

Nate's tape .... centimeters	
Jen's tape ...... centimeters	?

3. Write an equation you can use to find the difference in the lengths. Then find the difference.

4. Complete the sentence to compare the lengths.

   .... tape is .... centimeters

   longer than .... tape.

5. REFLECT

   Look back at your **Try It**, strategies by classmates, **Measure It** and **Model It**. Which models or strategies do you like best for finding differences between lengths? Explain.

   ....

   ....

   ....

APPLY IT

Use what you just learned to solve these problems.

Use these stickers for problems 6 and 7.

 Circle the sticker that is longer.

7 Measure and write the length of each sticker in centimeters. How much longer is the long sticker than the short sticker?

 Choose *Yes* or *No* to tell if you can use the equations to compare the lengths of the worms.

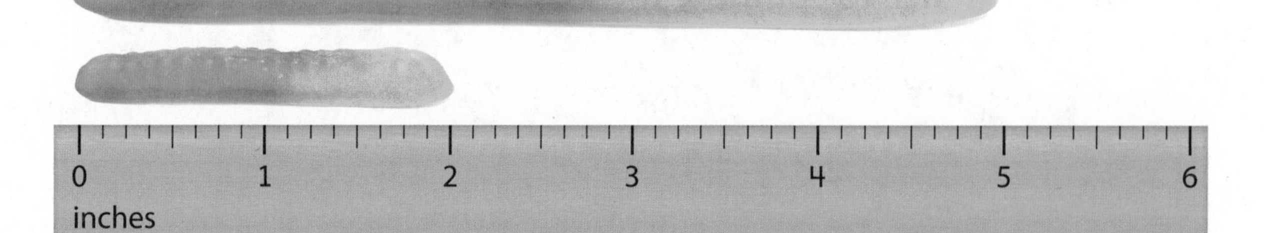

	Yes	No
$? = 5 + 2$	Ⓐ	Ⓑ
$5 = 2 + ?$	Ⓒ	Ⓓ
$? = 5 - 2$	Ⓔ	Ⓕ
$2 = 5 - ?$	Ⓖ	Ⓗ

Practice Finding Differences Between Lengths

Study the Example showing how to find the difference between two lengths. Then solve problems 1–8.

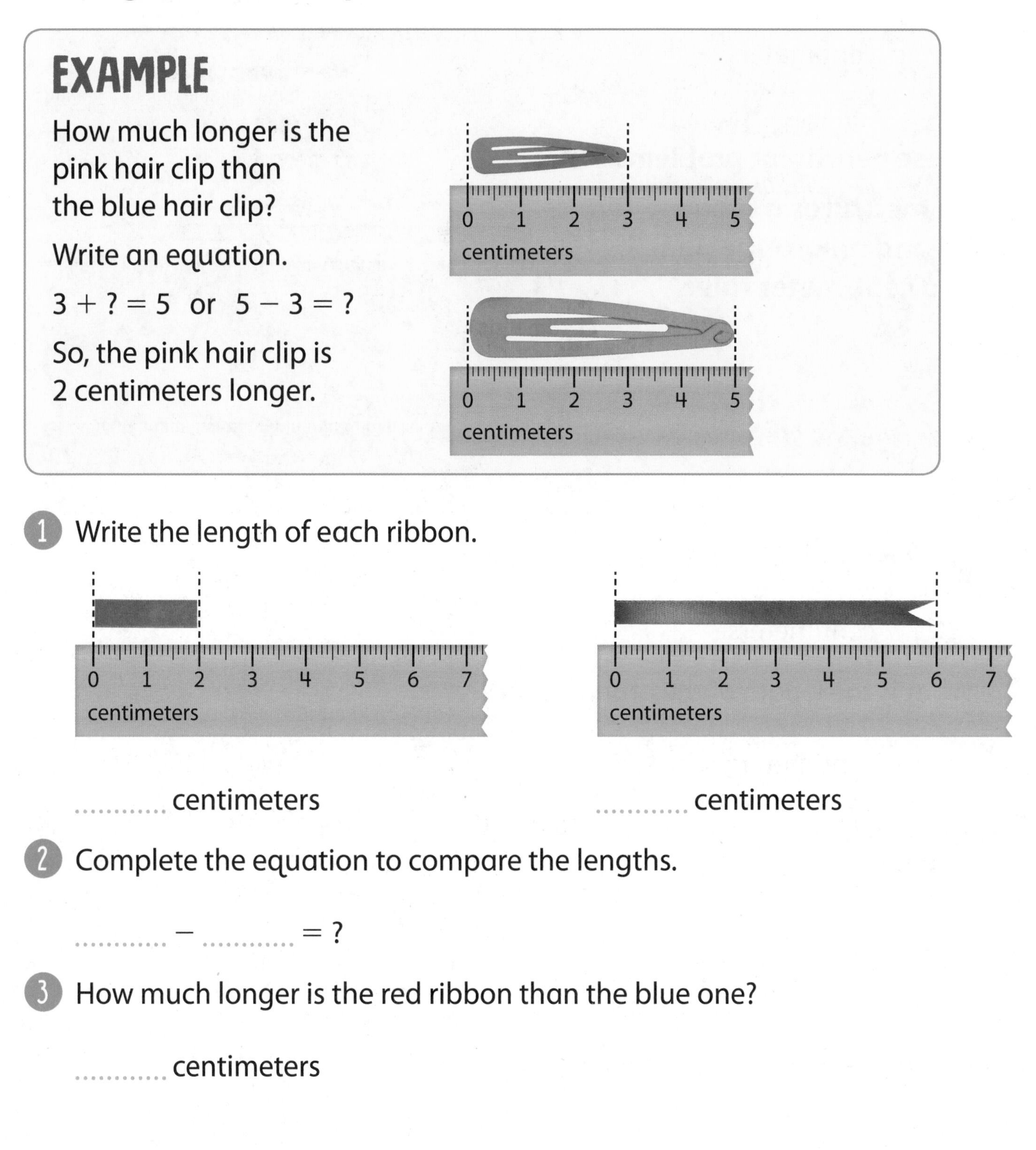

EXAMPLE

How much longer is the pink hair clip than the blue hair clip?

Write an equation.

$3 + ? = 5$ or $5 - 3 = ?$

So, the pink hair clip is 2 centimeters longer.

1. Write the length of each ribbon.

   .... centimeters　　　　............ centimeters

2. Complete the equation to compare the lengths.

   .... − .... = ?

3. How much longer is the red ribbon than the blue one?

   .... centimeters

4 How much longer is the purple paper clip than the green paper clip? Show your work.

.... centimeters

Use these pencils for problems 5–8.

Aruna measures a green pencil and an orange pencil using a centimeter ruler.

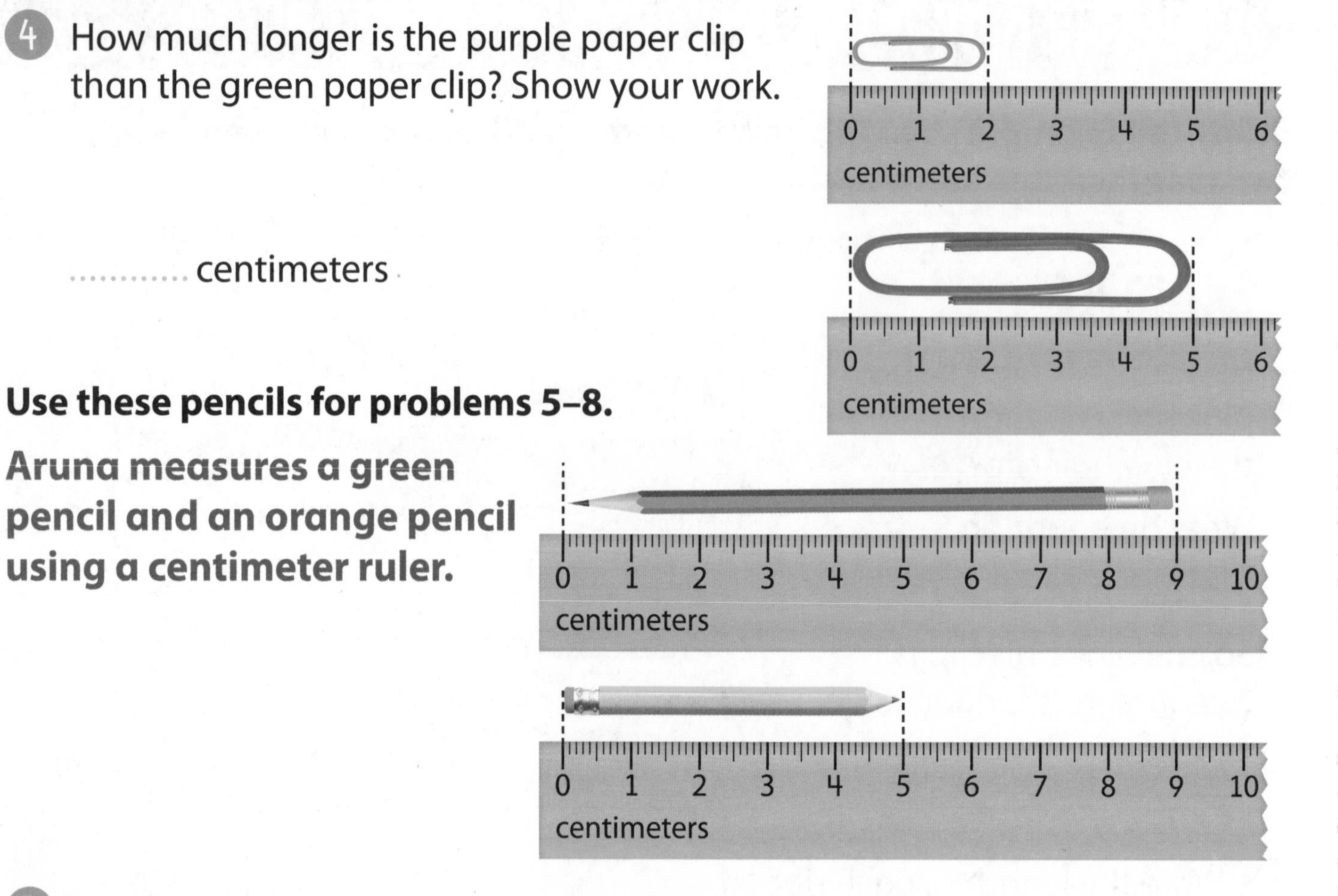

5 What is the length of the green pencil?

.... centimeters

6 What is the length of the orange pencil?

.... centimeters

7 Write an equation you can use to find the difference in lengths.

8 How much longer is the green pencil than the orange pencil? .... centimeters

Develop Ways to Compare Lengths

Read and try to solve the problem below.

How much shorter in inches is the eraser than the crayon?

TRY IT

DISCUSS IT

Ask your partner: Do you agree with me? Why or why not?

Tell your partner: I agree with you about . . . because . . .

Explore different ways to understand comparing lengths.

How much shorter in inches is the eraser than the crayon?

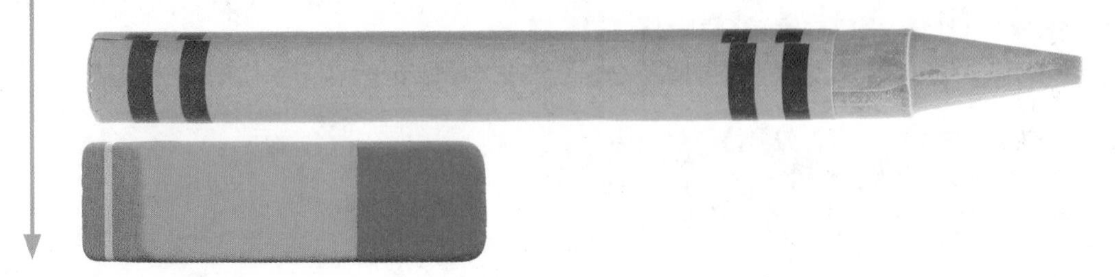

MEASURE IT

You can measure each object and find the difference.

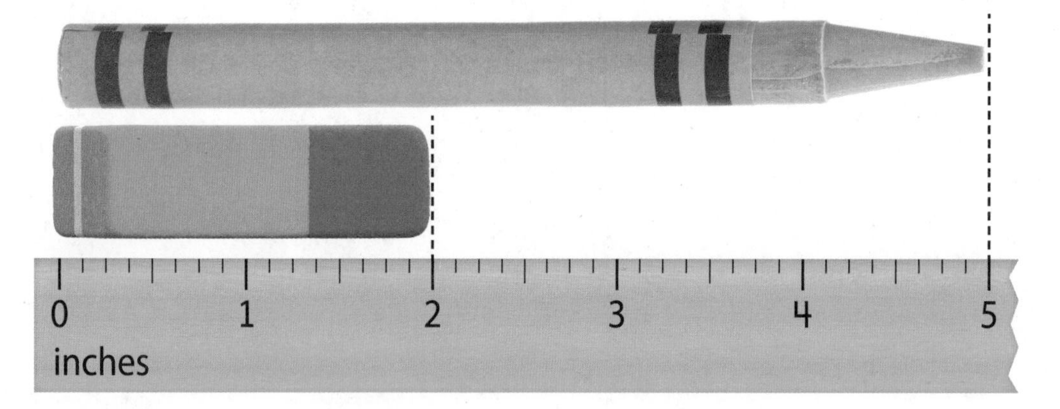

MODEL IT

You can measure the difference.

Line up one end of the eraser and the crayon. Then use a ruler to measure the difference.

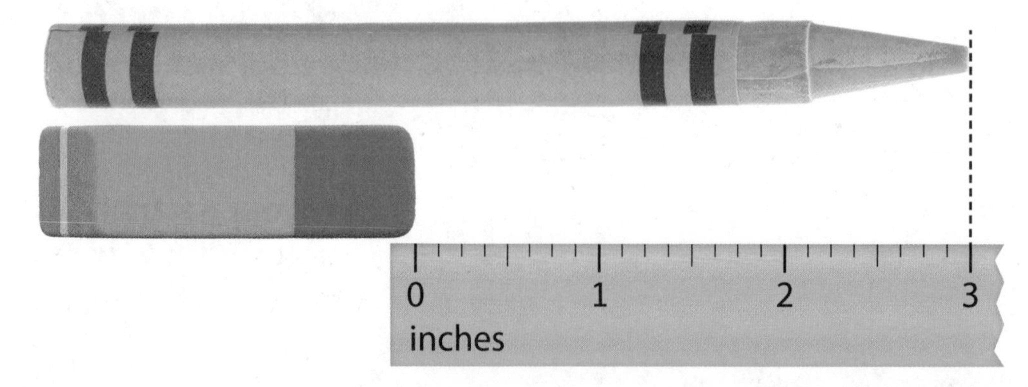

CONNECT IT

Now you will use the problem from the previous page to help you understand different ways to compare lengths.

1. Look at **Measure It**. Explain how to find how much shorter the eraser is than the crayon.

2. How much shorter is the eraser than the crayon?

3. What is measured in **Model It**?

4. ## REFLECT

   Look back at your **Try It**, strategies by classmates, and **Measure It** and **Model It**. Which models or strategies do you like best for comparing lengths? Explain.

   ....

   ....

   ....

APPLY IT

Use what you just learned to solve these problems.

5. Henry has two paper clips.

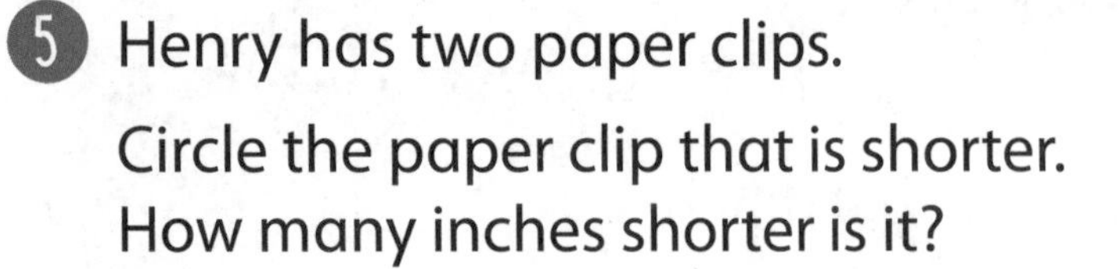

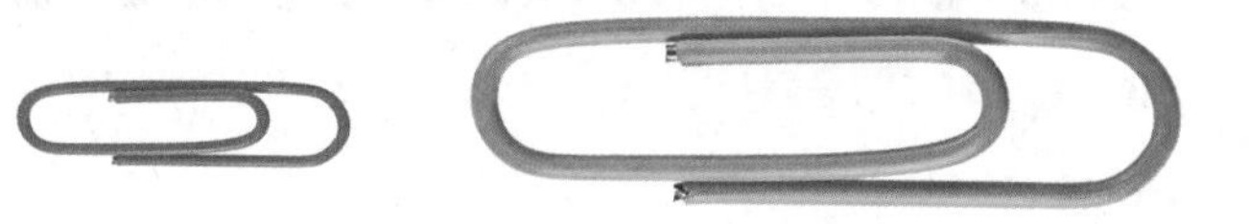

Circle the paper clip that is shorter.
How many inches shorter is it?

6. Sharon has two pieces of ribbon. What is the difference in the lengths of the pieces of ribbon, in centimeters? Show your work.

7. Explain how you could find the difference between the length of the bean and the length of the carrot in two different ways.

First way:

Second way:

Practice Ways to Compare Lengths

Study the Example showing two ways to find the difference between lengths. Then solve problems 1–4.

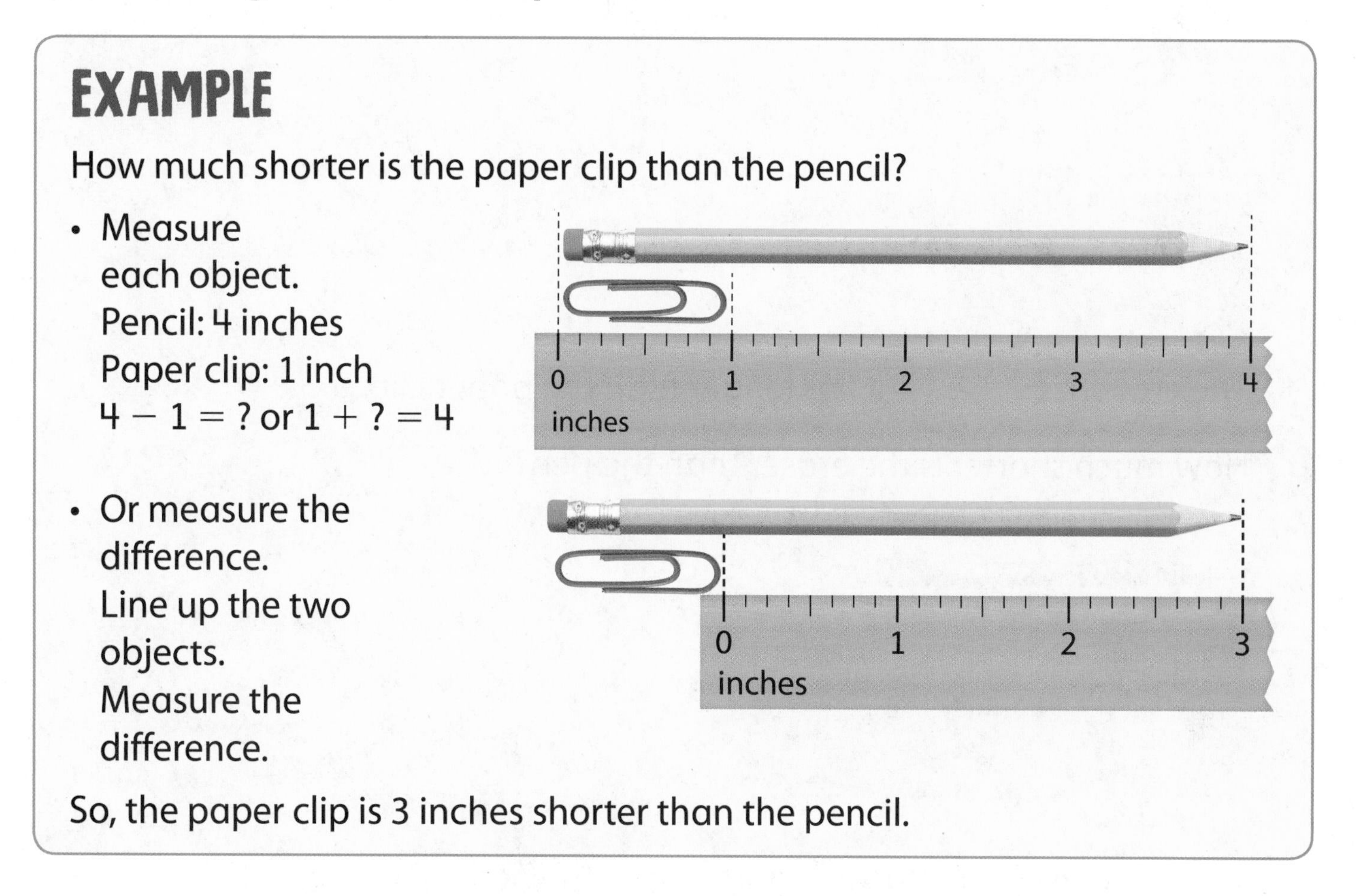

EXAMPLE

How much shorter is the paper clip than the pencil?

- Measure each object.
  Pencil: 4 inches
  Paper clip: 1 inch
  $4 - 1 = ?$ or $1 + ? = 4$
- Or measure the difference.
  Line up the two objects.
  Measure the difference.

So, the paper clip is 3 inches shorter than the pencil.

1 How many inches shorter is the hair clip than the marker?

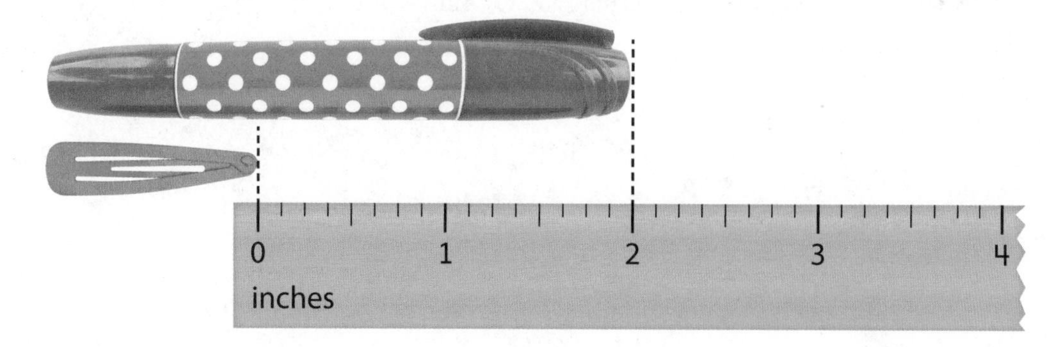

The hair clip is .... inches shorter than the marker.

How much longer is the crayon than the paper clip?

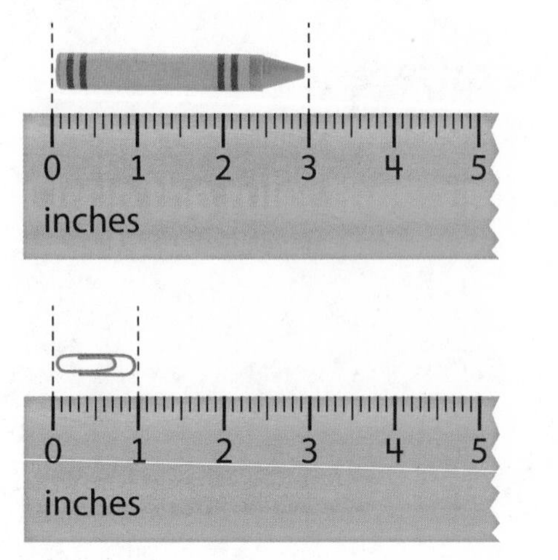

The rulers on this page are not life-sized.

The crayon is .... inches longer than the paper clip.

3 How much shorter is the eraser than the pen?

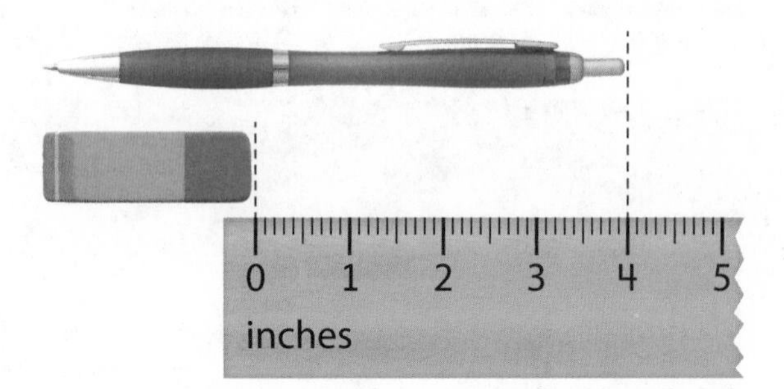

The eraser is .... inches shorter than the pen.

4 Do you like the method shown in problem 2 or in problem 3 better? Explain why.

Refine Comparing Lengths

Complete the Example below. Then solve problems 1–3.

EXAMPLE

Jonah is 52 inches tall. His sister Sophia is 43 inches tall. How much taller is Jonah than Sophia?

You can use a bar model and equation.

52	
43	?

$52 - 43 = 9$

Solution ....

APPLY IT

1 Anna measures the paper strips below in centimeters. What is the difference in the lengths of the paper strips? Show your work.

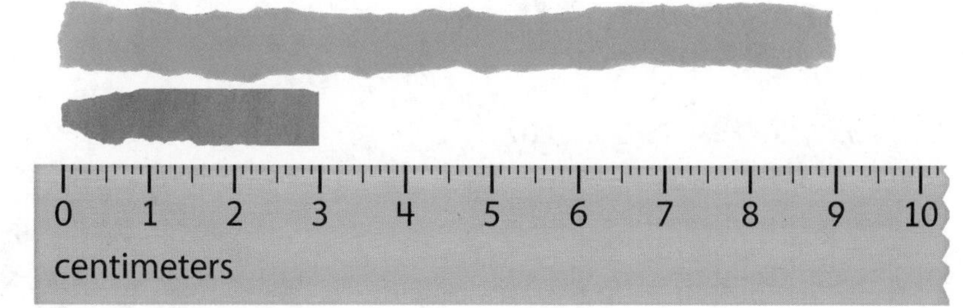

The difference in the lengths of the paper strips is how much longer or shorter one is than the other.

Solution ....

2 Circle the nail that is shorter. Then tell how much shorter it is. Use a ruler. Measure using centimeters. Show your work.

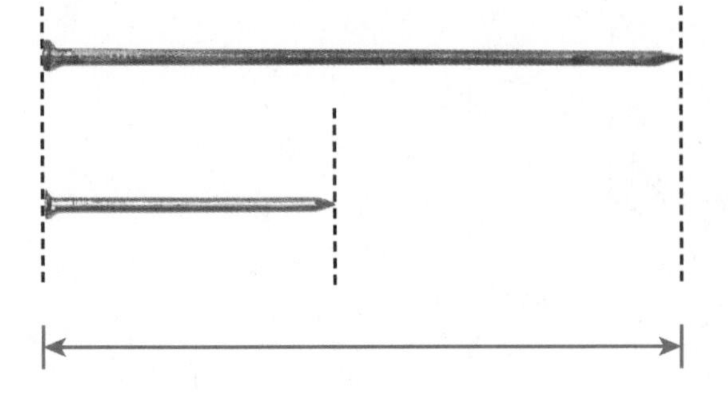

What equation can you write to help you find the answer?

Solution ....

3 Tim has a piece of yarn that is 3 inches long. Which piece of yarn is 1 inch shorter than Tim's yarn?

Will the length of the correct piece of yarn be more or less than 3 inches?

Ⓐ

Ⓑ

Ⓒ

Ⓓ

Ben chose Ⓐ as the answer. How did Ben get his answer?

Name: ____________________

Practice Comparing Lengths

1. What is the difference in the lengths of the two pieces of yarn? The ruler shows centimeters. Show your work.

0 1 2 3 4 5 6 7 8 9
centimeters

> Remember: finding the difference in length means you tell how much longer or shorter one piece of yarn is than the other.

Solution ....

2. How much longer is the eraser than the paper clip?

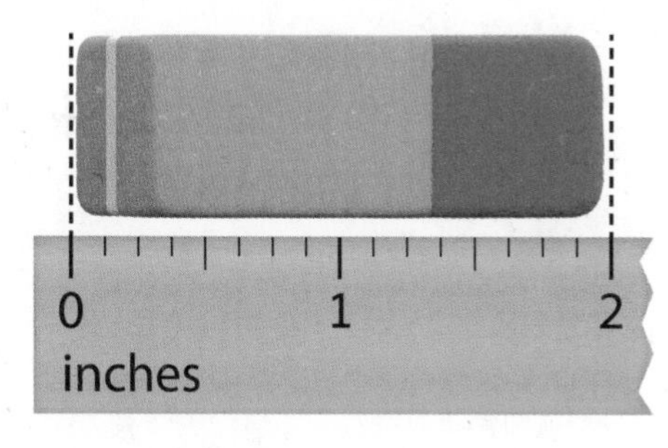

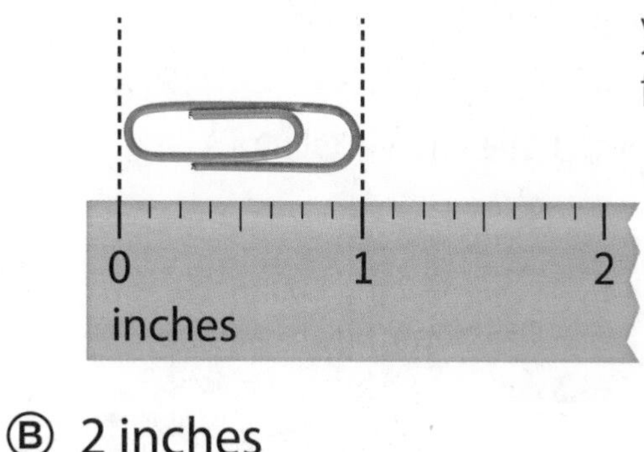

Ⓐ 1 inch Ⓑ 2 inches

Ⓒ 3 inches Ⓓ 4 inches

Jane chose Ⓒ. How did Jane get her answer?

> What equation can you write to help you find the answer?

3 Frank drew the line below. Draw a line below it that is 3 centimeters shorter.

How many centimeters long should your line be?

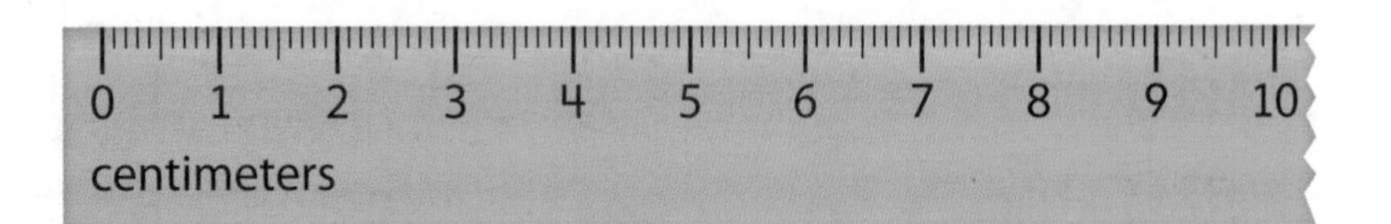

4 Keith's tower is 37 centimeters tall. Ruby's tower is 45 centimeters tall. Which equations could you use to find out how much taller Ruby's tower is than Keith's tower?

Can you use a bar model to help you decide which equations you could use?

Ⓐ $45 + 37 = ?$

Ⓑ $45 - ? = 37$

Ⓒ $37 + ? = 45$

Ⓓ $45 - 37 = ?$

Ⓔ $37 - 45 = ?$

5 Sadie says the marker is 1 inch longer than the pencil. What did Sadie do wrong?

What do you need to do first when you measure the difference?

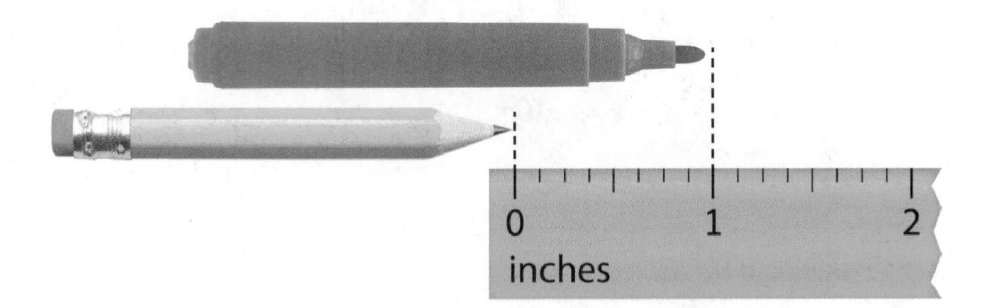

Refine Comparing Lengths

APPLY IT

Solve the problems.

 How much longer in inches is the bottom bandage than the top bandage?

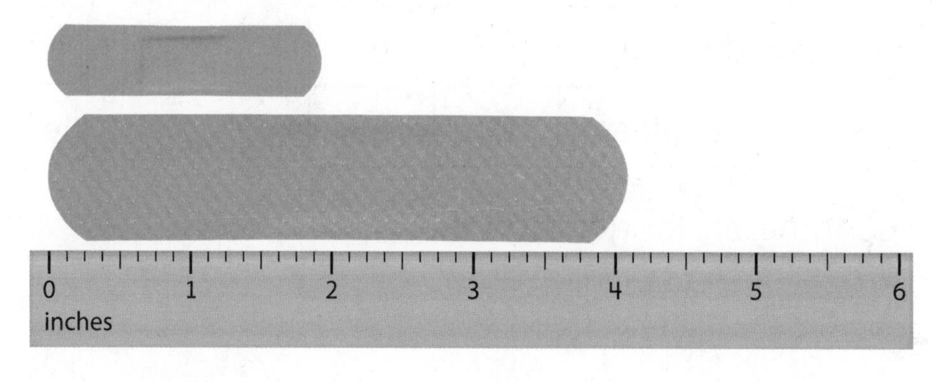

Ⓐ 2 inches

Ⓑ 3 inches

Ⓒ 4 inches

Ⓓ 5 inches

2 What is the difference in the lengths of the two straws? Measure using centimeters.

Ⓐ 3 centimeters

Ⓑ 4 centimeters

Ⓒ 7 centimeters

Ⓓ 10 centimeters

 A table is 10 feet long. A desk is 3 feet long. Choose *True* or *False* for each statement.

	True	False
The table is 7 feet shorter than the desk.	Ⓐ	Ⓑ
The table is 7 feet longer than the desk.	Ⓒ	Ⓓ
The desk is 7 feet shorter than the table.	Ⓔ	Ⓕ
The desk is 7 feet longer than the table.	Ⓖ	Ⓗ

4 Draw a line that is 6 centimeters longer than the line below.

How long is your line in centimeters? How did you know the length your line should be?

 MATH JOURNAL

When you find the difference in length of two objects, why do you get the same answer whether you measure each object and find the difference or you just measure the difference?

SELF CHECK Go back to the Unit 4 Opener and see what you can check off.

Prepare for Adding and Subtracting Lengths

1. Think about what you know about finding solutions. Fill in each box. Use words, numbers, and pictures. Show as many ideas as you can.

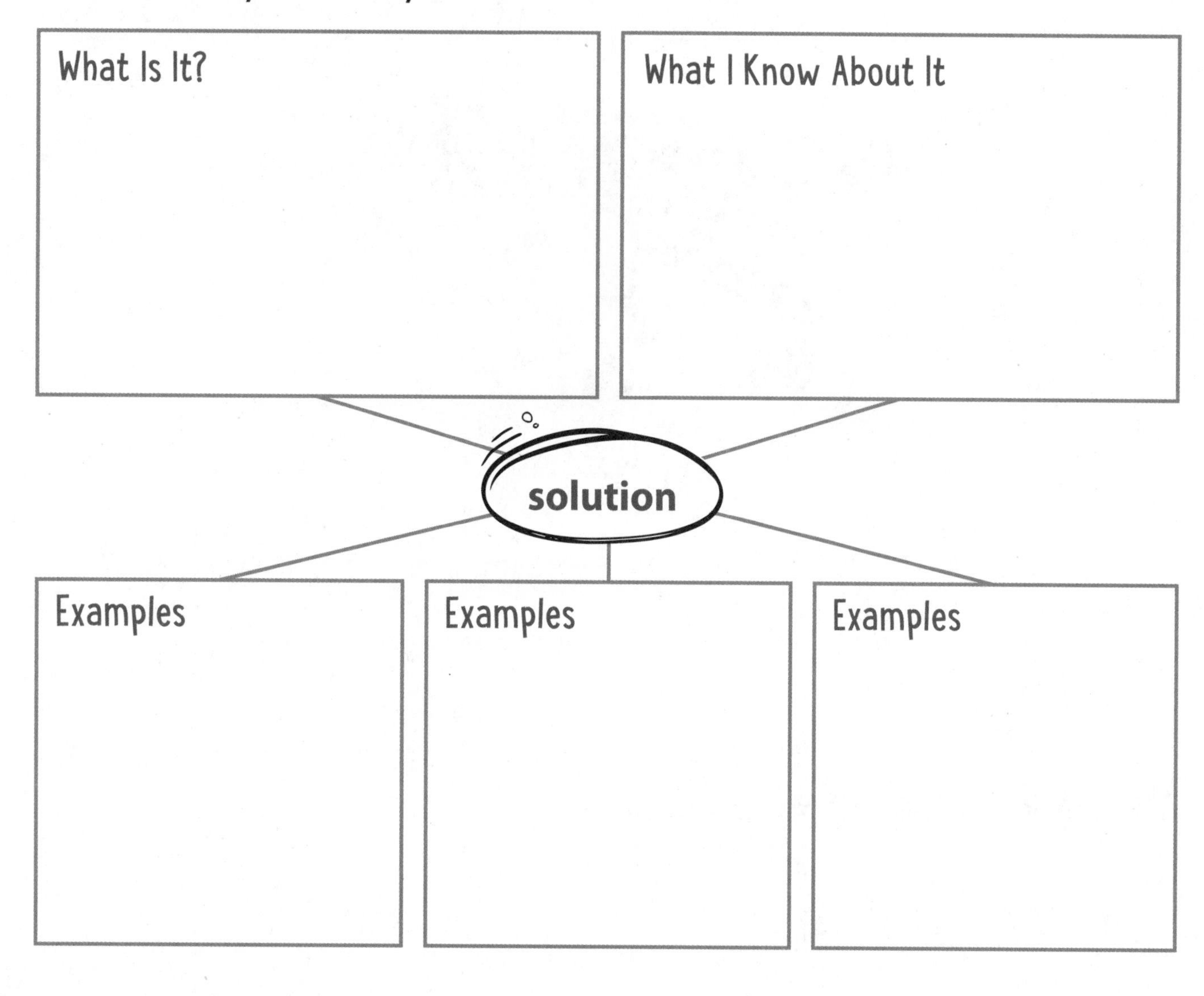

2. Together the cars of a toy train are 17 inches long. The engine is 5 inches long. What is the total length of the train?

.... inches + ... inches = ... inches

Solution ....

3 Solve the problem. Show your work.

The tail of a model dinosaur is 8 inches shorter than the rest of its body. The rest of its body is 36 inches long. How long is the dinosaur's tail?

Solution ....

4 Check your answer. Show your work.

Develop Solving Problems About Length

Read and try to solve the problem below.

Michaela has a string of beads that is 56 centimeters long. She cuts off 8 centimeters to make it the right length for a necklace. How long is the string of beads now?

TRY IT

Math Toolkit
- bar models
- open number lines
- measuring tape
- meter stick

DISCUSS IT

Ask your partner: How did you get started?

Tell your partner: I started by . . .

Explore different ways to understand solving problems about length.

Michaela has a string of beads that is 56 centimeters long. She cuts off 8 centimeters to make it the right length for a necklace. How long is the string of beads now?

PICTURE IT

You can draw a picture.

The string of beads is **56** centimeters long.

Michaela cuts off **8** centimeters.

56 centimeters

8 centimeters

MODEL IT

You can make a bar model.

The total length is **56** centimeters.

The part cut off is **8** centimeters.

56

? 8

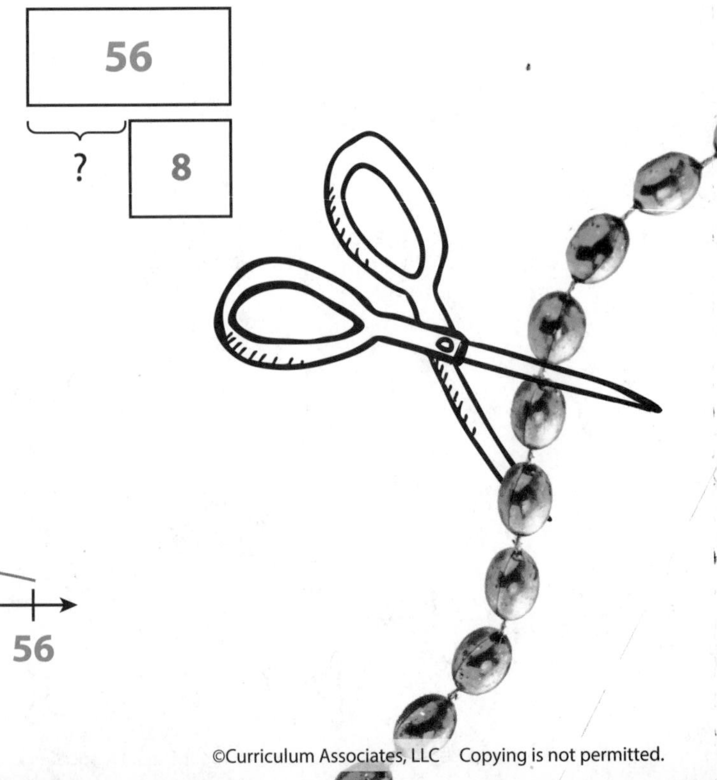

MODEL IT

You can use an open number line.

Start at **56**. Subtract to a tens number. Then subtract the rest.

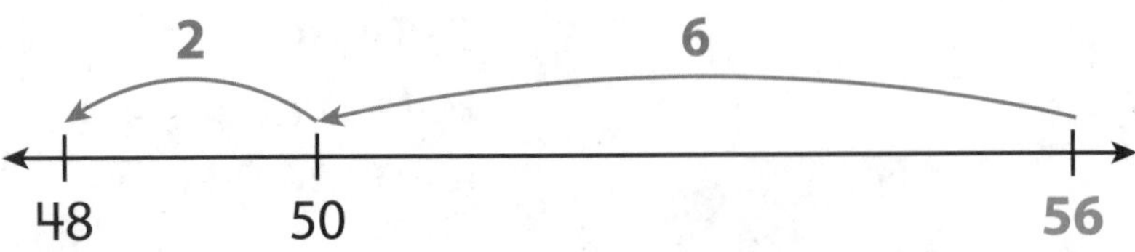

CONNECT IT

Now you will use the problem from the previous page to help you understand how to solve problems about length.

 Look at the models on the previous page. Write a subtraction equation you can use to solve the problem.

 Explain how the jumps on the open number line show that Michaela cuts off 8 centimeters.

 How long is the string of beads now? ....

4 How much shorter is a string of beads that is 34 centimeters long than a string that is 56 centimeters long? Explain how you found your answer.

5 REFLECT

Look back at your **Try It**, strategies by classmates, **Picture It**, and **Model Its**. Which models or strategies do you like best for solving problems about length? Explain.

....

....

APPLY IT

Use what you just learned to solve these problems.

6. Jose throws a ball 59 feet. Oscar throws a ball 15 feet less than Jose. How far does Oscar throw the ball? Show your work.

Solution ....

7. Kelly has a piece of string that is 70 inches long. She uses some of the string to wrap a package. Now she has 24 inches of string left. How many inches of string does Kelly use? Show your work.

Solution ....

8. Tom's first track is 54 centimeters long. His second track is 82 centimeters long. How much shorter is the first track than the second track? Show your work.

Solution ....

Name: ____________________

Practice Solving Problems About Length

Study the Example showing how to solve a problem about length. Then solve problems 1–6.

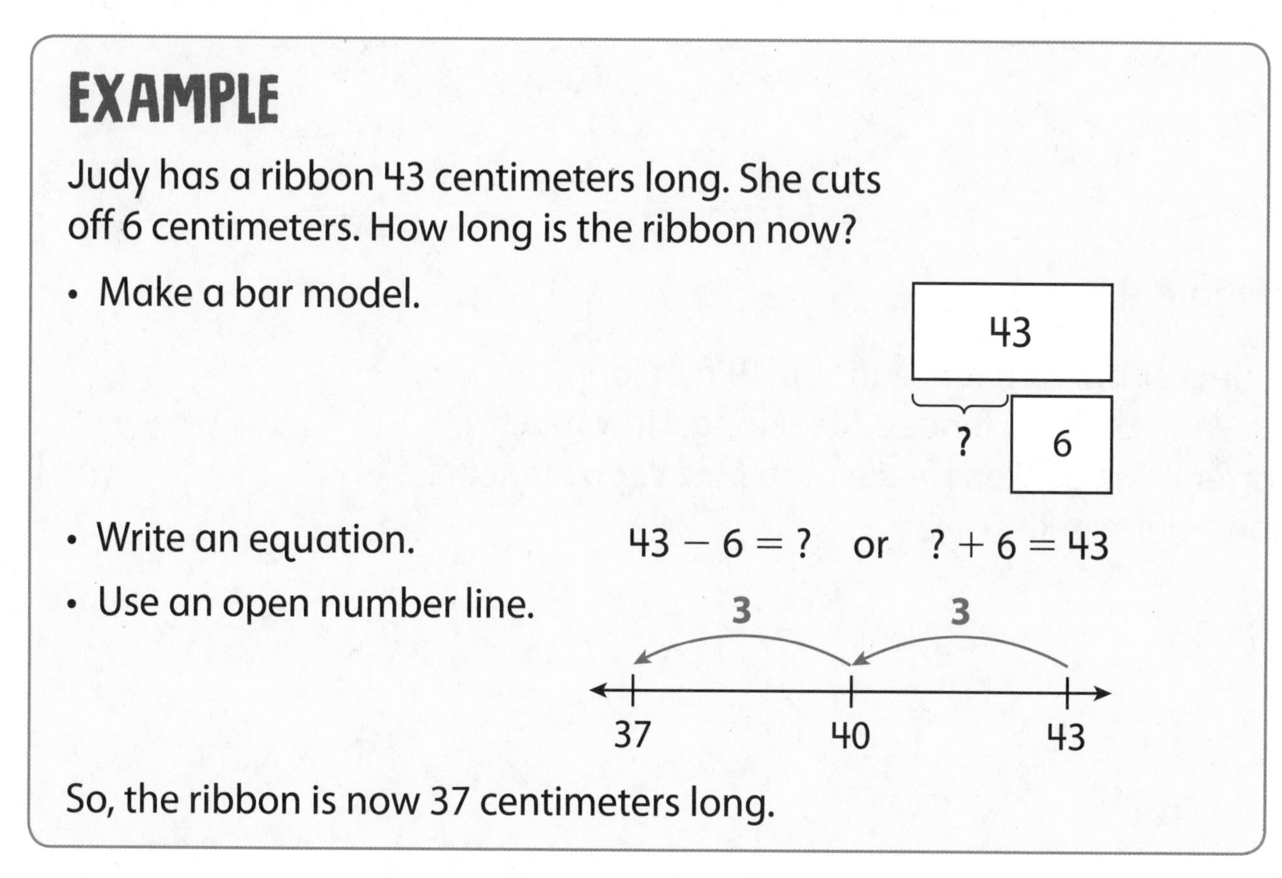

EXAMPLE

Judy has a ribbon 43 centimeters long. She cuts off 6 centimeters. How long is the ribbon now?

- Make a bar model.

- Write an equation. $43 - 6 = ?$ or $? + 6 = 43$
- Use an open number line.

So, the ribbon is now 37 centimeters long.

Marie kicks a ball 68 feet. Liam kicks a ball that goes 17 feet less than that. How far does Liam kick the ball?

1. Fill in the bar model to show this problem.

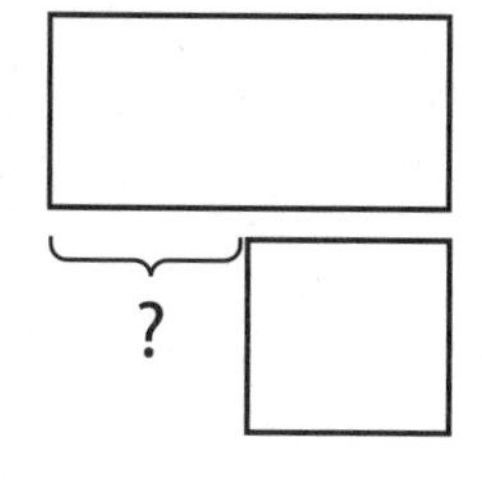

2. Complete the equations.

$68 -$ .... $= ?$ $? +$ .... $= 68$

3. How far does Liam kick the ball? ....

 Ms. Rom puts together two hoses. One hose is 24 meters long. When she puts the hoses together, they are 76 meters long.

What is the length of the other hose? Show your work.

Solution ....

5 Mr. Becker builds a fence that is 14 feet long. Mrs. Vega builds a fence 37 feet long. How much shorter is Mr. Becker's fence than Mrs. Vega's fence? Show your work.

Solution ....

6 Jackson has a piece of yarn that is 89 centimeters long. He cuts off 19 centimeters to make it the right length for a craft project. How long is the piece of yarn now? Show your work.

Solution ....

Develop Solving Two-Step Problems About Length

Read and try to solve the problem below.

Sam and Sadie are making a poster with a border. Sam has a piece of border 23 inches long. Sadie has a border that is 7 inches longer than Sam's. The top of their poster is 50 inches long. Do they have enough border to cover the top of the poster? Explain your reasoning.

TRY IT

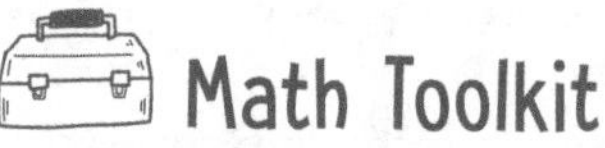

Math Toolkit
- bar models
- open number lines
- measuring tape
- yardstick

DISCUSS IT

Ask your partner: Do you agree with me? Why or why not?

Tell your partner: I disagree with this part because . . .

Explore different ways to understand solving two-step problems about length.

Sam and Sadie are making a poster with a border. Sam has a piece of border 23 inches long. Sadie has a border that is 7 inches longer than Sam's. The top of their poster is 50 inches long. Do they have enough border to cover the top of the poster? Explain your reasoning.

PICTURE IT

You can draw a picture.

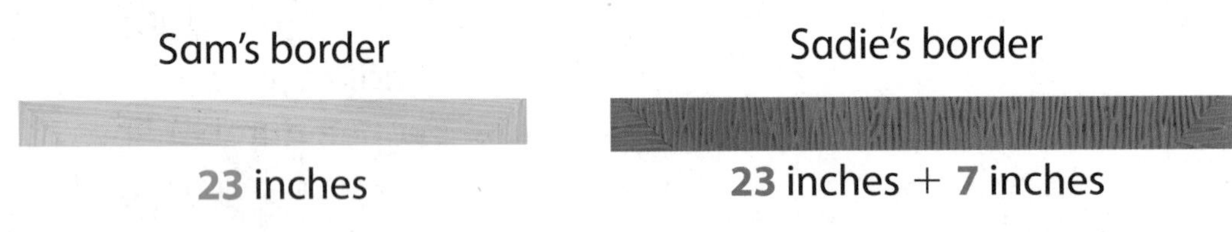

MODEL IT

You can use an open number line.

Start at 23.
Add 7 first to get to the next ten.

To add 23 more, jump 20 and then 3.

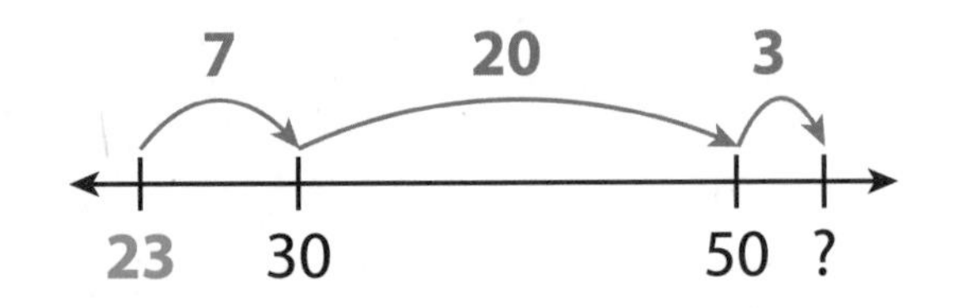

MODEL IT

You can use bar models.

Add 23 + 7. Then, add 23 more.

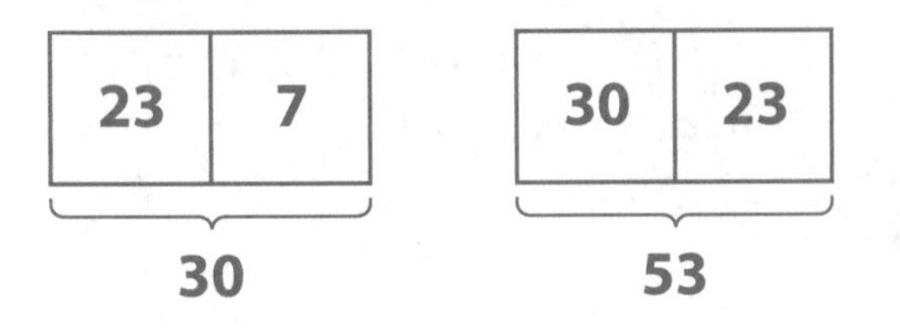

CONNECT IT

Now you will use the problem from the previous page to help you understand how to solve two-step problems about length.

1 Explain how you know the length of Sadie's border is 23 + 7.

2 Write an equation you can use to find the length of the two pieces together.

3 Cameron has two pieces of border. One is 24 inches long, and the other is 5 feet long. He says that the total length is 29 inches. What did he do wrong?

4 REFLECT

Look back at your **Try It**, strategies by classmates, **Picture It**, and **Model Its**. Which models or strategies do you like best for solving two-step problems about length? Explain.

....

....

APPLY IT

Use what you just learned to solve these problems.

5. Sarah buys 18 yards of rope. She uses 6 yards to hang a swing and 4 yards to hang a birdfeeder. How much rope is left? Show your work.

6. Luisa has a piece of yarn that is 38 inches long. Daryl has a piece of yarn that is 4 inches shorter than Luisa's. They need 75 inches of yarn for their craft project. Do they have enough yarn? Explain your answer.

7. Carey uses 23 centimeters of wire to hang up a clock. Then she uses 53 centimeters of wire to hang up posters. Now she has 14 centimeters of wire left. How many centimeters of wire did Carey have at the start?

   Ⓐ 90 centimeters

   Ⓑ 76 centimeters

   Ⓒ 67 centimeters

   Ⓓ 39 centimeters

Practice Solving Two-Step Problems About Length

Study the Example showing how to solve a two-step problem about length. Then solve problems 1–6.

EXAMPLE

Fay makes a paper chain that is 34 inches long. Liz makes a paper chain that is 6 inches longer than Fay's. They put their chains together. How long is the paper chain now?

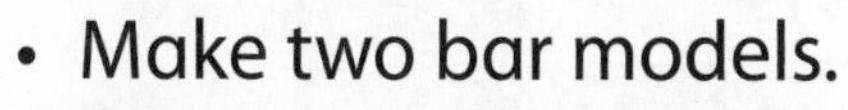

- Make two bar models.
- Write two equations.

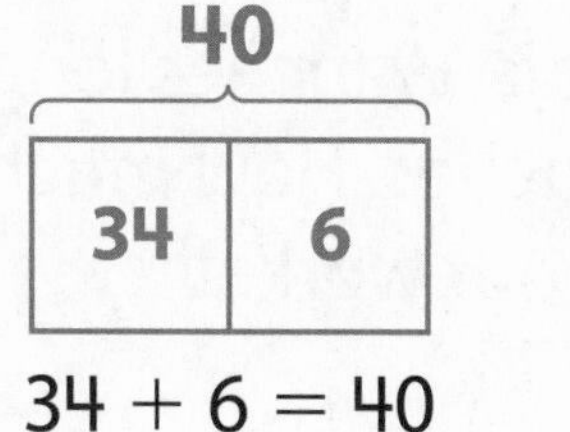

$34 + 6 = 40$

74

40	34

$40 + 34 = 74$

So, the paper chain is now 74 inches long.

1 Fill in the boxes on the number line to model the Example.

30 ☐ 4

34 64 70 ☐

Lester makes a string of beads 17 inches long. Jill makes a string of beads that is 3 inches longer than Lester's. They put their strings together.

2 Complete the equation to find the total length of the string of beads.

$17 + \ldots\ldots = ?$

3 How long is the string of beads now?

.... inches

Solve.

4. Olga has 13 meters of ribbon. She uses 4 meters. Then she uses 2 meters.

   How much ribbon is left? Show your work.

   Solution ....

5. Raj has a paper strip that is 19 inches long. He uses 5 inches. Then he uses 6 inches. How much of the paper strip is left? Show your work.

   Solution ....

6. Al wants his toy train tracks to be 30 inches long. Al has one track that is 12 inches long. He has another track that is 3 inches longer than the first one. Together, are these two tracks long enough? Explain. Show your work.

Refine Adding and Subtracting Lengths

Complete the Example below. Then solve problems 1–3.

EXAMPLE

Mr. Yee has 12 nonfiction books and 28 fiction books for sale. He sells 17 books. How many books does Mr. Yee have left to sell?

Look at how you can show your work with two bar models.

40	
12	28

40	
23	17

$12 + 28 = 40$ $40 - 17 = 23$

Solution ....

APPLY IT

1. Jude's sunflower grows 8 inches this week. It is 26 inches tall now. How tall was Jude's sunflower at the beginning of the week? Show your work.

Was the sunflower taller or shorter at the beginning of the week?

Solution ....

 A path in the park is 22 meters long. Then a new section is added. Now the path is 50 meters long. How long is the new section? Show your work.

Does the path get longer or shorter?

Solution ....

3 Lisa uses 37 centimeters of string to hang a picture and 46 centimeters of string to hang another picture. She has 12 centimeters of string left. How much string did she start with?

Ⓐ 21 cm

Ⓑ 71 cm

Ⓒ 83 cm

Ⓓ 95 cm

Chase chose Ⓒ as the answer. How did Chase get his answer?

The amount of string at the start is the amount of string Lisa used plus what other amount?

Refine Adding and Subtracting Lengths

1 Mina has 11 yards of ribbon. She uses 3 yards to tie onto balloons and 2 yards to wrap presents. How much ribbon is left?

Ⓐ 16 yards Ⓑ 14 yards

Ⓒ 8 yards Ⓓ 6 yards

Dennis chose Ⓐ. How did Dennis get his answer?

To find how much is left, should you add or subtract the ribbon that Mina uses?

2 Stu's block tower is 39 inches tall. Jen's block tower is 17 inches shorter than Stu's. How tall is Jen's block tower?

Which equations can you use to solve the problem?

Ⓐ $39 - ? = 17$

Ⓑ $39 - 17 = ?$

Ⓒ $39 + 17 = ?$

Ⓓ $17 + 39 = ?$

Ⓔ $17 + ? = 39$

Can you use a model to help you solve the problem?

3. Ed has two dog leashes. The purple leash is 84 inches long. The red leash is 75 inches long. How much shorter is the red leash than the purple leash? Show your work.

When you compare, you find the difference.

Solution ....

4. Anjali crosses a playground that is 45 meters long. First, she walks for 5 meters. Then she skips for 23 meters. She runs the rest of the way. How many meters does Anjali run?

Which equations show a step in solving the problem?

Ⓐ $45 + 5 = ?$

Ⓑ $45 - 5 = ?$

Ⓒ $? + 23 = 40$

Ⓓ $23 + 45 = ?$

Ⓔ $40 - 23 = ?$

After Anjali walks 5 meters, how much of the playground does she have left to cross?

5. Ms. Bard uses 24 centimeters of thread to sew a button. Then she uses 31 centimeters of thread to sew another button. She has 9 centimeters of thread left. How much thread did Ms. Bard start with? Show your work.

To find the amount Ms. Bard started with, should you add or subtract the amount she used?

Solution ....

Refine Adding and Subtracting Lengths

APPLY IT

Solve the problems.

1 Maddie's dresser is 44 inches shorter than her bedroom wall. The length of the dresser is 36 inches. What is the length of the wall?

Ⓐ 8 inches
Ⓑ 12 inches
Ⓒ 70 inches
Ⓓ 80 inches

2 Jordan has two tracks for his toy cars. One track is 25 inches longer than the other. Which could be the lengths of the tracks?

Ⓐ 12 inches and 13 inches
Ⓑ 75 inches and 50 inches
Ⓒ 20 inches and 45 inches
Ⓓ 5 inches and 20 inches
Ⓔ 17 inches and 42 inches

3 Willa draws three lines.

- a blue line 55 cm long
- a red line 14 cm shorter than the blue line
- a green line 23 cm shorter than the red line

What is the length of the green line?

Ⓐ 18 cm
Ⓑ 22 cm
Ⓒ 32 cm
Ⓓ 41 cm

 Bella hangs a string of lights in her room. Then she adds two more strings of lights that are 12 feet and 9 feet long. Altogether, the length of all the lights is 32 feet. How long is the first string of lights?

Fill in the blanks. Then select all the answers that show a step in solving the problem.

Ⓐ $12 + 9 =$ ....

Ⓑ $12 - 9 =$ ....

Ⓒ $21 + 32 =$ ....

Ⓓ $32 - 21 =$ ....

Ⓔ $21 - 9 =$ ....

5 Josh is on a path 100 meters long. He runs 35 meters and then starts walking. He runs again for the last 15 meters. How far does Josh walk? Show your work.

Solution ....

6 MATH JOURNAL

Write an addition word problem that uses lengths. Then solve your problem.

☑ SELF CHECK Go back to the Unit 4 Opener and see what you can check off.

Add and Subtract on the Number Line

LESSON 26

Dear Family,

This week your child is learning how to use a number line to represent numbers as lengths, and to use a number line to add and subtract.

Your child will use **number lines** like the one shown below. He or she will learn that the numbers on a number line must be evenly spaced, and that a number can be represented as a length starting at 0. He or she will learn how to use a number line to solve problems.

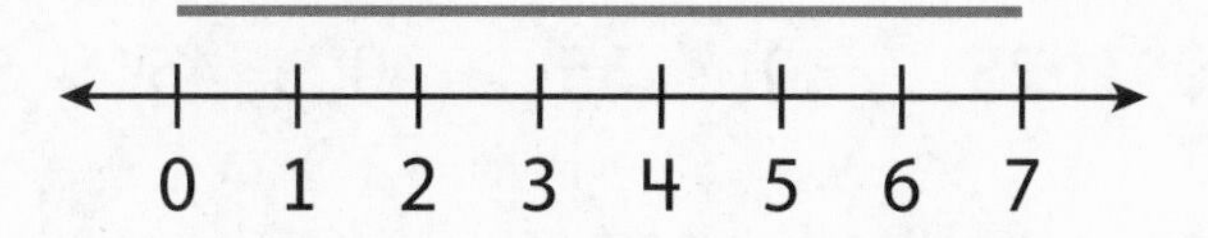

Your child might see a problem like this:

Janie was 21 inches tall when she was born. Now she is 48 inches tall. How many inches has Janie grown since she was born?

You can draw segments above a number line to solve this problem. Draw a line segment from 0 to 21. Then draw a second line segment from 21 to 48. The length of the second line segment is 27.

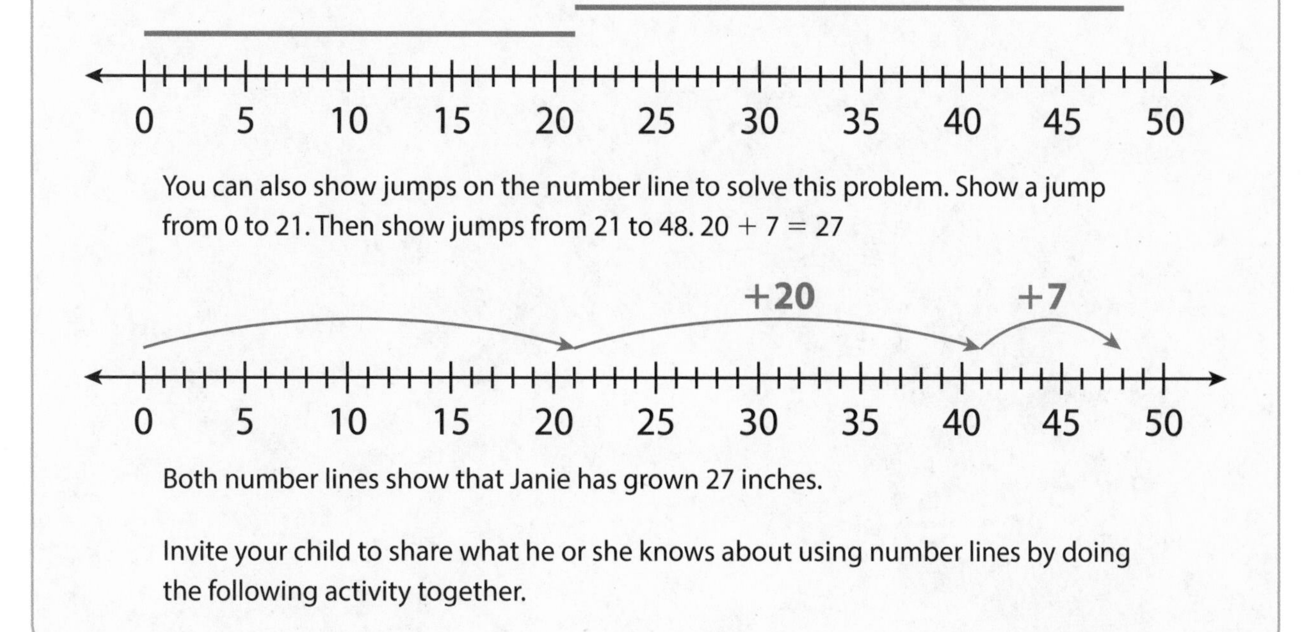

You can also show jumps on the number line to solve this problem. Show a jump from 0 to 21. Then show jumps from 21 to 48. $20 + 7 = 27$

Both number lines show that Janie has grown 27 inches.

Invite your child to share what he or she knows about using number lines by doing the following activity together.

ACTIVITY USING A NUMBER LINE TO ADD AND SUBTRACT

Do this activity with your child to add and subtract on a number line.

- Ask your child to name a number between 10 and 25.
- Have your child ask a family member to select a different number between 10 and 25.
- Ask your child to use the number line below to add his or her number to the family member's number. Have your child explain how he or she used the number line to find the answer.

- Ask your child to select a number between 26 and 50 and have your child ask another family member to select a number between 10 and 25.
- Have your child use a second number line to subtract the family member's number from his or her number. Have your child explain how he or she used the number line to find the answer.
- Ask your child: *How can you use the number line to add and subtract?*

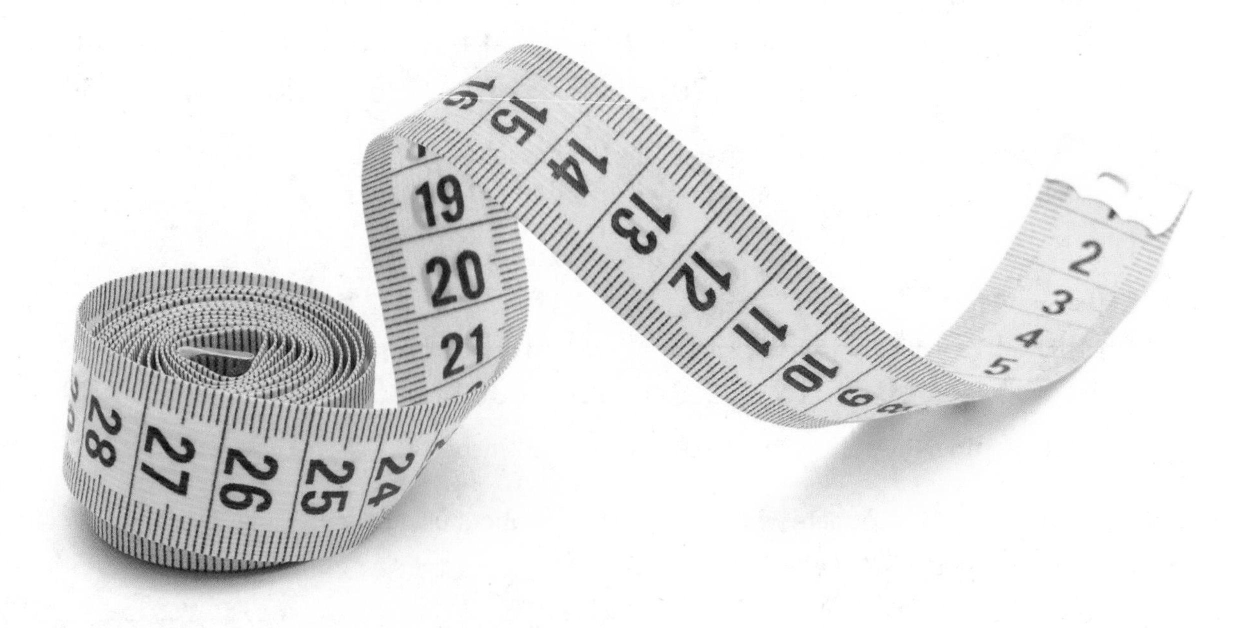

Explore Adding and Subtracting on the Number Line

You have used an open number line to show numbers. Now you will think about numbers as lengths on a number line. Use what you know to try to solve the problem below.

Learning Target

- Represent whole numbers as lengths from 0 on a number line diagram with equally spaced points corresponding to the numbers 0, 1, 2, . . . , and represent whole-number sums and differences within 100 on a number line diagram.

SMP 1, 2, 3, 4, 5, 6, 7

Carol has started to make a number line to show a length of 8. How can you complete the number line and show a length of 8?

0 1 2 3 4

TRY IT

Math Toolkit

- ruler
- connecting cubes
- sticky notes
- centimeter tiles
- string
- number lines

DISCUSS IT

Ask your partner: Why did you choose that strategy?

Tell your partner: The strategy I used to find the answer was . . .

CONNECT IT

1 LOOK BACK

Explain how to show a length of 8 on the **number line**.

2 LOOK AHEAD

You can show sums on a number line. Think about 15 + 18.

0 5 10 15 20 25 30 35 40 45 50

a. Show a length of 15 on the number line starting at 0.

b. Show a length of 18 more on the number line starting at 15.

c. What total length have you shown on the number line? ....

3 REFLECT

Explain how the number line shows the sum 15 + 18.

....

....

....

Name: ______________________________

Prepare for Adding and Subtracting on the Number Line

1 Think about what you know about number lines. Fill in each box. Use words, numbers, and pictures. Show as many ideas as you can.

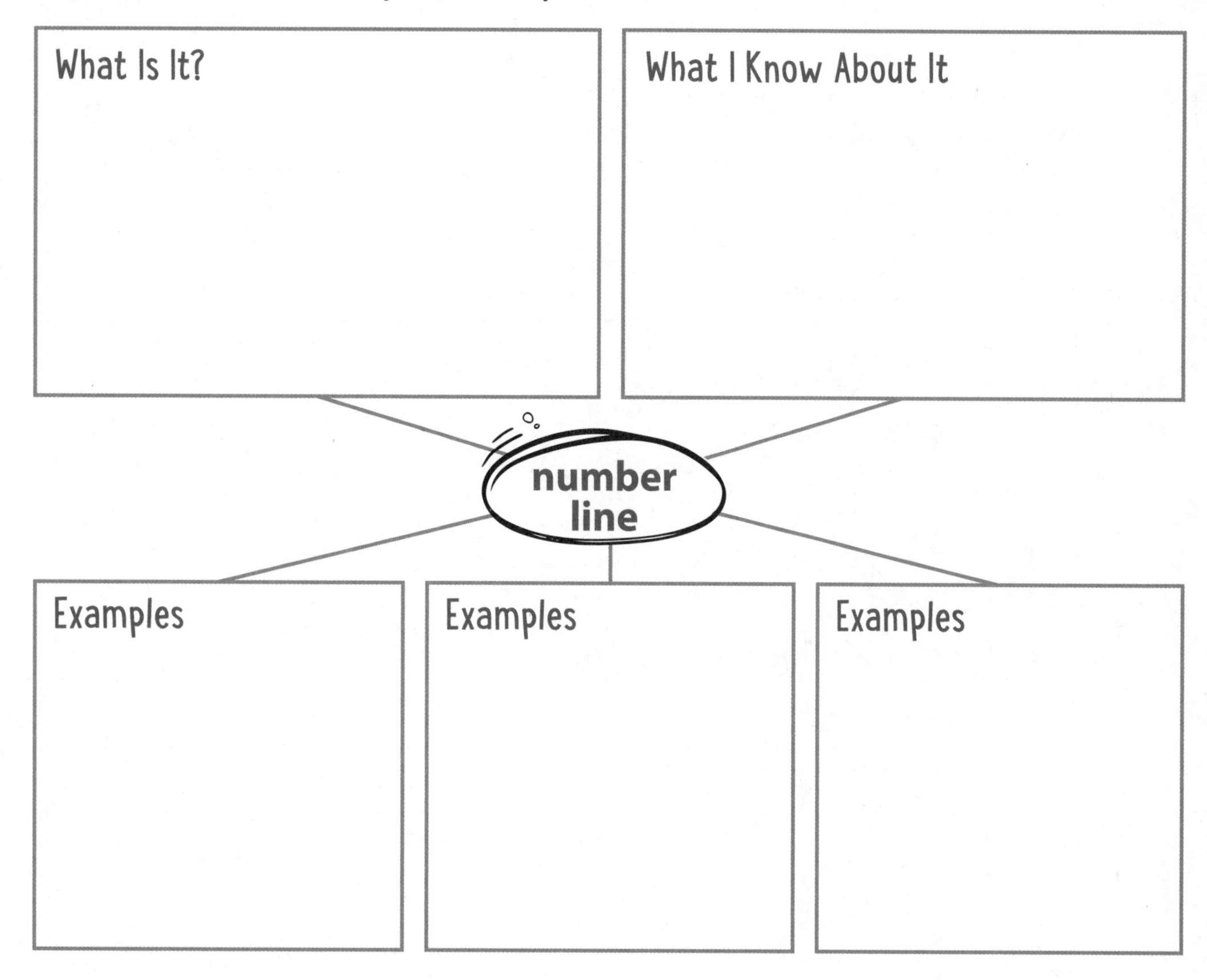

2 Show a length of 10 on the number line. Then show a length of 12 more on the number line.

0 5 10 15 20 25

What is the total length shown on the number line? ....

3 Solve the problem. Show your work.

Chin has started to make a number line to show a length of 10. How can you complete the number line and show a length of 10?

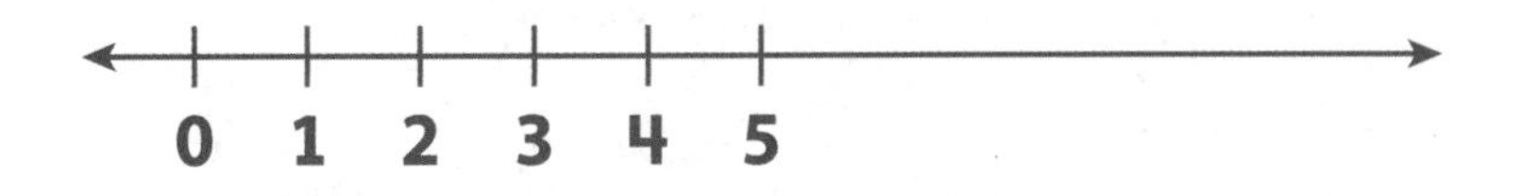

Solution ....

....

....

4 Check your answer. Show your work.

Develop Adding on the Number Line

Read and try to solve the problem below.

Sharon buys a plant that is 25 inches tall. Then the plant grows 13 more inches. How tall is the plant now? Use the number line to solve the problem.

TRY IT

Math Toolkit
- base-ten blocks
- tens place-value mats
- connecting cubes
- string
- measuring tape
- number lines

DISCUSS IT

Ask your partner: Can you explain that again?

Tell your partner: At first, I thought . . .

Explore different ways to understand adding on the number line.

Sharon buys a plant that is 25 inches tall. Then the plant grows 13 more inches. How tall is the plant now? Use the number line to solve the problem.

0 5 10 15 20 25 30 35 40 45 50

MODEL IT

Use the number line to add by drawing lengths.

Draw a length from 0 to 25, to show that the plant was 25 inches tall when Sharon bought it.

Then draw another length starting from 25 to show that the plant grew 13 inches more.

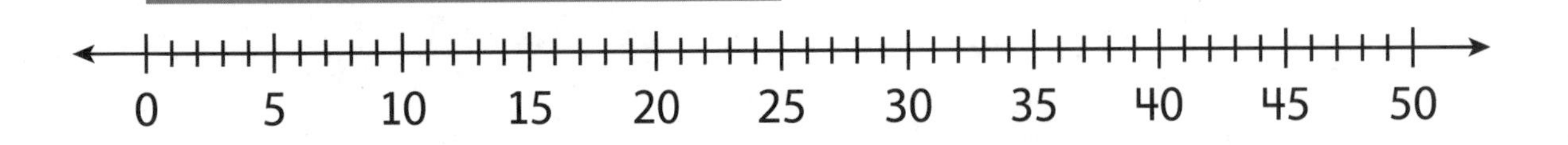

MODEL IT

Use the number line to add by showing jumps.

Draw a jump from 0 to 25 to show that the plant was 25 inches tall when Sharon bought it.

Then draw jumps to show that the plant grew 13 inches more.

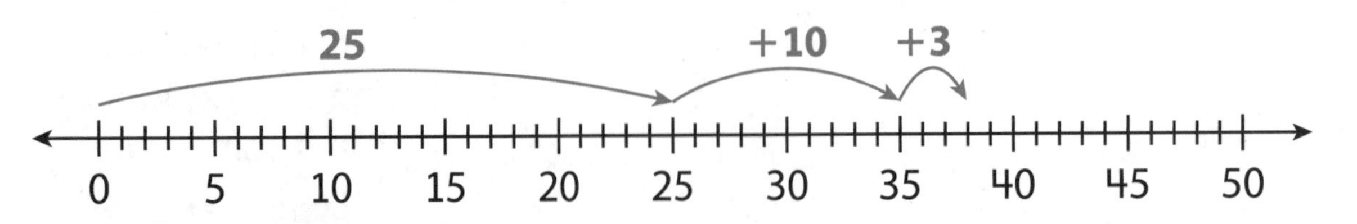

CONNECT IT

Now you will use the problem from the previous page to help you understand how to add on the number line.

1 Look at the **Model Its** on the previous page. Write an addition equation you can use to solve the problem.

2 Explain how the lines in the first **Model It** show the height of the plant when Sharon bought it and how much the plant grew.

3 How tall is the plant now? ....

4 **REFLECT**

Look back at your **Try It**, strategies by classmates, and **Model Its**. Which models or strategies do you like best for adding on the number line? Explain.

....

....

....

....

APPLY IT

Use what you just learned to solve these problems.

5 Dave has a piece of string that is 41 centimeters long. He cuts off a piece that is 26 centimeters long. How much string is left? Show your work. Use the number line.

Solution ....

6 Ellen's dog is 28 inches tall. Nadine's dog is 17 inches taller than Ellen's dog. How tall is Nadine's dog? Show your work. Use the number line.

7 Explain how to use a number line to solve this problem.

Gavin gets 20 dollars. Now he has 43 dollars. How much money did Gavin have at the start?

Name: ______________________________

Practice Adding on the Number Line

Study the Example showing one way to add on the number line. Then solve problems 1–4.

EXAMPLE

Jaime has 50 books. How many can he put on his desk and how many can he put on his shelf? Use the number lines to show two different ways.

Draw line segments to show pairs of numbers with a sum of 50.

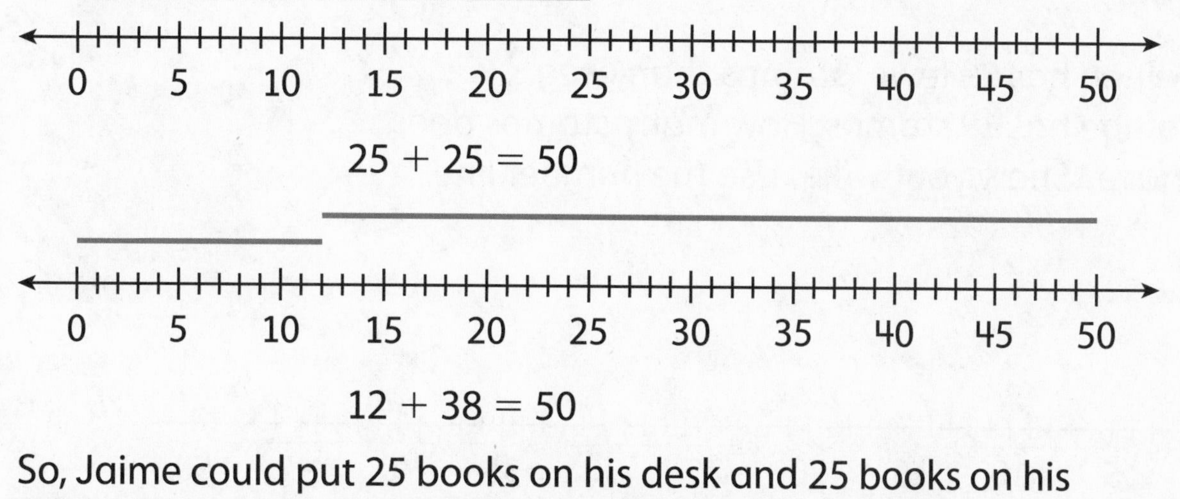

So, Jaime could put 25 books on his desk and 25 books on his shelf, or 12 books on his desk and 38 books on his shelf.

1. Use the problem in the Example and the number line below. Show another way Jaime could put books on his desk and books on his shelf.

0 5 10 15 20 25 30 35 40 45 50

.... books on the desk and .... books on the shelf

2 Greta has a strip of paper that is 42 centimeters long. She colors 15 centimeters yellow, and the rest green. How many centimeters does she color green? Show your work. Use the number line.

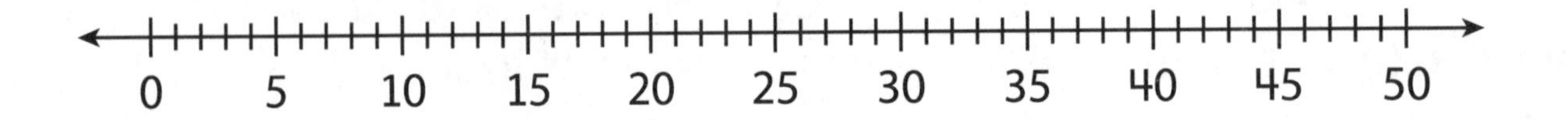

Solution ....

3 Guadalupe has 24 fewer stamps than Greg. Guadalupe has 19 stamps. How many stamps does Greg have? Show your work. Use the number line.

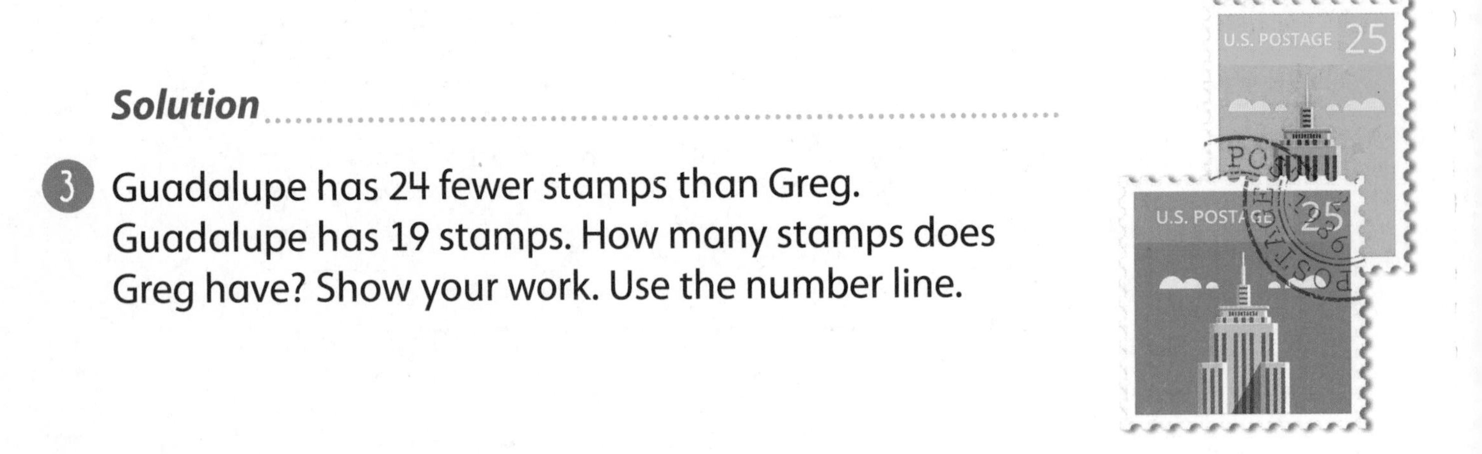

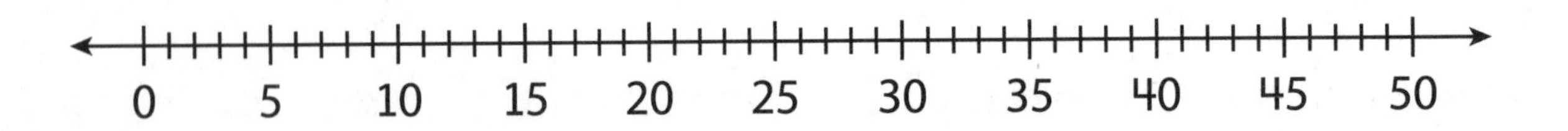

Solution ....

4 Which is shown on the number line below?

0 5 10 15 20 25 30 35 40 45 50

Ⓐ 23 + 18 Ⓑ 23 + 23

Ⓒ 23 + 41 Ⓓ 23 + 50

Develop Subtracting on the Number Line

Read and try to solve the problem below.

Lucas is 49 inches tall. His little sister is 27 inches tall. Use the number line to find how much taller Lucas is than his sister.

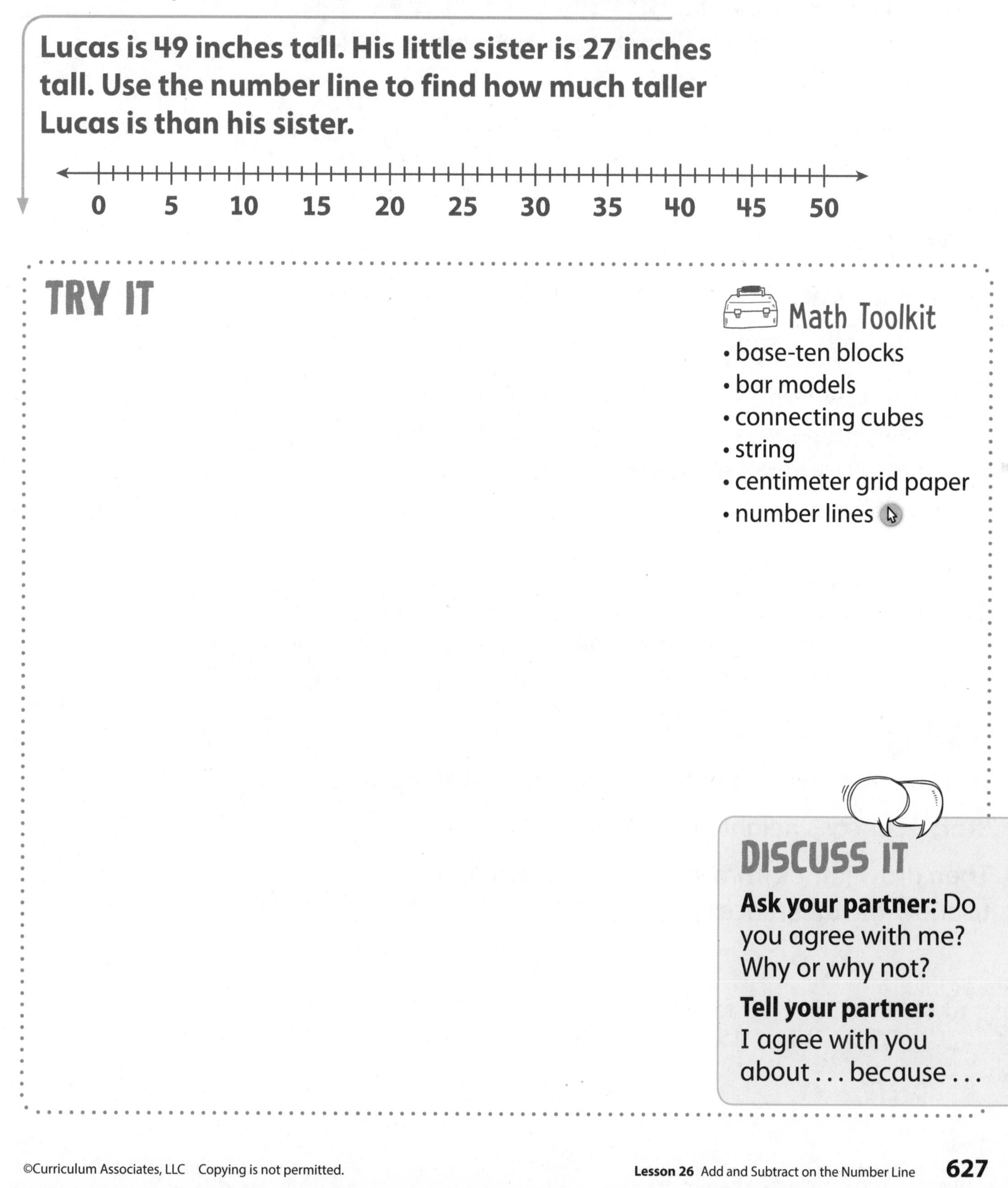

Explore different ways to understand subtracting on the number line.

Lucas is 49 inches tall. His little sister is 27 inches tall. Use the number line to find how much taller Lucas is than his sister.

0 5 10 15 20 25 30 35 40 45 50

MODEL IT

Use the number line to subtract by drawing lengths.

Draw a length to show that Lucas is **49 inches tall.**

Draw another length to show that his sister is **27 inches tall.**

Then find the **length between the ends** of the two line segments.

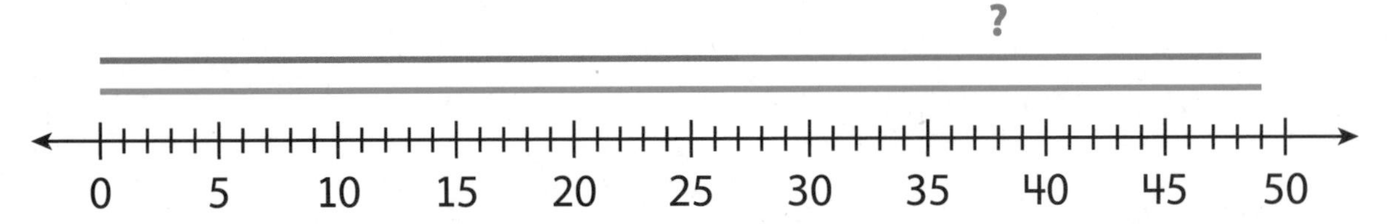

MODEL IT

Use the number line to subtract by showing jumps.

Start at Lucas's height of 49 inches.

Then draw jumps from 49 to his sister's height of 27 inches to show the difference.

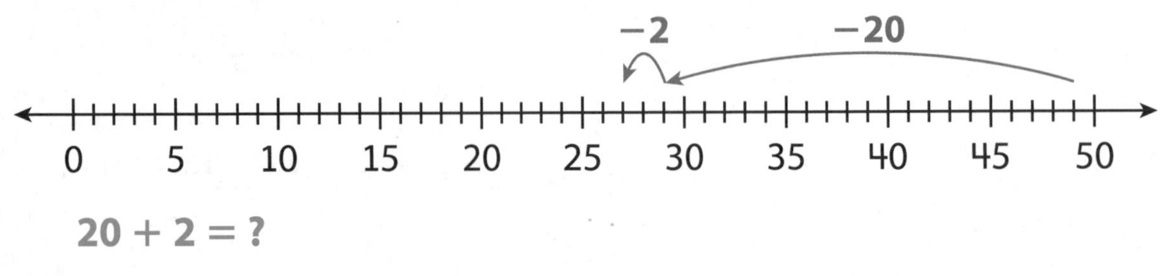

$20 + 2 = ?$

CONNECT IT

Now you will use the problem from the previous page to help you understand how to subtract on the number line.

1. Look at the models on the previous page. Write a subtraction equation that shows the problem.

2. How do the line segments above the number line in the first **Model It** show the heights of Lucas and his sister?

3. How much taller is Lucas than his sister? ....

4. Tino's plant is 47 centimeters tall. Nala's plant is 9 fewer centimeters tall than Tino's plant. How tall is Nala's plant? Use the number line to solve.

0 5 10 15 20 25 30 35 40 45 50

Nala's plant is .... centimeters tall.

5. ## REFLECT

Look back at your **Try It**, strategies by classmates, and **Model Its**. Which models or strategies do you like best for subtracting on the number line? Explain.

....

....

APPLY IT

Use what you just learned to solve these problems.

6 Dawn uses wire to hang up birdhouses. Her first piece of wire is 11 inches longer than her second piece of wire. Her first piece of wire is 36 inches. How long is Dawn's second piece of wire? Show your work. Use the number line.

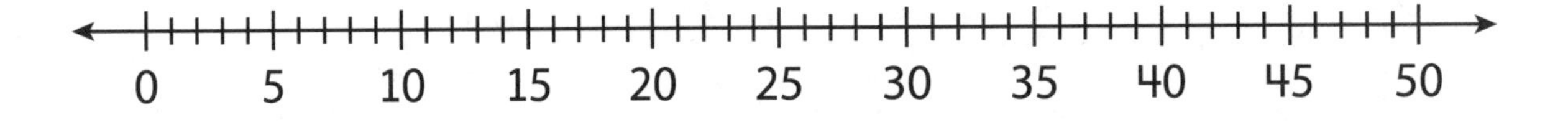

Solution ....

7 Explain how you would use subtraction on a number line to solve this problem.

Gary brings juice boxes for his class. The class drinks 19 juice boxes. Then there are 8 juice boxes left. How many juice boxes did Gary bring?

Which difference is shown on the number line below?

0 5 10 15 20 25 30 35 40 45 50

Ⓐ $48 - 12 = 36$

Ⓑ $36 - 12 = 24$

Ⓒ $36 - 10 = 26$

Ⓓ $24 - 12 = 12$

Name: ____________________

Practice Subtracting on the Number Line

Study the Example showing one way to subtract on the number line. Then solve problems 1–4.

EXAMPLE

Larry earned 45 dollars taking care of pets. He spent 19 dollars for a baseball shirt. How much money does Larry have now?

Find 45 − 19.

Use jumps on the number line to subtract 19 from 45.

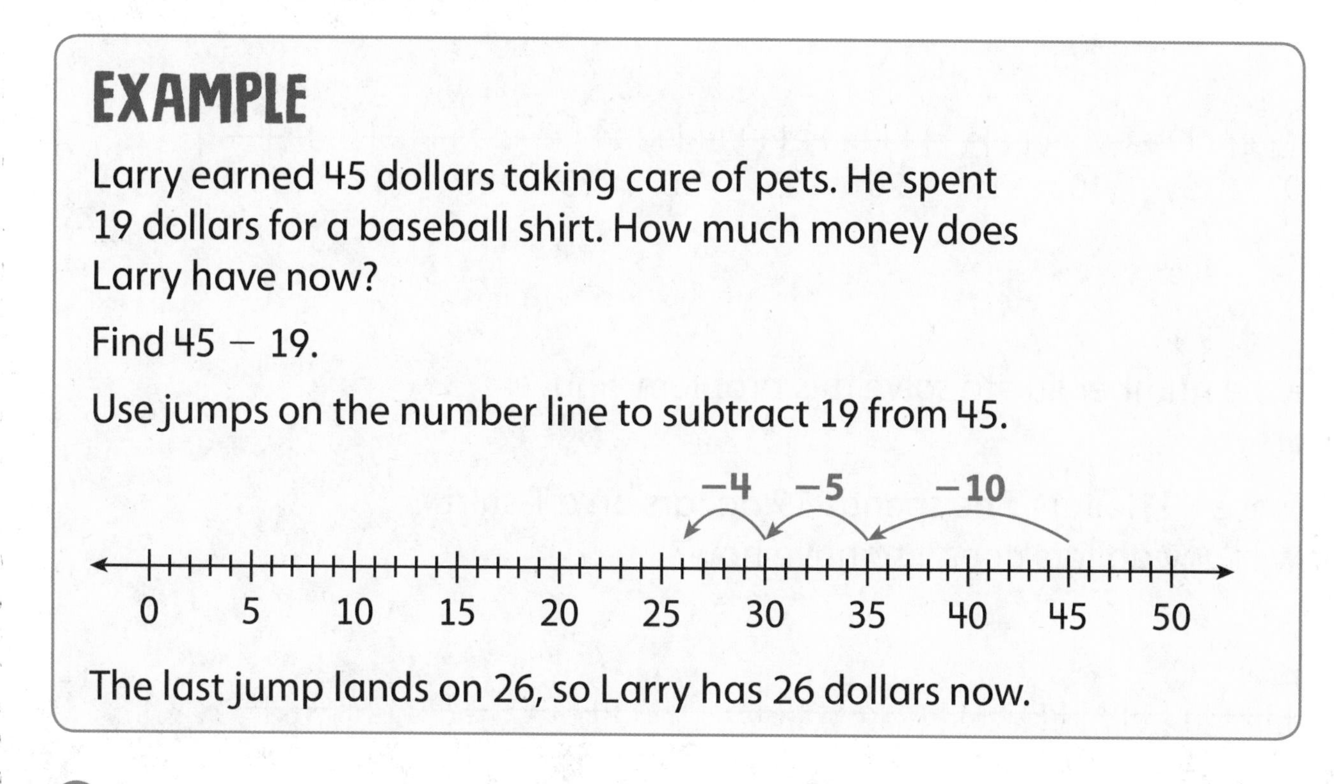

The last jump lands on 26, so Larry has 26 dollars now.

1 Larry has 26 dollars now. He decides to buy a computer game for 15 dollars. Complete the equation and use the number line to show how much money Larry will have after he buys the computer game.

0 5 10 15 20 25 30 35 40 45 50

.... − .... = ...

Larry will have .... dollars left.

2. Betty makes two sizes of posters. Large posters are 36 inches tall and small posters are 18 inches tall. How much taller are large posters than small posters? Show your work. Use the number line.

0 5 10 15 20 25 30 35 40 45 50

Solution ....

3. Use the number line to solve this problem. Show your work.

Lisa has 44 dollars. She spends 19 dollars on a T-shirt. How many dollars does Lisa have now?

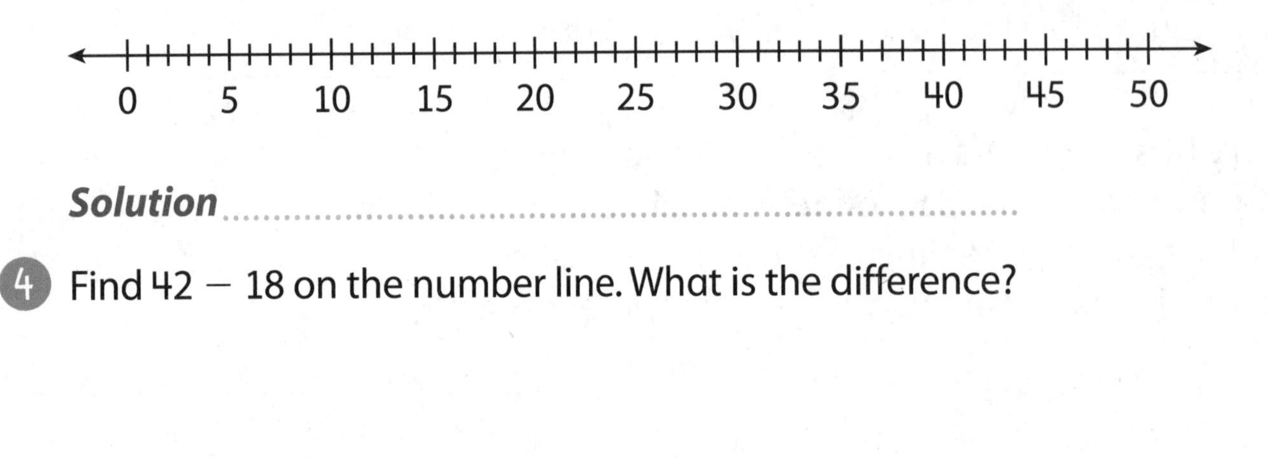

Solution ....

4. Find 42 − 18 on the number line. What is the difference?

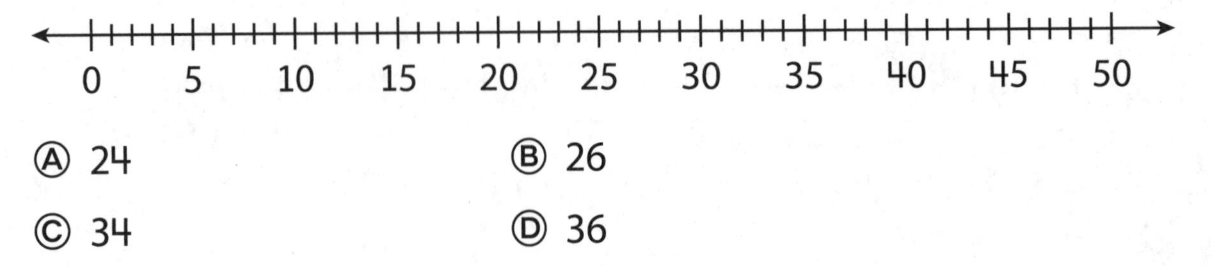

Ⓐ 24
Ⓑ 26
Ⓒ 34
Ⓓ 36

Refine Adding and Subtracting on the Number Line

Complete the Example below. Then solve problems 1–3.

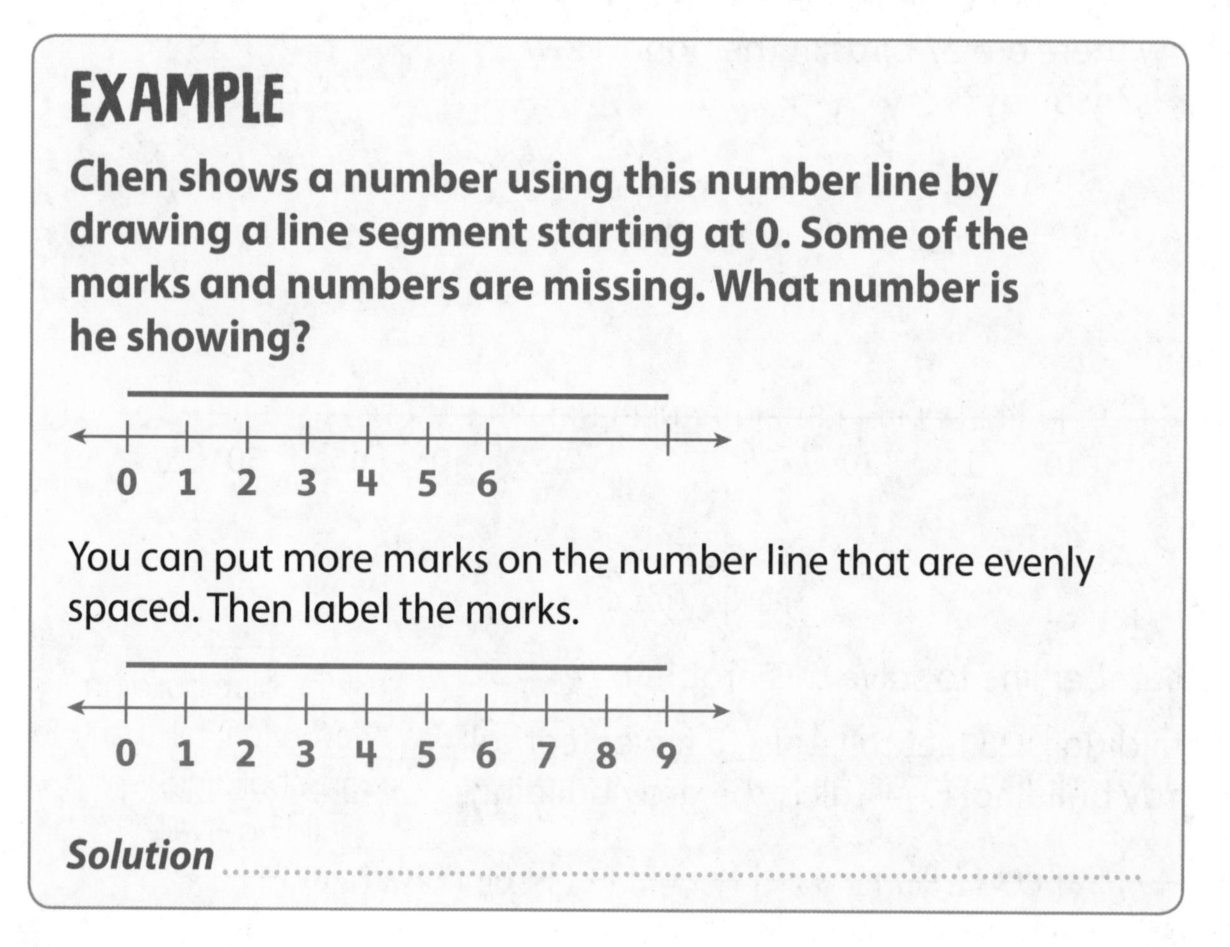

EXAMPLE

Chen shows a number using this number line by drawing a line segment starting at 0. Some of the marks and numbers are missing. What number is he showing?

You can put more marks on the number line that are evenly spaced. Then label the marks.

Solution ....

APPLY IT

1 Label the missing numbers on this number line. What number does the line segment show?

0 1 2 3

The line segment shows ....

Is the space between each pair of numbers the same?

Use the number line to solve this problem. Show your work.

50 birds are in a pond. Then some of them fly away. Now there are 27 birds in the pond. How many birds fly away?

Can drawing line segments or jumps above the number line help you solve this problem?

Solution ....

3 Use the number line to solve this problem.

A blue building is 25 feet tall. It is 16 fewer feet tall than a gray building. How tall is the gray building?

If the blue building is fewer feet tall than the gray building, which building is taller?

0 5 10 15 20 25 30 35 40 45 50

Ⓐ 9 feet

Ⓑ 11 feet

Ⓒ 19 feet

Ⓓ 41 feet

Trevor chose Ⓐ as his answer. How did Trevor get his answer?

Name: ____________________

Practice Adding and Subtracting on the Number Line

1. Label the number line. Then start at 0 and show a length of 7.

Should there be equal space between the numbers?

2. Choose *Yes* or *No* to tell if the number line has been marked correctly.

How should the numbers be marked on the number line?

	Yes	No
Number line: 0 1 2 3 4 5 6	Ⓐ	Ⓑ
Number line: 0 1 2 3 4 5 6 (unequal spacing)	Ⓒ	Ⓓ
Number line: 0 1 2 3 4 5 6 7 8	Ⓔ	Ⓕ
Number line: 0 1 2 3 4 5 6 (unequal spacing)	Ⓖ	Ⓗ

3 Use the number line to solve this problem. Show your work.

Some students are on the playground. Then 25 of them go inside. Now 19 students are on the playground. How many students were on the playground to start?

Can drawing line segments or jumps above the number line help you solve this problem?

0 5 10 15 20 25 30 35 40 45 50

Solution ....

4 Use the number line to help solve the problem.

There are 35 daisies and roses in a vase. Which could be the number of daisies and roses in the vase?

Can you solve this using addition or subtraction?

0 5 10 15 20 25 30 35 40 45 50

Ⓐ 14 daisies and 21 roses

Ⓑ 13 roses and 12 daisies

Ⓒ 30 daisies and 15 roses

Ⓓ 26 daisies and 19 roses

Lisa chose Ⓑ as the answer. How did Lisa get her answer?

Refine Adding and Subtracting on the Number Line

APPLY IT

Solve the problems.

1 What is 47 − 19? Use the number line.

0 5 10 15 20 25 30 35 40 45 50

Ⓐ 38

Ⓑ 32

Ⓒ 28

Ⓓ 22

2 Use the number line to solve the problem. Show your work.

One part of a path is 23 meters long. Another part of the path is 18 meters long. How long are the two parts together?

0 5 10 15 20 25 30 35 40 45 50

Together, the two parts are .... meters long.

3 Which number lines show 46 − 21?

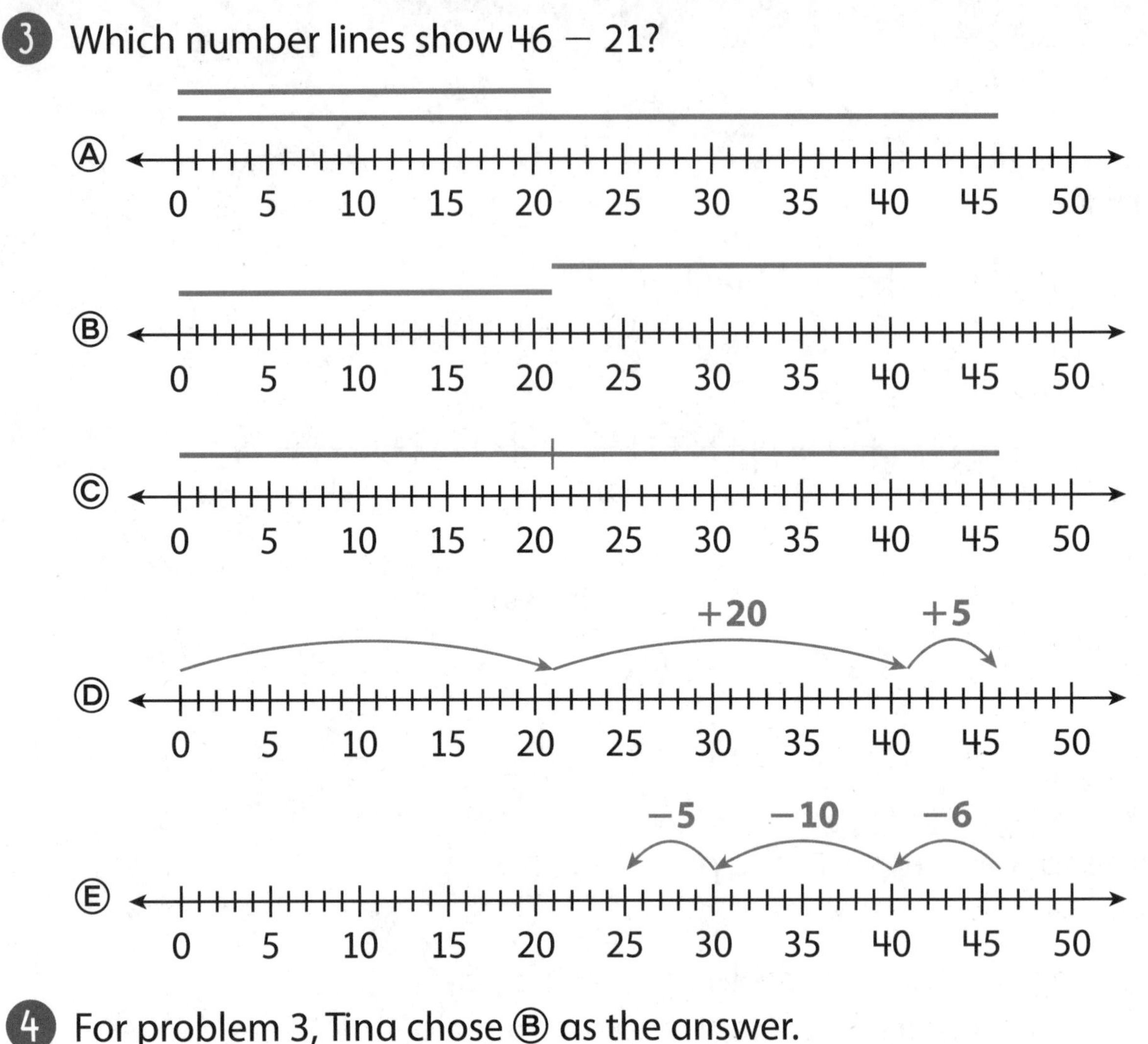

4 For problem 3, Tina chose Ⓑ as the answer.
How did Tina get her answer?

5 MATH JOURNAL

Explain how you can add and subtract on the number line.

☑ SELF CHECK Go back to the Unit 4 Opener and see what you can check off.

Read and Make Line Plots

LESSON 27

Dear Family,

This week your child is learning how to organize a set of measurements using a line plot.

Here is a table showing the lengths of four crayons. A line plot can show how many crayons of each length there are.

Crayon	Length (inches)
A	3
B	2
C	4
D	2

A **line plot** is made up of a number line, a title, and a label that tells what is being shown. It has an X for each measurement.

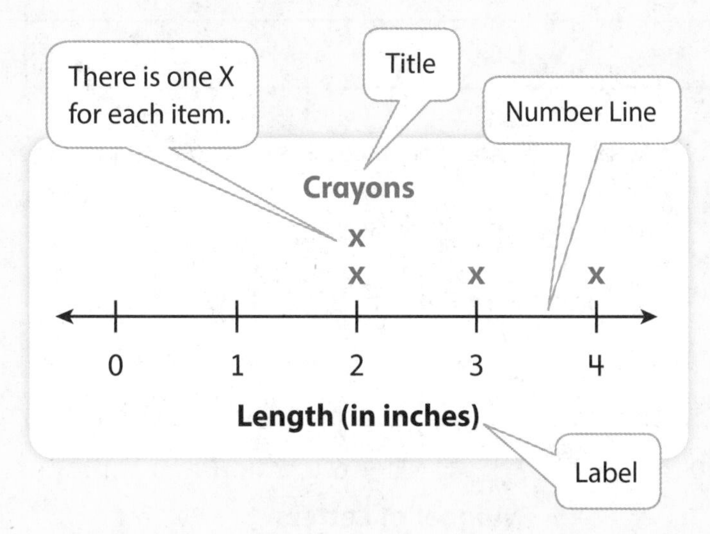

Invite your child to share what he or she knows about line plots by doing the following activity together.

ACTIVITY MAKING LINE PLOTS

Do this activity with your child to read and make line plots.

Together make a line plot of the number of letters in the first names of several of your child's classmates.

- First gather the data. Choose up to six classmates and count the number of letters in each name.
- Organize the data in the table below.

Name	Number of Letters

- Fill in the line plot. Mark one "X" for each name, above the correct number of letters.

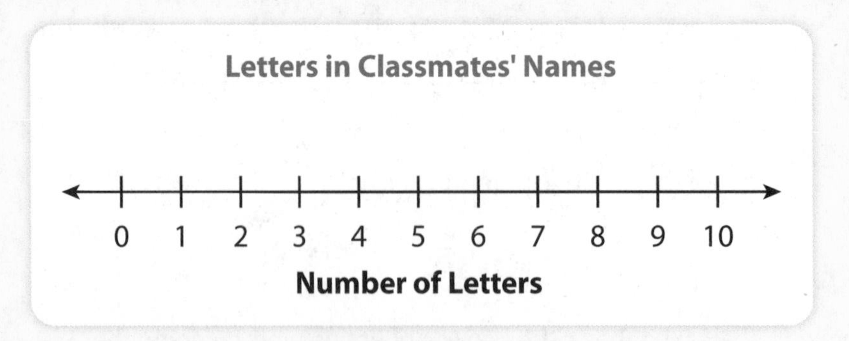

- Ask your child how the line plot would change if you added in the names Dan, Jon, and Sam.

Explore Sorting and Organizing Data

Learning Target

- Generate measurement data by measuring lengths of several objects to the nearest whole unit, or by making repeated measurements of the same object. Show the measurements by making a line plot, where the horizontal scale is marked off in whole-number units.

SMP 1, 2, 3, 4, 5, 6

You know how to sort, count, and organize data. Use what you know to try to solve the problem below.

How many of each shape does the picture show? Draw a table to organize what you see in the picture.

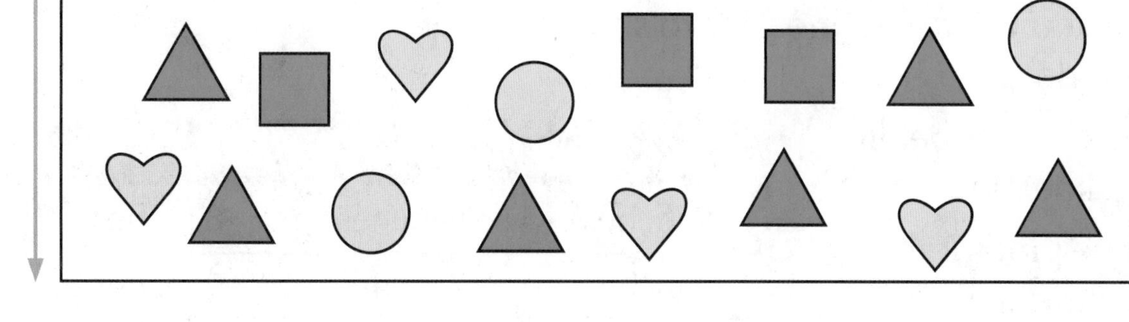

TRY IT

Math Toolkit

- centimeter grid paper
- rulers
- counters
- sticky notes
- stickers

DISCUSS IT

Ask your partner: How did you get started?

Tell your partner: I knew . . . so I . . .

CONNECT IT

1 LOOK BACK

How many of each shape are in the picture?

2 LOOK AHEAD

In this lesson you will use a **line plot** to show measurement data.

a. You can use a number line to make a line plot.

This is a line plot for the data at the right.

Lengths of Toy Dinosaurs		
9 inches	5 inches	8 inches
8 inches	7 inches	9 inches

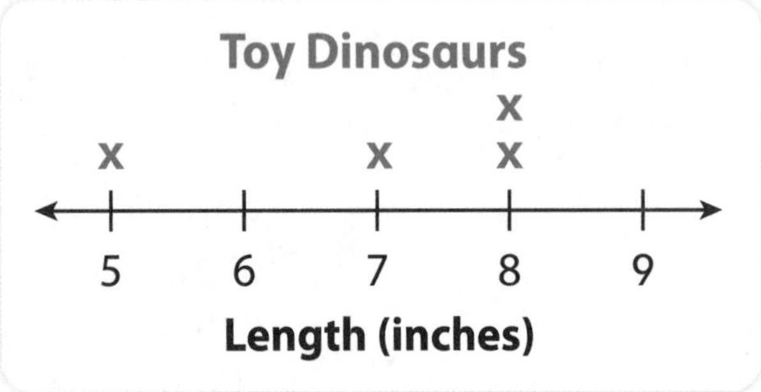

Why is there an X above the mark for 5 inches?

b. Two dinosaurs are 9 inches long. Draw two Xs to complete the line plot.

3 REFLECT

Why is it helpful to organize data?

....

Prepare for Sorting and Organizing Data

1. Think about what you know about data displays. Fill in each box. Use words, numbers, and pictures. Show as many ideas as you can.

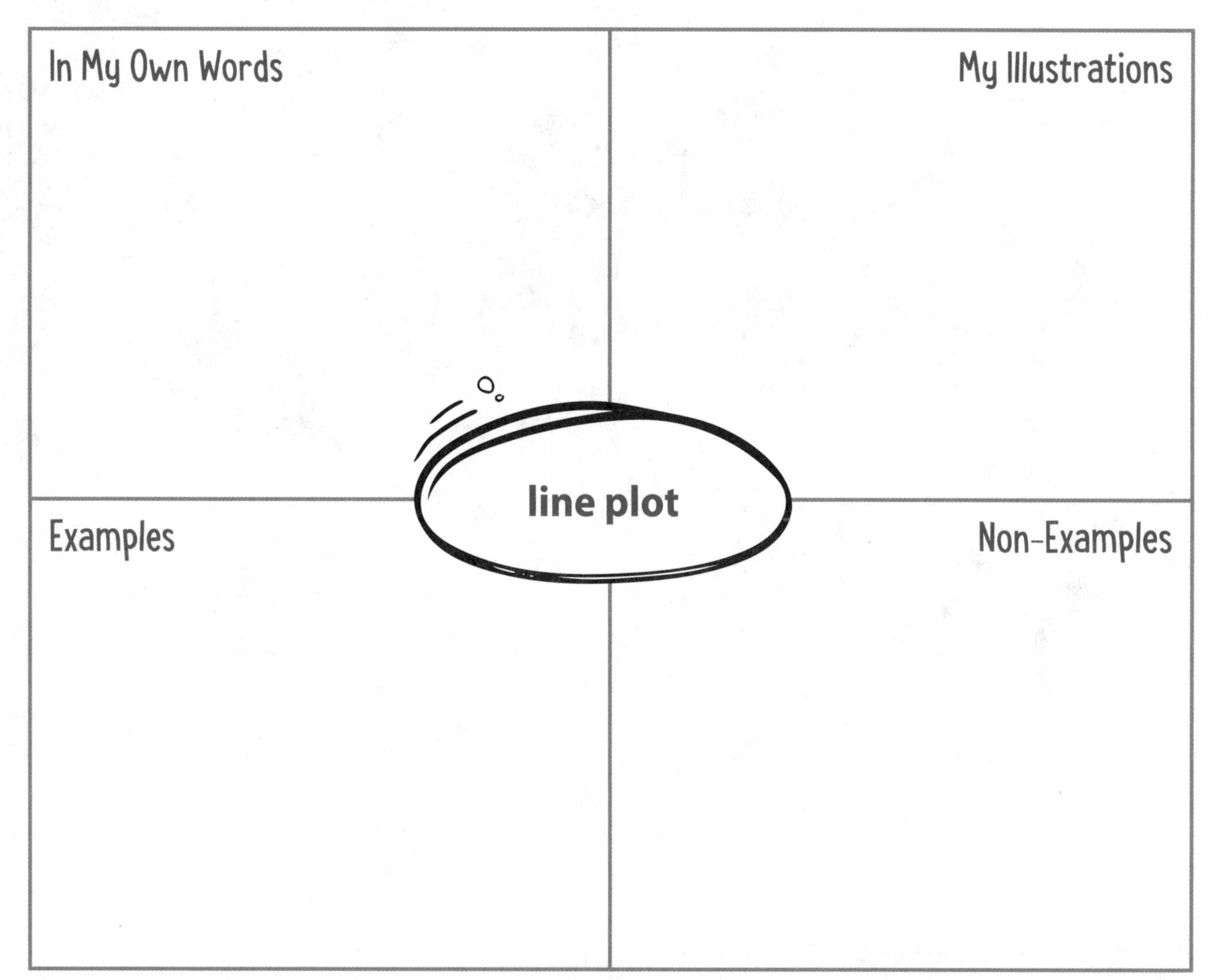

2. Neda starts to make a line plot for the length of his toy cars. He forgot two toy cars that are each 8 inches long. Draw two Xs to complete the line plot.

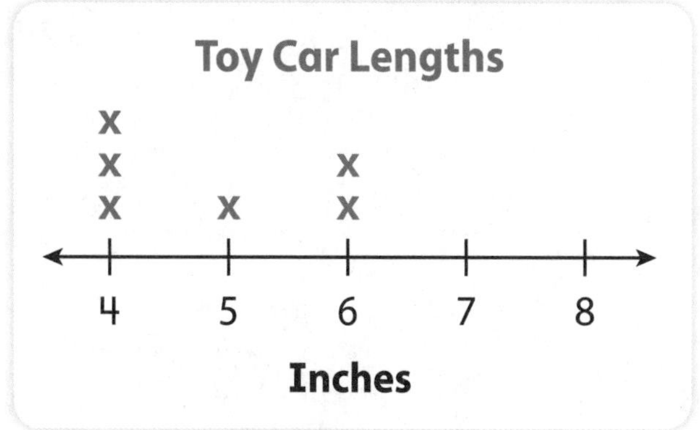

3 Solve the problem. Show your work.

How many of each animal does the picture show? Draw a table to organize what you see in the picture.

Solution ....

4 Check your answer. Show your work.

Develop Reading and Making Line Plots

Read and try to solve the problem below.

The lengths of young sea lions at an aquarium are shown below. Show these measurements on a line plot. What strategy can you use to find which length is the most common?

52 inches, 49 inches, 50 inches, 52 inches,

52 inches, 48 inches, 49 inches

TRY IT

Math Toolkit

- 1-centimeter grid paper
- whiteboard
- counters
- sticky notes
- stickers

DISCUSS IT

Ask your partner: Do you agree with me? Why or why not?

Tell your partner: I agree with you about . . . because . . .

Explore different ways to understand reading and making line plots.

The lengths of young sea lions at an aquarium are shown below. Show these measurements on a line plot. How do you know which length is most common?

52 inches, 49 inches, 50 inches, 52 inches,

52 inches, 48 inches, 49 inches

PICTURE IT

Think about where the measurements would be on a measuring tape. A number line is like a measuring tape.

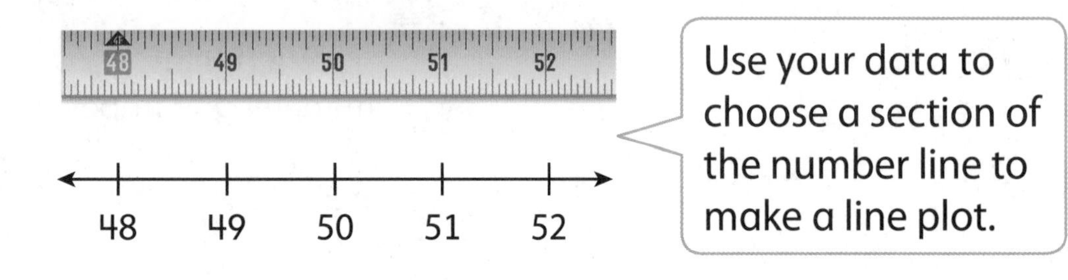

Use your data to choose a section of the number line to make a line plot.

MODEL IT

A line plot can help you show measurements.

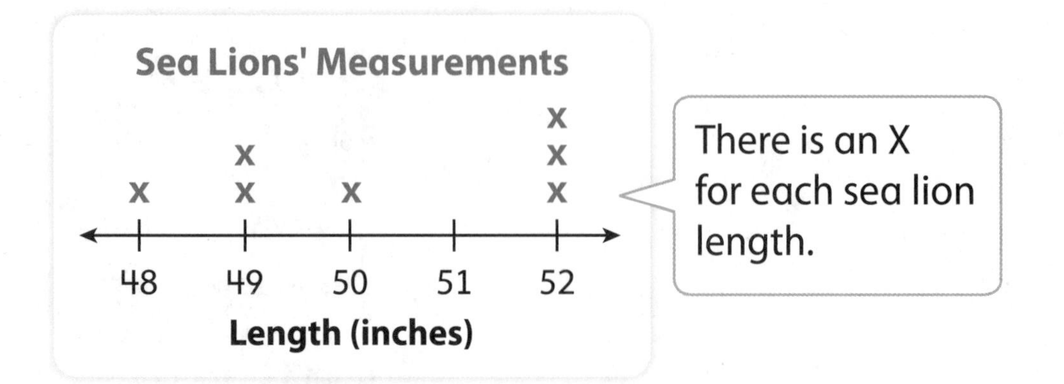

There is an X for each sea lion length.

CONNECT IT

Now you will use the problem from the previous page to understand reading and making line plots.

1 Look at **Picture It**. How is a number line like a measuring tape?

2 Look at **Model It**. How do you know what the line plot is about?

3 What do the numbers along the bottom of the line plot stand for?

4 How long is the shortest sea lion? The longest?

5 Which length of sea lion is the most common? ....

6 **REFLECT**

Look back at your **Try It**, strategies by classmates, and **Picture It** and **Model It**. Which models or strategies do you like best for reading and making line plots? Explain.

....

....

....

APPLY IT

Use what you just learned to solve these problems.

7 Sam measures the length of each feather in her collection. She writes the lengths in a table. Complete the line plot to show the data.

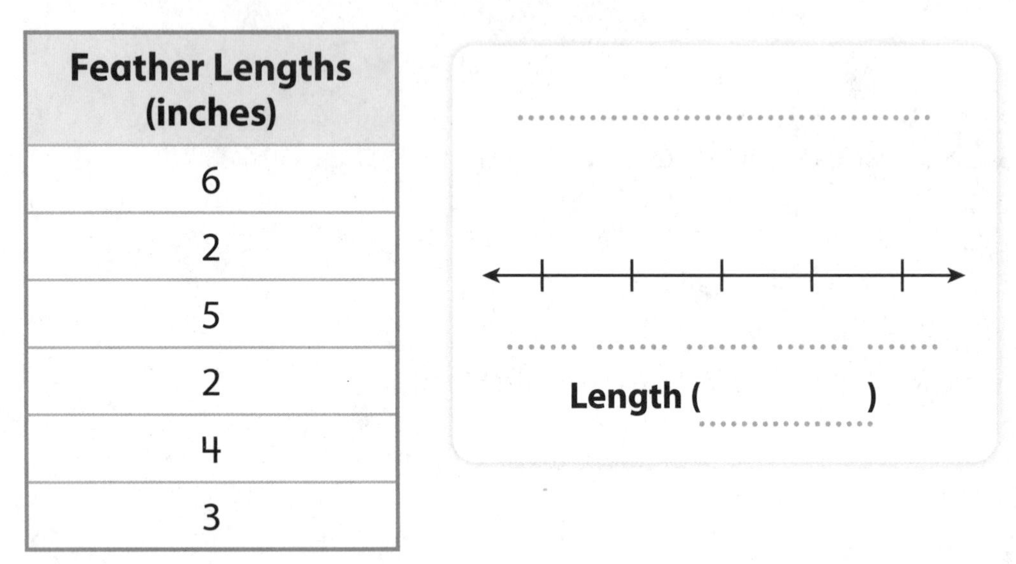

Feather Lengths (inches)
6
2
5
2
4
3

8 Darious measures each of his toy cars using centimeters. How many toy cars are 16 centimeters long?

Ⓐ 2

Ⓑ 3

Ⓒ 4

Ⓓ 5

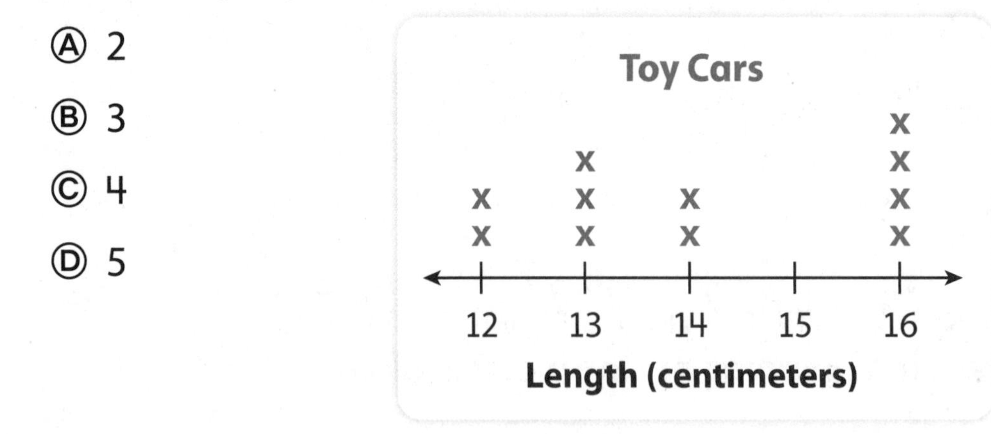

9 Explain how you found the answer to problem 8.

Practice Reading and Making Line Plots

Study the Example showing how to make a line plot to show length data. Then solve problems 1–3.

EXAMPLE

Lexi measures the lengths of her toy cars. The lengths are shown in the table. She follows these steps to make a line plot.

1. Write a title for the line plot.
2. Fill in the numbers for length on the line plot.
3. Draw an X on the line plot for each toy car.

Toy Car	Length (inches)
A	4
B	3
C	7
D	5
E	3
F	5

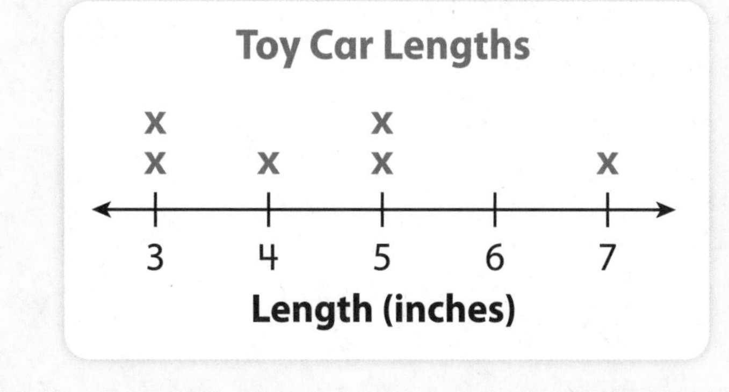

1. Why do some numbers have two Xs above them?

Paco measures the lengths of the bookmarks he has in his desk. The lengths are shown in the chart.

Bookmark	Length (inches)
A	8
B	7
C	4
D	6
E	7
F	4

2 Use the lengths to make a line plot.

- Write a title for the line plot.
- Fill in the numbers for length on the line plot.
- Draw an X on the line plot for each bookmark.

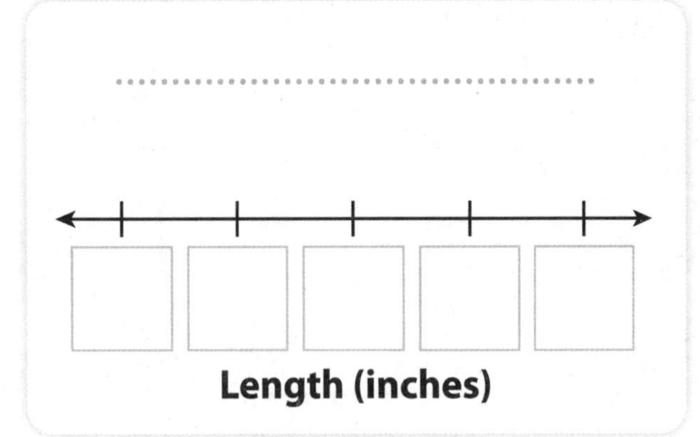

3 How did you decide where to draw the Xs on the number line? Explain.

Develop Reading and Making Line Plots

Read and try to solve the problem below.

Julia spills a box of spaghetti. She picks up the broken pieces. Measure each piece using centimeters. Show how the measurement data might be organized.

A
B
C
D
E
F
G
H

TRY IT

Math Toolkit
- centimeter rulers
- centimeter grid paper
- whiteboards
- counters
- sticky notes
- stickers

DISCUSS IT

Ask your partner: Why did you choose that strategy?

Tell your partner: The strategy I used to find the answer was . . .

Explore more different ways to understand making and reading line plots.

Julia spills a box of spaghetti. She picks up the broken pieces. She measures each piece using centimeters. How many of each size piece does Julia have?

PICTURE IT

You can group the pieces by length and put them in order.

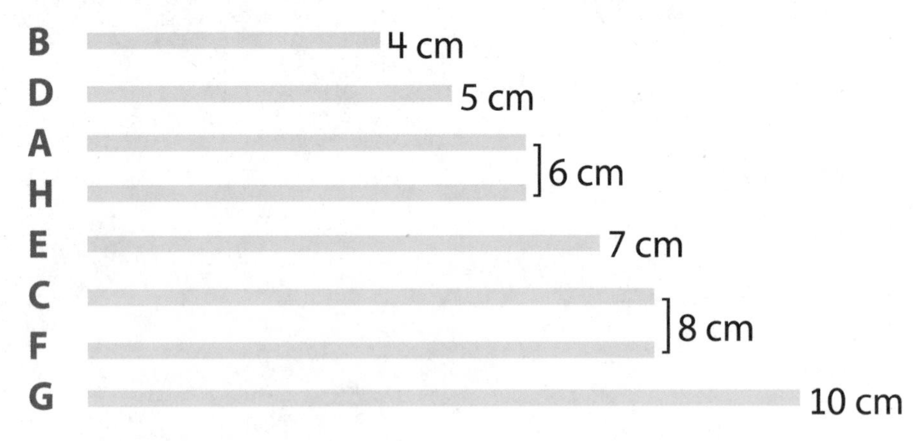

MODEL IT

You can make a line plot to show the measurements.

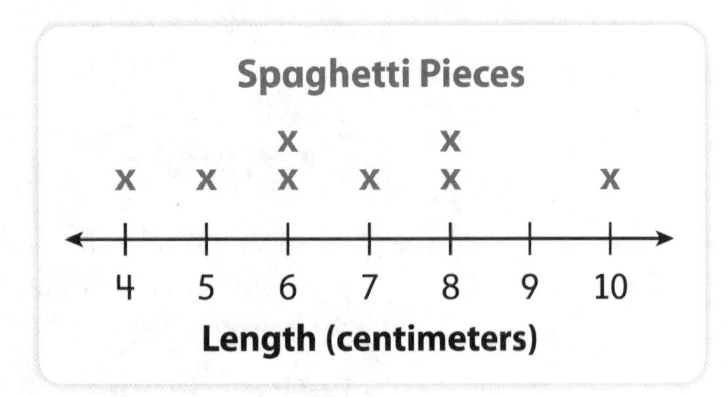

CONNECT IT

Now you will read the line plot to solve the problem from the previous page.

 Look at the **Picture It**. What are the lengths of the shortest and longest spaghetti pieces?

shortest .... cm longest .... cm

2 Look at the **Model It**. What does each number on the line plot show?

3 What does each X on the line plot show?

 Why does the line plot start at 4 instead of 0?

 REFLECT

Look back at your **Try It**, strategies by classmates, and **Picture It** and **Model It**. Which models or strategies do you like best for reading and making line plots? Explain.

....

....

....

APPLY IT

Use what you just learned to solve these problems.

6 Lana has several pieces of yarn. Measure the lengths below in centimeters. Then use the lengths to complete the line plot. Explain how you decided where to draw the Xs on the line plot.

A
B
C
D
E
F

Length (centimeters)

Solution ....

....

....

7 How many Xs should be on the on the yarn line plot in all?

Ⓐ 1 Ⓑ 2

Ⓒ 5 Ⓓ 6

8 Lin puts 7 in the left square on the line plot above and ends with 3 in the last square. Why is Lin wrong? Explain.

Practice Reading and Making Line Plots

Study the Example showing how to read a line plot. Then solve problems 1–9.

EXAMPLE

Kyle measures each leaf in his collection using centimeters. He makes this line plot.

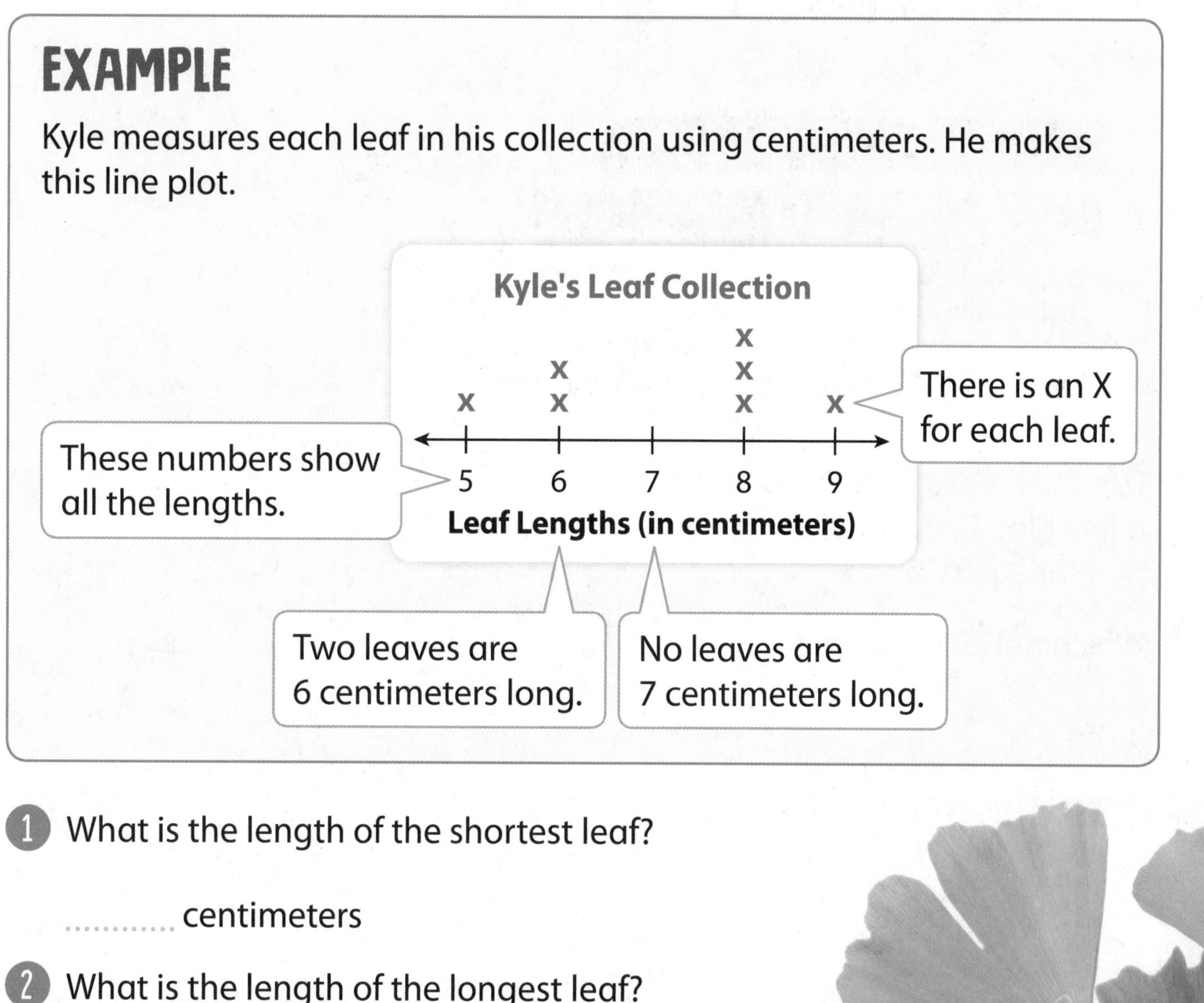

1. What is the length of the shortest leaf?

   .... centimeters

2. What is the length of the longest leaf?

   .... centimeters

3. How many leaves are 8 centimeters long? ....

4. How many leaves are in Kyle's collection? ....

5 Rita uses these ribbons from her craft box. Measure the ribbons in centimeters and write the length beside each ribbon.

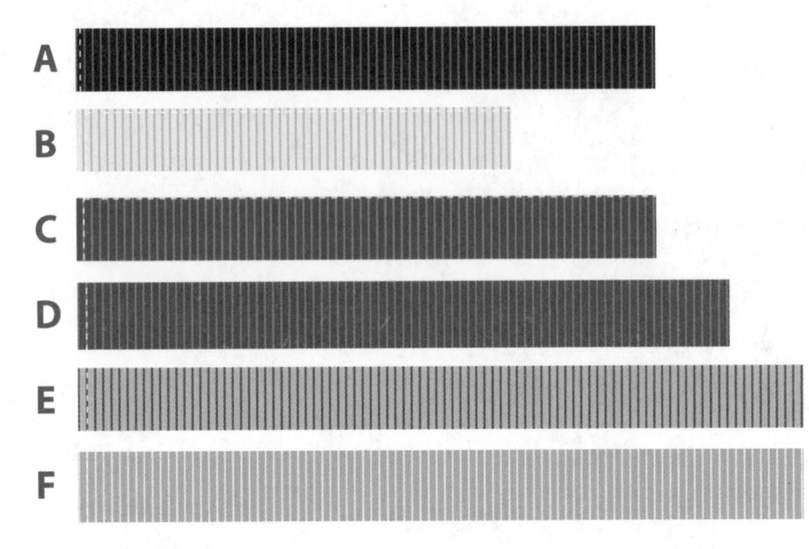

6 Use the measurements to make a line plot. Draw an X on the line plot for each ribbon.

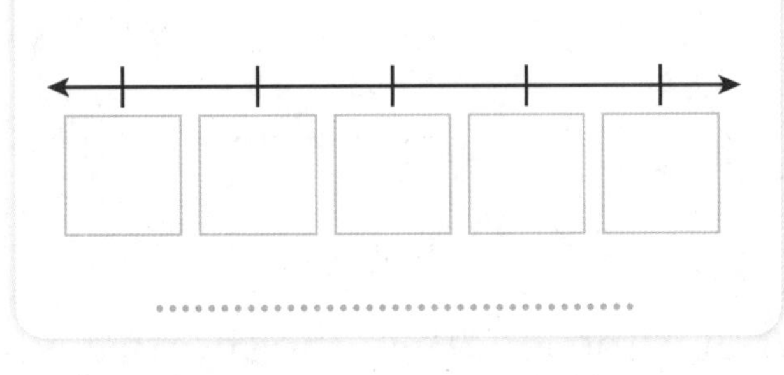

7 Which ribbon(s) are the

longest? ....

8 What is the length of the shortest ribbon?

.... centimeters

9 How many ribbons are longer than

8 centimeters? ....

Refine Reading and Making Line Plots

Complete the Example below. Then solve problems 1–4.

EXAMPLE

Rachel wants to make a line plot to show the lengths of six rooms. Complete Rachel's labeling of the line plot.

Room Lengths

6 7 8 ☐ ☐ ☐

Length (meters)

Room	Length (meters)
A	8
B	6
C	10
D	9
E	11
F	10

APPLY IT

1. Why is 7 on the line plot when there is no 7 in the data?

What does the line plot need to show?

2. Nate says that the length of the longest room is the one with the most Xs over it.
Explain why Nate is wrong.

How does a line plot show data?

3 Bo is using straws to make a design. Measure the straws below in centimeters. Then make a line plot that shows the lengths of all of Bo's straws. Show your work.

How can you make a line plot to show different lengths?

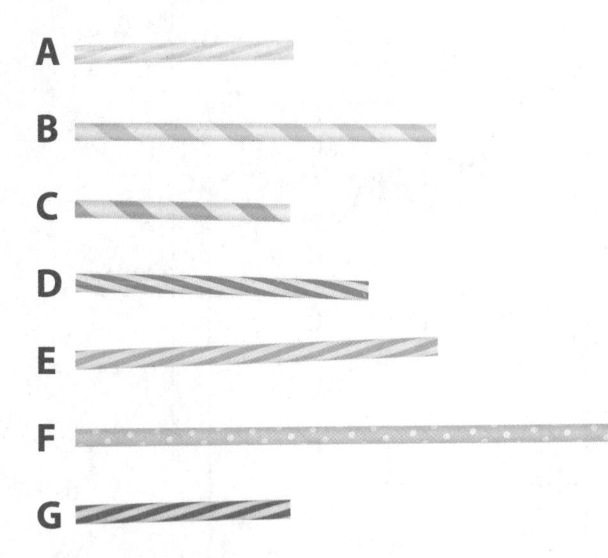

4 Daquan makes a line plot to show the heights of his basketball teammates. What is the most common height of the teammates?

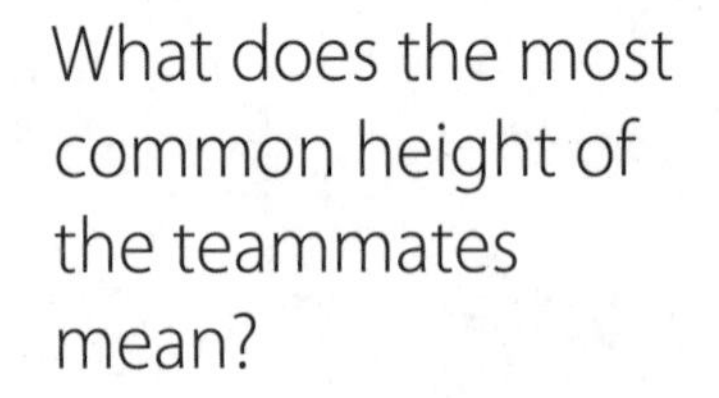

What does the most common height of the teammates mean?

Ⓐ 49 inches

Ⓑ 50 inches

Ⓒ 51 inches

Ⓓ 53 inches

Basketball Teammates

Height (inches)	49	50	51	52	53
Number of X's	X	X X X	X X		X

Nadia chose Ⓓ. How did Nadia get her answer?

Name: ______________________

Practice Reading and Making Line Plots

1. Natalie measures each book on her shelf. The lengths are shown in the table. Use the lengths to make a line plot.

How can you show data on a line plot?

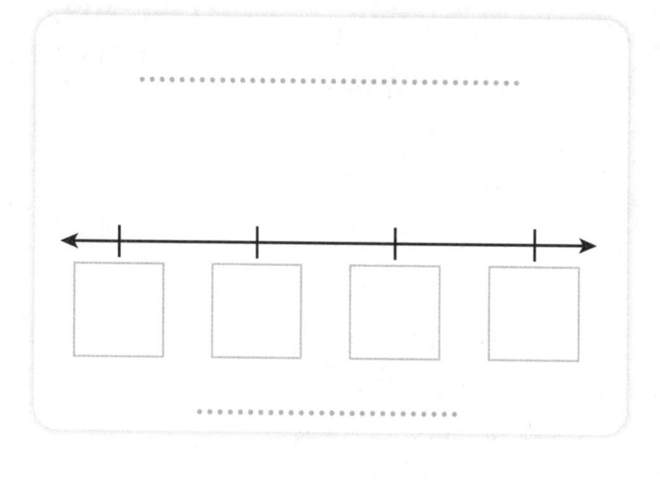

Book	Length (inches)
A	6
B	3
C	6
D	5
E	3
F	6

2. What is the length of the shortest book? ....

3. What is the length of the longest book? ....

4. What is the most common book length? ....

How can you read line plots?

5 Rena has the beads shown below. Measure each string of beads using centimeters. Write the lengths in the table. Use the measurements to make a line plot and then answer the questions.

What do you need to do first?

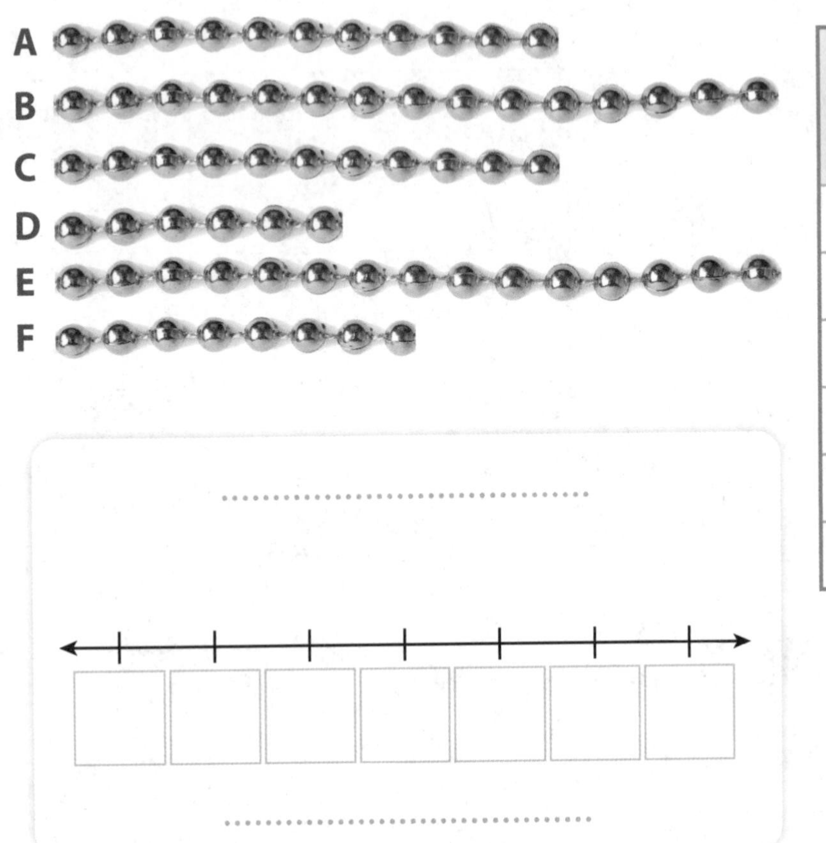

String of Beads	Length (centimeters)
A	
B	
C	
D	
E	
F	

6 How many strings of beads of each length are there?

What lengths are the same?

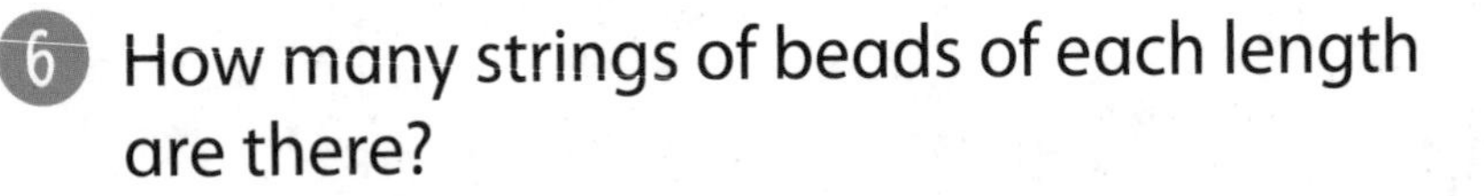

7 How would the line plot change if Rena added a string of beads measuring 9 centimeters long?

How would you show this extra string on the line plot?

Refine Reading and Making Line Plots

APPLY IT

Solve the problems.

1 Use the page of shells your teacher gives you.

Measure the length of each shell in inches. Write the lengths in the table.

Shell	Length (inches)
A	
B	
C	
D	
E	
F	
G	

2 Use your measurements to make a line plot.

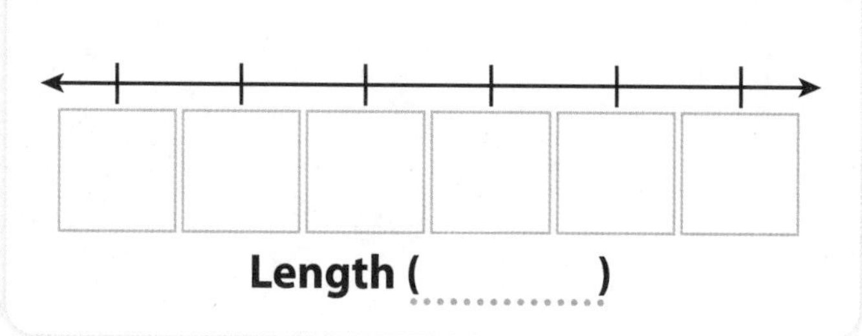

3 The length of the longest shell is .... inches.

The length of the shortest shell is .... inches.

The most shells have a length of .... inches.

4 Two more shells are each 4 inches long. Explain how the line plot would change if the lengths of these shells were added to the line plot.

5 Why does the line plot start at 2 instead of 0?

Why are 5 and 6 included on the line plot?

How would you use the line plot to find out how many shells there are of each length?

How do you know that the correct number of Xs are shown on the line plot?

MATH JOURNAL

What are two ways you can organize data to help you make a line plot?

☑ SELF CHECK Go back to the Unit 4 Opener and see what you can check off.

UNIT 4

Self Reflection

In this unit you learned to . . .

Skill	Lesson
Use a ruler to measure the length of an object.	20, 21
Choose the correct tool for measuring an object.	21
Measure the same object using different units.	22
Estimate the length of an object.	23
Compare lengths to tell which of two objects is longer and how much longer that object is.	24
Add and subtract lengths to solve problems.	25
Add and subtract lengths on a number line.	26
Measure lengths and show data on a line plot.	27

Think about what you learned.

Use words, numbers, and drawings.

1. Three examples of what I learned are . . .

2. The hardest thing I learned to do is .... because . . .

3. A question I still have is . . .

Use Measurement

Study an Example Problem and Solution

SMP 1 Make sense of problems and persevere in solving them.

Read this problem about measuring in centimeters. Then look at Yoop's solution to the problem.

Buttons

Bella saves buttons to decorate things she makes. Bella wants to glue some buttons on the top of a pencil box. Each button is the same distance across.

?

- Put buttons in a line around all 4 edges.
- The buttons do not have to touch.
- Measure the button to help you plan.

Top of Box

9 centimeters

7 centimeters

How can Bella decorate the pencil box? Draw a picture. Tell how many buttons she needs.

Show how Yoop's solution matches the checklist.

PROBLEM-SOLVING CHECKLIST

- ☐ Tell what is known.
- ☐ Tell what the problem is asking.
- ☐ Show all your work.
- ☐ Show that the solution works.

a. Circle something that is known.

b. Underline something that you need to find.

c. Draw a box around what you do to solve the problem.

d. Put a checkmark next to the part that shows the solution works.

YOOP'S SOLUTION

Hi, I'm Yoop. Here's how I solved this problem.

- **First, I can measure the button.**
  It is 1 centimeter across.
- **I need 4 lines of buttons.**
  I'll put 1 centimeter of space between the buttons.
- **I can make a drawing to show my thinking.**
  - Start with the long sides.
  - Draw and count 9 centimeters.
  - Then make the top and bottom.
  - Draw and count 7 centimeters.

I made a drawing to help me solve the problem.

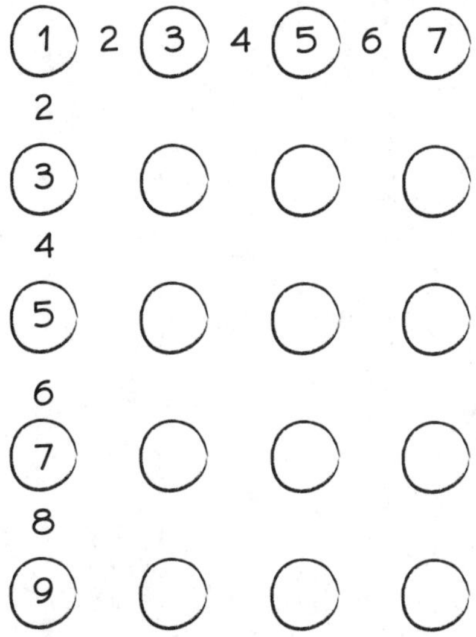

(1) 2 (3) 4 (5) 6 (7)
2
(3) ○ ○ ○
4
(5) ○ ○ ○
6
(7) ○ ○ ○
8
(9) ○ ○ ○

Both sides have 5 buttons and 4 spaces.
$5 + 4 = 9$

The bottom and top each have 4 buttons and 3 spaces.
$4 + 3 = 7$

9 centimeters and 7 centimeters match the drawing.

I checked my work by adding.

- **I can count all the buttons to see how many I need.**
  There are 14 buttons.

Try Another Approach

There are many ways to solve problems. Think about how you might solve the Buttons problem in a different way.

Buttons

Bella saves buttons to decorate things she makes. Bella wants to glue some buttons on the top of a pencil box. Each button is the same distance across.

- Put buttons in a line around all 4 edges.
- The buttons do not have to touch.
- Measure the button to help you plan.

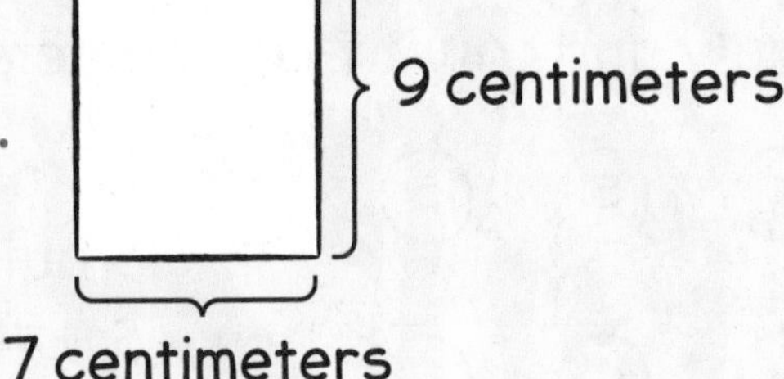

How can Bella decorate the pencil box? Draw a picture. Tell how many buttons she needs.

PLAN IT

Answer this question to help you start thinking about a plan.

Yoop's solution has spaces between each button. How could you make a design with no space between the buttons?

SOLVE IT

Find a different solution for the Buttons problem.
Show all your work on a separate sheet of paper.

You may want to use the Problem-Solving Tips to get started.

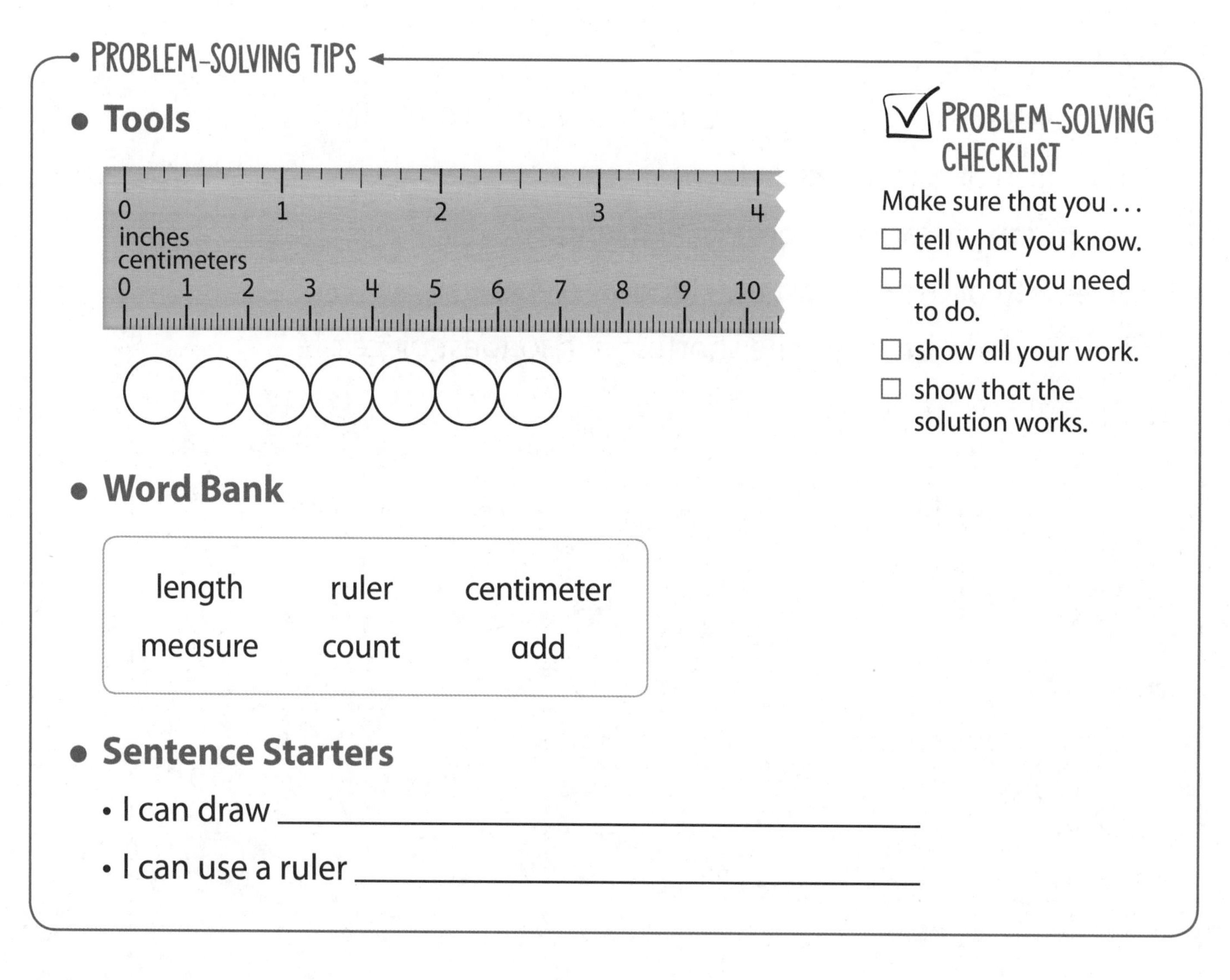

PROBLEM-SOLVING TIPS

- **Tools**

- **Word Bank**

length	ruler	centimeter
measure	count	add

- **Sentence Starters**
  - I can draw ______
  - I can use a ruler ______

PROBLEM-SOLVING CHECKLIST

Make sure that you . . .

- ☐ tell what you know.
- ☐ tell what you need to do.
- ☐ show all your work.
- ☐ show that the solution works.

REFLECT

Use Mathematical Practices Talk about this question with a partner.

- **Persevere** What can you do if you get to a difficult part of the problem?

Discuss Models and Strategies

Solve the problem on a separate sheet of paper. There are different ways you can solve it.

Wood Scraps

Bella saves scraps of wood to reuse. She wants you to find:

- the length of each piece in inches.
- how many pieces there are of each length.
- the length of the shortest and longest pieces.
- the difference between the shortest and longest pieces.

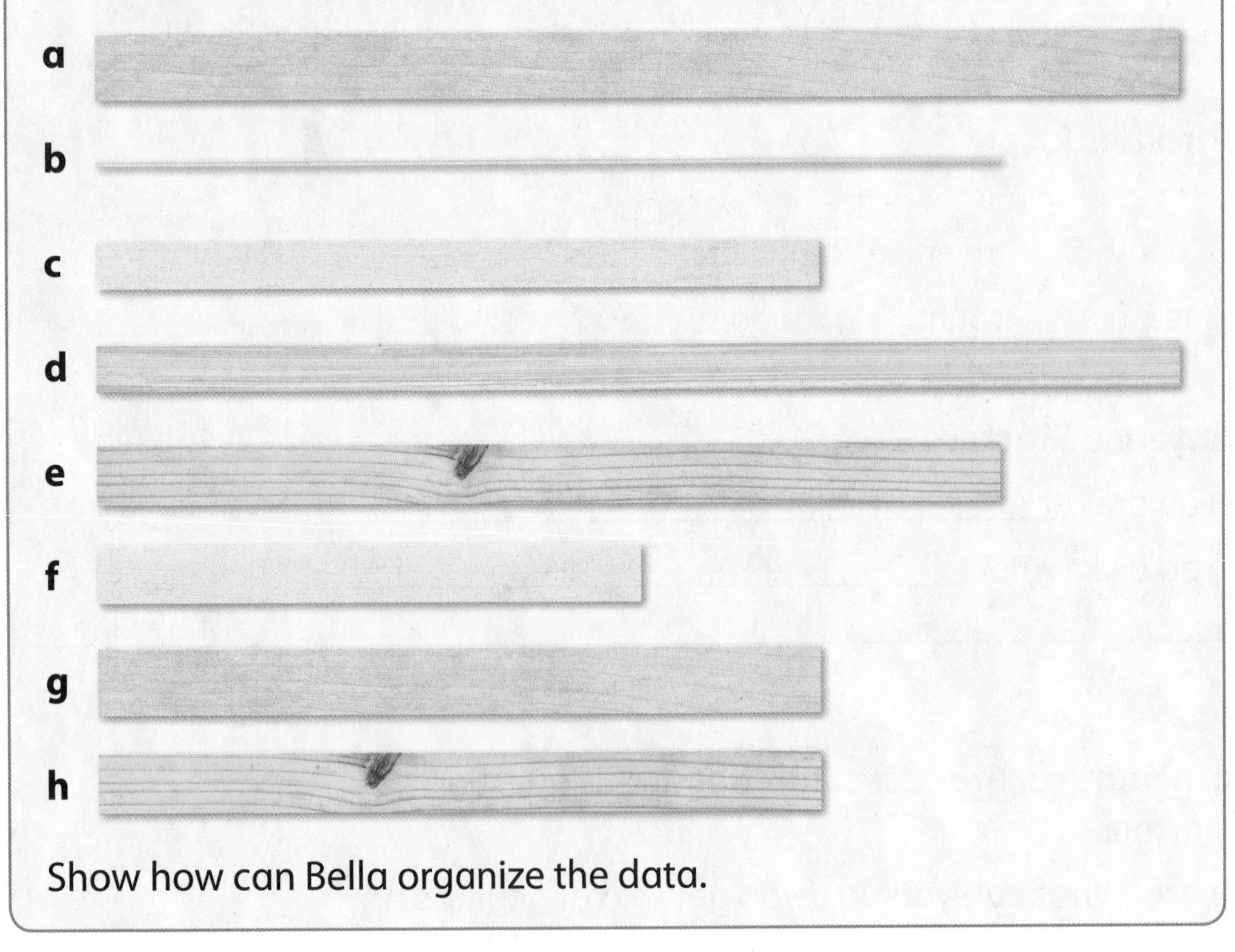

Show how can Bella organize the data.

PLAN IT AND SOLVE IT

Find a solution to Bella's Wood Scraps problem.

Make sure to do all parts of the task.

- Measure each piece of wood.
- Organize the data in a line plot or bar graph.
- Use words to describe the lengths of the scraps of wood.

You may want to use the Problem-Solving Tips to get started.

PROBLEM-SOLVING TIPS

- **Questions**
  - What tool should I use to measure?
  - How will I show the data?
- **Word Bank**

length	longer	shorter
difference	inches	longest
shortest	compare	

- **Sentence Starters**
  - The length of ______
  - The longest piece ______

PROBLEM-SOLVING CHECKLIST

Make sure that you . . .

- ☐ tell what you know.
- ☐ tell what you need to do.
- ☐ show all your work.
- ☐ show that the solution works.

REFLECT

Use Mathematical Practices Talk about this question with a partner.

- **Use Tools** How can you decide what measuring tool to use?

Persevere On Your Own

Solve each problem on a separate sheet of paper.

Craft Supplies

Bella likes to recycle items for her projects. But she still has to buy some things. Bella wants to buy at least one wooden heart and at least one wooden letter. She can spend up to $2.

Wooden hearts: 44¢ each **Wooden letters: 28¢ each**

How many hearts and letters can Bella buy? How many cents will she have left?

SOLVE IT

Help Bella decide what to buy.

- Tell how many hearts and letters to buy.
- Give the cost for the hearts and for the letters.
- Give the total cost.
- Tell how much money is left.

REFLECT

Use Mathematical Practices Talk about this question with a partner.

- **Use Structure** How did you use how many cents are in a dollar to solve the problem?

Bella's Bottles

Bella wants to make a garden border.

She will use red and blue recycled bottles to make it.

Read Bella's notes.

Garden	
Part A	**Part B**
Red Bottles	Blue Bottles

My Notes

- The whole border is between 60 and 72 inches.
- Part A is between 45 and 55 inches.
- Part B is between 15 and 25 inches.

How can Bella design her border?

SOLVE IT

Help Bella make a plan for her border.

- Write the length for each part.
- Show all your work.
- Tell why your measurements work.

REFLECT

Use Mathematical Practices Talk about this question with a partner.

- **Make an Argument** How did you show that your measurements work?

UNIT 4

Unit Review

1 Teddy has a pencil and a crayon.

Use a ruler to measure the length of each item in inches. Then compare the lengths. Write your answers in the blanks.

The crayon is .... inches long.

The pencil is .... inches long.

The crayon is .... inches shorter than the pencil.

2 Roger has an iguana and a gecko. The iguana is 32 inches long. The gecko is 14 inches long. Use the number line to find how many inches longer the iguana is than the gecko. Show your work.

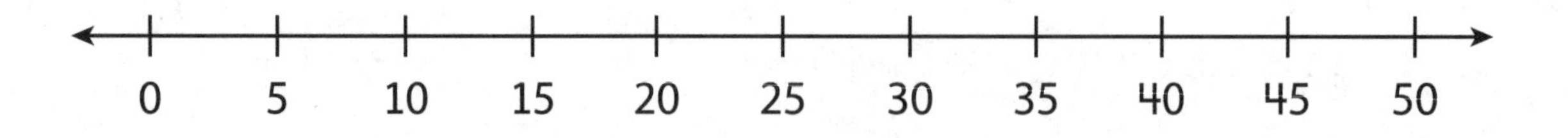

The iguana is .... inches longer than the gecko.

3. Catelyn has a rope that is 66 inches long. She cuts it into two pieces. Decide if each pair of lengths could be the lengths of the two pieces.
Choose *Yes* or *No* for each pair of lengths.

	Yes	No
44 inches and 24 inches	Ⓐ	Ⓑ
40 inches and 26 inches	Ⓒ	Ⓓ
35 inches and 32 inches	Ⓔ	Ⓕ
33 inches and 33 inches	Ⓖ	Ⓗ

4. Brett wants to measure the length of his car. Which unit should Brett measure with if he wants the length to be the fewest number of units?

Ⓐ yards

Ⓑ feet

Ⓒ inches

Ⓓ centimeters

5. Jay measures the lengths of some blocks. Use the measurements shown in the table to help Jay complete the line plot. Show your work.

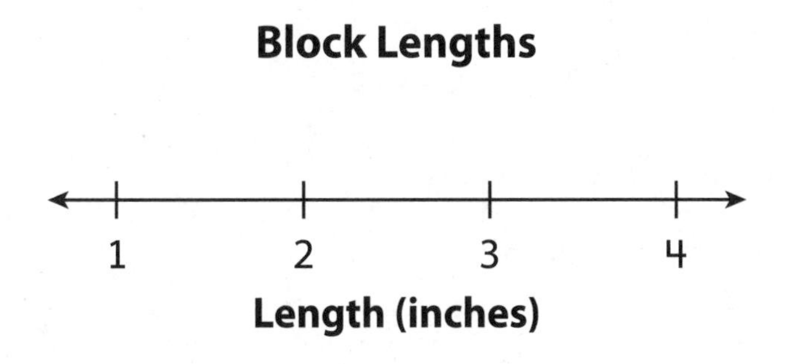

Block	Length (Inches)
A	3
B	2
C	1
D	4
E	4
F	3

Performance Task

Answer the questions. Show all your work on separate paper.

Measure 5 objects in inches and in centimeters. Make a table like the one below. Write the names of the objects and the lengths in the table.

Object	Length in Inches	Length in Centimeters

- What is the total length of all the objects in inches? What is the total length in centimeters?
- Compare the total lengths. Is there a greater number of centimeters or inches? Explain why.
- Use your measurements to make a line plot like the one below. The line plot can show inches or centimeters.

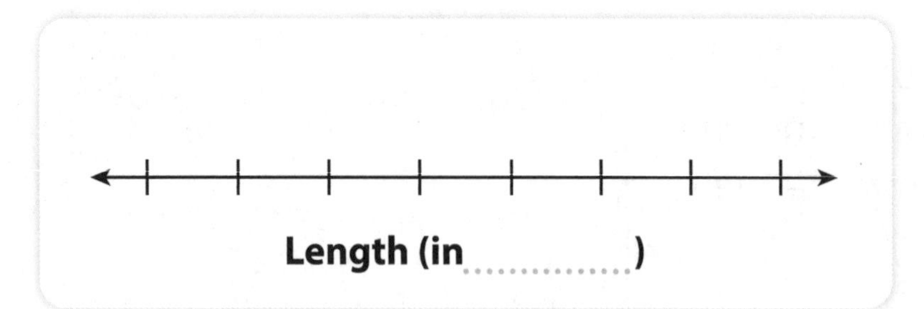

Checklist

Did you . . .

- ☐ measure each object using both units?
- ☐ check your answers?
- ☐ explain your answers?

REFLECT

Look for Structure What was different about measuring the objects using inches and measuring them using centimeters? What was the same?

UNIT 4

Vocabulary

Draw or write to show examples for each term.

centimeter (cm) a unit of length. There are 100 centimeters in 1 meter. Your little finger is about 1 centimeter across.

My Example

estimate (noun) a close guess made using mathematical thinking.

My Example

estimate (verb) to make a close guess based on mathematical thinking.

My Example

foot (ft) a unit of length. There are 12 inches in 1 foot.

My Example

inch (in.) a unit of length. There are 12 inches in one foot. A quarter is about 1 inch across.

My Example

length measurement that tells the distance from one point to another, or how long something is.

My Example

line plot a data display that shows data as marks above a number line.

My Example

measure to find length, height, or weight by comparing it to a known unit.

My Example

measuring tape a flexible measuring strip that shows inches and centimeters.

My Example

meter (m) a unit of length. There are 100 centimeters in 1 meter.

My Example

meter stick a measuring stick that is 1 meter long and shows 100 centimeters.

My Example

number line a straight line marked at equal spaces to show numbers.

My Example

ruler a measuring stick that is marked in inches and centimeters. It shows 12 inches and 30 centimeters.

My Example

yard (yd) a unit of length. There are 3 feet, or 36 inches, in 1 yard.

My Example

yardstick a measuring stick that is 1 yard long and shows 36 inches.

My Example

My Word: ____________________

____

____

My Example

My Word: ____________________

____

____

My Example

My Word: ____________________

____

____

My Example

My Word: ______________________

____

____

My Example

My Word: ______________________

____

____

My Example

My Word: ______________________

____

____

My Example

My Word: ______________________

____

____

My Example

My Word: ______________________

____

____

My Example

My Word: ______________________

____

____

My Example

UNIT

5

Shapes and Arrays

Partitioning and Tiling Shapes, Arrays, Evens and Odds

SELF CHECK

Before starting this unit, check off the skills you know below. As you complete each lesson, see how many more skills you can check off!

I can . . .	Before	After
Recognize and draw different shapes.	☐	☐
Break up a rectangle into squares.	☐	☐
Divide shapes into equal parts.	☐	☐
Find the total number of squares used to tile a rectangle by counting them.	☐	☐
Use addition to find the total number of objects in an array.	☐	☐
Find even and odd numbers.	☐	☐

Build Your Vocabulary

REVIEW

equal parts
halves
fourths
quarters
whole
unequal parts

Math Vocabulary

Use the review words to describe each picture.

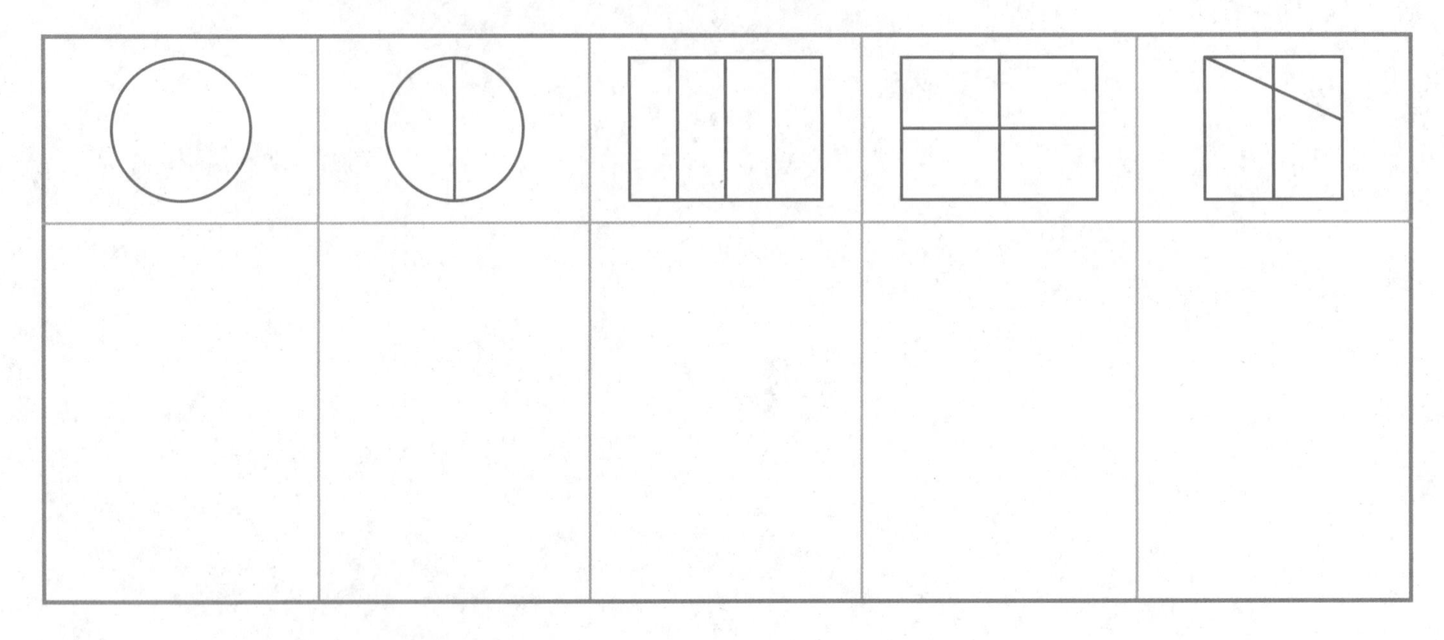

Academic Vocabulary

Put a check next to the academic words you know. Then use the words to complete the sentences.

☐ create ☐ restate ☐ category ☐ characteristic

1. Another word for trait is .... It describes something about a person or object.

2. A .... is a group of similar items.

3. To .... is to build things such as ideas, models, objects, and inventions.

4. When I .... my argument, I repeat or change the way I say it to make it clearer.

Recognize and Draw Shapes

LESSON 28

Dear Family,

This week your child is learning about recognizing and drawing shapes by paying attention to the characteristics they have.

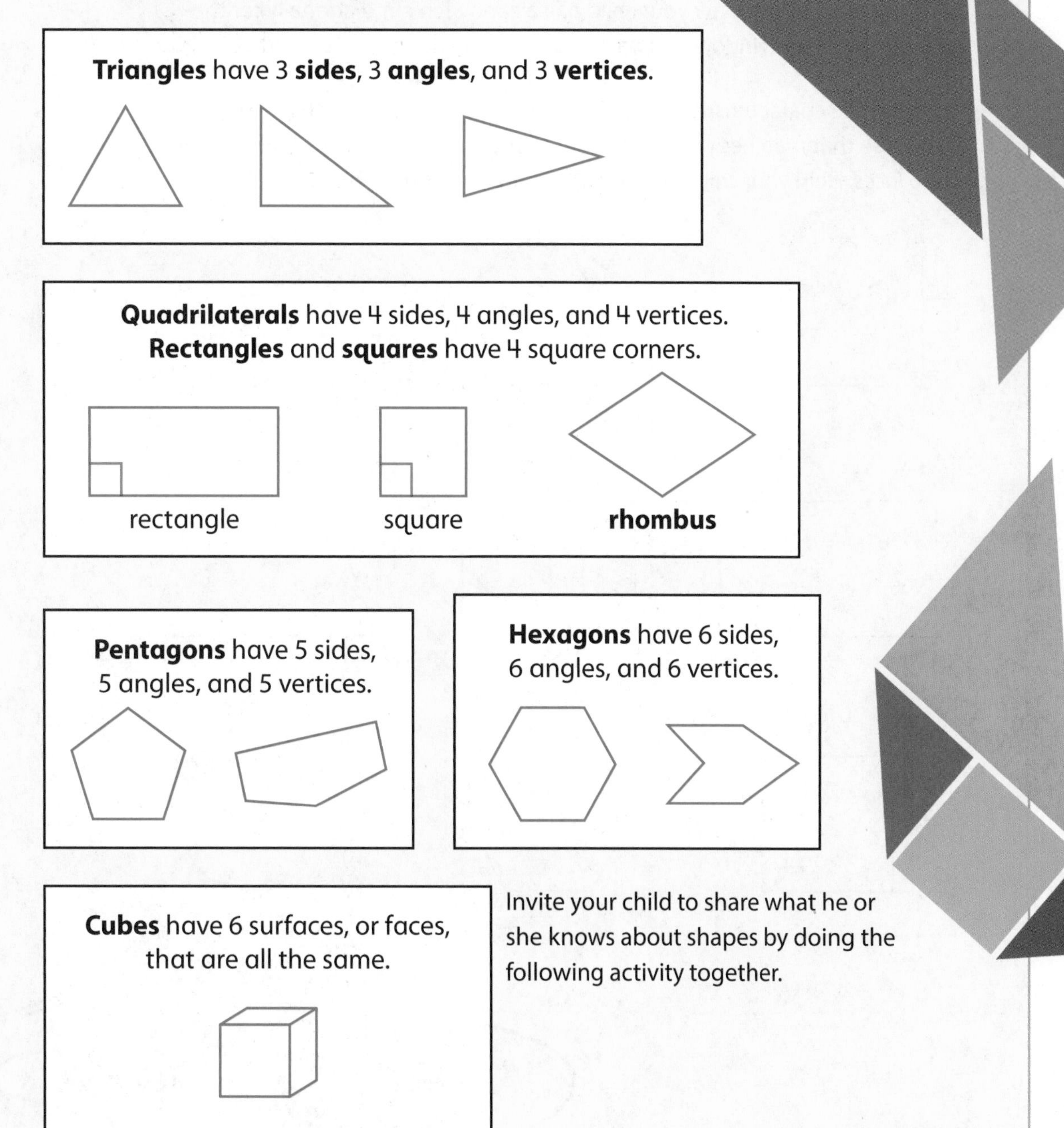

Invite your child to share what he or she knows about shapes by doing the following activity together.

ACTIVITY SHAPES

Do this activity with your child to explore shapes.

Materials real-world objects with geometric shapes, pencil

Work with your child to look for and name shapes based on their characteristics.

- Display real-world objects that match some of the shapes shown below. For example, you might show your child half a sandwich cut diagonally for the triangle, a square window that has 4 sides of same length and 4 vertices.
- Describe the characteristics of a shape shown below. Ask your child to circle the shape that matches your description. For example, say: *Circle the shape that has 6 faces*. Help your child to correctly identify and name the shape. Repeat.

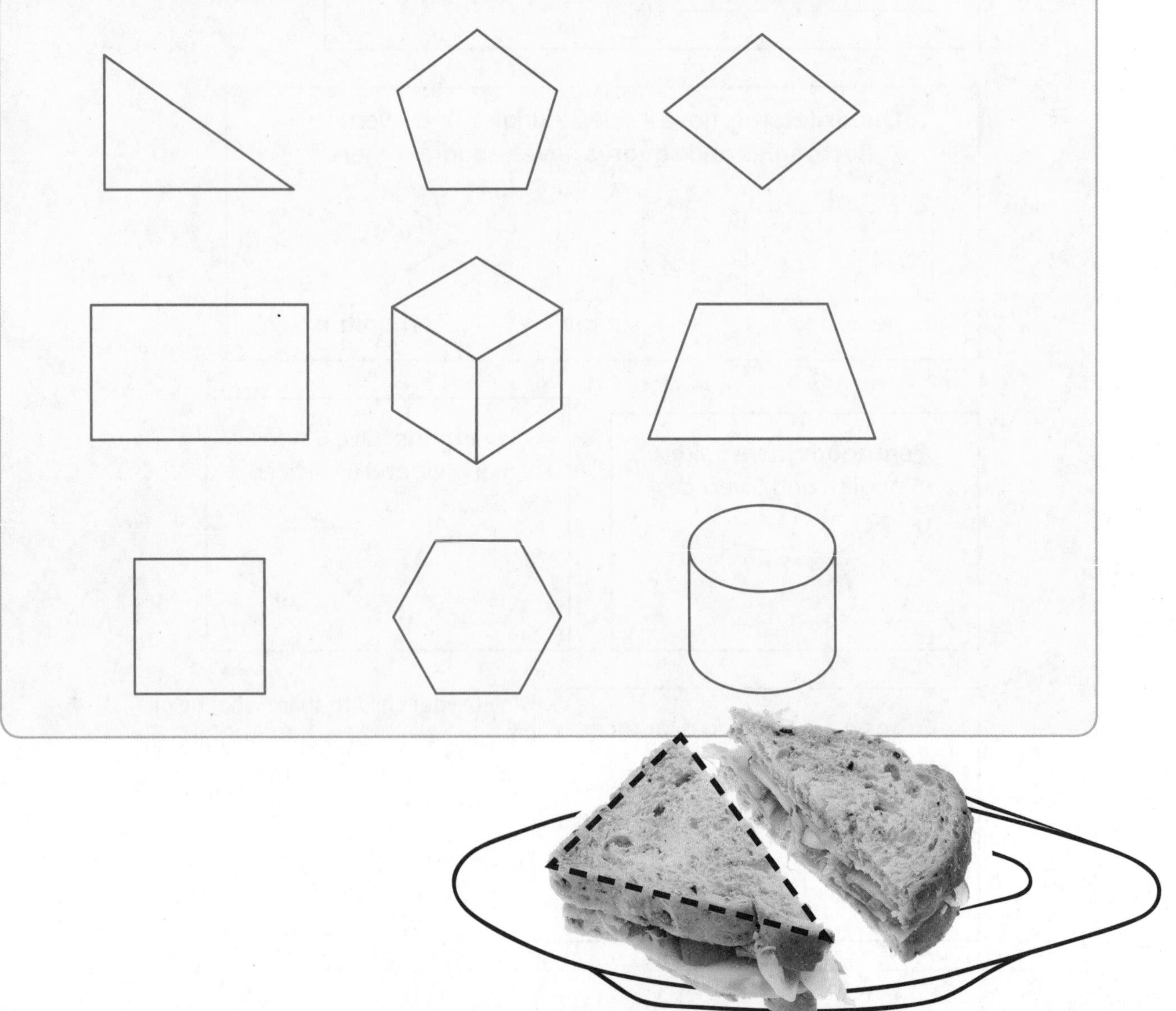

Explore Recognizing and Drawing Shapes

Learning Target

- Recognize and draw shapes having specified attributes, such as a given number of angles or a given number of equal faces. Identify triangles, quadrilaterals, pentagons, hexagons, and cubes.

SMP 1, 2, 3, 4, 5, 6, 7

You have worked with flat and solid shapes in different ways. Use what you know to try to solve the problem below.

Macy makes this collage. Use the key to color each shape.

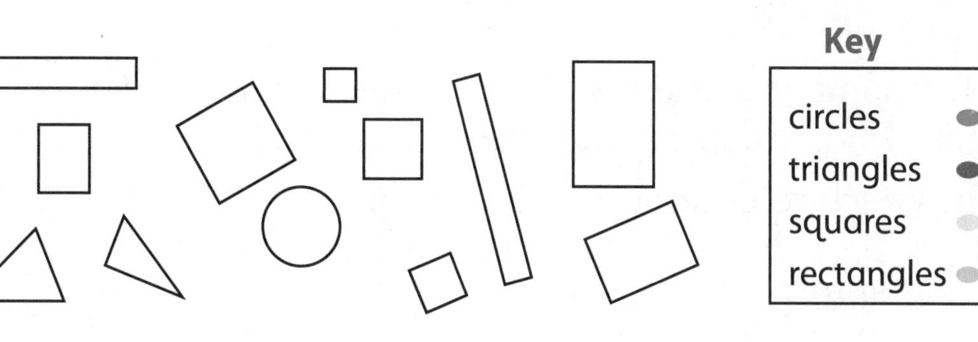

Key

- circles
- triangles
- squares
- rectangles

How many of each shape does she use?

TRY IT

Math Toolkit

- 1-centimeter grid paper
- ruler
- counters
- sticky notes
- color tiles

DISCUSS IT

Ask your partner: Do you agree with me? Why or why not?

Tell your partner: I agree with you about . . . because . . .

CONNECT IT

1 LOOK BACK

How many of each shape (circles, **triangles, squares, rectangles**) are in Macy's collage?

2 LOOK AHEAD

The number of **sides, vertices** (corners), and **angles** tells what group a shape belongs to.

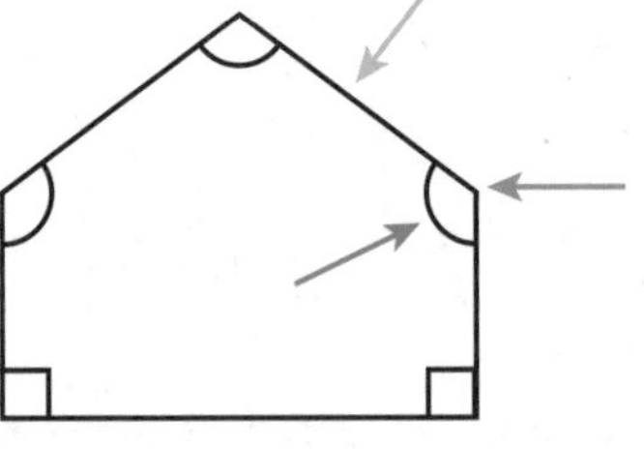

a. Which color arrow is pointing to:

a side? ....

a vertex? ....

an angle? ....

b. The shape formed by two sides at an angle is a vertex. How many vertices does this shape have?

....

c. A **quadrilateral** is a shape with 4 sides, 4 vertices, and 4 angles. Name a quadrilateral shape:

3 REFLECT

A **pentagon** has 5 sides, 5 vertices, and 5 angles. Is the shape above a pentagon? Explain.

....

....

Name: ______________________________

Prepare for Recognizing and Drawing Shapes

1. Think about what you know about shapes. Fill in each box. Use words, numbers, and pictures. Show as many ideas as you can.

Word	In My Own Words	Example
circle		
triangle		
rectangle		
square		

2. Is the shape below a rectangle? Explain.

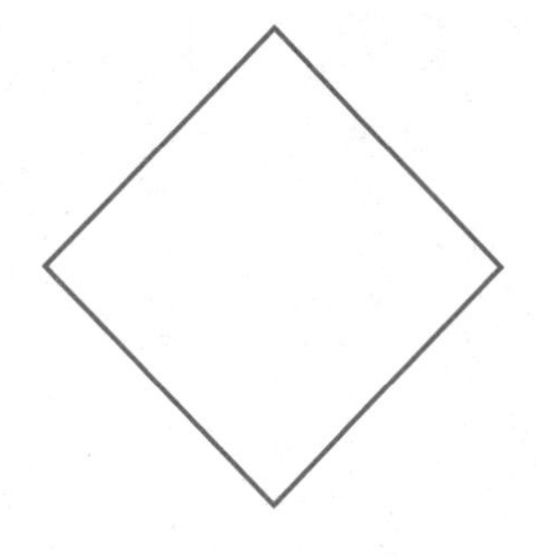

 Solve the problem.

Percy makes this collage. Use the key to color each shape.

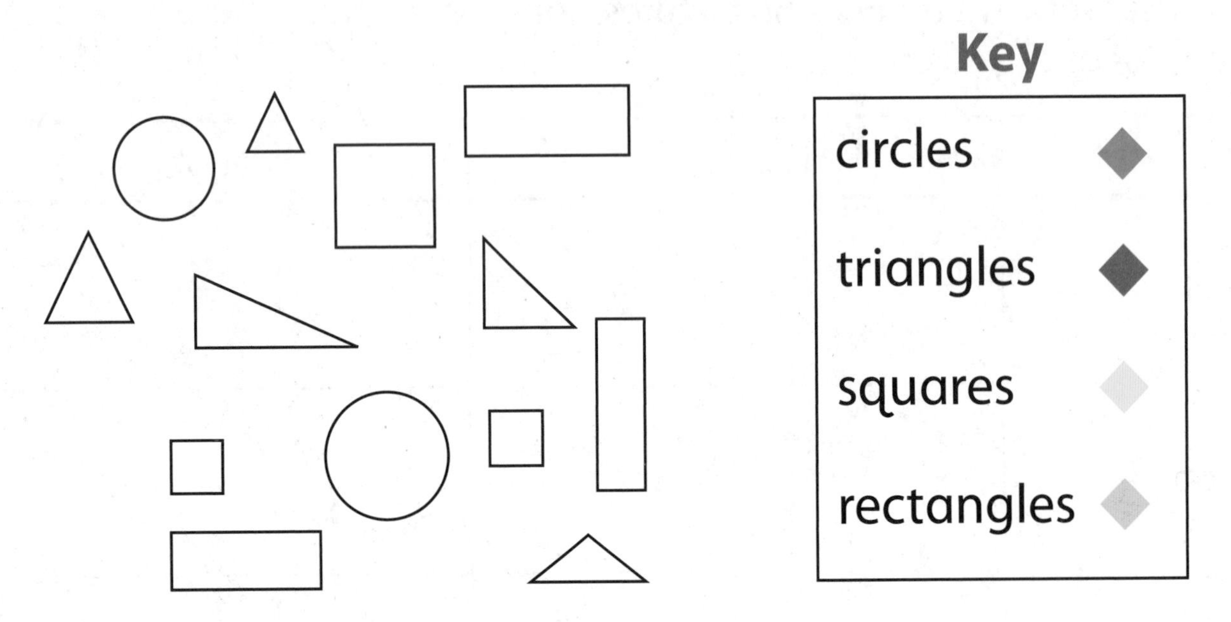

How many of each shape does he use?

Solution 

4 Check your answer. Show your work.

Name: ____________________

Practice Recognizing and Drawing Shapes

Study the Example showing how to name shapes and describe shapes. Then solve problems 1–5.

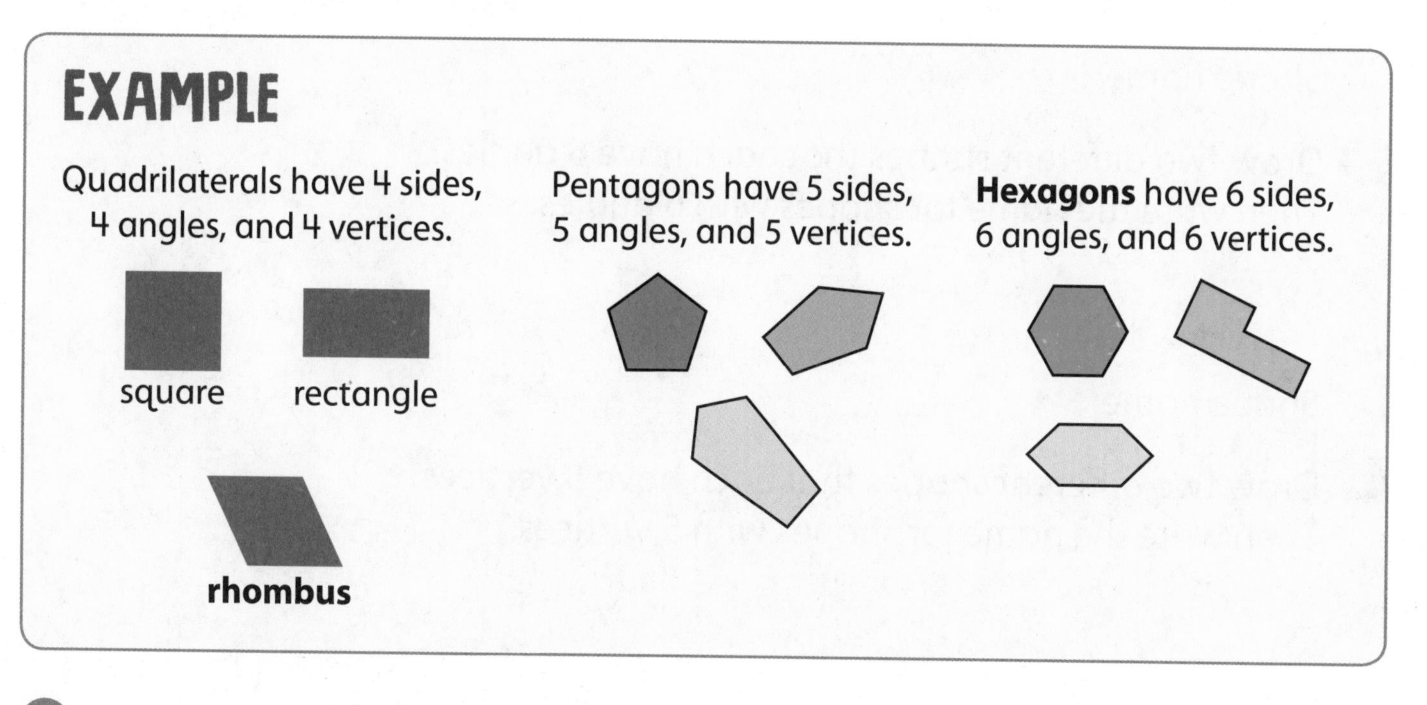

1. Look at the shapes below. Fill in the chart to name and describe each shape.

Shape A Shape B Shape C

Shape	Shape Name	Sides	Angles	Vertices
A				
B				
C				

Vocabulary

angle one of the corners of a shape where two sides meet.

vertex the point where two rays, lines, or line segments meet to form an angle.

2 Draw two different shapes that each have 3 sides.
Then write the name for shapes with 3 sides.

Shape name: ....

3 Draw two different shapes that each have 6 angles.
Then write the name for shapes with 6 angles.

Shape name: ....

4 Draw two different shapes that each have 5 vertices.
Then write the name for shapes with 5 vertices.

Shape name: ....

5 Fill in the blanks. Use the words in the box.

a. .... quadrilaterals have 4 vertices.

b. .... quadrilaterals have 5 angles.

c. .... quadrilaterals have sides the same length.

Some
No
All

Develop Recognizing and Describing Cubes

Read and try to solve the problem below.

Which shape is a cube? Tell how you know.

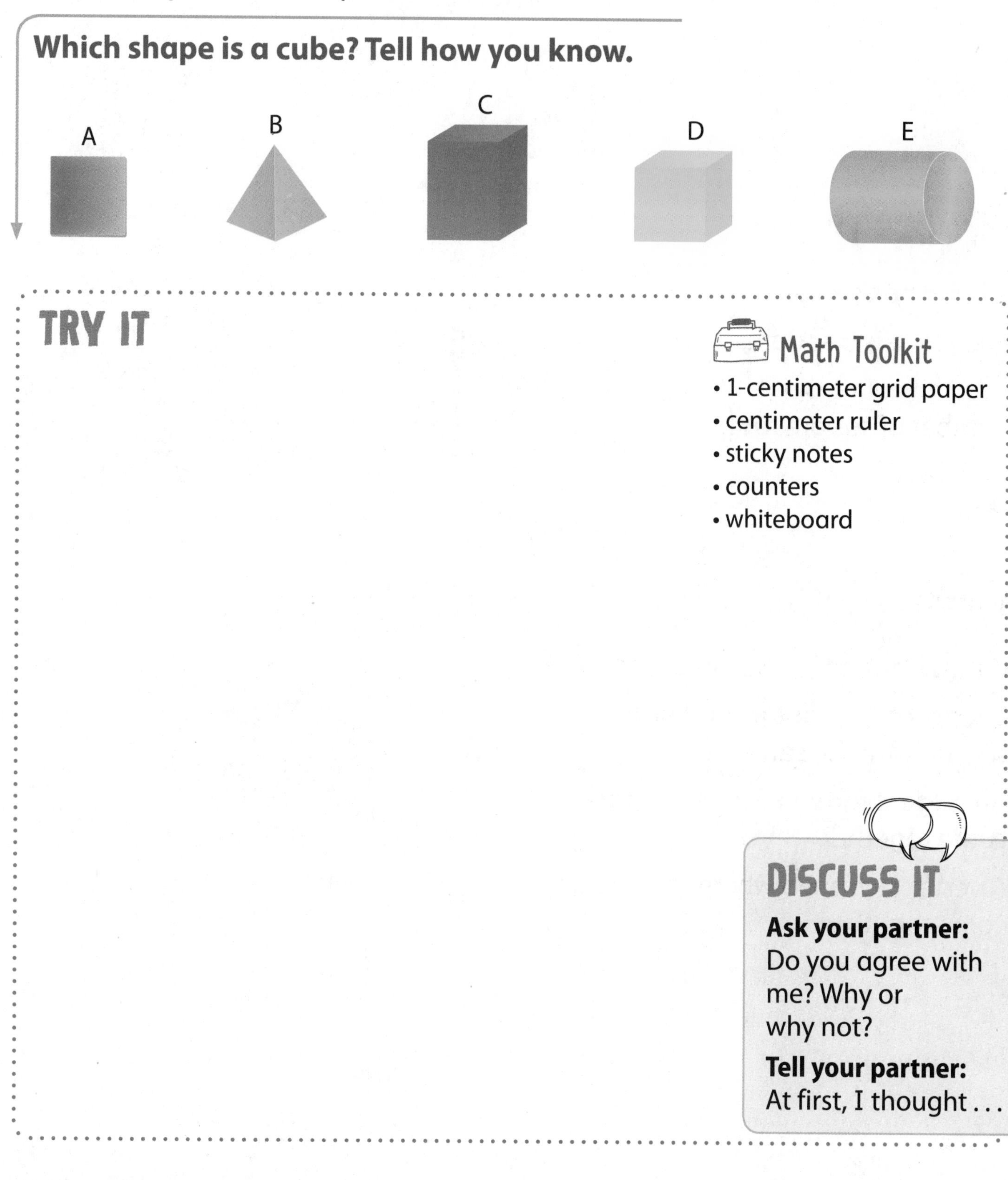

TRY IT

Math Toolkit

- 1-centimeter grid paper
- centimeter ruler
- sticky notes
- counters
- whiteboard

DISCUSS IT

Ask your partner: Do you agree with me? Why or why not?

Tell your partner: At first, I thought . . .

Explore different ways of recognizing cubes.

Which shape is a cube? Tell how you know.

A

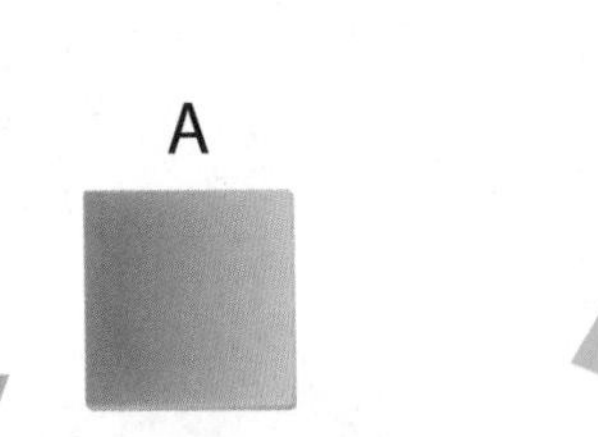

B

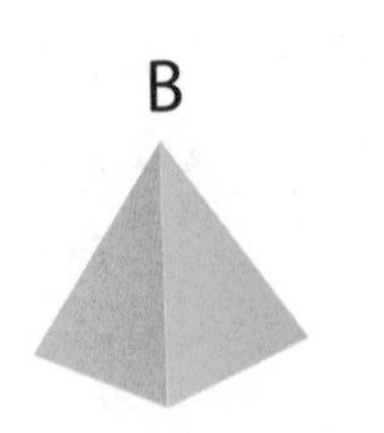

C

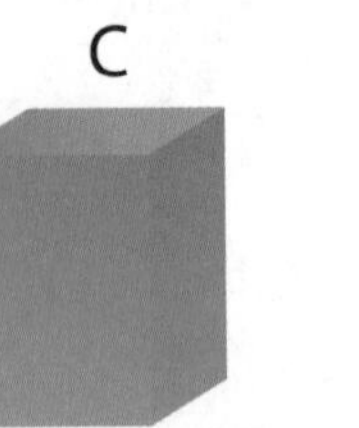

D

E

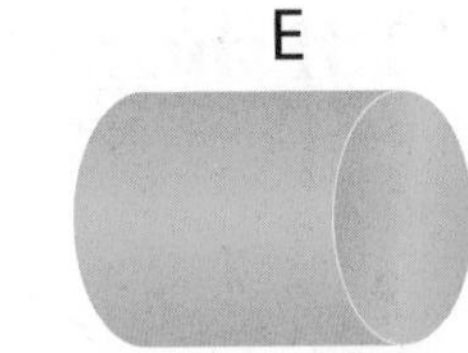

PICTURE IT

A **cube** has six faces.

Each face is a square.

You can count the number of square faces.

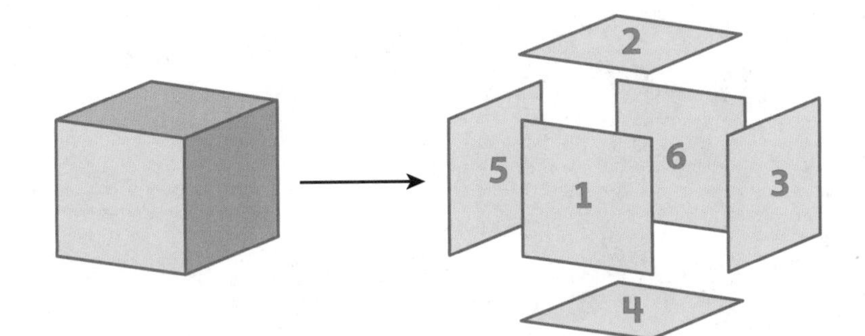

PICTURE IT

Cubes have edges, vertices, and faces.

Each face is a square, and all of the squares are the same size.

An **edge** is formed where two faces come together.

A vertex is formed where three edges come together.

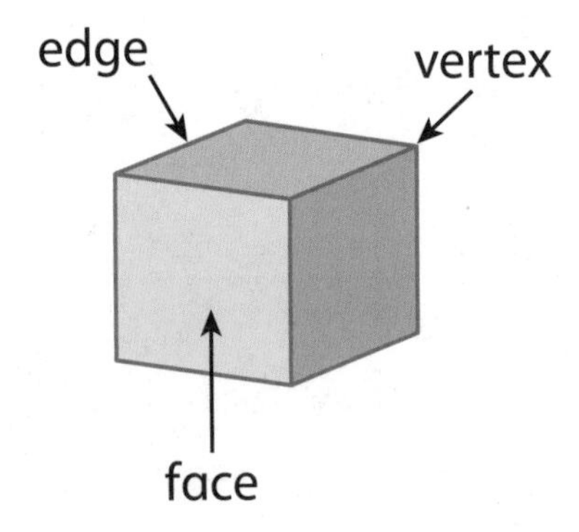

CONNECT IT

Now you will use the problem from the previous page to help you understand naming and describing cubes.

1 Look at the first **Picture It**. How many faces does a cube have? ....

2 Draw any face of a cube.

3 Which shape on the previous page is a cube? ....

4 Why is Shape C on the previous page not a cube?

5 Pick up a cube. How many edges does a cube have? How many vertices?

A cube has .... edges and .... vertices.

6 REFLECT

Look back at your **Try It**, strategies by classmates, and the **Picture Its**. Which models or strategies do you like best for identifying cubes? Explain.

....

....

....

APPLY IT

Use what you just learned to solve these problems.

7 Bonnie says this figure is a square. Marty says it is a cube. Who is correct? Explain.

Solution ....

....

....

 Which description is true for all cubes?

Ⓐ 6 square faces that are all the same

Ⓑ 6 sides and 6 vertices

Ⓒ 4 square faces that are all the same

Ⓓ 4 sides and 4 vertices

9 Tam puts together two cubes that are the same size and says his new solid shape is also a cube. Is Tam correct? How do you know? Use two cubes to model the problem.

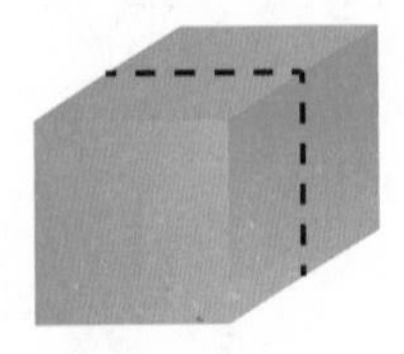

Name: ____________________

Practice Recognizing and Describing Cubes

Study the Example showing flat shapes and solid shapes. Then solve problems 1–3.

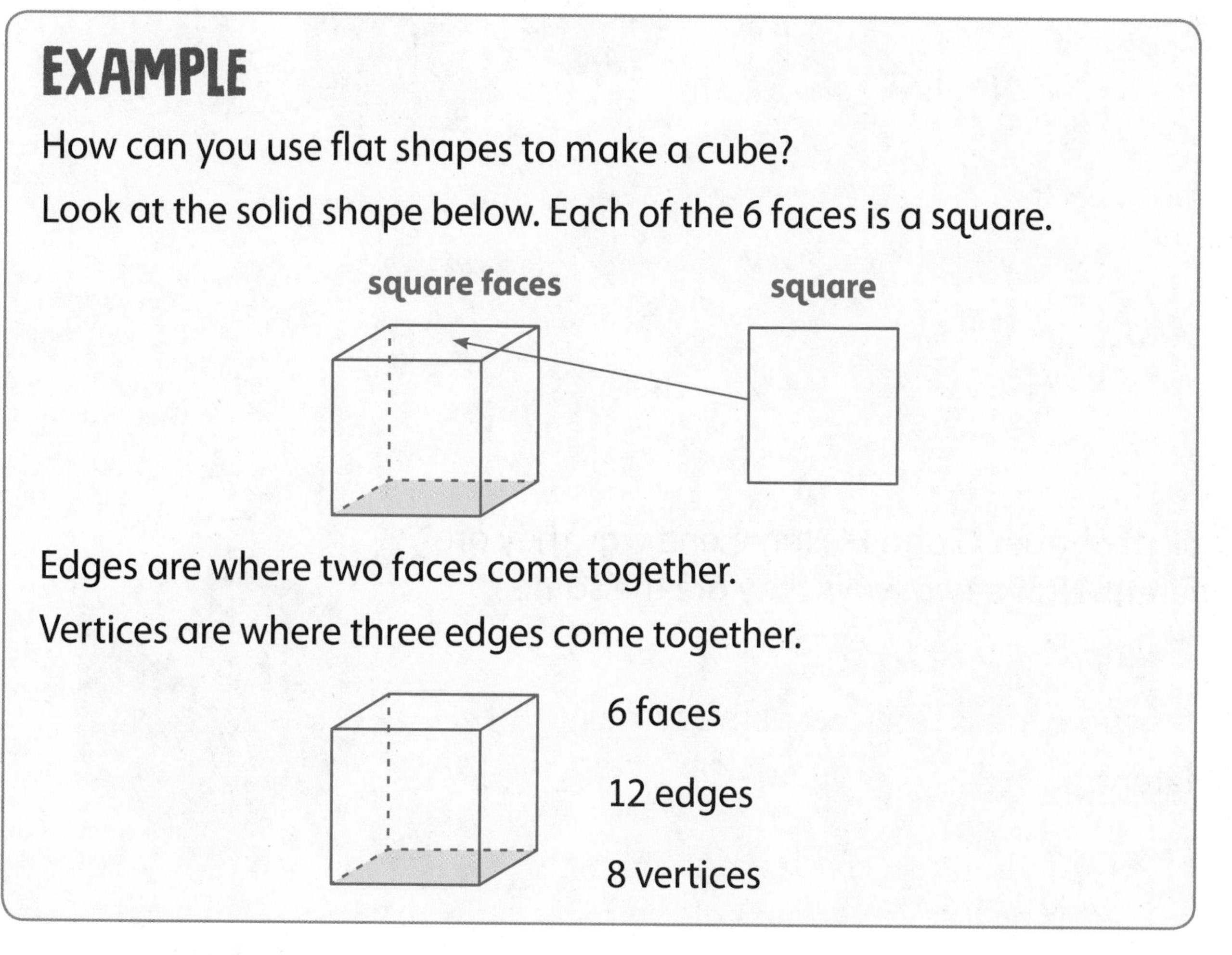

EXAMPLE

How can you use flat shapes to make a cube?

Look at the solid shape below. Each of the 6 faces is a square.

Edges are where two faces come together.

Vertices are where three edges come together.

6 faces

12 edges

8 vertices

APPLY IT

1 What does it mean for faces to be the same?

2 Which of these shapes are cubes? Write the letter of each shape that is a cube. Explain how you know.

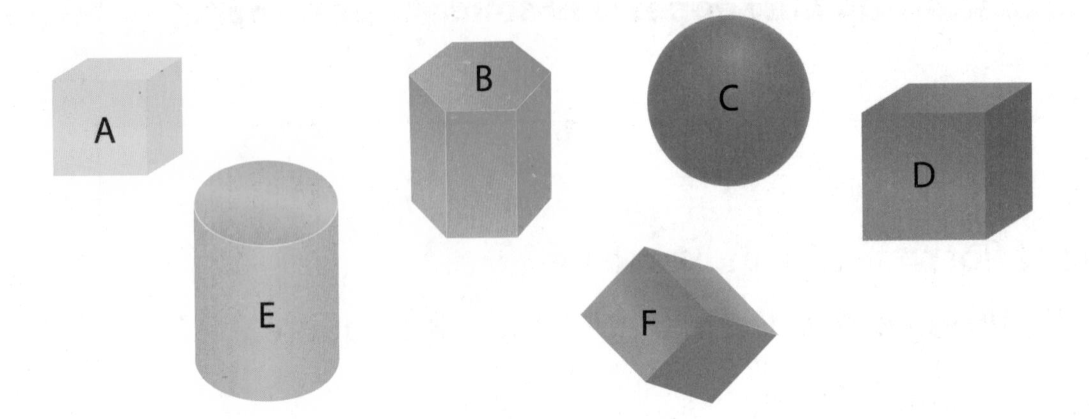

3 Look at Shapes G and H. Name one way they are different. Name two ways they are the same.

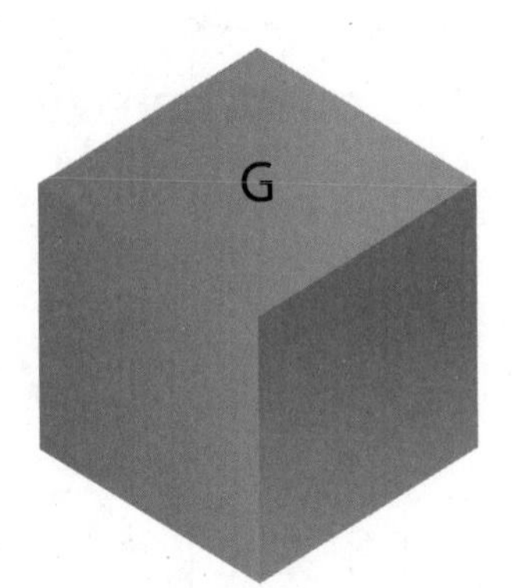

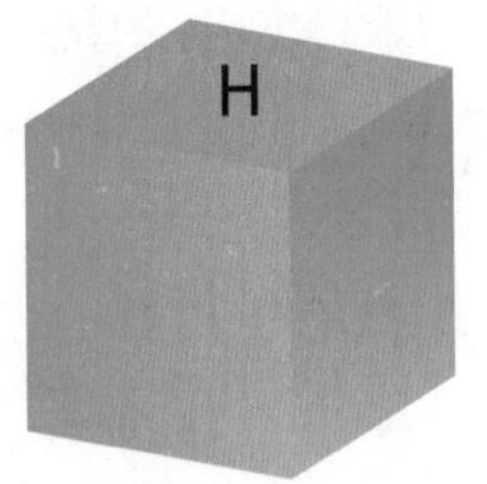

Different:

1. ....

The same:

1. ....

2. ....

Refine Recognizing and Drawing Shapes

Complete the Example below. Then solve problems 1–3.

EXAMPLE

Lin draws a shape with 6 sides. Draw a shape that could be Lin's on the dot grid below. Number the sides and tell the name of the shape.

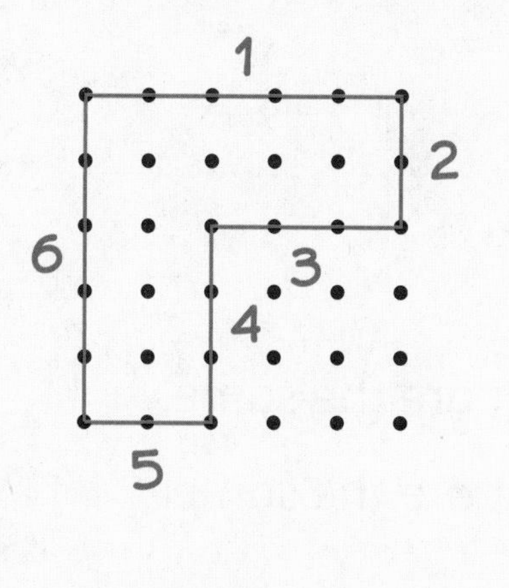

Solution ....

APPLY IT

1 Draw a shape that has 5 sides. Write the name of the shape. Show your work.

You can use the dots as the corners of your shape.

Solution ....

2 Solve the riddle.

I have fewer sides than a pentagon.

I am not a quadrilateral.

What am I? Show your work.

What shapes have fewer sides than a pentagon?

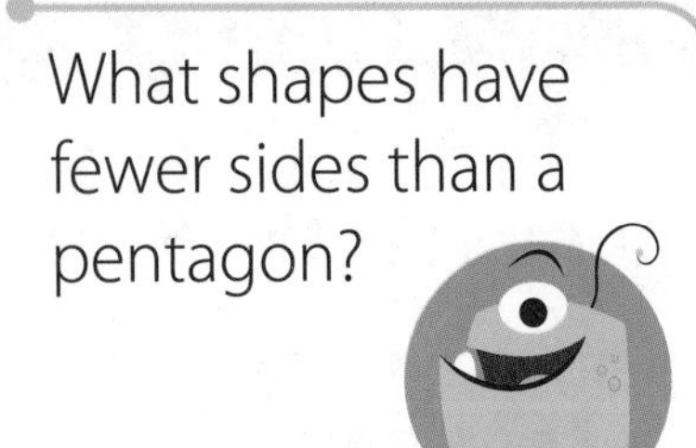

Solution ....

3 Which statement is true?

Ⓐ Cubes are not solid shapes.

Ⓑ Cubes have exactly 4 faces that are the same.

Ⓒ Cubes have exactly 6 faces that are the same.

Ⓓ Cubes have exactly 6 vertices.

Alma chose Ⓓ as the answer. How did Alma get her answer?

Draw a cube. Draw an arrow that points to each corner. Label the arrows to show the number of corners.

Practice Recognizing and Drawing Shapes

1 Choose *True* or *False* for each sentence.

	True	False
All hexagons have 5 angles.	Ⓐ	Ⓑ
All squares have 4 vertices.	Ⓒ	Ⓓ
All triangles have 3 equal sides.	Ⓔ	Ⓕ
All hexagons have more sides than triangles have.	Ⓖ	Ⓗ

You can draw a picture of each shape to help you.

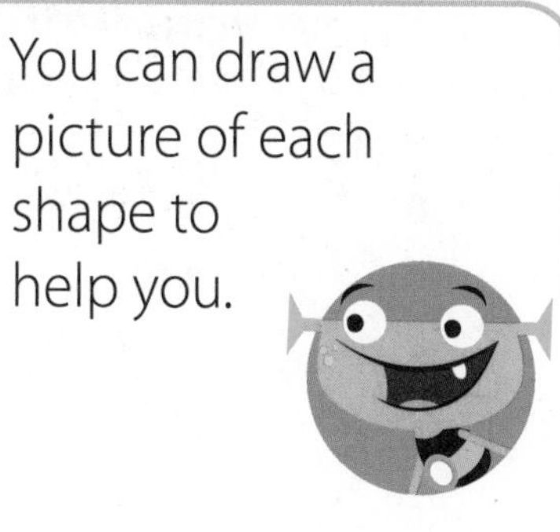

2 Which shape has fewer sides than a quadrilateral? Circle the correct answer.

Ⓐ pentagon

Ⓑ hexagon

Ⓒ triangle

Ⓓ square

How many sides does a quadrilateral have?

Nina chose Ⓓ. How did Nina get her answer?

3 Draw a flat shape that has 6 sides. Write the name of the shape. You may use the dots to help you. Show your work.

You can use the dots as the corners of your shape.

Solution ....

4 Draw a flat shape that has 5 vertices. Write the name of the shape. You may use the dots to help you. Show your work.

How many sides are made when you connect 5 vertices?

Solution ....

5 Which of the following are true?

Ⓐ A triangle never has equal sides.

Ⓑ A quadrilateral has 6 angles.

Ⓒ A pentagon has 5 vertices.

Ⓓ A hexagon has 6 sides.

Ⓔ A cube always has faces that are the same.

What do you know about each of these shapes?

Refine Recognizing and Drawing Shapes

APPLY IT

Solve the problems.

1 Fill in the blanks. Use the words in the box.

a. .... triangles have 3 sides.

b. .... triangles have sides the same length.

c. .... triangles have 4 angles.

Some
No
All

2 Ross draws a shape with exactly 6 angles. Which are true about his shape?

Ⓐ It is a pentagon.

Ⓑ It has exactly 6 sides.

Ⓒ It has exactly 5 vertices.

Ⓓ It is a hexagon.

Ⓔ It cannot be a quadrilateral.

Ⓕ It could be a triangle.

3 Which are true about this shape?

Ⓐ It is a pentagon.

Ⓑ It is a quadrilateral.

Ⓒ It has 5 vertices.

Ⓓ It has exactly 3 angles.

Ⓔ It is a hexagon.

 Sort the shapes. Write the letter in the correct column.

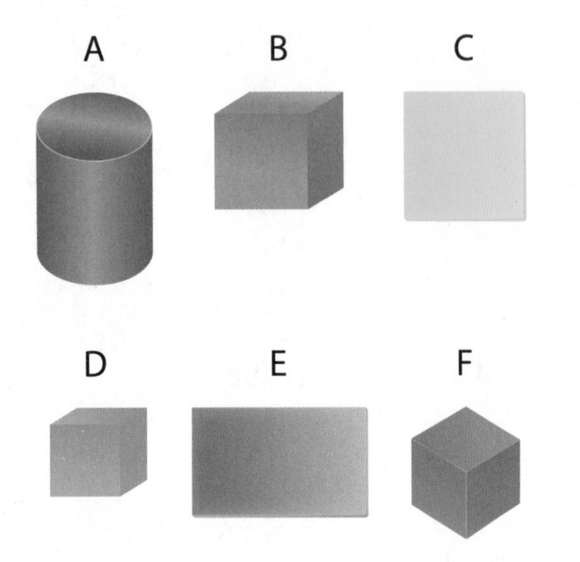

Cube	Not a Cube

5 Marisol stores blocks in a shoe box. Is a shoe box usually a cube? Explain why or why not.

 MATH JOURNAL

Draw a shape that has between 3 and 6 sides. Use the dots below. What is the name of your shape? Explain how you know.

SELF CHECK Go back to the Unit 5 Opener and see what you can check off.

Understand Partitioning Shapes into Halves, Thirds, and Fourths

LESSON 29

Dear Family,

This week your child is exploring the idea of equal parts of whole rectangles and circles to get ready for working with fractions next year.

Your child will see whole rectangles and circles cut into 2, 3, or 4 equal parts.

2 equal parts are called halves. Each of these parts is called **one half** of the whole.

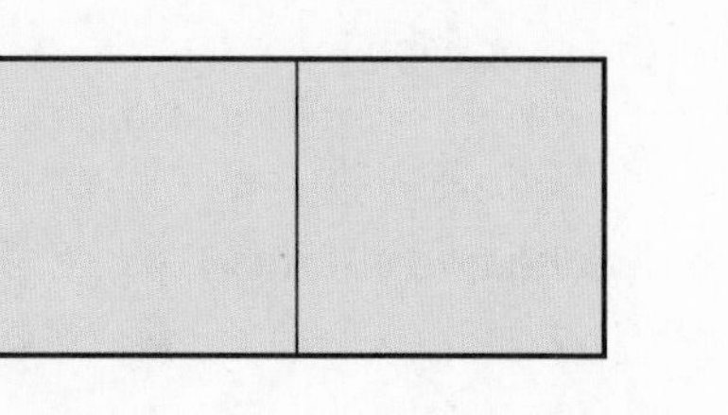
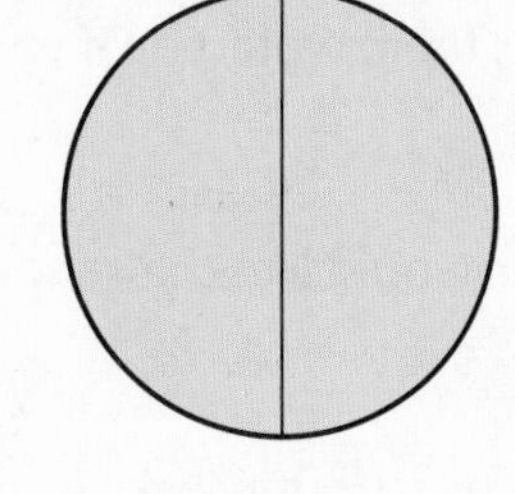

3 equal parts are called **thirds**. Each of these parts is called **one third** of the whole.

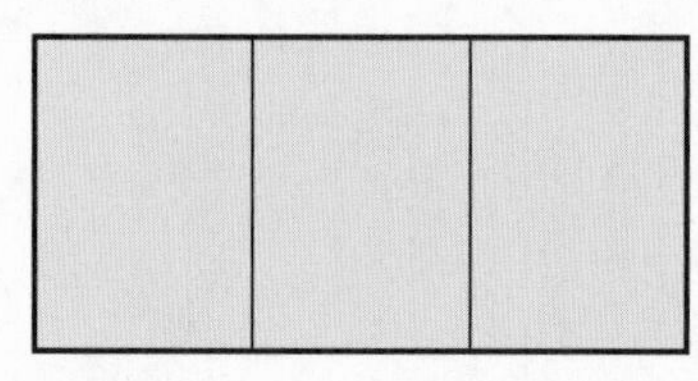
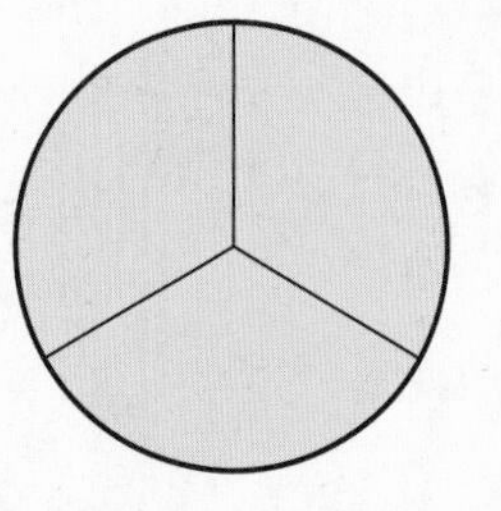

4 equal parts are called fourths. Each of these parts is called **one fourth** of the whole.

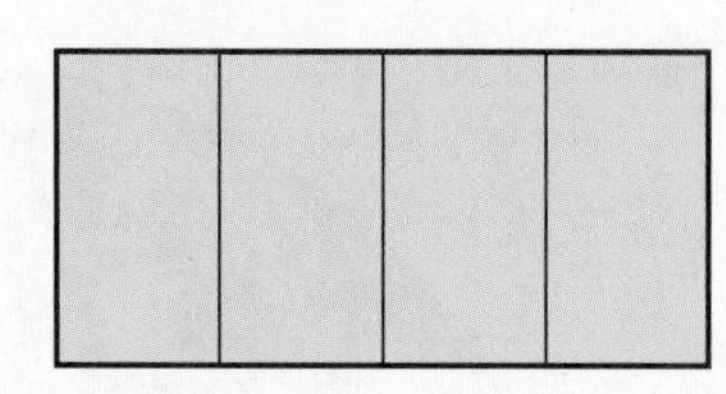
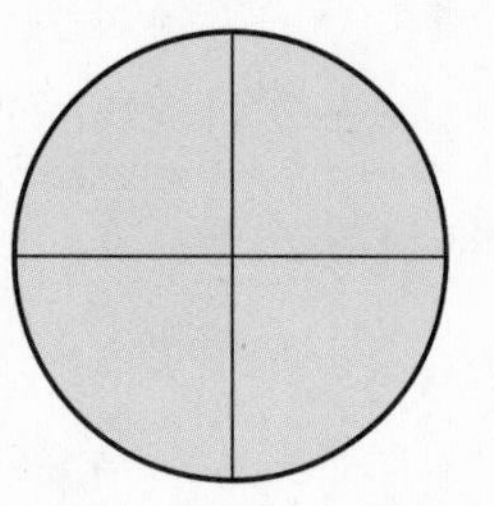

Invite your child to share what he or she knows about halves, thirds, and fourths by doing the following activity together.

ACTIVITY EQUAL PARTS

Do this activity with your child to understand halves, thirds, and fourths in shapes.

Materials sandwich ingredients, including square bread slices

Along with your child, make a sandwich using square pieces of bread.

- Ask your child to show with his or her finger how to cut the sandwich into halves. Ask your child to show you more than one way. Talk about how many pieces there would be if you cut the sandwich into halves.
- Ask your child to show you how to cut the sandwich into thirds and fourths. Talk about how many pieces there would be if you cut the sandwich into thirds or into fourths.
- Ask your child how he or she would like the sandwich divided and cut the sandwich accordingly.

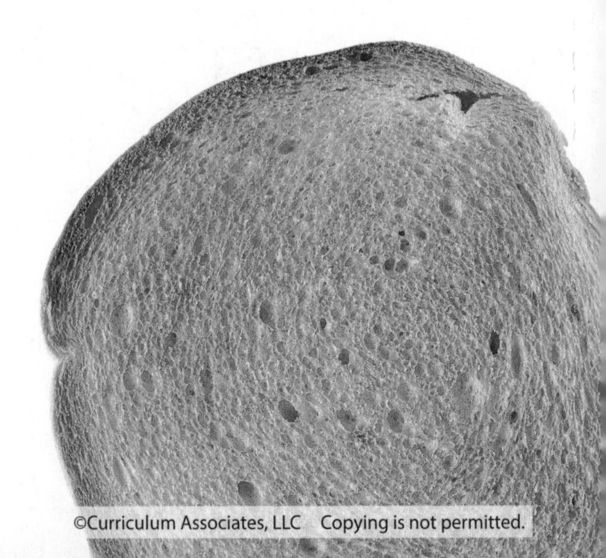

Explore Partitioning Shapes into Halves, Thirds, and Fourths

How do you divide shapes into 2, 3, and 4 equal parts?

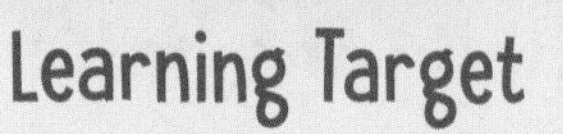

Learning Target

- Partition circles and rectangles into two, three, or four equal shares, describe the shares using the words *halves, thirds, half of, a third of*, etc., and describe the whole as two halves, three thirds, four fourths. Recognize that equal shares of identical wholes need not have the same shape.

SMP 1, 2, 3, 4, 5, 6, 7

MODEL IT

Complete the models and sentences below.

1. Shade **one fourth** of this square.

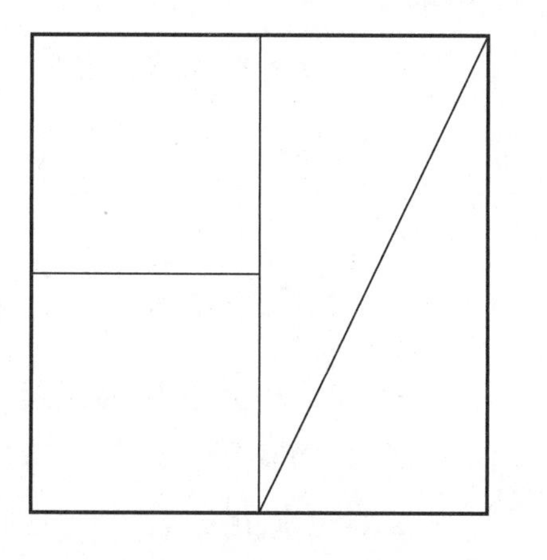

The whole square is .... fourths.

2. Shade one fourth of this square.

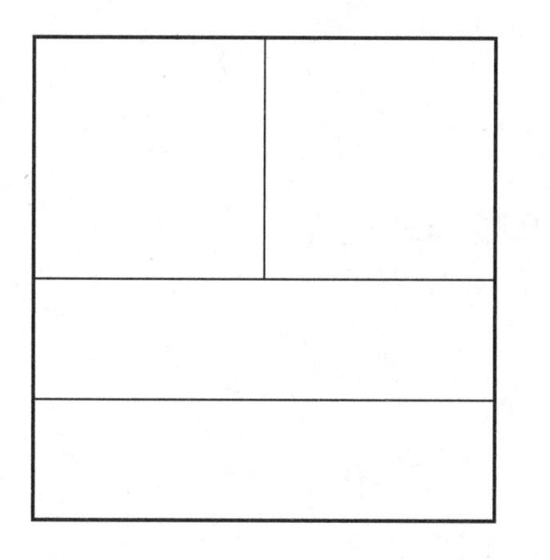

The whole square is .... fourths.

DISCUSS IT

- Compare your shaded fourths to your partner's shaded fourths. Are they the same?
- I know I have shaded one fourth of the square because . . .

MODEL IT

Complete the models and sentences below.

3 Shade **one half** of each square.

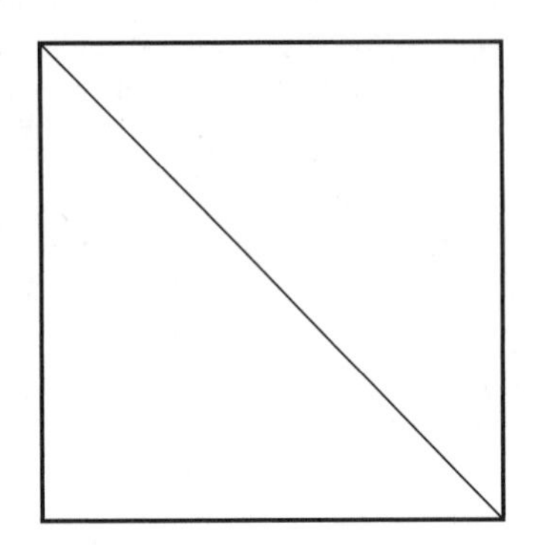

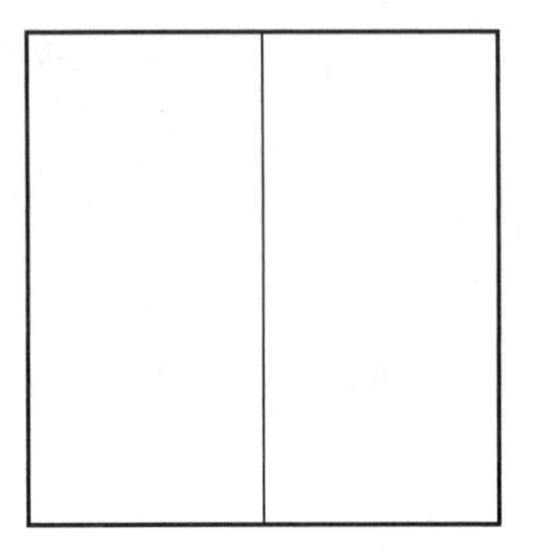

Each whole square is .... halves.

4 Shade **one third** of each square.

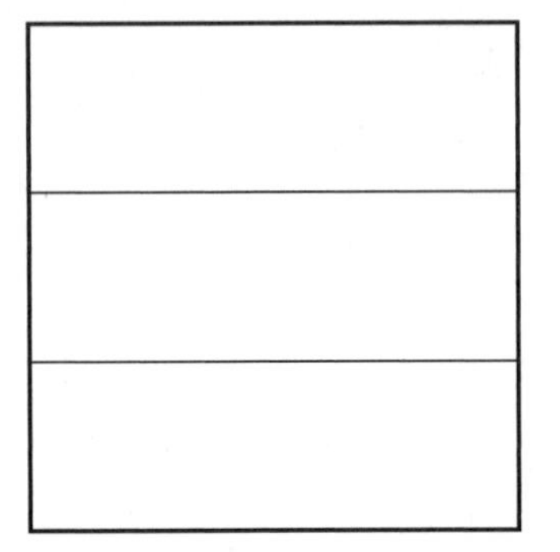

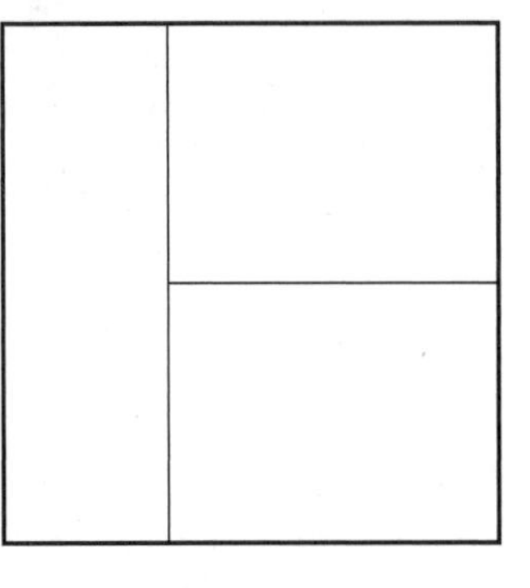

Each whole square is .... **thirds**.

DISCUSS IT

- What tells you the name of the part?
- I knew the square was divided into thirds because . . .

5 REFLECT

Look at all the squares divided above. Which parts are bigger, the halves or thirds? Explain.

....

....

....

Prepare for Partitioning Shapes into Halves, Thirds, and Fourths

1. Think about what you know about equal parts. Fill in each box. Use words, numbers, and pictures. Show as many ideas as you can.

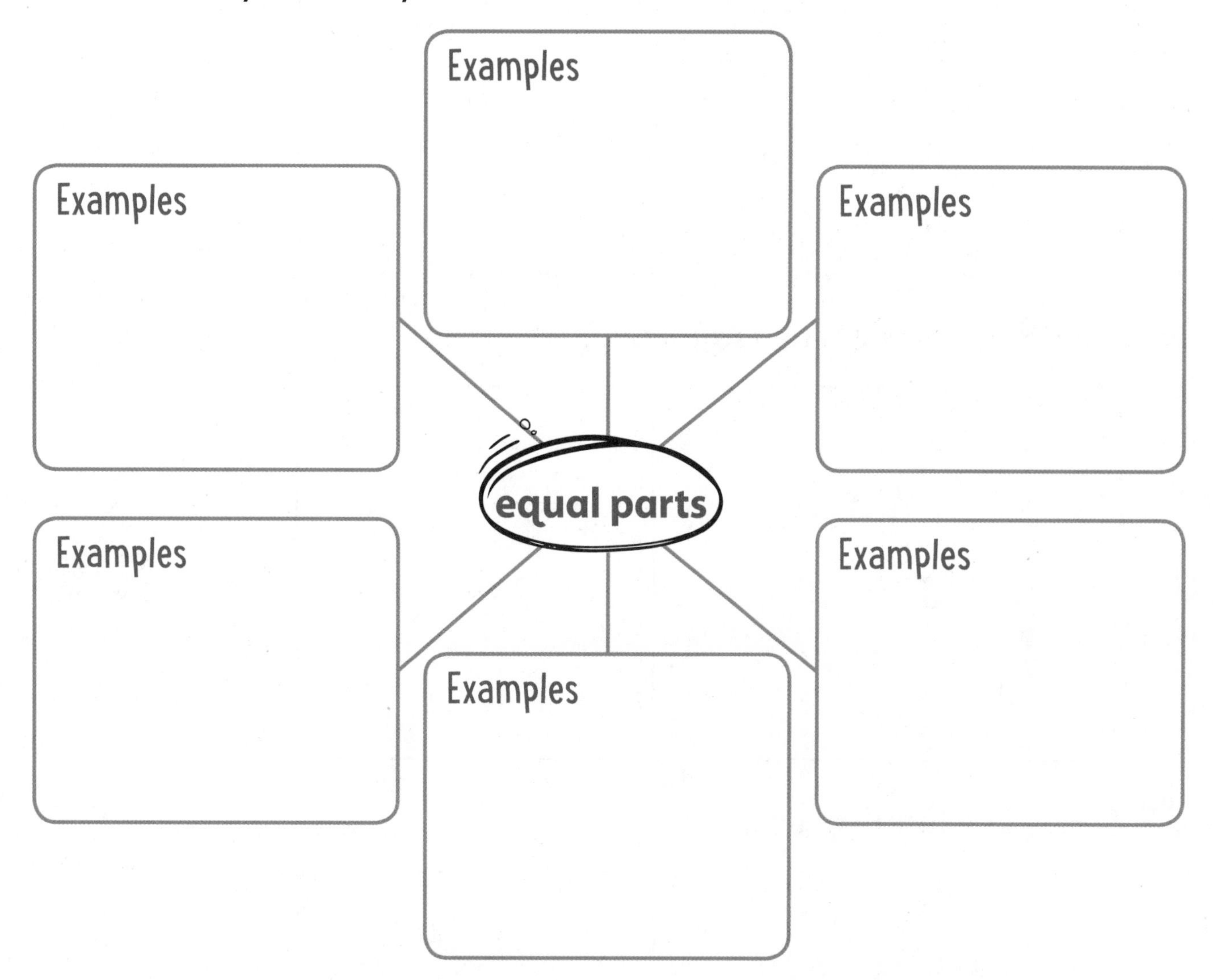

2. Jenna says that she has shaded one third of this square. Do you agree? Explain.

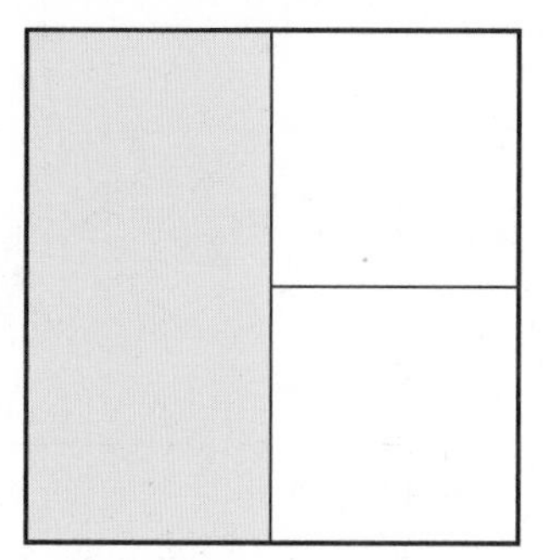

Solve.

3 Shade one half of each square.

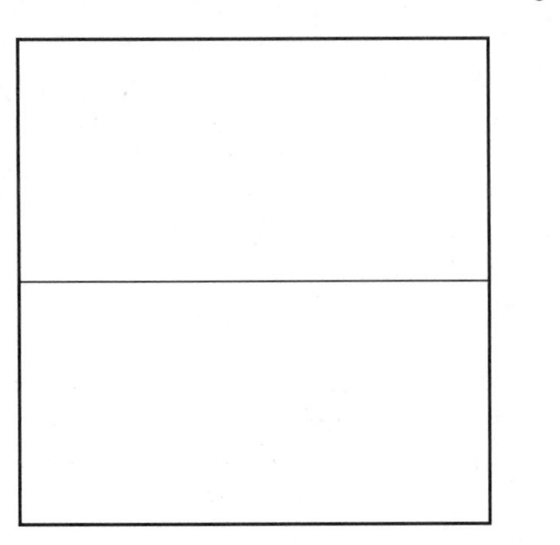

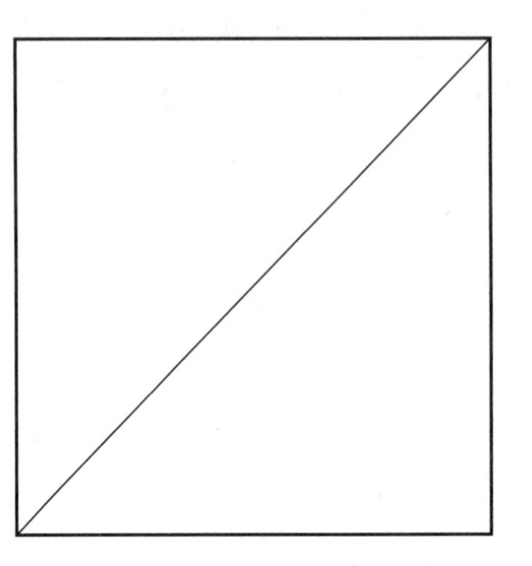

4 Shade one third of each square.

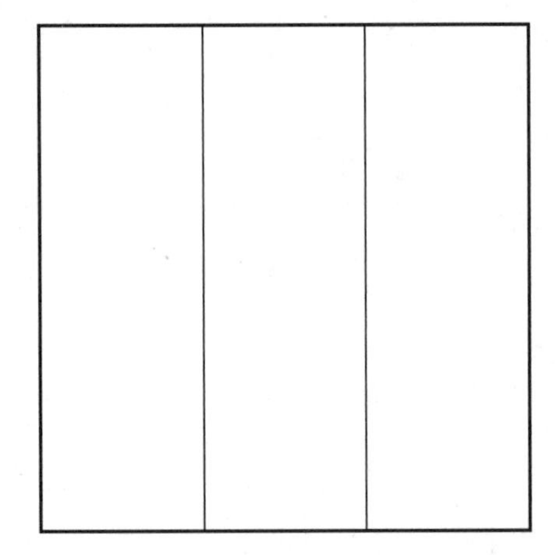

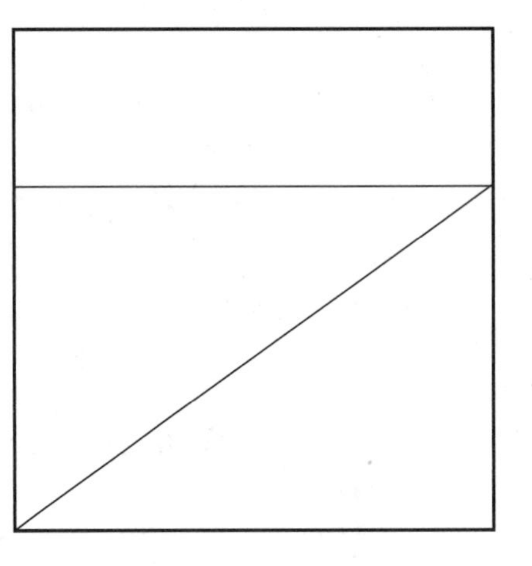

5 Shade one fourth of each square.

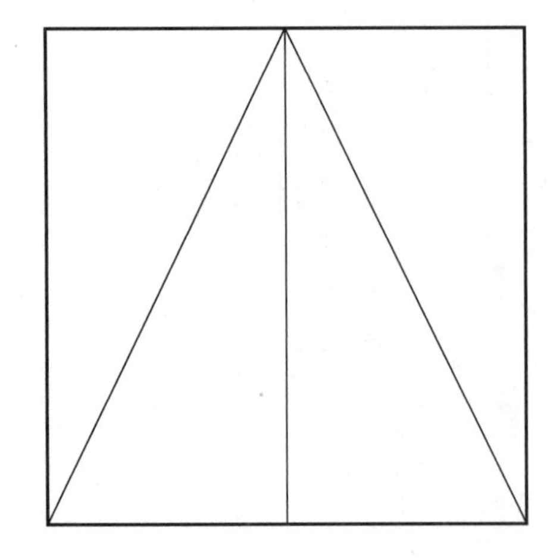

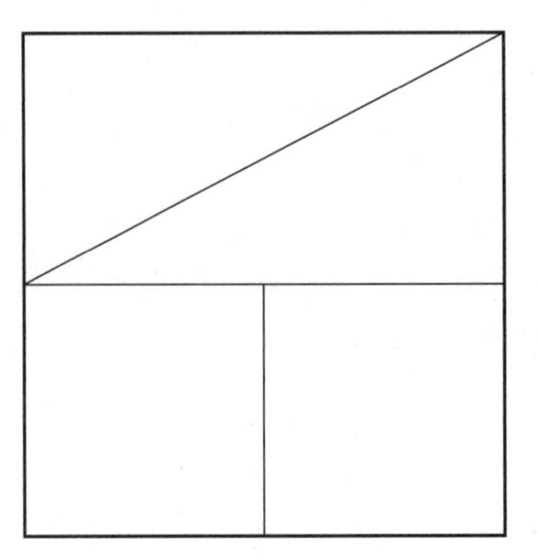

Develop Understanding of Partitioning Shapes Into Equal Parts

MODEL IT: RECTANGLE AREA MODELS

Try these three problems.

Divide the rectangles into the number of equal parts shown. Then use words from the box to complete the sentences.

half
third
fourth

1 Four equal parts

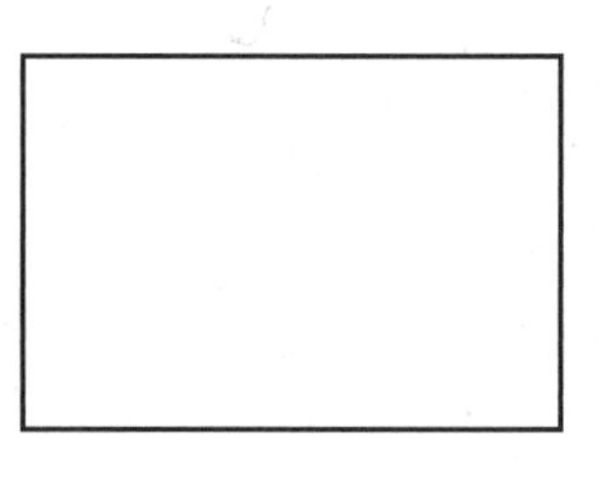

Each part is a .... of the whole rectangle.

2 Two equal parts

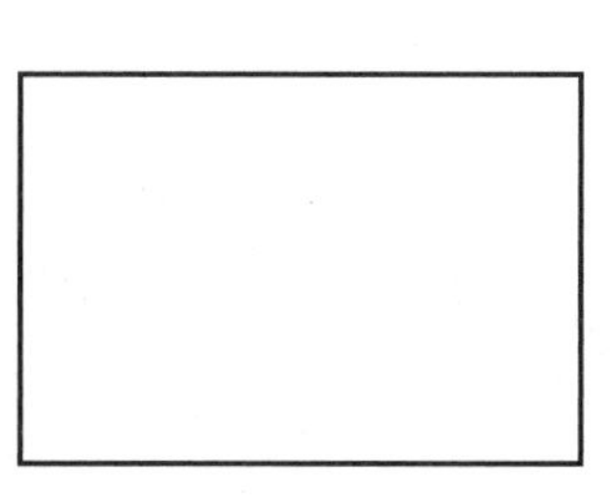

Each part is a .... of the whole rectangle.

3 Three equal parts

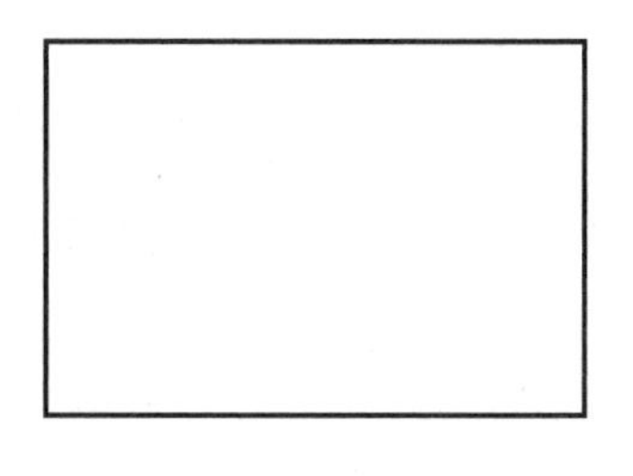

Each part is a .... of the whole rectangle.

DISCUSS IT

- How can you check that each third takes up the same amount of the rectangle?
- I think two is less than three but halves are larger than thirds because . . .

MODEL IT: CIRCLE AREA MODELS

Divide the circles into the number of equal parts shown.

4 Two equal parts

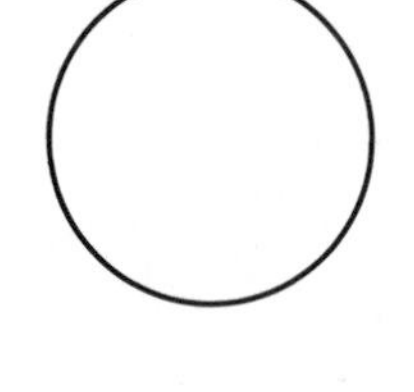

5 Three equal parts

DISCUSS IT

- How can you describe the parts of each circle?
- I know the parts are equal because . . .

6 Four equal parts

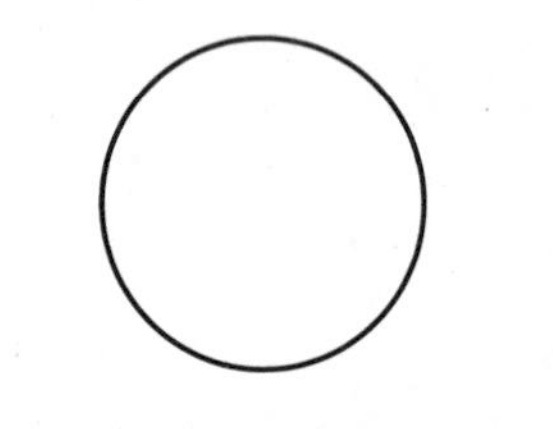

CONNECT IT

Answer the questions below.

7 How are the rectangle and the circle models the same? How are they different?

8 The rectangle is divided into halves. Show a way to divide it again, so that each part is one fourth of the rectangle.

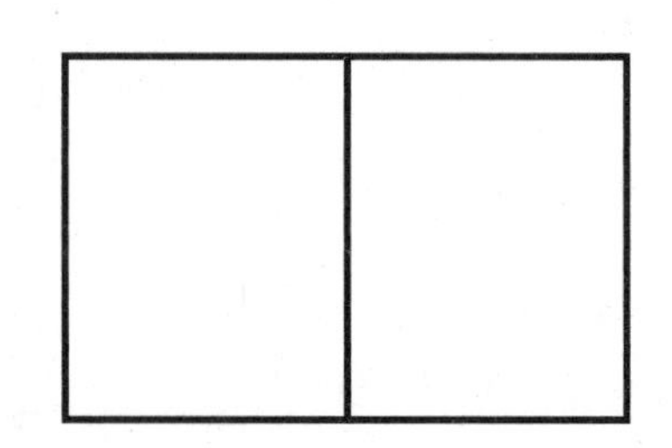

Practice Partitioning Shapes into Equal Parts

Study the Example showing how to divide a rectangle into equal parts. Then solve problems 1–9.

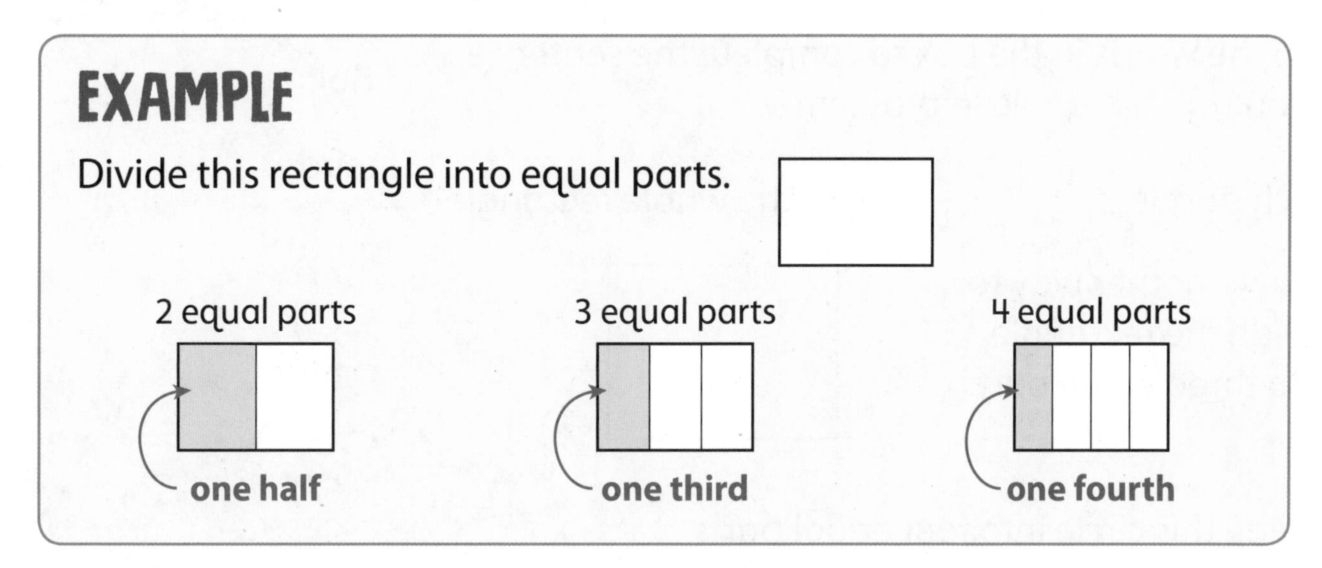

1. Divide this rectangle into two equal parts.

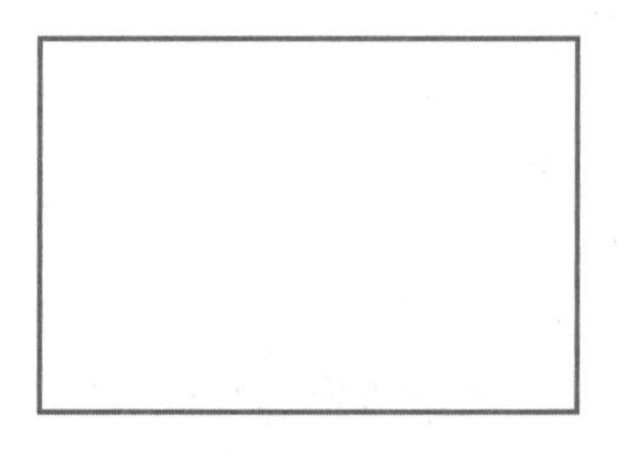

2. Use the words in the box to complete the sentence about the rectangle in problem 1.

   Each part is a .... of the whole rectangle.

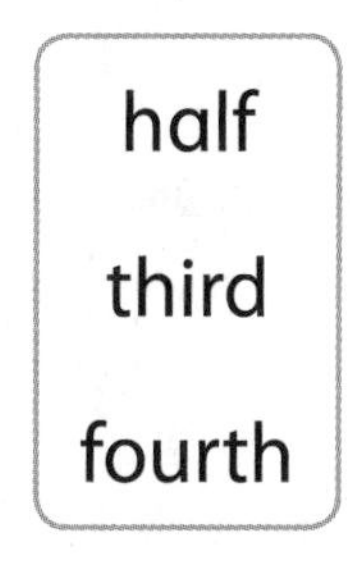

3. Show another way to divide the rectangle into two equal parts.

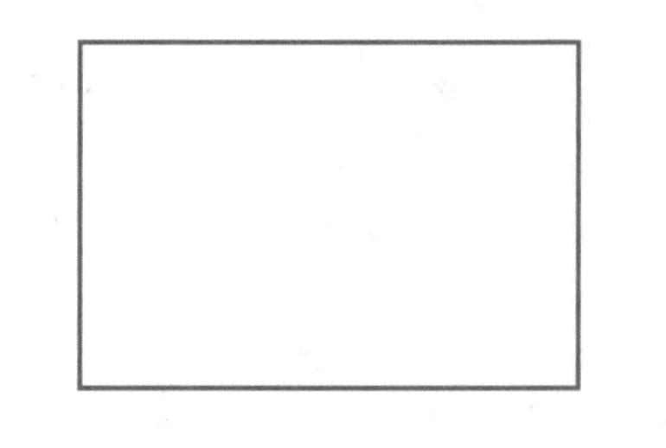

4 Divide this rectangle into three equal parts.

5 Use the words in the box to complete the sentence about the rectangle in problem 4.

half
third
fourth

Each part is a .... of the whole rectangle.

6 Show another way to divide the rectangle into three equal parts.

7 Divide this circle into four equal parts.

8 Use the words in the box to complete the sentence about the circle in problem 7.

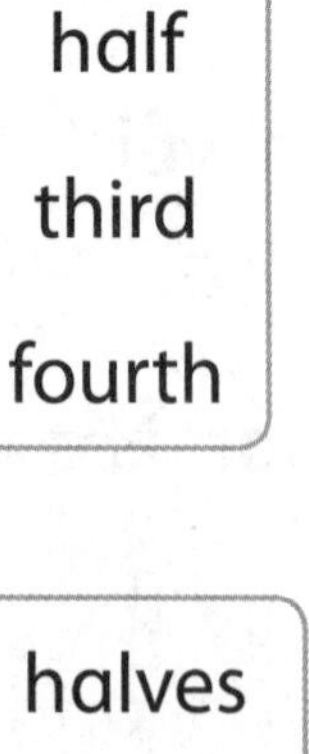

Each part is a .... of the whole circle.

9 Use the words in the box to complete the sentence about the circle in problem 7.

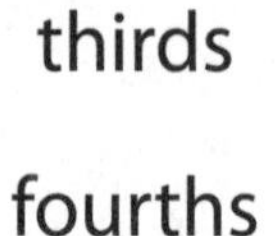

The circle is divided into ....

Refine Ideas About Partitioning Shapes into Halves, Thirds, and Fourths

APPLY IT

Complete these problems on your own.

1 COMPARE

Which circle is divided into thirds? Explain.

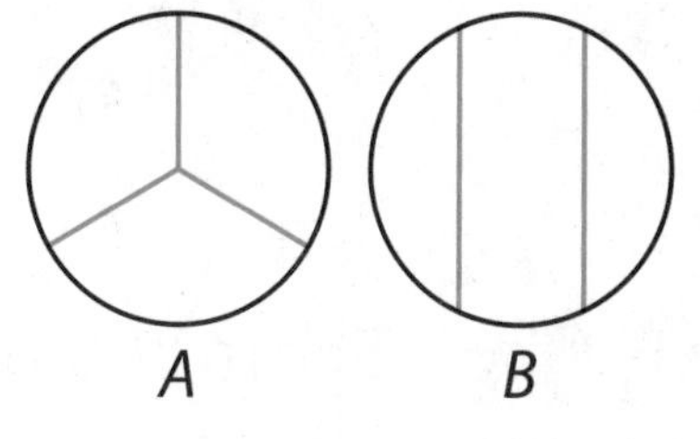

2 DRAW

Divide the squares in half two different ways. Make the halves of one square different shapes than the halves of the other square. Try doing the same with the circles. What do you notice?

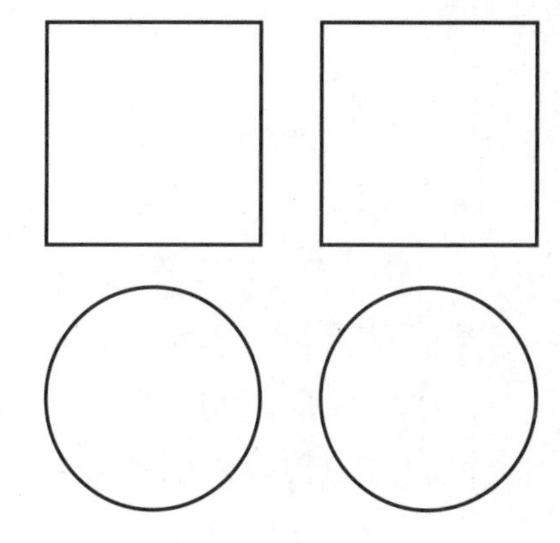

3 EXPLAIN

Carlo and Abe buy the same sandwich. Carlo's sandwich is cut in thirds. Abe's sandwich is cut in fourths. Which sandwich has smaller pieces? Explain.

PAIR/SHARE
Discuss your solutions for these three problems with a partner.

Use what you have learned to complete problem 4.

4 Shara and her mom make these 3 pizzas for a party.

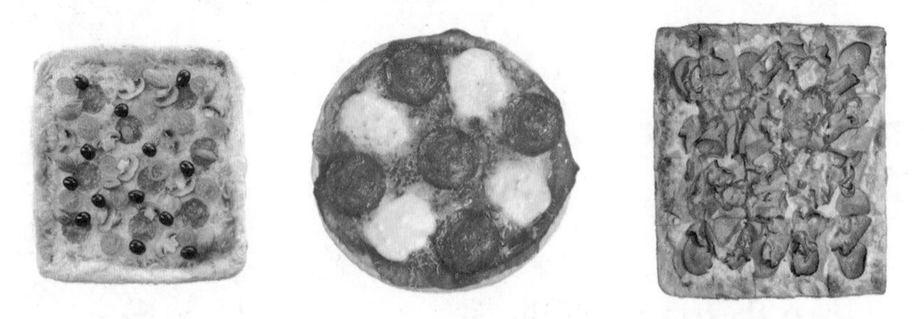

Part A Shara will have 10 people at the party. Draw how Shara could cut each pizza into halves, thirds, or fourths to get exactly 10 pieces of pizza in all.

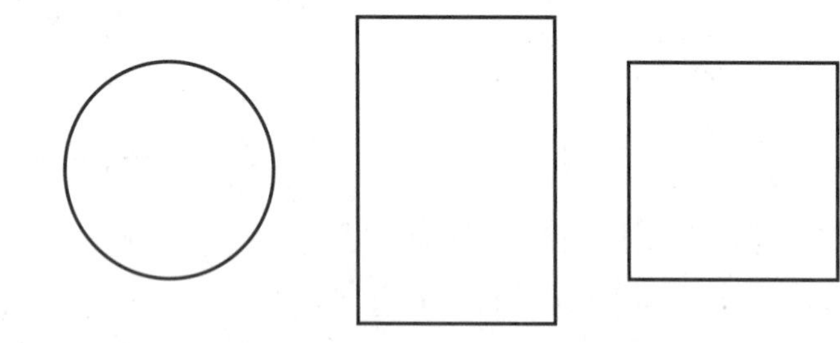

Part B Shara asks more people to the party. Now there will be 12 people. Draw how Shara could cut each pizza into halves, thirds, or fourths to get exactly 12 pieces of pizza in all.

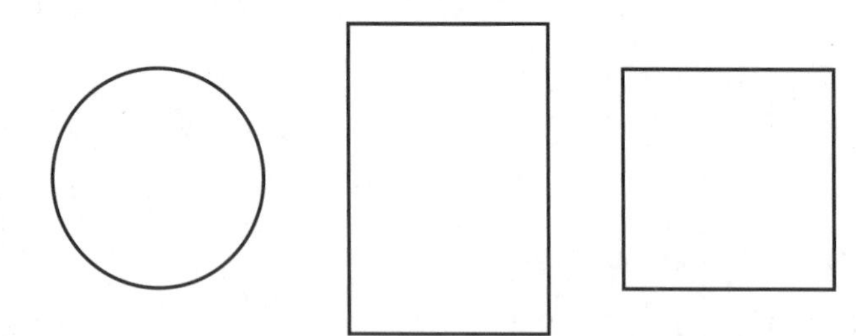

5 MATH JOURNAL

Can equal parts of a whole be different shapes? Explain.

Partition Rectangles

Dear Family,

This week your child is learning how to partition rectangles into same-sized squares.

Rectangles can be partitioned into squares in different ways. For example:

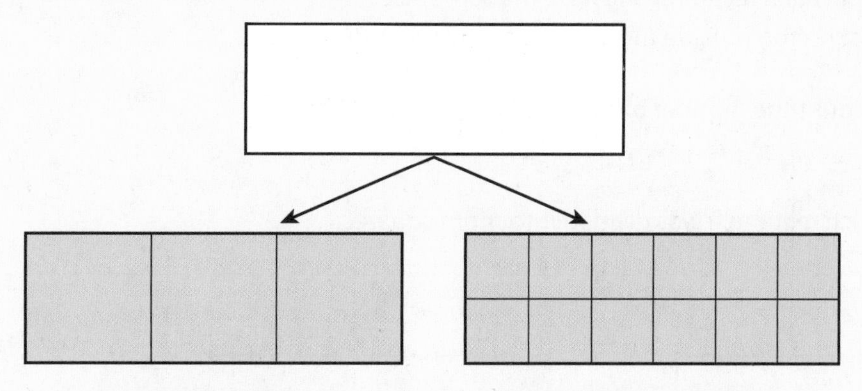

1 **row** and 3 **columns**
3 large squares

2 rows and 6 columns
12 small squares

Your child is exploring partitioning rectangles to get ready for learning how to find the area of rectangles next year.

Examples of partitioning can be found throughout your daily life. You may find square tiles covering the kitchen floor, the bathroom wall, or a ceiling. You may see squares filling a game board or a wall calendar.

Invite your child to share what he or she knows about partitioning by doing the following activity together.

ACTIVITY PARTITIONING

Do this activity with your child to partition rectangles.

Materials markers or crayons

- Work with your child to finish partitioning the two rectangles shown below.
  - The squares must fill the whole rectangle.
  - The squares within each rectangle must be the same size.
  - The squares must not go outside the borders of the rectangle.
- Ask your child to count the number of rows and columns of squares in each rectangle.
- Ask your child which rectangle was divided into more squares.

Explore Partitioning Rectangles

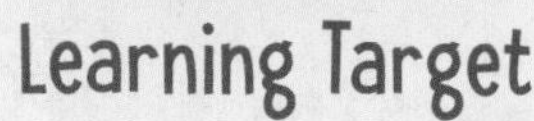

Learning Target

- Partition a rectangle into rows and columns of same-size squares and count to find the total number of them.

SMP 1, 2, 3, 4, 5, 6, 7, 8

You have worked with dividing rectangles into equal parts. Use what you know to try to solve the problem below.

Jen is using 12 squares to make a design in the shape of a rectangle.

Use 12 square tiles to show what Jen's rectangle could look like.

TRY IT

Math Toolkit

- 1-inch tiles
- 1-centimeter tiles
- 1-inch grid paper
- 1-centimeter grid paper
- half-inch grid paper

DISCUSS IT

Ask your partner: Do you agree with me? Why or why not?

Tell your partner: I knew . . . so I . . .

CONNECT IT

1 LOOK BACK

How many **rows** and **columns** could Jen's rectangle have?

 LOOK AHEAD

Al is filling the large rectangle with 15 of the squares shown below.

Draw lines to show how to fill the rectangle with the squares.

 REFLECT

How did you check your work to know that you used 15 squares to fill Al's rectangle?

Name: ______________________

Prepare for Partitioning Rectangles

1 Think about what you know about filling rectangles with same-sized squares. Fill in each box. Use words, numbers, and pictures. Show as many ideas as you can.

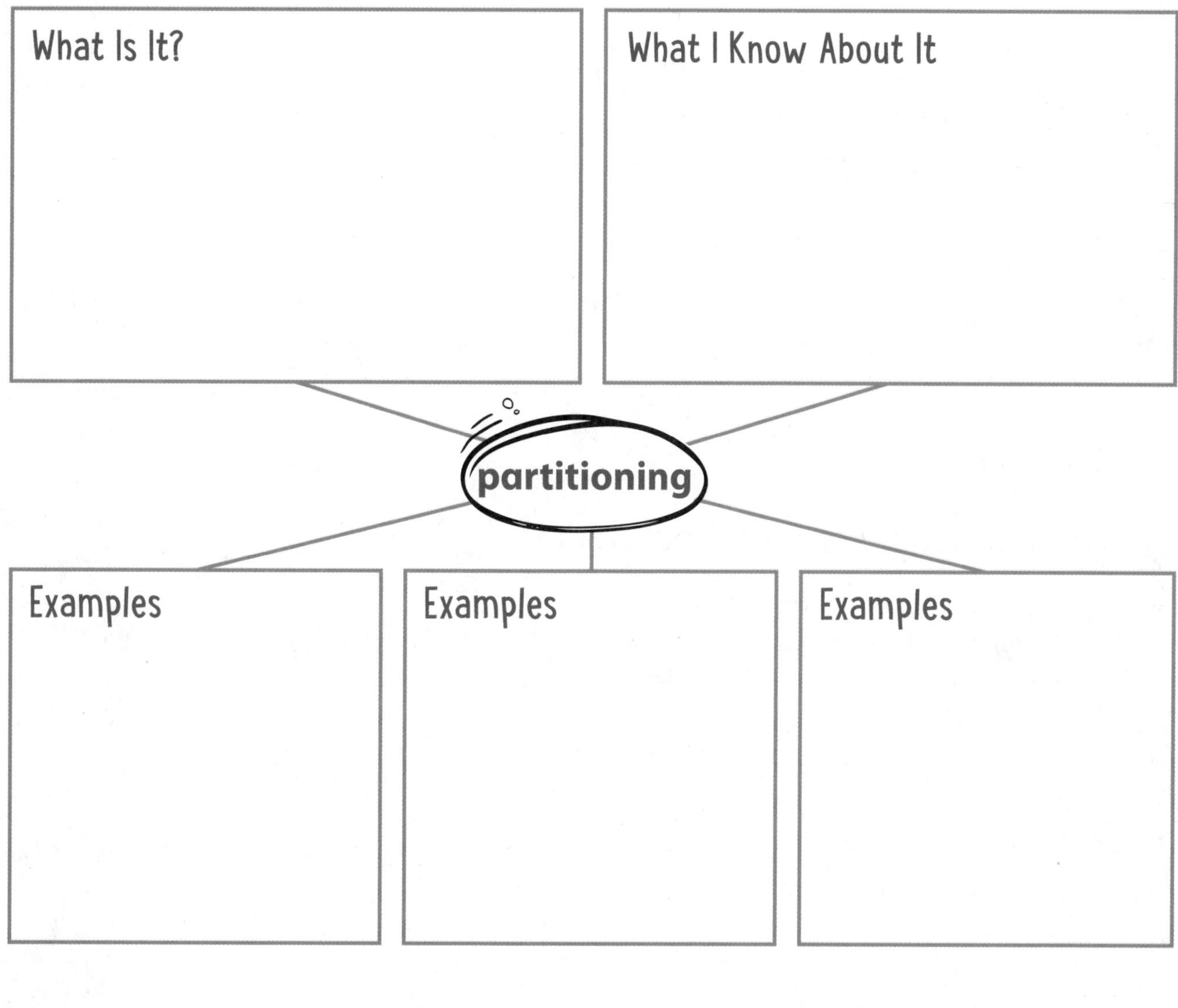

2 Tanya is filling this rectangle with 10 of the square tiles shown. Draw lines to show how to fill the rectangle.

 Solve the problem. Show your work.

Juan is using 18 squares to make a design in the shape of a rectangle. Show what Juan's rectangle could look like.

Solution ....

4 Check your answer. Show your work.

Develop Partitioning a Rectangle into Squares

Use what you know to try to solve the problem below.

Bella starts filling this rectangle with squares. How many total squares does it take to fill the rectangle without going outside the edges?

TRY IT

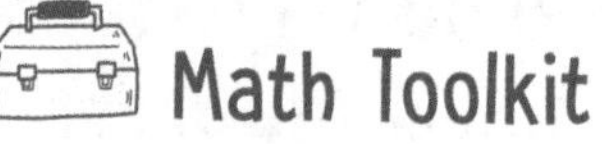

Math Toolkit
- 1-inch tiles
- 1-centimeter tiles
- 1-inch grid paper
- 1-centimeter grid paper
- $\frac{1}{2}$-inch grid paper

DISCUSS IT

Ask your partner: Why did you choose that strategy?

Tell your partner: A model I used was . . . It helped me . . .

Develop different ways to understand using squares to fill a rectangle.

Bella starts filling this rectangle with squares. How many total squares does it take to fill the rectangle without going outside the edges?

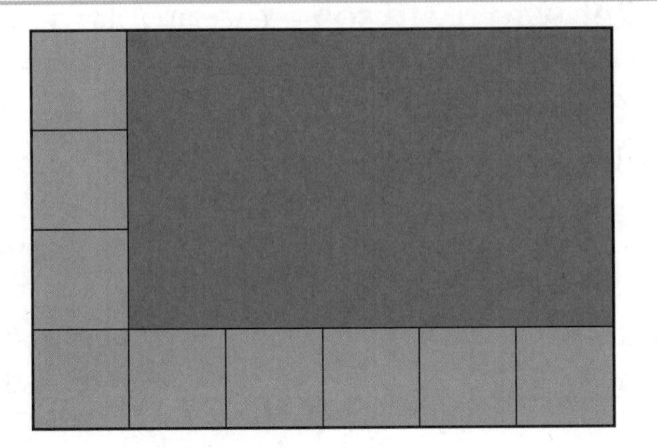

MODEL IT

Use grid paper to fill a rectangle with same-sized squares.

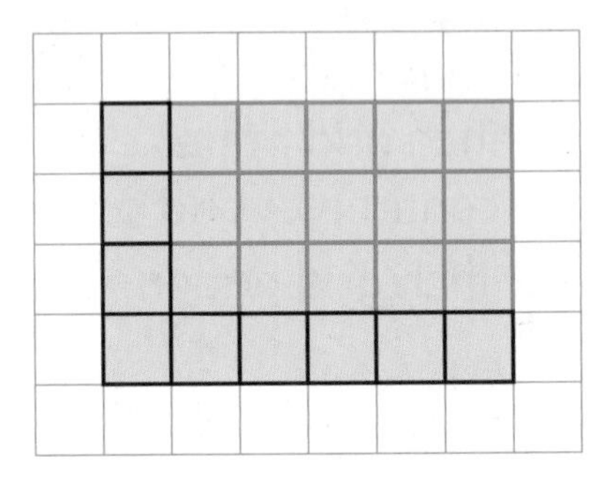

MODEL IT

Use dot paper to fill a rectangle with same-sized squares.

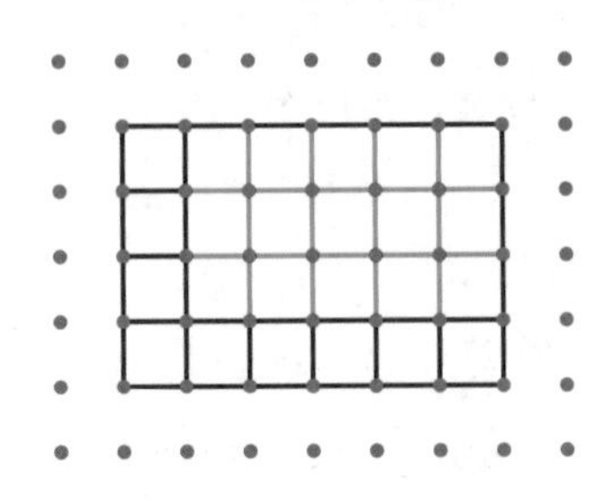

CONNECT IT

Now you will use the problem from the previous page to help you understand how to use squares to fill a rectangle.

1 **a.** Complete the equation to show how many squares Bella breaks the rectangle into.

4 + ... + ... + ... + ... + ... = ...

b. It takes .... squares to fill the rectangle.

2 Jaime and Ava both draw lines to break apart same-sized rectangles into squares. Why is there a different number of squares in each of their rectangles?

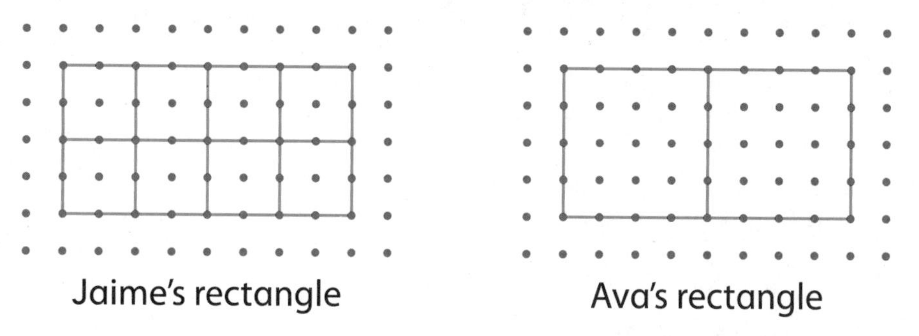

Jaime's rectangle

Ava's rectangle

3 REFLECT

Look back at your **Try It**, strategies by classmates, and **Model Its**. Which models or strategies do you like best for filling a rectangle? Explain.

....

....

APPLY IT

Use what you just learned to solve these problems.

4 Tam starts breaking apart this rectangle into squares. Draw lines to finish breaking it apart. How many total squares is the rectangle broken into?

The rectangle is broken into .... total squares.

5 Gia breaks apart this rectangle into squares. How many squares does Gia use?

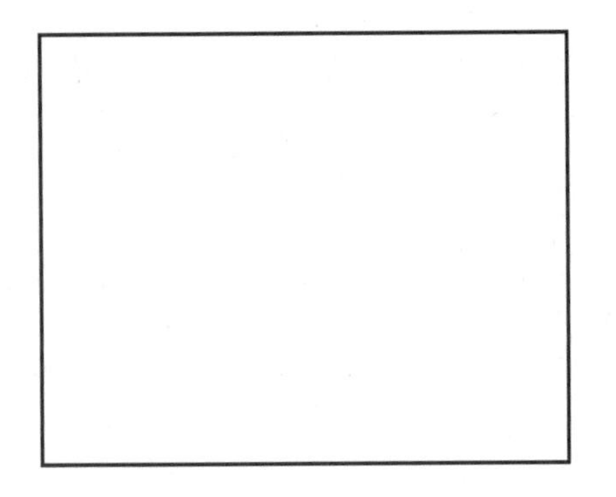

Gia uses .... squares to fill the rectangle.

6 Kyle wants to make this design using square letter and number tiles.

A	B	C	D	E	F
G	H	I	J	K	L
M	N	O	P	Q	R
S	T	U	V	W	X
Y	Z	0	1	2	3

Which equations could Kyle use to find the number of square tiles he will need in all?

Ⓐ $5 + 5 + 5 + 5 + 5 = ?$

Ⓑ $5 + 5 + 5 + 5 + 5 + 5 = ?$

Ⓒ $6 + 6 + 6 + 6 = ?$

Ⓓ $6 + 6 + 6 + 6 + 6 = ?$

Ⓔ $6 + 6 + 6 + 6 + 6 + 6 = ?$

Name: ______________________

Practice Partitioning a Rectangle into Squares

Study the Example showing how to draw and count squares. Then solve problems 1–8.

EXAMPLE

Sal draws squares on dot paper to fill a rectangle. How many squares does he draw in all?

- You can count each square.
- Or you can count the rows and number of squares in each row. Then add: $4 + 4 = ?$

2 rows

4 squares in each row

Sal draws 8 squares in all.

Break apart the rectangle into same-size squares. Then answer the questions below.

1. How many rows of squares are there?

   .... rows

2. How many squares are in each row?

   .... squares in each row

3. Complete the equation to find how many squares in all.

   .... + ... + ... = ...

4. How many squares are in the rectangle?

   .... squares

5 Write an equation to find how many squares are in the rectangle.

.... + ... + ... = ...

How many squares are in the rectangle?

.... squares

6 Write an equation to find how many squares are in the rectangle.

How many squares are in the rectangle?

.... squares

7 The rectangles in problems 5 and 6 are the same size. Why does the rectangle in problem 6 have more squares than the other rectangle?

8 Draw lines to show two different ways to break apart the rectangles into same-size squares.

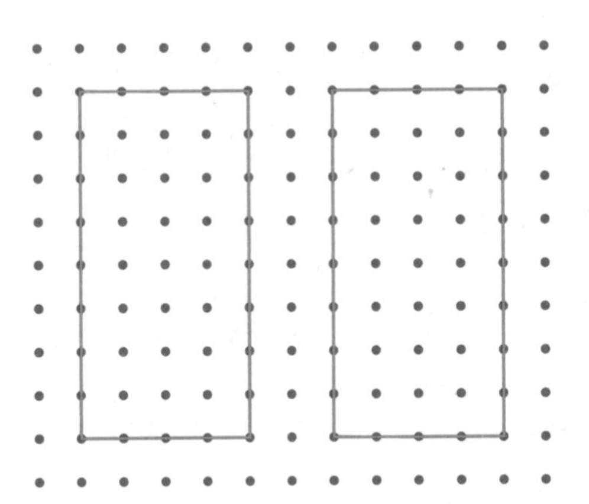

Refine Partitioning Rectangles

Complete the Example below. Then solve problems 1–3.

EXAMPLE

You can break apart a rectangle into same-size squares and count to find the total number of squares it takes.

How can you add to find the total number of squares it takes to partition the rectangle?

You can add the rows.

There are 6 rows, with 3 squares in each row.

$3 + 3 + 3 + 3 + 3 + 3 = ?$

You can add the columns.

There are 3 columns, with 6 squares in each column.

$6 + 6 + 6 = ?$

Solution ....

APPLY IT

1 Tim says this shows it takes a total of 9 squares to fill this rectangle. Do you agree? Explain.

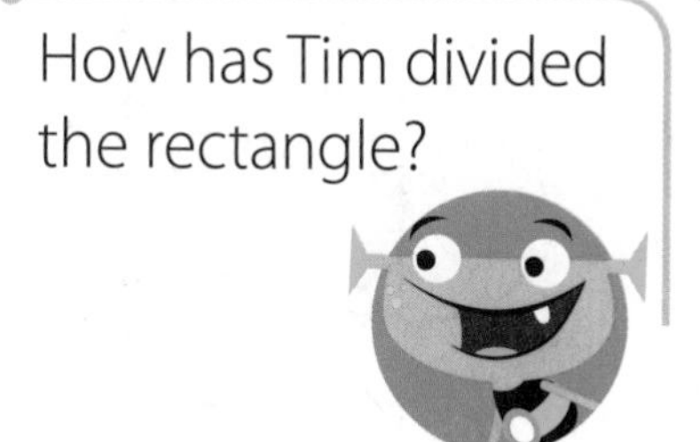

2 Nina pastes a square on a poster. She will fill the rest of the poster with squares that are the same size as the first one. How many squares will there be on Nina's filled poster? Show your work.

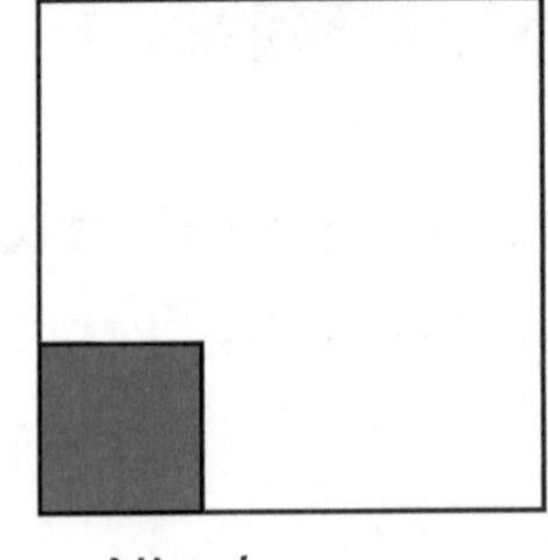

Nina's square

What does it mean to fill a rectangle with squares?

There will be .... squares on Nina's filled poster.

3 Juan breaks apart a rectangle into same-size squares. He writes the equation $2 + 2 + 2 = 6$ to find the total number of squares. Which could be Juan's rectangle?

You can look at the rows and columns of each rectangle.

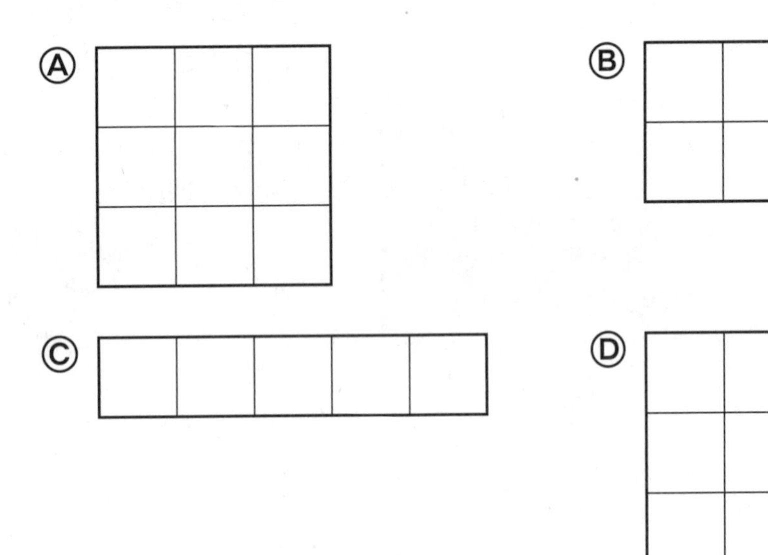

Name: ______________________________

Practice Partitioning Rectangles

1 Nick drew this rectangle.

Count the squares inside the rectangle.

He says that there are a total of 8 squares in his rectangle. What is Nick's mistake, and how can he fix it?

2 The two outlined rectangles are the same size.

Think about the size of the squares.

a. Break apart the rectangle into the fewest number of same-size squares you can.

How many squares did you use? ....

b. Break apart the rectangle into the greatest number of same-size squares you can.

How many squares did you use? ....

3. Anuj has 21 squares of colored paper. Show how he can arrange the squares to form a rectangle.

Make sure each square is the same size.

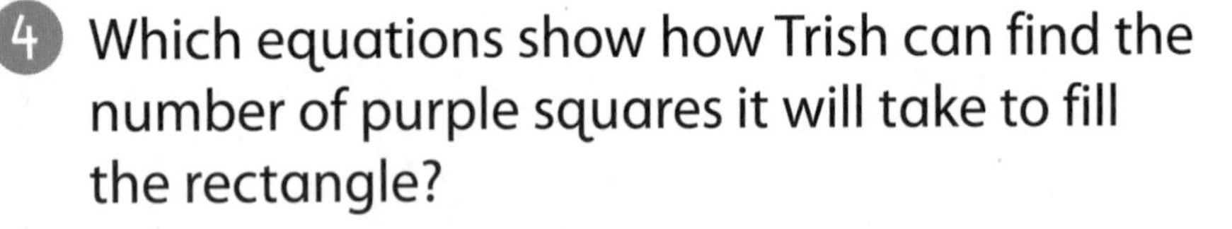

4. Which equations show how Trish can find the number of purple squares it will take to fill the rectangle?

You can think about rows and columns.

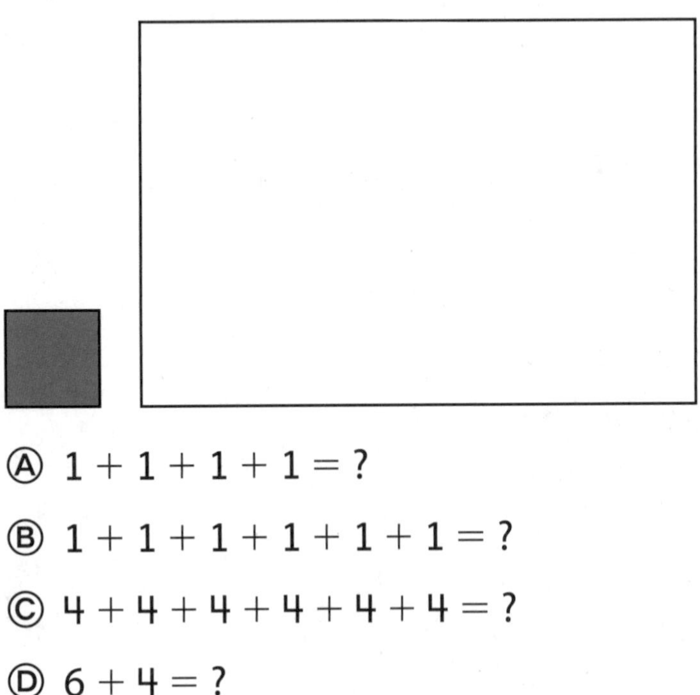

Ⓐ $1 + 1 + 1 + 1 = ?$

Ⓑ $1 + 1 + 1 + 1 + 1 + 1 = ?$

Ⓒ $4 + 4 + 4 + 4 + 4 + 4 = ?$

Ⓓ $6 + 4 = ?$

Ⓔ $6 + 6 + 6 + 6 = ?$

Refine Partitioning Rectangles

APPLY IT

1 Winny fills this rectangle with squares. Which statements describe her rectangle?

Ⓐ There are 3 rows of 7 squares.

Ⓑ There are 7 rows of 2 squares.

Ⓒ There are 8 rows of 3 squares.

Ⓓ There are 6 columns of 3 squares.

Ⓔ There are 7 columns of 3 squares.

2 Craig is partitioning this rectangle with squares. Will he find the correct number of squares that fills the rectangle? Explain.

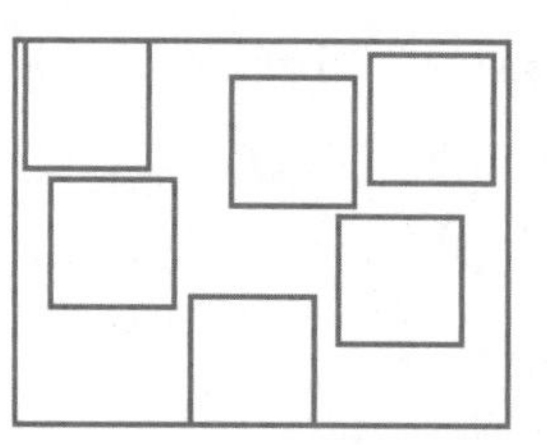

3 Luis fills this rectangle with equal-sized squares. Which equation could he use to find the total number of squares?

Ⓐ $4 + 7 = 11$

Ⓑ $7 + 7 + 7 = 21$

Ⓒ $7 + 7 + 7 + 7 = 28$

Ⓓ $4 + 4 + 4 + 4 + 4 + 4 = 24$

4 Jamal starts making a design with orange squares.

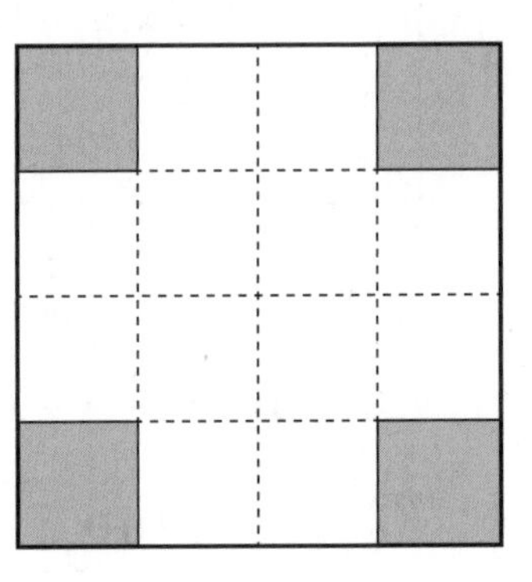

a. How many more squares does Jamal need to fill the rectangle?

b. How many squares will Jamal use in all? ....

5 MATH JOURNAL

What are two different ways you can find the total number of squares in this partitioned rectangle?

☑ SELF CHECK Go back to the Unit 5 Opener and see what you can check off.

Add Using Arrays

LESSON 31

Dear Family,

This week your child is learning about adding with arrays.

Your child is working with arrays to build skills related to addition. An **array** is a set of objects arranged in equal rows and equal columns.

The array of stars below has 3 rows and 4 columns. You can find the number of stars in the array by breaking apart the array into groups (rows or columns) and using addition strategies.

Break apart the array into 3 groups of 4 stars.

- You can use an equation.

  $4 + 4 + 4 = 12$

- Or you can skip-count by fours.

  4, 8, 12

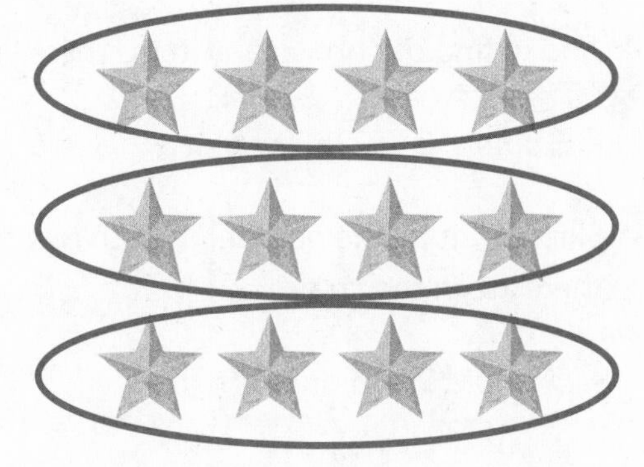

Here is another way to find the number of stars.

Break apart the array into 4 groups of 3 stars.

- You can use an equation.

  $3 + 3 + 3 + 3 = 12$

- Or you can skip-count by threes.

  3, 6, 9, 12

Invite your child to share what he or she knows about arrays by doing the following activity together.

ACTIVITY ARRAYS

- With your child, look for arrays in and around your home.
  - *Examples:* floor or wall tiles, window panes, a carton of eggs, a pack of bottles or cans, a package of English muffins, plants in a garden, shoes on shelves, or arrays made with buttons, fruit, or coins.
- For each array, ask your child to say how he or she could split up the array into groups and the number of items in each group.
  - *Example:* For a pack of water bottles, your child might say: *2 groups of 3 bottles* or *3 groups of 2 bottles*.
- Add to find out how many items there are in the array.
  - *Example:* $2 + 2 + 2 = 6$ or $3 + 3 = 6$
- Skip-count by the number in each row or column to find out how many items there are in the array.
  - *Example:* 2, 4, 6 or 3, 6

Explore Adding Using Arrays

Learning Target

- Use addition to find the total number of objects arranged in rectangular arrays with up to 5 rows and up to 5 columns; write an equation to express the total sum of equal addends.

SMP 1, 2, 3, 4, 5, 6, 7

You have worked with addition strategies. Use what you know to try to solve the problem below.

Rob's team has shelves for their hats. How many hats are there in all?

TRY IT

Math Toolkit

- counters
- connecting cubes
- hundred charts
- number lines
- multiplication models

DISCUSS IT

Ask your partner: Do you agree with me? Why or why not?

Tell your partner: I started by . . .

CONNECT IT

1 LOOK BACK

Explain how you can find the number of hats in all.

2 LOOK AHEAD

An **array** can be used to represent the numbers in the problem. Arrays have equal rows that go across. Arrays have equal columns that go up and down.

a. Circle one row and label it "row." Circle one column and label it "column."

b. How do the number of hats in every row compare?

c. How do the number of hats in every column compare?

d. Write an equation to show the total number of hats.

3 REFLECT

Explain how the array represents the problem. Tell how the equation you wrote matches the array.

Name: ______________________

Prepare for Adding Using Arrays

1. Think about what you know about grouping objects. Fill in each box. Use words, numbers, and pictures. Show as many ideas as you can.

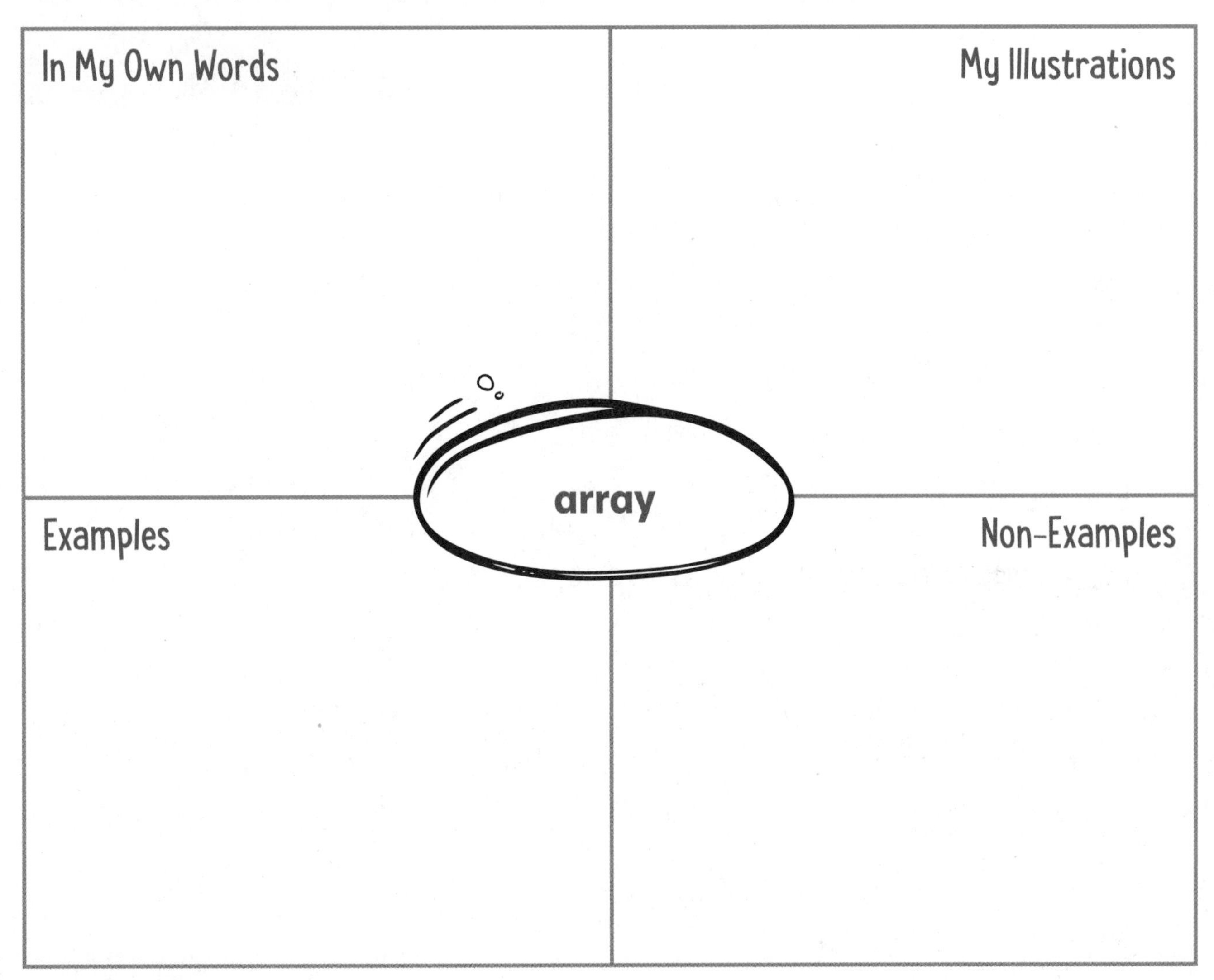

2. Write an equation to show the total number of stars in the array.

3 Solve the problem. Show your work.

Natasha's team has shelves for their basketballs. How many basketballs are there in all? Show how you can use addition to find how many in all.

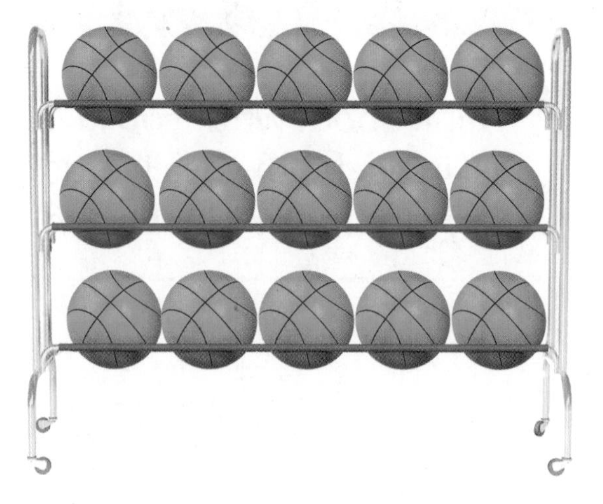

Solution ....

4 Check your answer. Show your work.

Develop Adding Using Arrays

Use what you know to try to solve the problem below.

Mike puts some stickers into an array. Each row has 5 stickers. Each column has 4 stickers. How many stickers are there in all?

TRY IT

Math Toolkit

- counters
- connecting cubes
- hundred charts
- number lines
- multiplication models
- perimeter and area tool

DISCUSS IT

Ask your partner: Why did you choose that strategy?

Tell your partner: At first, I thought . . .

Develop different ways to understand adding using an array.

Mike puts some stickers into an array. Each row has 5 stickers. Each column has 4 stickers. How many stickers are there in all?

PICTURE IT

You can draw an array.

MODEL IT

You can use the rows in the array to write an equation.

Add the number of stickers in each row.

Each row has 5 stickers. ⟶ $5 + 5 + 5 + 5 = ?$

MODEL IT

You can use the rows in the array to skip-count.

There are 5 stickers in each row.
Skip-count by fives. ⟶ 5, 10, 15, ?

CONNECT IT

Now you will use the problem from the previous page to help you understand how to add using arrays.

1 Look at the first **Model It** on the previous page. Why is 5 written four times in the equation?

2 Write an equation you could use to find the total number of stickers using the columns.

3 Look at the second **Model It** on the previous page. Why do you skip-count by fives?

4 Do you need to see the array from **Picture It** to solve the problem on the previous page? Explain.

5 REFLECT

Look back at your **Try It**, strategies by classmates, **Picture It**, and **Model Its**. Which models or strategies do you like best for adding using arrays? Explain.

APPLY IT

Use what you just learned to solve these problems.

6 Write two equations you could use to find the total number of shapes in this array. Show your work.

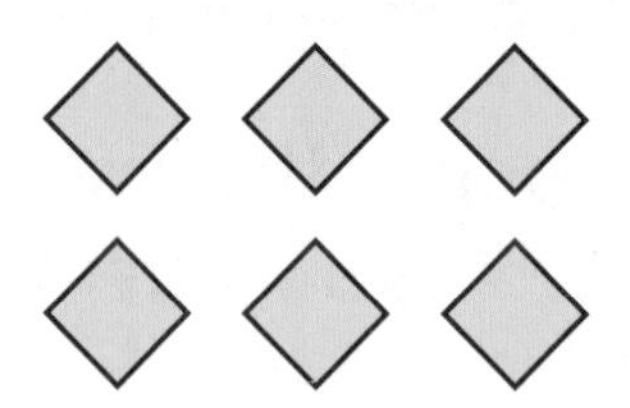

Solution ....

7 Andre makes an array of toy cars on the table.

Write two equations you could use to find the total number of cars in Andre's array. Show your work.

There are .... cars in Andre's array.

8 There are 4 rows of muffins in a pan. Each row has 3 muffins. Draw an array to show the muffins in the pan. Then write and solve an equation to find the total number of muffins in the pan. Show your work.

Solution ....

Name: ____________________

Practice Adding Using Arrays

Study the Example showing two ways to find the number of shapes in an array. Then solve problems 1–5.

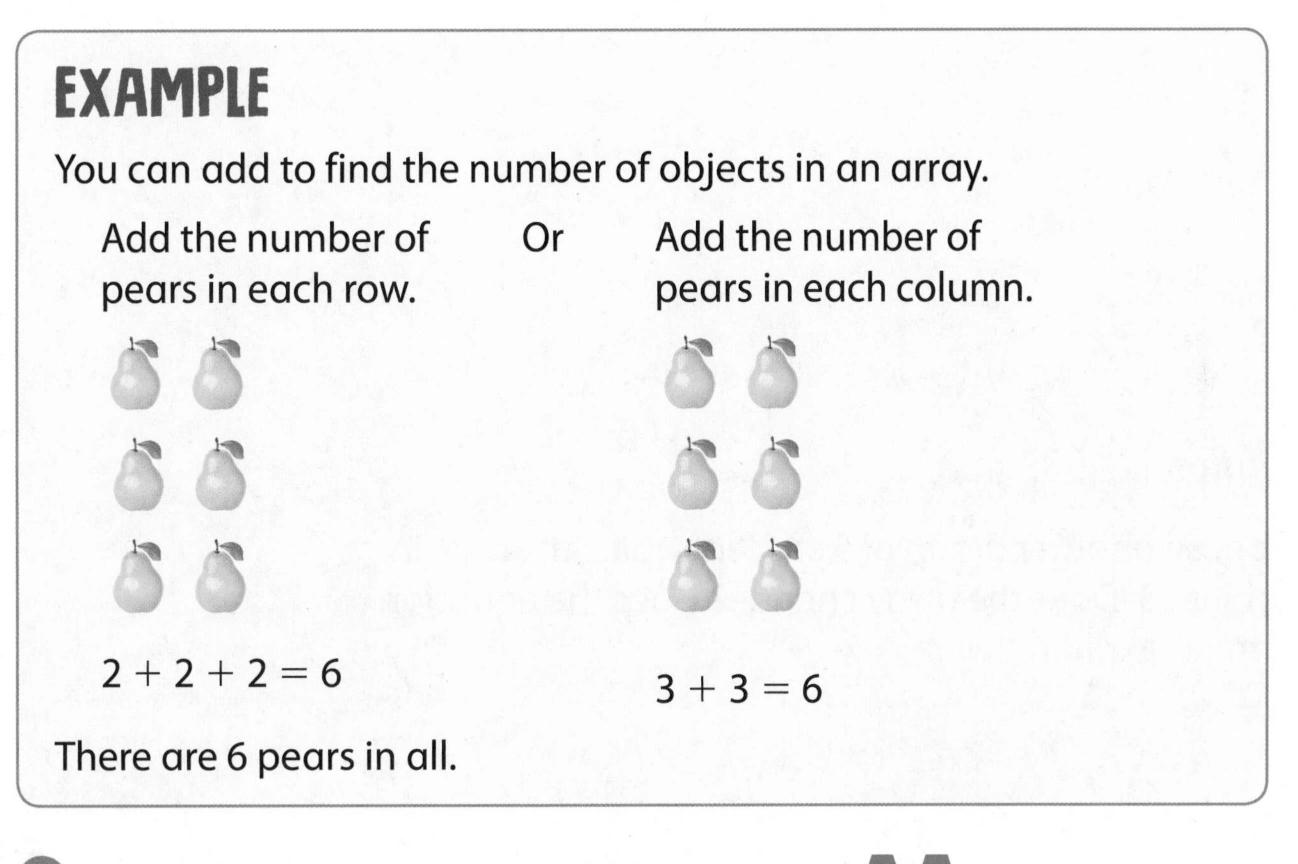

EXAMPLE

You can add to find the number of objects in an array.

Add the number of pears in each row.

$2 + 2 + 2 = 6$

Or

Add the number of pears in each column.

$3 + 3 = 6$

There are 6 pears in all.

1. Write two equations you could use to find the total number of shapes in this array.

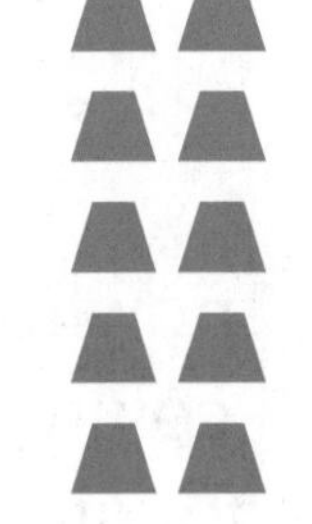

2. Use the rows in problem 1. Show how you could skip-count to find the total number of shapes.

Vocabulary

array a set of objects arranged in equal rows and equal columns.

3 Students line up in 3 rows for a relay race. There are 5 students in each row. How many students are in the race? Draw an array to show your answer. Show your work.

Solution ....

4 Suppose another group of 5 students joins the race in problem 3. Does the array change? Does the equation change? Explain.

5 Lee makes 18 paper snowflakes. He wants to make an array of 4 rows and 4 columns of snowflakes on the wall. Does he have enough snowflakes? Explain.

Refine Adding Using Arrays

Complete the Example below. Then solve problems 1–3.

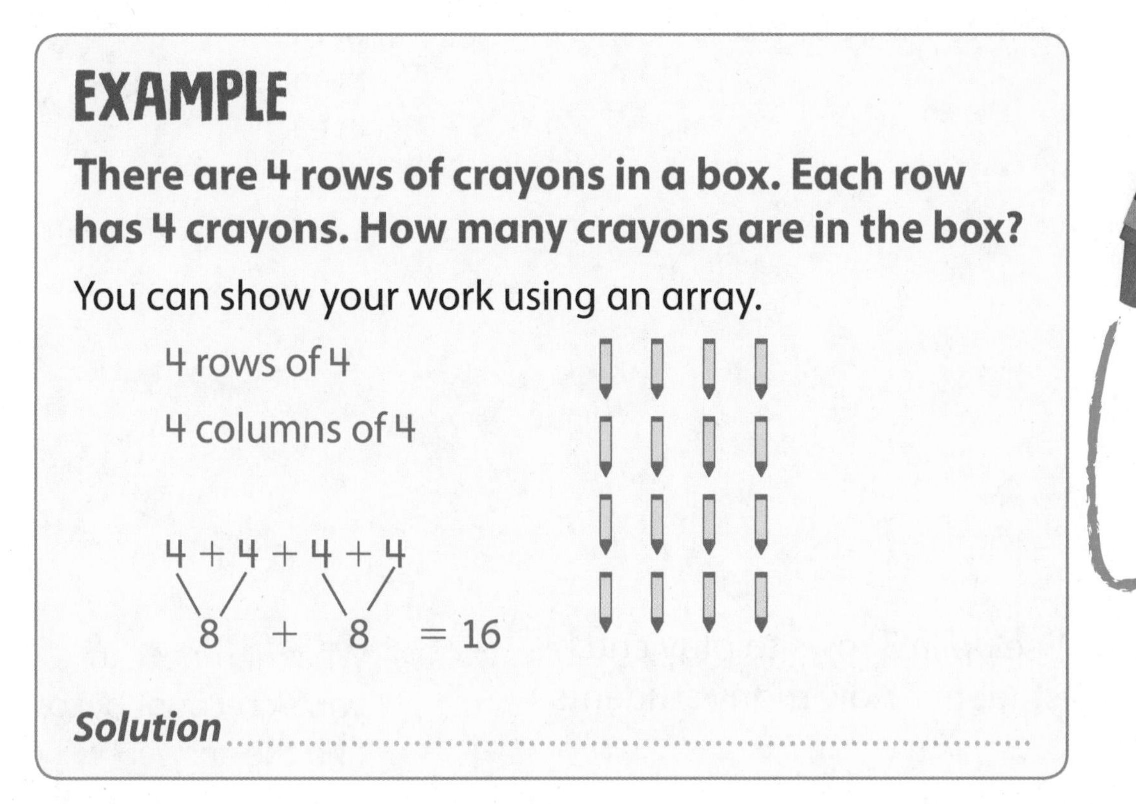

EXAMPLE

There are 4 rows of crayons in a box. Each row has 4 crayons. How many crayons are in the box?

You can show your work using an array.

4 rows of 4

4 columns of 4

$4 + 4 + 4 + 4$

$8 + 8 = 16$

Solution ....

APPLY IT

Can you skip-count to find the answer?

1 In a game, players place game pieces in 3 columns. Each column holds 5 pieces. How many pieces fill all 3 columns? Draw an array and write an equation as part of your answer. Show your work.

Solution ....

2 A package has 2 rows of soup cans. Each row has 3 cans. How many cans of soup are in the package? Draw an array and write an equation as part of your answer. Show your work.

You can add the numbers in each row or the numbers in each column.

Solution ....

3 Some students line up in 3 rows to play catch. Each row has 5 students. How many students play catch?

What number can you skip-count by to find the answer?

Ⓐ 8

Ⓑ 5

Ⓒ 15

Ⓓ 13

Vic chose Ⓐ as the answer. How did Vic get his answer?

Practice Adding Using Arrays

1. Does the equation show the total number of leaves in the array?

   Choose *Yes* or *No* for each equation.

	Yes	No
$4 + 3 = 7$	Ⓐ	Ⓑ
$4 + 4 + 4 = 12$	Ⓒ	Ⓓ
$3 + 3 + 3 + 3 = 12$	Ⓔ	Ⓕ
$3 + 3 + 4 + 4 = 14$	Ⓖ	Ⓗ

How can you use the rows to write an equation? How can you use the columns?

2. Write two different ways you can skip-count to find the number of leaves in problem 1.

How can you use the rows to skip-count? The columns?

3. An array has 3 rows with 3 items in each row. How many equations can you write to show the total? Explain.

Can you draw a picture to help?

 Which sum describes the total number of squares in this array?

Ⓐ 2 + 2

Ⓑ 2 + 3

Ⓒ 3 + 3

Ⓓ 3 + 3 + 3

Nikki chose Ⓑ as the answer. How did Nikki get her answer?

What numbers do you use to find the total?

 This picture shows a box filled with water bottles. They are packed in an array. Some of the bottles are covered by the lid.

Which could be the total number of bottles in the box?

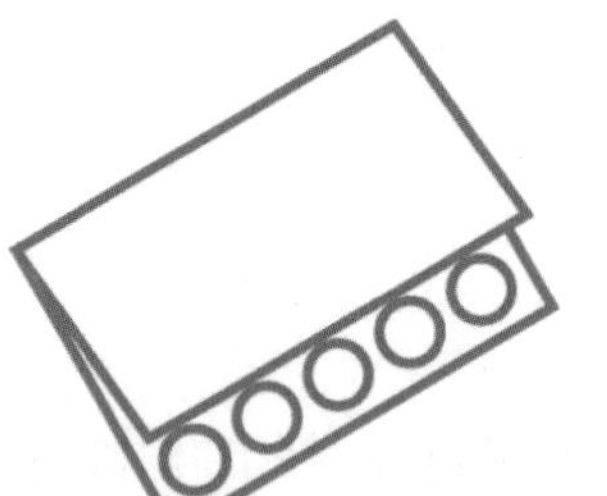

Ⓐ 8

Ⓑ 15

Ⓒ 12

Ⓓ 10

Ⓔ 20

What does the picture tell you about the array?

Prepare for Even and Odd Numbers

1. Think about what you know about grouping objects. Fill in each box. Use words, numbers, and pictures. Show as many ideas as you can.

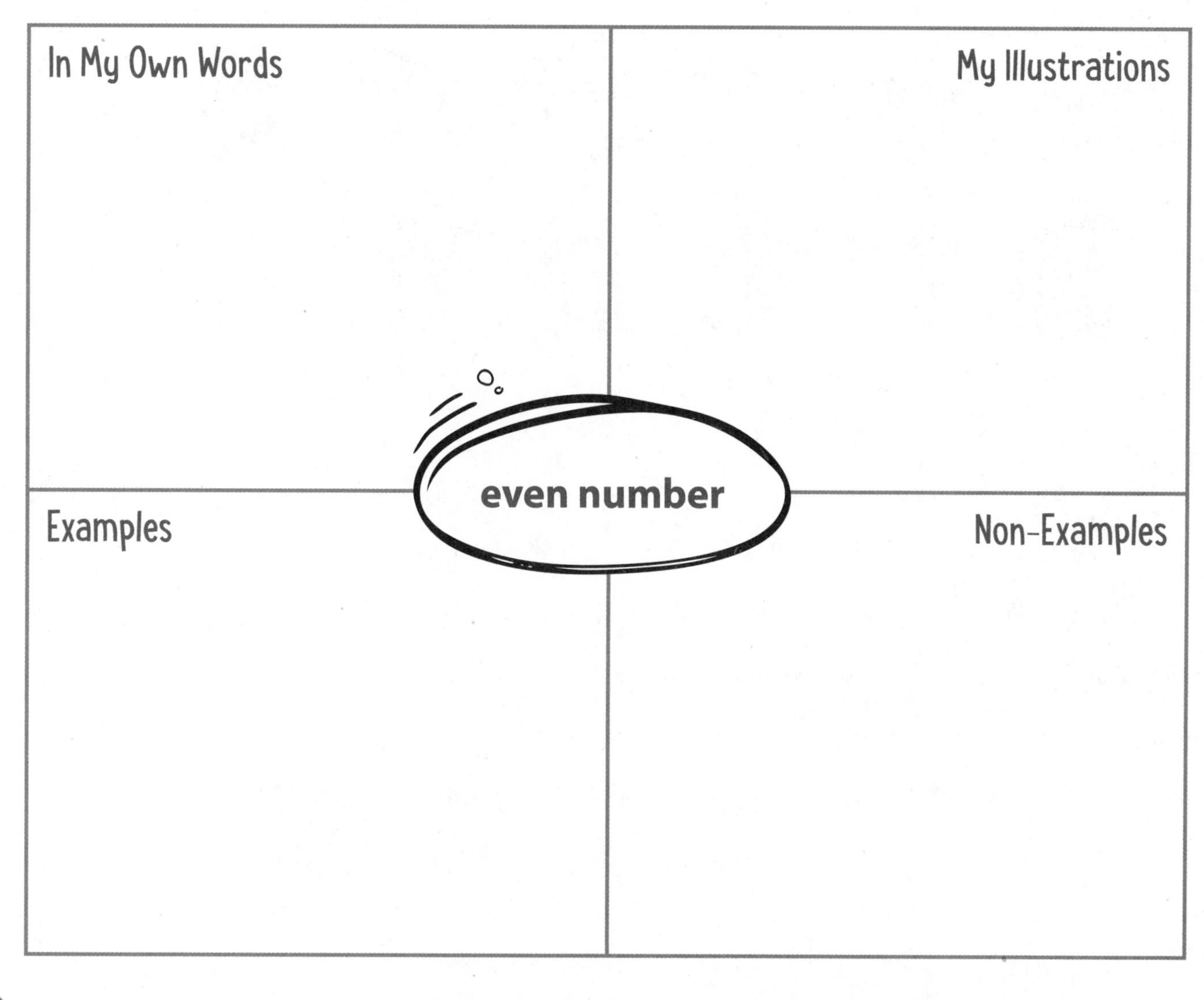

2. Try to make groups of 2. Circle your groups. Complete the sentences with *even* or *odd*.

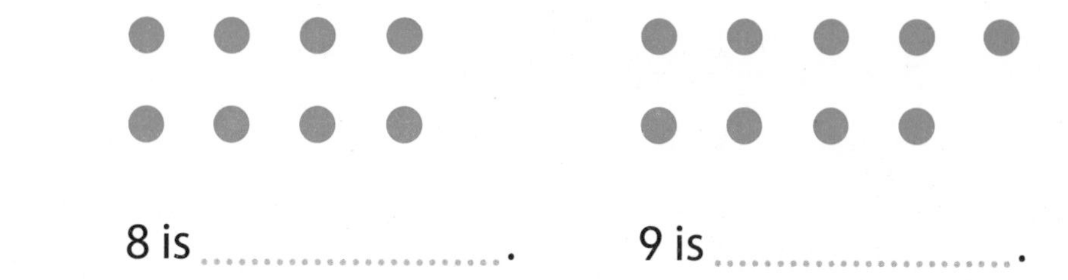

8 is ______________.   9 is ______________.

3 Solve the problem. Show your work.

Joy's mother gives her 12 shirts to fold. Can Joy put all the shirts into groups of 2 or 2 equal groups?

Solution ....

....

4 Check your answer. Show your work.

Develop Modeling Even and Odd Numbers

Use what you know to try to solve the problem below.

Ms. Ruiz brings 15 footballs and 14 soccer balls to gym class. Which number is odd?

TRY IT

Math Toolkit
- counters
- hundred charts
- 0–20 number lines
- sticky notes

DISCUSS IT

Ask your partner: Do you agree with me? Why or why not?

Tell your partner: I started by . . .

Develop different ways to identify even and odd numbers.

Ms. Ruiz brings 15 footballs and 14 soccer balls to gym class. Which number is odd?

MODEL IT

Write the equation of a doubles fact for even numbers.

$7 + 7 = 14$

MODEL IT

Write the equation of a doubles plus 1 fact for odd numbers.

$7 + 7 + 1 = 15$

MODEL IT

Count by twos to find even numbers.

2, 4, 6, 8, 10, 12, 14, 16, 18, 20

Is 14 or 15 on the list of even numbers?

CONNECT IT

Now you will use the problem from the previous page to help you understand even and odd numbers.

Look at the first **Model It** about soccer balls. Explain how a doubles fact helps you identify an even number.

2. Look at the second **Model It** about footballs.

   a. What does the 1 in a doubles plus 1 fact represent? Explain.

   b. Do doubles plus 1 facts represent odd or even numbers? Explain.

3. Look at the list of even numbers in the third **Model It**.

   a. Is the number of footballs even or odd? ....

   b. Is the number of soccer balls even or odd? ....

4. REFLECT

   Look back at your **Try It**, strategies by classmates, and **Model Its**. Which models or strategies do you like best for identifying even and odd numbers? Explain.

   ....

   ....

   ....

APPLY IT

Use what you just learned to solve these problems.

5 Circle the even numbers. Underline the odd numbers.

11 14 16 17

6 Write a doubles fact for each even number in problem 5.

Which statements describe the mice? Select all the correct answers.

Ⓐ $8 + 8 = 16$

Ⓑ $8 + 8 + 1 = 17$

Ⓒ The mice do not make 2 equal groups.

Ⓓ The number of mice is even.

Ⓔ The number of mice is odd.

Name: ____________________

Practice Modeling Even and Odd Numbers

Study how the Example shows different ways to decide if a number is odd or even. Then solve problems 1–6.

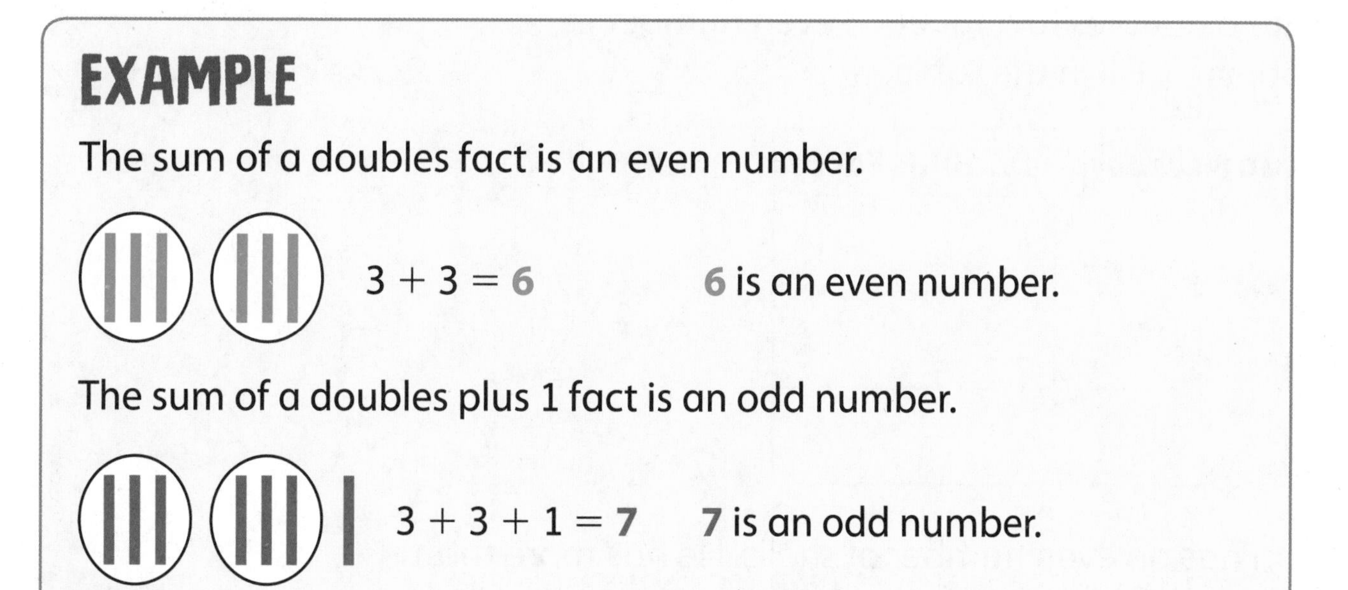

1. Write a doubles fact for 12. Is 12 odd or even? Circle the correct answer.

   .... + ... = ...

   odd even

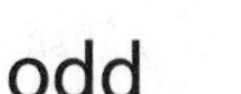

2. Write a doubles plus 1 fact for 15. Is 15 odd or even? Circle the correct answer.

   .... + ... + 1 = ...

   odd even

Vocabulary

even number
an even number of objects can be put into pairs or two equal groups without any leftovers.

odd number
an odd number of objects cannot be put into pairs or two equal groups without a leftover.

3 Circle the even numbers.

12 19 10 18 15

4 Write a doubles fact for each even number in problem 3. Fill in the table.

Even Numbers	Doubles Facts

5 Evan has an even number of shells. He has more than 10 shells and fewer than 15 shells. How many could he have? Tell how you know.

6 Think of different ways to tell if a number is odd or even. Which way do you think you will use most often? Why?

Refine Identifying Even and Odd Numbers

Complete the Example below. Then solve problems 1–3.

EXAMPLE

Ms. Lane's class is on a field trip. There are 9 students who each have a partner. There is also 1 student paired with Ms. Lane. How many students in all are on the trip?

Is the number even or odd? Explain.

There are 9 pairs with 1 leftover.

$2 + 2 + 2 + 2 + 2 + 2 + 2 + 2 + 2 + 1 = 19$

Solution ....

....

APPLY IT

1 Pat looks at this picture of 14 apples. He says 14 is an odd number. Do you agree? Explain.

How can the apples be organized?

2 Mimi says that when she adds doubles, the sum is always even. It doesn't matter if the doubles fact addends are odd or even numbers. Do you agree? Explain.

Think about the totals when you add.

3 Which equations show a sum that is an odd number?

Ⓐ $5 + 5 = 10$

Ⓑ $6 + 6 + 1 = 13$

Ⓒ $7 + 7 = 14$

Ⓓ $8 + 8 + 1 = 17$

Ⓔ $9 + 9 + 1 = 19$

What is each equation showing?

Practice Identifying Even and Odd Numbers

1. Show two different ways to tell if the number 15 is odd or even. Show your work.

How can you show 15?

Solution ....

2. Show two different ways to tell if the number 18 is odd or even. Show your work.

How can you show 18?

Solution ....

3 Tell whether each number is even or odd. Then write a doubles or doubles plus 1 fact for each number.

Number	Even or Odd?	Doubles Fact or Doubles Plus 1 Fact
11		
14		
19		

What do you know about even and odd numbers?

4 Ezra has two equal groups of toy cars. Each of the groups has an odd number of cars. Does Ezra have an even or an odd number of cars in all? Explain.

What does equal groups mean?

5 Luis says counting by twos only helps find even numbers. Julia says counting by twos helps find even and odd numbers. Who is correct? Explain.

What numbers do you say when you count by twos?

Refine Even and Odd Numbers

APPLY IT

 Use this number chart to answer the questions.

1	2	3	4	5	6	7	8	9	10
11	12	13	14	15	16	17	18	19	20

a. Color squares with odd numbers red. Color squares with even numbers blue.

b. How are the patterns of even and odd numbers shown by the patterns of the colors?

c. Look at the number 19. Is the ones digit odd or even? Is 19 odd or even?

d. Look at 12, 14, 16, and 18. Amy says that if a two-digit number has an even number in the ones place, the number is also even. Is she correct? Why or why not?

2. Noah gives these clues for a secret number:

- The number is between 10 and 18.
- Its ones digit is an odd number.
- The sum of its two digits is greater than 2.

Which could be Noah's number?

Ⓐ 11
Ⓑ 13
Ⓒ 14
Ⓓ 15
Ⓔ 18

3. Marie writes a doubles fact to match the cats.

She writes $8 + 8 = 16$. How can you tell without counting that Marie's fact does not match the cats?

4. MATH JOURNAL

Raj has 13 shoes in his closet. Describe three different ways to tell if 13 is even or odd.

SELF CHECK Go back to the Unit 5 Opener and see what you can check off.

Self Reflection

In this unit you learned to . . .

Skill	Lesson
Recognize and draw different shapes.	28
Break up a rectangle into squares.	29
Divide shapes into equal parts.	29
Find the total number of squares used to tile a rectangle by counting them.	30
Use addition to find the total number of objects in an array.	31
Find even and odd numbers.	32

Think about what you learned.

Use words, numbers, and drawings.

1. The most important topic I learned was .... because . . .

2. A mistake I made that helped me learn was . . .

3. One thing I am still confused about is . . .

Use Shapes and Even and Odd Numbers

Study an Example Problem and Solution

SMP 1 Make sense of problems and persevere in solving them.

Read this problem about breaking shapes into equal parts. Then look at Plory's solution to the problem.

Cake Shapes

Luna makes 3 cakes. She wants to cut each cake into equal-size pieces. Read Luna's notes.

My Notes
My cakes are in the shape of a circle, a rectangle, and a square.

- Cut one cake into halves.
- Cut one into thirds.
- Cut one into fourths.

Show one way Luna can cut the cakes.

Show how Plory's solution matches the checklist.

PROBLEM-SOLVING CHECKLIST

- ☐ Tell what is known.
- ☐ Tell what the problem is asking.
- ☐ Show all your work.
- ☐ Show that the solution works.

a. Circle something that is known.

b. Underline something that you need to find.

c. Draw a box around what you do to solve the problem.

d. Put a checkmark next to the part that shows the solution works.

PLORY'S SOLUTION

Hi, I'm Plory. Here's how I solved this problem.

- **I know what** halves, thirds, and fourths are.
  Halves are 2 equal parts.
  Thirds are 3 equal parts.
  Fourths are 4 equal parts.

I thought about what I already know.

- **I need to cut each shape into a different number of equal parts.**

2 half-circles
(2 halves)

1	2	3

3 same-size rectangles
(3 thirds)

4 same-size triangles
(4 fourths)

- **I can tell how I cut the cakes.**
  I cut the circle cake in halves.
  I cut the rectangle cake in thirds.
  I cut the square cake in fourths.

I labeled the pictures to check my thinking.

Try Another Approach

There are many ways to solve problems. Think about how to solve the Cake Shapes problem in a different way.

Cake Shapes

Luna makes 3 cakes. She wants to cut each cake into equal-size pieces. Read Luna's notes.

My Notes

My cakes are in the shape of a circle, a rectangle, and a square.

- Cut one cake into halves.
- Cut one into thirds.
- Cut one into fourths.

Show one way Luna can cut the cakes.

PLAN IT

Answer this question to help you start thinking about a plan.

Look at Plory's solution. How can you cut each shape into a different number of pieces?

SOLVE IT

Find a different solution for the Cake Shapes problem. Show all your work on a separate sheet of paper.

You may want to use the Problem-Solving Tips to get started.

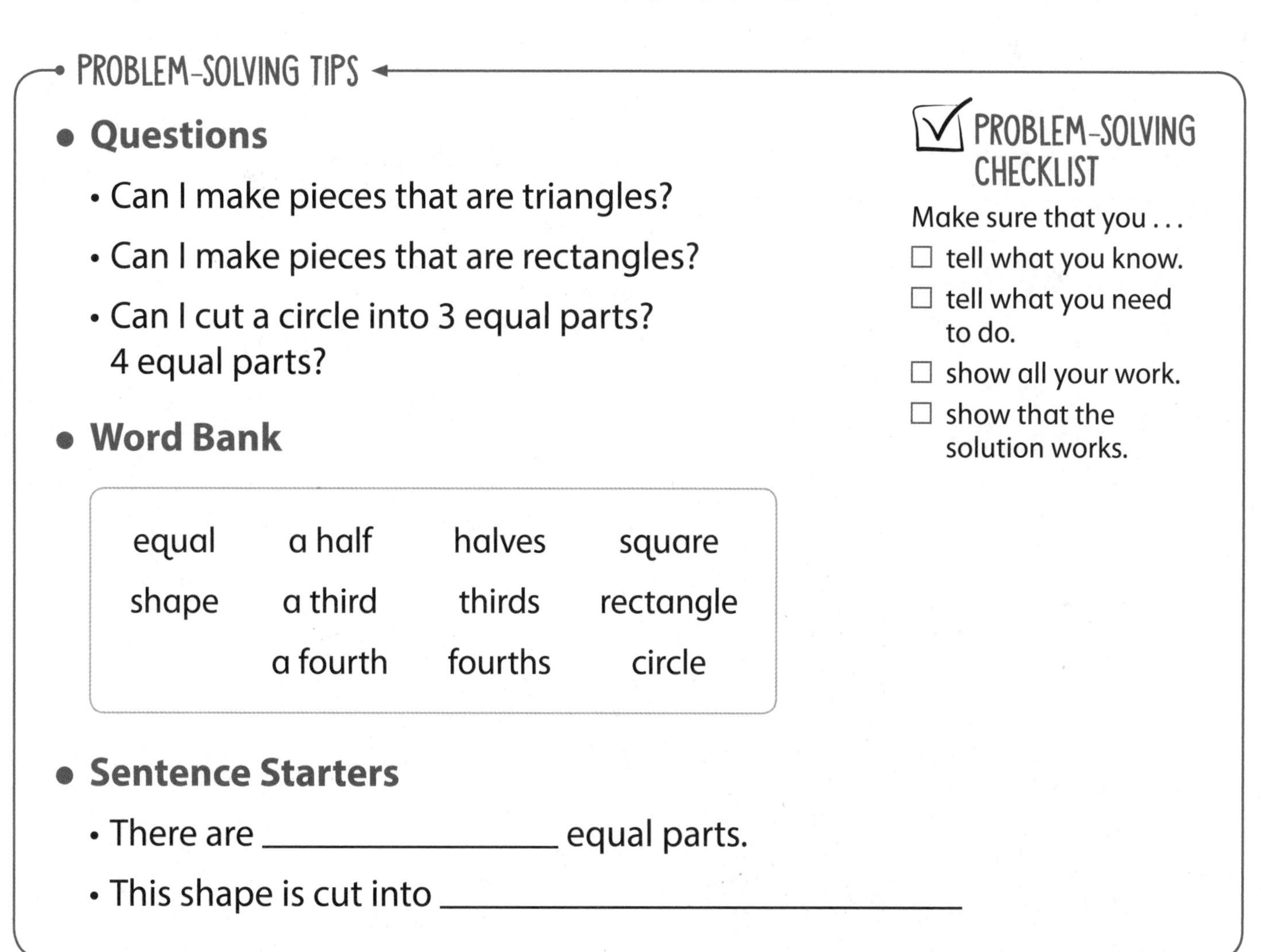

PROBLEM-SOLVING TIPS

- **Questions**
  - Can I make pieces that are triangles?
  - Can I make pieces that are rectangles?
  - Can I cut a circle into 3 equal parts? 4 equal parts?
- **Word Bank**

equal	a half	halves	square
shape	a third	thirds	rectangle
	a fourth	fourths	circle

- **Sentence Starters**
  - There are ________________ equal parts.
  - This shape is cut into ____________________________

PROBLEM-SOLVING CHECKLIST

Make sure that you . . .

☐ tell what you know.

☐ tell what you need to do.

☐ show all your work.

☐ show that the solution works.

REFLECT

Use Mathematical Practices Talk about this question with a partner.

- **Use Structure** How can you use the name of the fraction to tell how many equal parts it describes?

Discuss Models and Strategies

Solve the problem on a separate sheet of paper.
There are different ways you can solve it.

Cutting Cakes

Luna's friends make cakes in all shapes and sizes. Luna helps them plan ways to cut the cakes into pieces of different sizes. Here is one plan.

My Cake Cutting Plan

- Draw squares on the top of the cake to show how to cut it into pieces.
- Each square must be the same size.

Luna has a square cake like this one.
Each side is 6 inches long.

What size squares can Luna cut the cake into?

PLAN IT AND SOLVE IT

Find a solution for the Cutting Cakes problem.

- Divide the square into same-size smaller squares.
- Then write the length of the sides of your squares.
- Last, tell why the pieces work with Luna's plan.

You may want to use the Problem-Solving Tips to get started.

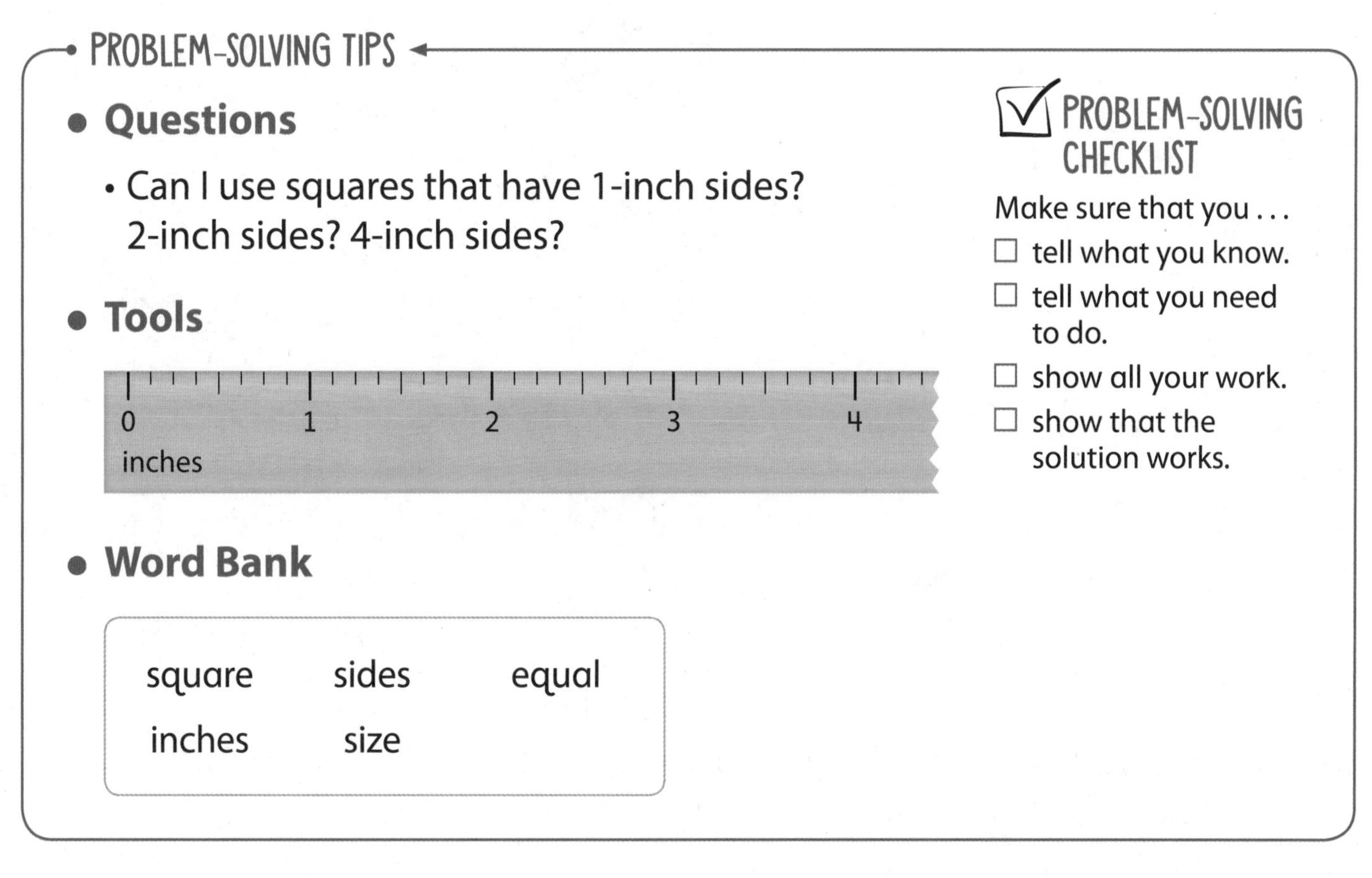

REFLECT

Use Mathematical Practices Talk about this question with a partner.

- **Use Tools** How can you put the square tiles together to make different-size squares?

Persevere On Your Own

Solve each problem on a separate sheet of paper.

Create a Cake

Luna wants to make a cake that looks like this fish.

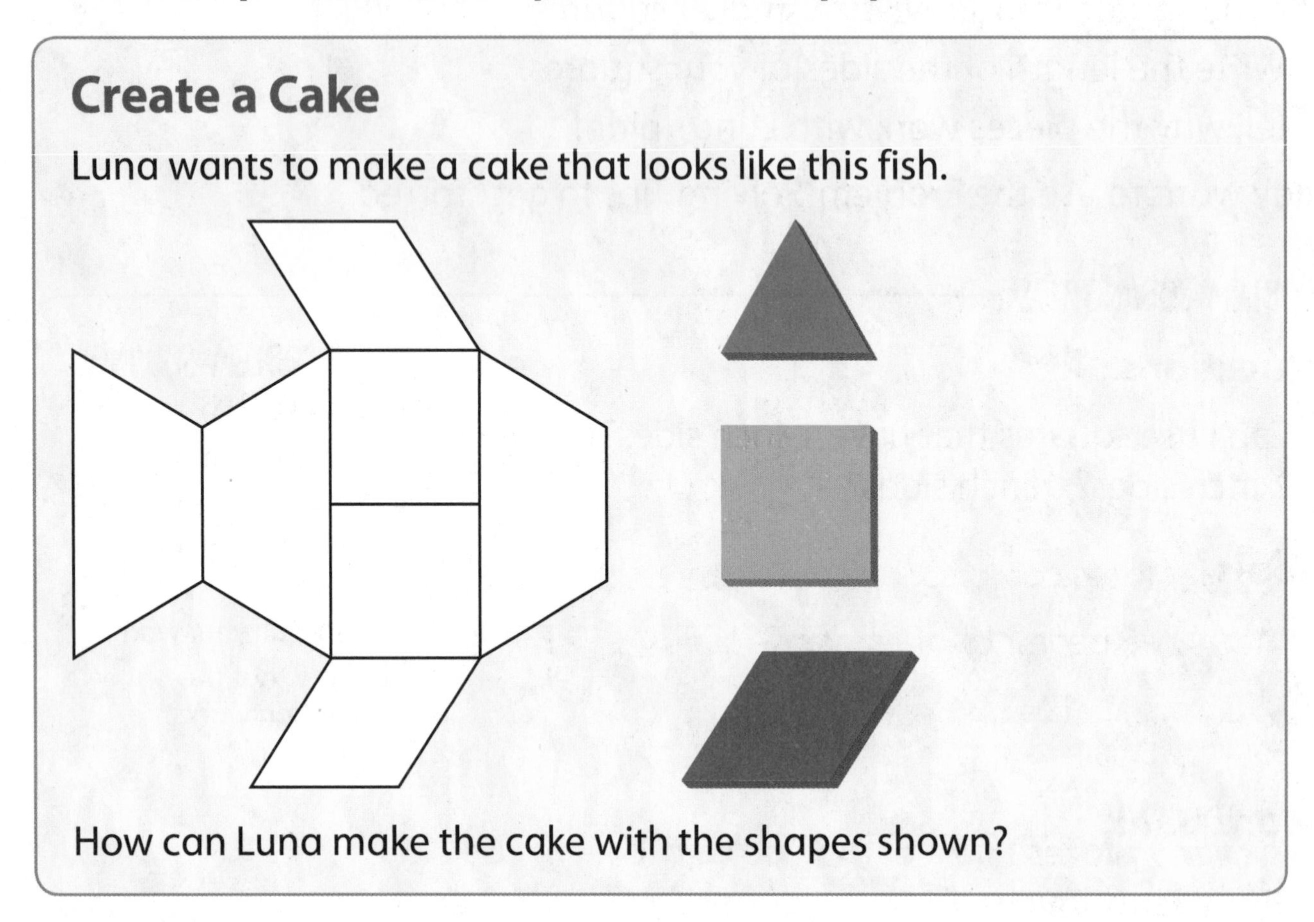

How can Luna make the cake with the shapes shown?

SOLVE IT

Help Luna make the cake shown above.

- Find a way to use Luna's pieces to make the fish.
- List and name the shapes that you used.
- Tell how many of each shape you used.

REFLECT

Use Mathematical Practices Talk about this question with a partner.

- **Make an Argument** How do you know that you named each shape correctly?

Serving Cake

Luna has 13 plates. She needs an even number to serve her cake. She will put the rest of the plates away.

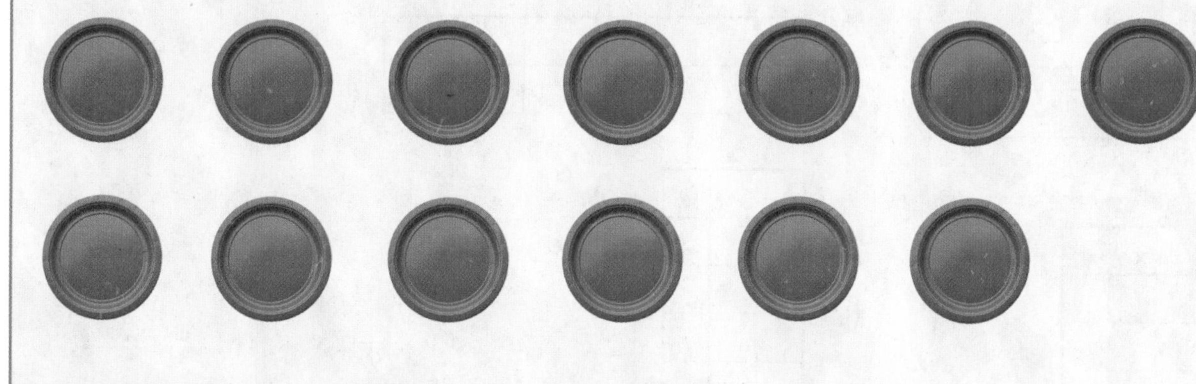

How many plates could Luna use to serve her cake?

How many will be left to put away?

SOLVE IT

Tell how many plates Luna could use and how many will be left to put away.

- Draw a picture.
- Circle an even number of plates Luna can use.
- Find the number of plates Luna will put away.
- Show that the total number of plates is 13.

REFLECT

Use Mathematical Practices Talk about this question with a partner.

- **Check Your Answer** What did you do to check that your answer makes sense?

Unit Review

Kate makes rectangles. She uses 18 same-sized square tiles to make each rectangle. Which rectangles can Kate make? Choose all the correct answers.

Ⓐ 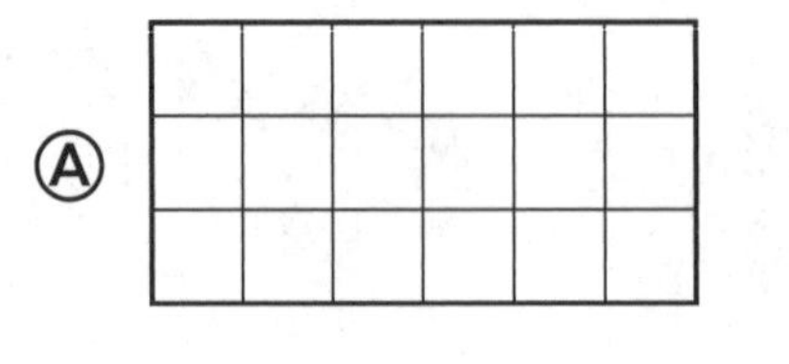

Ⓑ 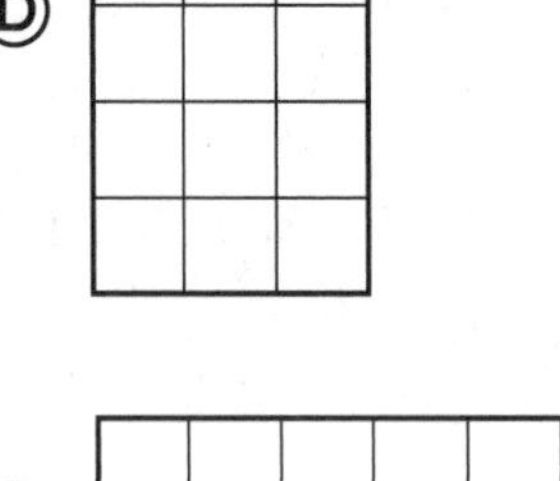

Ⓒ 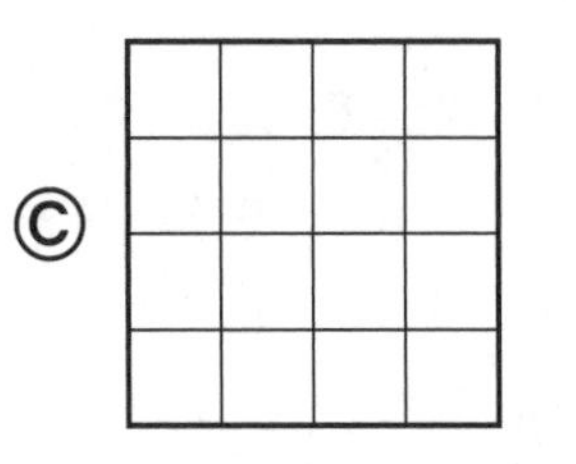

Ⓓ 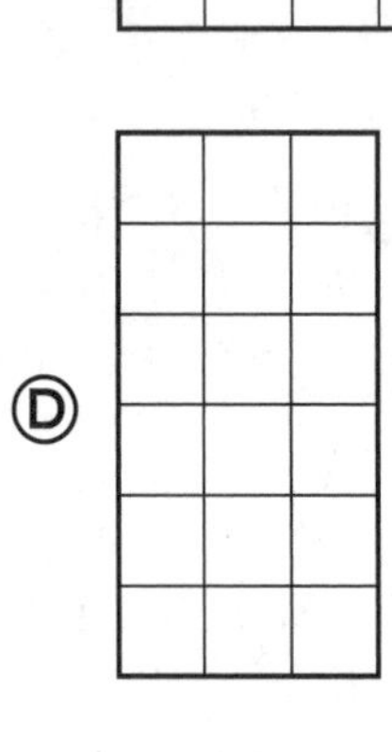

Ⓔ 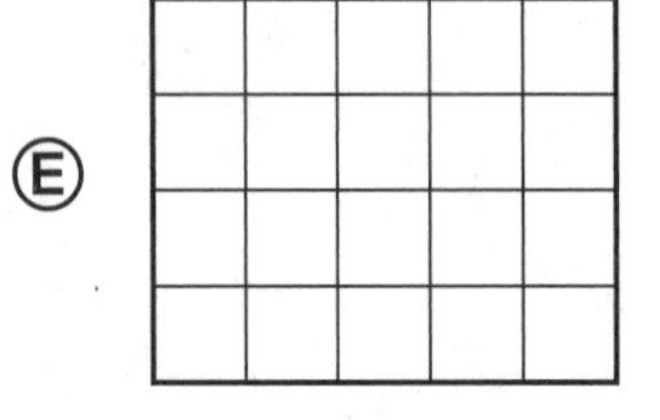

Ⓕ 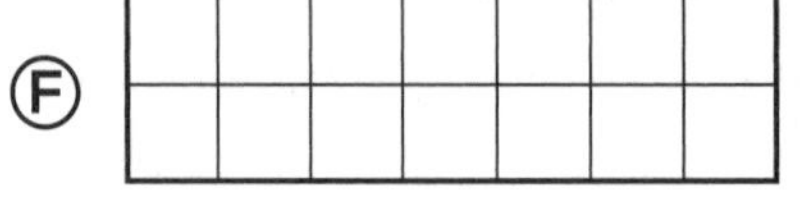

Mason put his toy cars in an array.

Which equation shows the total number of cars in the array?

Ⓐ $4 + 5 = 9$

Ⓑ $4 + 4 + 4 + 4 = 16$

Ⓒ $5 + 5 + 5 + 5 + 5 = 25$

Ⓓ $4 + 4 + 4 + 4 + 4 = 20$

3 Dennis drew a hexagon. Decide if each statement about the hexagon is true.

Choose *True* or *False* for each statement.

	True	False
It has 6 angles.	Ⓐ	Ⓑ
It is a quadrilateral.	Ⓒ	Ⓓ
It has more than 5 sides.	Ⓔ	Ⓕ
It has fewer angles than a rectangle.	Ⓖ	Ⓗ

4 Seth has two bags of dog treats. Each bag has the same number of dog treats. Which could be the number of dog treats Seth has in all?
Choose all the correct answers.

Ⓐ 4

Ⓑ 7

Ⓒ 12

Ⓓ 14

Ⓔ 15

5 The two squares below are the same size. Each square is divided into equal parts in a different way.

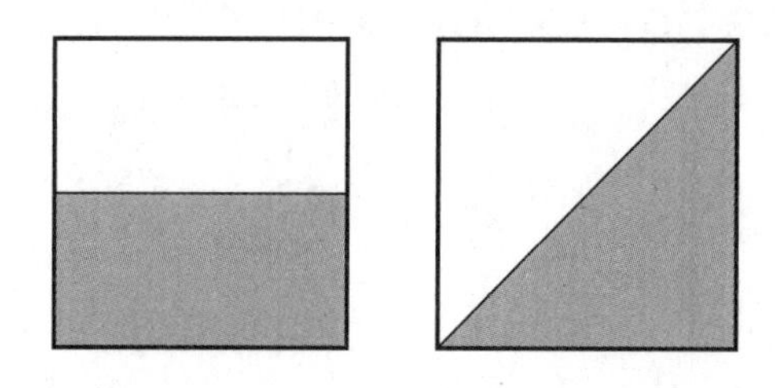

Are the shaded parts equal in size? Explain your answer.

....

....

....

Performance Task

Answer the questions. Use the shapes on this page. Show the rest of your work on separate paper.

Keeth Elementary School is having Field Day. Each grade plays on a separate field.

- Grade 1 has two classes. Draw a line to divide the rectangular field into 2 equal parts. What shape is each part? Choose a word from the box to tell the name of each equal part.

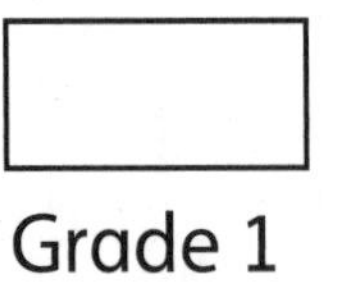

Grade 1

- Explain how you could divide the same field into 2 equal parts that are each a different shape than the parts in your drawing above. What shape is each part?
- There are four Grade 2 classes and four Grade 3 classes. Draw lines to divide each square field into 4 equal parts. Divide the two fields in different ways. Use a word from the box to name each equal part.

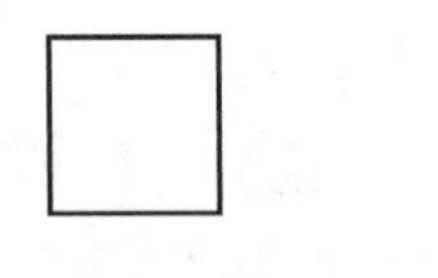

Grade 2

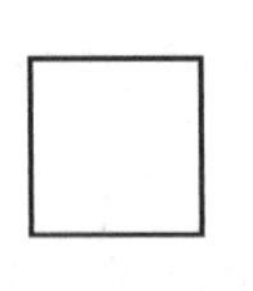

Grade 3

Checklist

Did you . . .

- ☐ make the parts equal in size?
- ☐ check your answers?
- ☐ explain your answers?

one half
one third
one fourth

REFLECT

Use a Tool How could you fold a piece of square paper to show that both squares have 4 equal parts?

UNIT 5

Vocabulary

Draw or write to show examples for each term. Then draw or write to show other math words in the unit.

angle one of the corners of a shape where two sides meet.

My Example

array a set of objects arranged in equal rows and equal columns.

My Example

column a top-to-bottom (vertical) line of objects or numbers, such as in an array or table.

My Example

cube a two-dimensional closed shape with 6 square faces and all sides of equal length.

My Example

edge a line segment where two faces meet in a three-dimensional shape.

My Example

even number a whole number that always has 0, 2, 4, 6, or 8 in the ones place. An even number of objects can be put into pairs or into two equal groups without any leftovers.

My Example

hexagon a two-dimensional closed shape with 6 straight sides and 6 angles.

My Example

odd number a whole number that always has 1, 3, 5, 7, or 9 in the ones place. An odd number of objects cannot be put into pairs or into two equal groups without a leftover.

My Example

one fourth one of four equal parts of a whole.

My Example

one half one of two equal parts of a whole.

My Example

one third one of three equal parts of a whole.

My Example

pentagon a two-dimensional closed shape with exactly 5 sides and 5 angles.

My Example

quadrilateral a two-dimensional closed shape with exactly 4 sides and 4 angles.

My Example

rectangle a quadrilateral with 4 square corners. Opposite sides of a rectangle have the same length.

My Example

rhombus a quadrilateral with all sides the same length.

My Example

row a side-by-side (horizontal) line of objects or numbers, such as in an array or table.

My Example

side a line segment that forms part of a two-dimensional shape.

My Example

square a quadrilateral with 4 square corners and 4 sides of equal length.

My Example

thirds the parts formed when a whole is divided into three equal parts.

My Example

vertex the point where two rays, lines, or line segments meet to form an angle.

My Example

My Word: ____________

____

____

My Example

My Word: ____________

____

____

My Example

My Word: ____________

____

____

My Example

My Word: ____________

____

____

My Example

UNIT 3

Cumulative Practice

Name: ______________________________

Set 1: Add Two-Digit Numbers

Solve the problems. Show your work.

1. Find 27 + 41.

27 + 41 = ...

2. Find 36 + 18.

36 + 18 = ...

Set 2: Subtract Two-Digit Numbers

Solve the problems. Show your work.

1. Find 37 − 24.

37 − 24 = ...

2. Find 42 − 28.

42 − 28 = ...

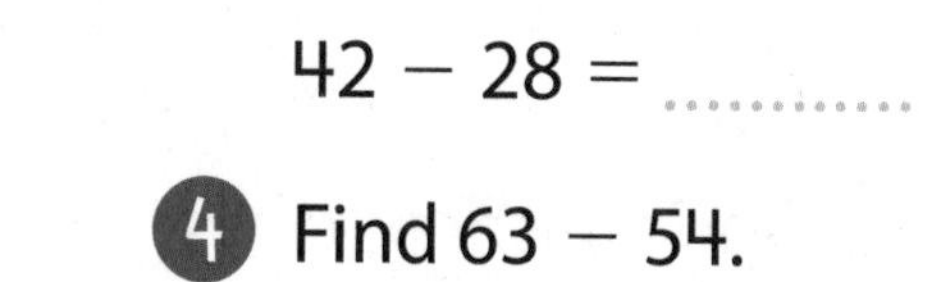

3. Find 58 − 29.

58 − 29 = ...

4. Find 63 − 54.

63 − 54 = ...

Set 3: Add and Subtract with Two-Digit Numbers

Solve the problems.

1. 23 + 24 = ...
2. 32 + 48 = ...
3. 45 − 23 = ...
4. 36 − 19 = ...
5. 42 + 49 = ...
6. 60 − 38 = ...
7. 84 − 58 = ...
8. 64 + 34 = ...

Set 4: Solve Word Problems with Two-Digit Numbers

Solve the word problems. Show your work.

1. Some chickens drink from a water bowl. Then 12 chickens walk away. Now 21 chickens drink from the water bowl. How many chickens drink from the water bowl at the start?

2. Dana picks 28 apples. Her sister picks 19 apples. Then they give away 11 apples. How many apples do they have now?

3. Dillon eats 76 almonds in three days. He eats 29 almonds on the first day and 34 almonds on the second day. How many almonds does Dillon eat on the third day?

Name: ____________________

Set 5: Mental Math Strategies for Addition

Use mental math to solve the problems.

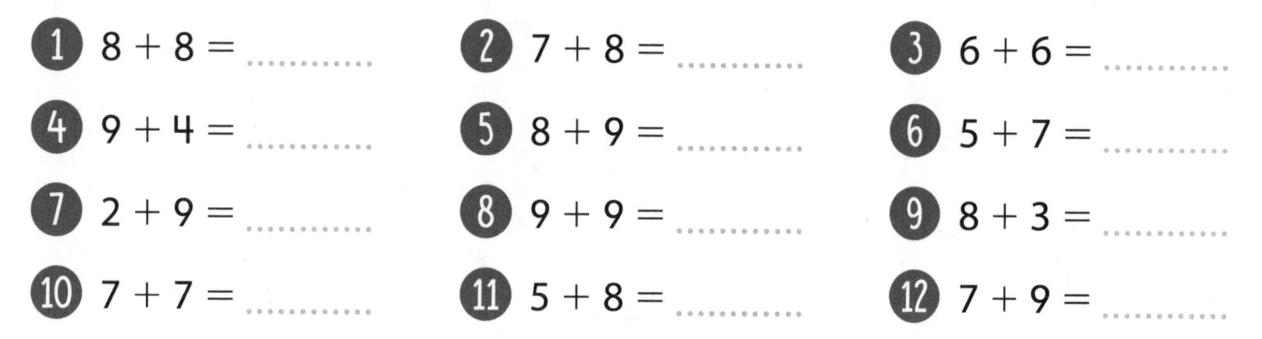

1. $8 + 8 =$ ....
2. $7 + 8 =$ ....
3. $6 + 6 =$ ....
4. $9 + 4 =$ ....
5. $8 + 9 =$ ....
6. $5 + 7 =$ ....
7. $2 + 9 =$ ....
8. $9 + 9 =$ ....
9. $8 + 3 =$ ....
10. $7 + 7 =$ ....
11. $5 + 8 =$ ....
12. $7 + 9 =$ ....

Set 6: Solve One-Step Word Problems

Solve the word problems. Show your work.

1. Tom has 32 toys. He puts 18 toys on the bottom shelf. The rest are on the top shelf. How many toys are on the top shelf?

2. A small box holds 21 fewer water bottles than a big box. The small box holds 9 water bottles. How many water bottles does the big box hold?

3. Rita makes 46 keychains and Dee makes 39 keychains. How many more keychains does Rita make than Dee?

4. Carl makes 19 headbands. He keeps 4 headbands. He gives the rest to friends. How many headbands does Carl give to his friends?

Set 7: Mental Math Strategies for Subtraction

Use mental math to solve the problems.

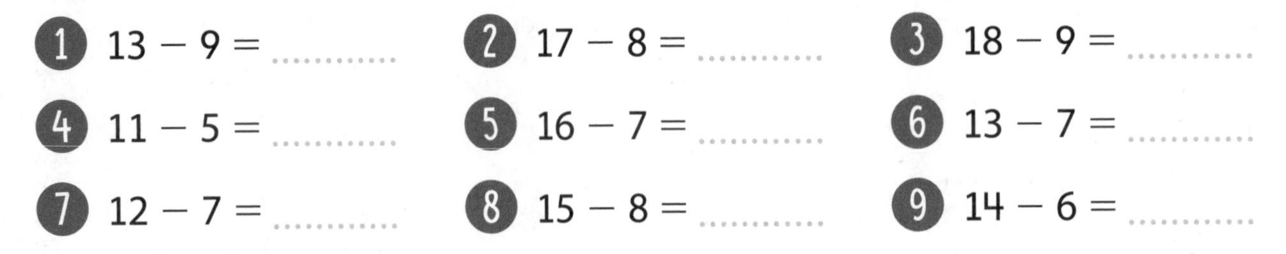

1. $13 - 9 =$ ....
2. $17 - 8 =$ ....
3. $18 - 9 =$ ....
4. $11 - 5 =$ ....
5. $16 - 7 =$ ....
6. $13 - 7 =$ ....
7. $12 - 7 =$ ....
8. $15 - 8 =$ ....
9. $14 - 6 =$ ....

Set 8: Solve Two-Step Word Problems

Solve the word problems. Show your work.

1. There are 19 geese in a pond. 6 geese fly away. Then 9 more geese land in the pond. How many geese are in the pond now?

2. Simon has \$56. He spends \$12 on a new shirt. Then he spends \$38 on a pair of shoes. How much money does Simon have left?

3. A baker has 15 pounds of flour. A shipment of 25 pounds of flour arrives. The baker then uses 11 pounds of flour. How many pounds of flour are left?

4. Anu has 14 long shells and 9 round shells. Then she finds 7 more long shells. How many shells does Anu have now?

UNIT 4

Cumulative Practice

Name: ______________________

Set 1: Three-Digit Numbers

Fill in the blanks to show the numbers in different ways.

1. 300 = ______ hundreds 300 = ______ tens 300 = ______ ones
2. 500 = ______ hundreds 500 = ______ tens 500 = ______ ones

Set 2: Write Three-Digit Numbers

Use the chart below for problems 1–3.

Hundreds	Tens	Ones
2	3	7

1. Write the number using only digits. ______
2. Write the number in expanded form.
   ______ + ______ + ______
3. Write the number using words. ______________________

Fill in the blanks to show the numbers in different ways for problems 4 and 5.

4. Write eight hundred four using only digits. ______
5. Write eight hundred four in expanded form.
   ______ + ______ + ______

Set 3: Compare Three-Digit Numbers

Write >, <, or = in the circle to compare each pair of numbers.

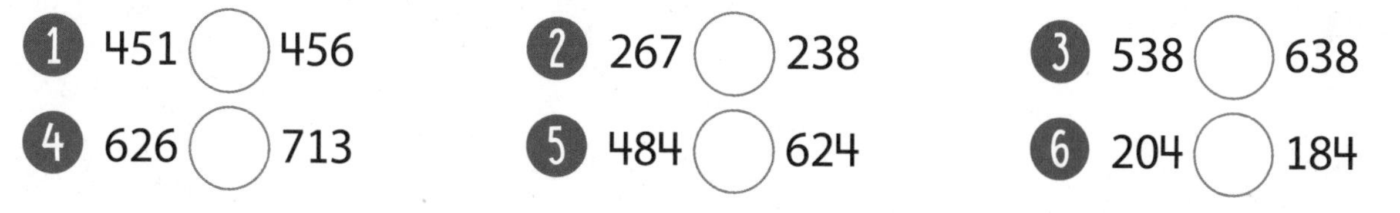

Set 4: Skip Count by Fives, Tens, and Hundreds

Continue each skip-counting pattern forward or backward for problems 1–4.

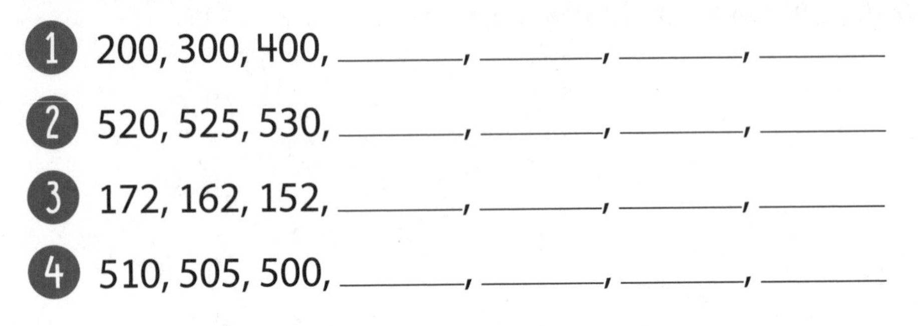

1. 200, 300, 400, ______, ______, ______, ______
2. 520, 525, 530, ______, ______, ______, ______
3. 172, 162, 152, ______, ______, ______, ______
4. 510, 505, 500, ______, ______, ______, ______

Solve problems 5–10. Fill in the blanks.

5. 746 + 10 = ...
6. 472 − 100 = ...
7. 228 + 100 = ...
8. 581 − 10 = ...
9. 356 − 10 = ...
10. 349 + 100 = ...

Set 5: Add Three-Digit Numbers

Find the sum. Show your work.

1. $\begin{array}{r} 423 \\ +\ 215 \\ \hline \end{array}$

2. $\begin{array}{r} 382 \\ +\ 536 \\ \hline \end{array}$

3. $\begin{array}{r} 286 \\ +\ 204 \\ \hline \end{array}$

4. $\begin{array}{r} 799 \\ +\ 152 \\ \hline \end{array}$

Name: ______________________

Set 6: Subtract Three-Digit Numbers

Find the difference. Show your work.

1. $\begin{array}{r} 363 \\ -\ 127 \\ \hline \end{array}$

2. $\begin{array}{r} 472 \\ -\ 298 \\ \hline \end{array}$

3. $\begin{array}{r} 629 \\ -\ 534 \\ \hline \end{array}$

4. $\begin{array}{r} 795 \\ -\ 737 \\ \hline \end{array}$

5. $\begin{array}{r} 536 \\ -\ 474 \\ \hline \end{array}$

6. $\begin{array}{r} 589 \\ -\ 364 \\ \hline \end{array}$

Set 7: Add Several Two-Digit Numbers

Find the sum. Show your work.

1. 27 + 25 + 13 + 35 = ?

   27 + 25 + 13 + 35 = ...

2. 34 + 52 + 26 + 15 = ?

   34 + 52 + 26 + 15 = ...

Set 8: Subtract Two-Digit Numbers

Find the difference. Show your work on the number line for problems 1 and 2.

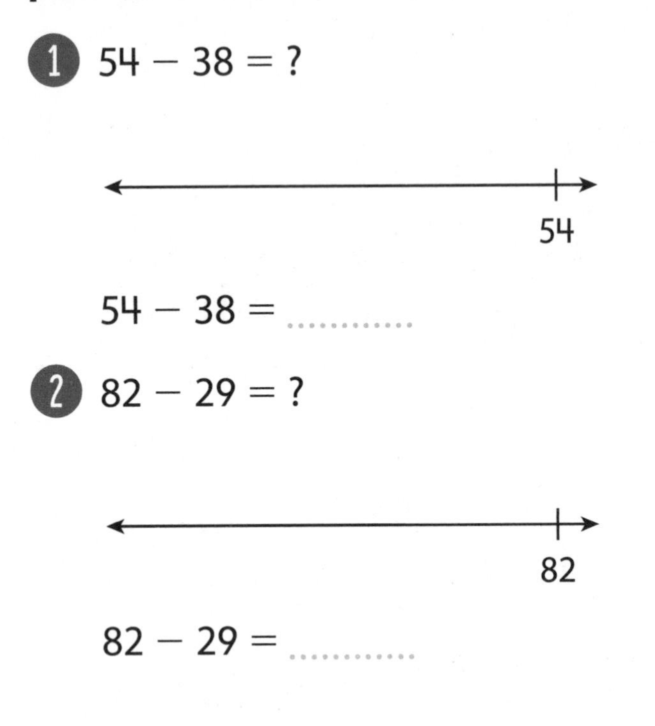

1. $54 - 38 = ?$

$54 - 38 =$ ....

2. $82 - 29 = ?$

$82 - 29 =$ ....

Find the difference for problems 3–6. Show your work.

3. $36 - 17 = ?$

$36 - 17 =$ ....

4. $42 - 14 = ?$

$42 - 14 =$ ....

5. $55 - 38 = ?$

$55 - 38 =$ ....

6. $67 - 29 = ?$

$67 - 29 =$ ....

UNIT 5

Cumulative Practice

Name: ______________________

Set 1: Measure in Inches and Centimeters

Use a ruler to measure the length of each pencil in inches for problems 1 and 2.

1. .... inches

2. .... inches

Use a ruler to measure the length of each pencil in centimeters for problems 3 and 4.

3. .... centimeters

4. .... centimeters

Set 2: Measure to the Nearest Unit

Solve the problems. Include the units.

1. What is the length of the wire to the nearest foot?

0 1 2 3 4 5 6 7 8 9 10 11 12 13 14 15 16 17 18 19 20 21 22 23 24 25 26
Inches 1 ft YARDSTICK 2 ft

The yardstick is not life-sized.

....

2. What is the length of the ribbon to the nearest inch?

0 1 2 3 4 5 6
inches

The ruler is not life-sized.

....

Set 3: Measure with Different Units

Use this marker to solve the problems.

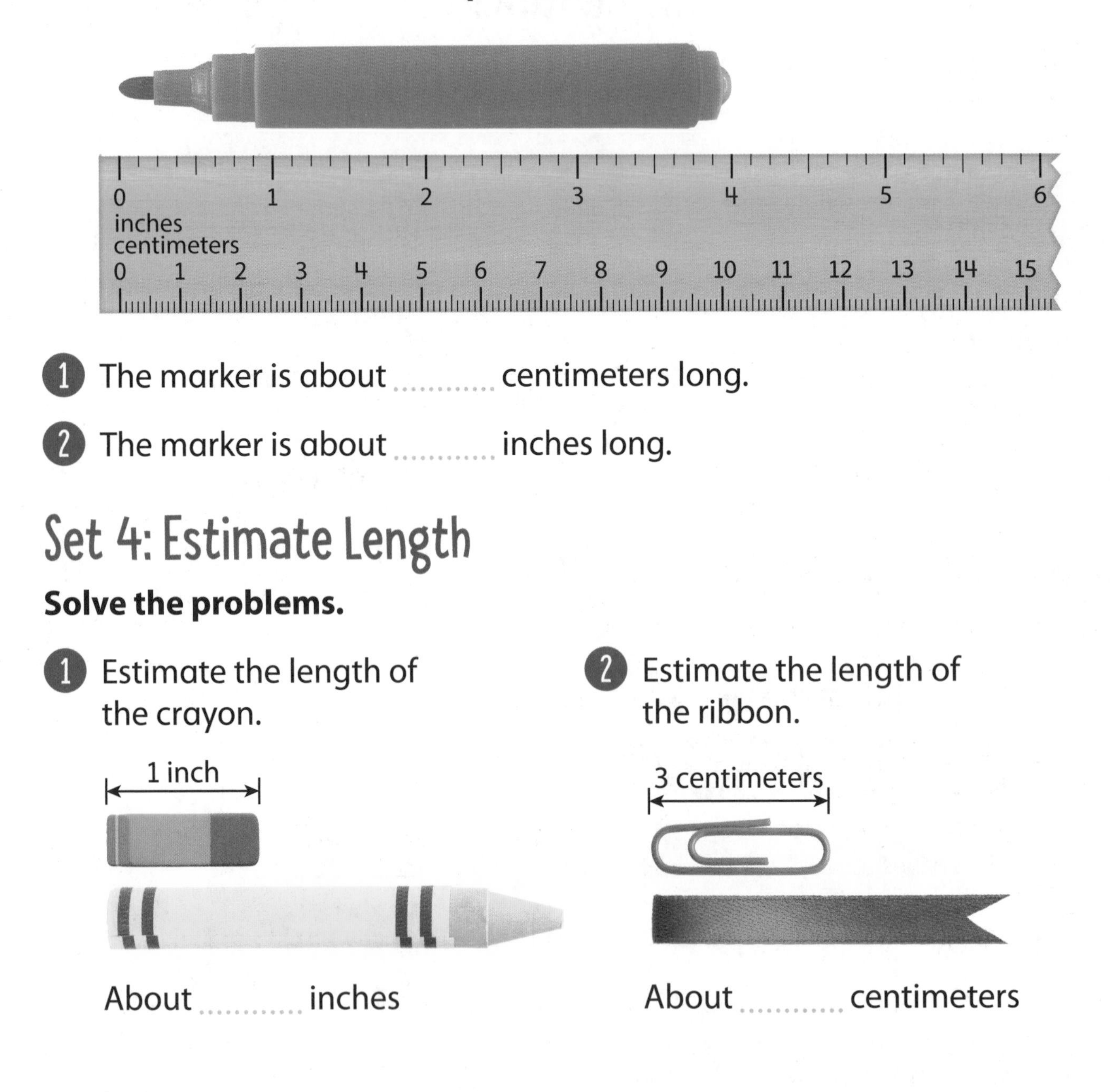

1. The marker is about .... centimeters long.

2. The marker is about .... inches long.

Set 4: Estimate Length

Solve the problems.

1. Estimate the length of the crayon.

   About .... inches

2. Estimate the length of the ribbon.

   About .... centimeters

Name: ____________________

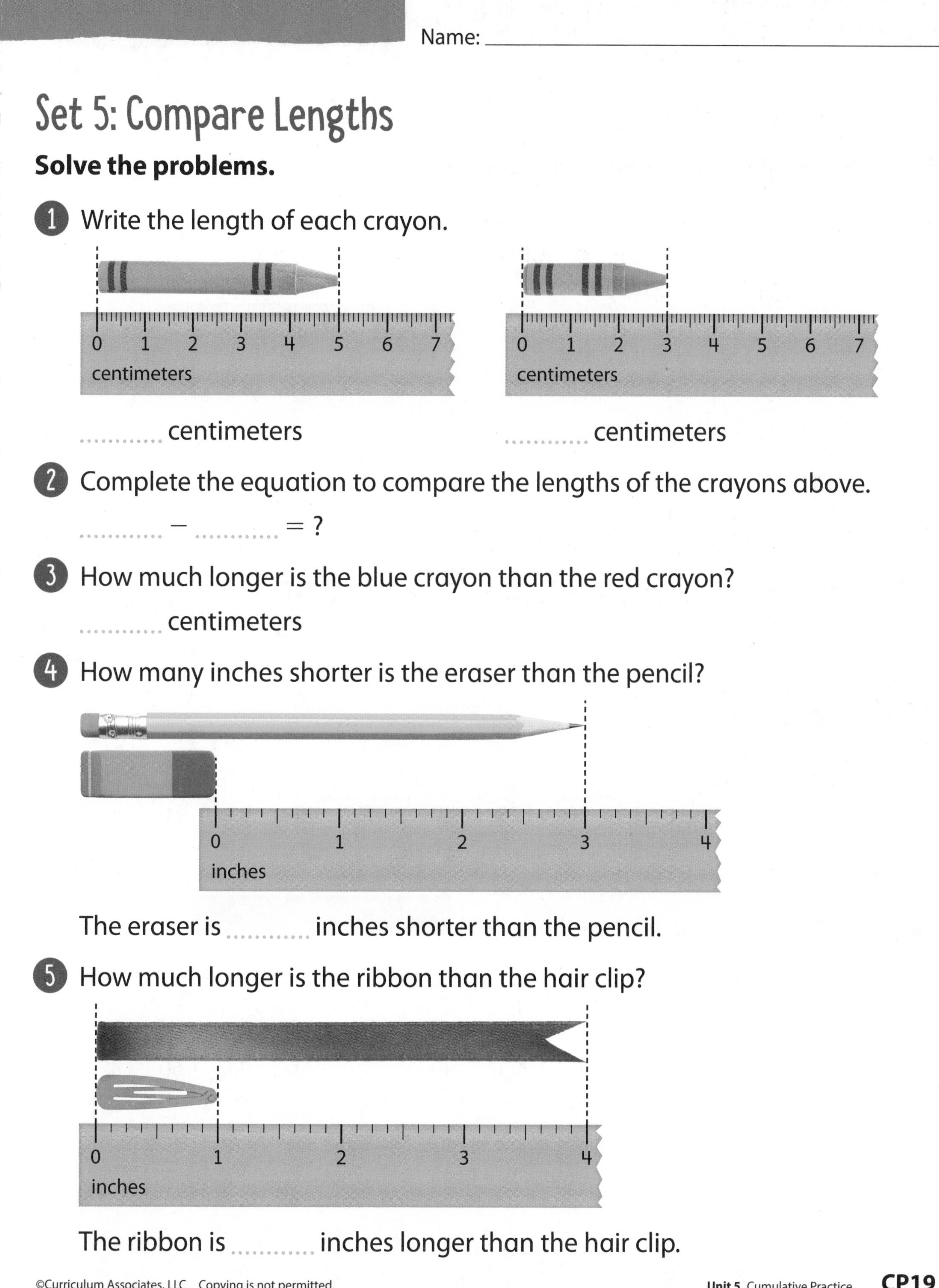

Set 5: Compare Lengths

Solve the problems.

1. Write the length of each crayon.

   .... centimeters .... centimeters

2. Complete the equation to compare the lengths of the crayons above.

   .... − .... = ?

3. How much longer is the blue crayon than the red crayon?

   .... centimeters

4. How many inches shorter is the eraser than the pencil?

   The eraser is .... inches shorter than the pencil.

5. How much longer is the ribbon than the hair clip?

   The ribbon is .... inches longer than the hair clip.

Set 6: Add and Subtract Lengths

Solve the word problem. Show your work.

1 Nicole has 24 inches of blue ribbon and 11 inches of red ribbon. She uses 18 inches of ribbon. How many inches of ribbon does Nicole have left?

.... inches of ribbon left

Set 7: Add and Subtract on the Number Line

Solve the problems.

1 Find 27 + 19 on the number line.

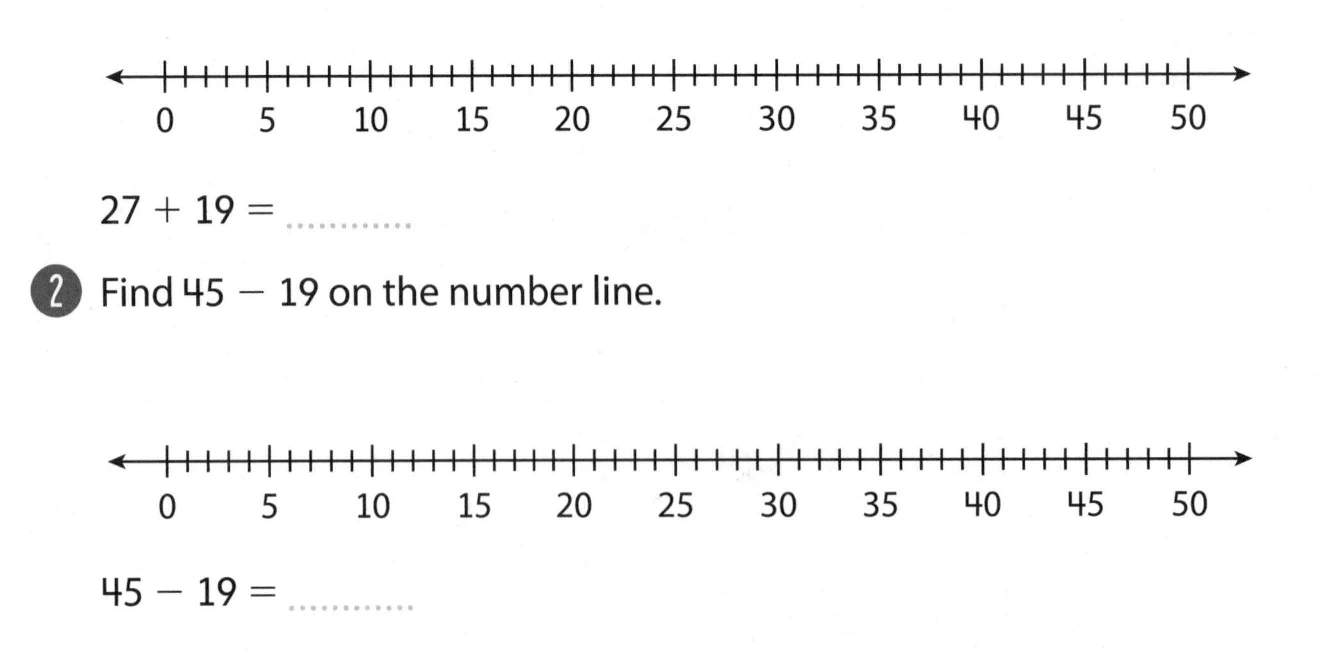

27 + 19 = ...

2 Find 45 − 19 on the number line.

45 − 19 = ...

Glossary/Glosario

English	Español	Example/Ejemplo

Aa

English	Español	Example/Ejemplo
add to put together two or more quantities, to find the total of two or more numbers, or to find how many in all.	**sumar** combinar dos o más cantidades, hallar el total de dos o más números, o hallar cuántos hay en total.	$27 + 15 = 42$
addend a number being added.	**sumando** número que se suma.	$4 + 7 = 11$ addends
AM (or a.m.) morning, or the time from midnight until before noon.	**a. m.** el tiempo que transcurre desde la medianoche hasta el mediodía.	AM 7:20
analog clock a clock that uses hour and minute hand positions to show time.	**reloj analógico** reloj que muestra la hora con una manecilla de la hora y un minutero.	hour hand, minute hand
angle one of the corners of a shape where two sides meet.	**ángulo** una de las esquinas de una figura en la que se unen dos lados.	angle
array a set of objects arranged in equal rows and equal columns.	**matriz** conjunto de objetos agrupados en filas y columnas iguales.	

English	Español	Example/Ejemplo
associative property of addition when the grouping of three or more addends is changed, the total does not change.	**propiedad asociativa de la suma** cambiar la agrupación de tres o más sumandos no cambia el total.	$(2 + 3) + 4 = 2 + (3 + 4)$

Bb

bar graph
a data display in which bars are used to show the number of items in each category.

gráfica de barras
representación de datos en la cual se usan barras para mostrar el número de elementos de cada categoría.

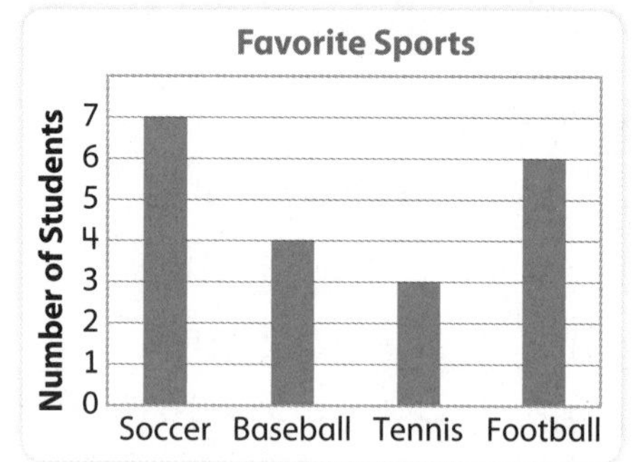

Cc

English	Español	Example/Ejemplo
cent (¢) the smallest unit of money in the U.S. One penny has a value of 1 cent. 100 cents is equal to 1 dollar.	**centavo (¢)** la menor unidad monetaria de Estados Unidos. 100 centavos equivalen a 1 dólar.	1 cent 1¢
centimeter (cm) a unit of length. There are 100 centimeters in 1 meter.	**centímetro (cm)** unidad de longitud. 100 centímetros equivalen a 1 metro.	Your little finger is about 1 **centimeter** (cm) across.

English	Español	Example/Ejemplo
column a top-to-bottom (vertical) line of objects or numbers, such as in an array or table.	**columna** línea de objetos o números vertical (que va de arriba abajo), como las de una matriz o una tabla.	
commutative property of addition changing the order of addends does not change the total.	**propiedad conmutativa de la suma** cambiar el orden de los sumandos no cambia el total.	$3 + 4 = 4 + 3$
compare to decide if numbers, amounts, or sizes are greater than, less than, or equal to each other.	**comparar** determinar si un número, una cantidad o un tamaño es mayor que, menor que o igual a otro número, otra cantidad u otro tamaño.	$421 > 312$
count on start with one addend and count to find a total.	**contar hacia delante** comenzar desde un sumando y contar para hallar un total.	$8 + 3 = ?$ 8, then **9, 10, 11** $8 + 3 = 11$
cube a solid shape with 6 square faces and all sides of equal length.	**cubo** figura sólida que tiene 6 caras cuadradas y todos los lados de igual longitud.	

English	Español	Example/Ejemplo
Dd		
data a set of collected information.	**datos** conjunto de información reunida.	Favorite Toys
difference the result of subtraction.	**diferencia** el resultado de la resta.	9 − 3 = **6**
digit a symbol used to write numbers.	**dígito** símbolo que se usa para escribir números.	The digits are 0, 1, 2, 3, 4, 5, 6, 7, 8, and 9.
digital clock a clock that uses digits to show the time.	**reloj digital** reloj que usa dígitos para mostrar la hora.	AM 7:20
dime a coin with a value of 10 cents (10¢).	**moneda de 10¢** moneda con un valor de 10 centavos (10¢).	10 cents 10¢
dollar ($) a unit of money in the U.S. There are 100 cents in 1 dollar ($1).	**dólar** unidad monetaria de Estados Unidos. 1 dólar ($1) equivale a 100 centavos.	

English	Español	Example/Ejemplo
Ee		
edge a line segment where two faces meet in a three-dimensional shape.	**arista** segmento de recta donde se encuentran dos caras de una figura tridimensional.	Edge
equal having the same value, same size, or same amount.	**igual** que tiene el mismo valor, el mismo tamaño, o la misma cantidad.	●●● + ● = ●●●● 3 + 1 is equal to 4.
equal sign (=) a symbol that means *is the same value as*.	**signo de igual (=)** símbolo que significa *tiene el mismo valor que*.	12 + 4 = 16
equation a mathematical statement that uses an equal sign (=) to show that two things have the same value.	**ecuación** enunciado matemático en el que se usa un signo de igual (=) para mostrar que dos cosas tienen el mismo valor.	25 − 15 = 10
estimate (noun) a close guess made using mathematical thinking.	**estimación** suposición aproximada que se hace usando el razonamiento matemático.	28 + 21 = ? 30 + 20 = 50 50 is an estimate of the sum.
estimate (verb) to make a close guess based on mathematical thinking.	**estimar / hacer una estimación** hacer una suposición aproximada usando el razonamiento matemático.	28 + 21 is about 50.

English	Español	Example/Ejemplo
even number a whole number that always has 0, 2, 4, 6, or 8 in the ones place. An even number of objects can be put into pairs or into two equal groups without any leftovers.	**número par** número entero que siempre tiene 0, 2, 4, 6, o 8 en la posición de las unidades. Un número par de objetos puede agruparse en parejas o en dos grupos iguales sin sobrantes.	20, 22, 24, 26, and 28 are even numbers.
expanded form a way a number is written to show the place value of each digit.	**forma desarrollada** manera de escribir un número para mostrar el valor posicional de cada dígito.	$249 = 200 + 40 + 9$

Ff

English	Español	Example/Ejemplo
face a flat surface of a solid shape.	**cara** superficie plana de una figura sólida.	face
fact family a group of related equations that use the same numbers, but in a different order and two different operation symbols. A fact family can show the relationship between addition and subtraction.	**familia de datos** grupo de ecuaciones relacionadas que tienen los mismos números ordenados de distinta manera y dos símbolos de operaciones diferentes. Una familia de datos puede mostrar la relación que existe entre la suma y la resta.	$7 - 3 = 4$ $7 - 4 = 3$ $3 + 4 = 7$ $4 + 3 = 7$

English	Español	Example/Ejemplo
foot (ft) a unit of length. There are 12 inches in 1 foot.	**pie (ft)** unidad de longitud. 1 pie equivale a 12 pulgadas.	12 inches = 1 foot
fourths the parts formed when a whole is divided into four equal parts.	**cuartos** partes que se forman cuando se divide un entero en cuatro partes iguales.	fourths 4 equal parts

Gg

English	Español	Example/Ejemplo
greater than symbol (>) a symbol used to compare two numbers when the first is greater than the second.	**símbolo de mayor que (>)** símbolo que se usa para comparar dos números cuando el primero es mayor que el segundo.	421 > 312

Hh

English	Español	Example/Ejemplo
halves the parts formed when a whole is divided into two equal parts.	**medios** partes que se obtienen cuando se divide un entero en dos partes iguales.	2 equal parts
hexagon a two-dimensional closed shape with 6 straight sides and 6 angles.	**hexágono** figura bidimensional cerrada que tiene 6 lados y 6 ángulos.	
hour (h) a unit of time. There are 60 minutes in 1 hour.	**hora (h)** unidad de tiempo. 1 hora equivale a 60 minutos.	60 minutes = 1 hour

English	Español	Example/Ejemplo
hour hand the shorter hand on a clock. It shows the hours.	**manecilla de la hora** la manecilla más corta de un reloj. Muestra las horas.	hour hand
hundreds groups of 10 tens.	**centenas** grupos de 10 decenas.	

Ii

English	Español	Example/Ejemplo
inch (in.) a unit of length. There are 12 inches in 1 foot.	**pulgada (pulg.)** unidad de longitud del sistema usual. 12 pulgadas equivalen a 1 pie.	A quarter is about 1 **inch** (in.) across.

Ll

English	Español	Example/Ejemplo
length measurement that tells the distance from one point to another, or how long something is.	**longitud** medida que indica la distancia de un punto a otro, o cuán largo es un objeto.	length

English	Español	Example/Ejemplo
less than symbol (<) a symbol used to compare two numbers when the first is less than the second.	**símbolo de menor que (<)** símbolo que se usa para comparar dos números cuando el primero es menor que el segundo.	321 < 421
line plot a data display that shows data as marks above a number line.	**diagrama de puntos** representación de datos en la cual se muestran datos como marcas sobre una recta numérica.	Sea Lion Lengths 48 49 50 51 52 Inches
longer having a length that is greater than that of another object.	**más largo** que tiene una longitud mayor que la de otro objeto.	longer

Mm

English	Español	Example/Ejemplo
measure to find length, height, or weight by comparing it to a known unit.	**medir** determinar la longitud, la altura o el peso de un objeto comparándolo con una unidad conocida.	0 1 2 inches 0 1 2 3 4 5 centimeters

English	Español	Example/Ejemplo
measuring tape a flexible measuring strip that shows inches and centimeters.	**cinta de medir** una tira flexible que se usa para medir y muestra pulgadas y centímetros.	
meter (m) a unit of length. There are 100 centimeters in 1 meter.	**metro (m)** unidad de longitud. 1 metro es igual a 100 centímetros.	100 centimeters = 1 meter
meter stick a measuring stick that is 1 meter long and shows 100 centimeters.	**metro** una regla que mide 1 metro de longitud y muestra 100 centímetros.	97 98 99 100
minute (min) a unit of time. There are 60 minutes in 1 hour.	**minuto (min)** unidad de tiempo. 60 minutos equivalen a 1 hora.	60 minutes = 1 hour
minute hand the longer hand on a clock. It shows minutes.	**minutero** la manecilla más larga de un reloj. Muestra los minutos.	minute hand

Nn

English	Español	Example/Ejemplo
nickel a coin with a value of 5 cents (5¢).	**moneda de 5¢** moneda con un valor de 5 centavos (5¢).	5 cents 5¢

English	Español	Example/Ejemplo
number line a straight line marked at equal spaces to show numbers.	**recta numérica** recta que tiene marcas separadas por espacios iguales; las marcas muestran números.	0 1 2 3 4

Oo

English	Español	Example/Ejemplo
odd number a whole number that always has 1, 3, 5, 7, or 9 in the ones place. An odd number of objects cannot be put into pairs or into two equal groups without a leftover.	**número impar** número entero que siempre tiene el dígito 1, 3, 5, 7, o 9 en a posición de las unidades. Un número impar de objetos no puede ordenarse en pares o en dos grupos iguales sin que queden sobrantes.	21, 23, 25, 27, and 29 are odd numbers.
one fourth one of four equal parts of a whole.	**un cuarto** una de las cuatro partes iguales de un entero.	4 equal parts
one half one of two equal parts of a whole.	**un medio** una de las dos partes iguales de un entero.	2 equal parts
one third one of three equal parts of a whole.	**un tercio** una de las tres partes iguales de un entero.	3 equal parts

English	Español	Example/Ejemplo
ones single units or objects.	**unidades** elementos u objetos individuales.	5 ones
open number line a straight line with only the numbers important to a problem labeled.	**recta numérica vacía** recta numérica que solo muestra los números que son importantes para el problema.	20, 20, 5 0, 20, 40, 45

Pp

English	Español	Example/Ejemplo
penny a coin with a value of 1 cent (1¢).	**moneda de 1¢** moneda con un valor de 1 centavo (1¢).	1 cent 1¢
pentagon a two-dimensional closed shape with exactly 5 sides and 5 angles.	**pentágono** figura bidimensional cerrada que tiene exactamente 5 lados y 5 ángulos.	
picture graph a data display in which pictures are used to show data.	**pictografía** representación de datos en la cual se usan dibujos para mostrar datos.	**Favorite Vegetables** 4 2 3 2 Carrots Beans Broccoli Corn

English	Español	Example/Ejemplo
place value the value assigned to a digit based on its position in a number. For example, the 2 in 324 is in the tens place and has a value of 2 tens, or 20.	**valor posicional** valor de un dígito según su posición en un número. Por ejemplo, el número 2 de 324 está en el lugar de las decenas; entonces, tiene un valor de 2 decenas, o 20.	Hundreds / Tens / Ones: 3 / 2 / 4 → 300 / 20 / 4
PM (or p.m.) the time from noon until before midnight.	**p. m.** tiempo desde el mediodía hasta la medianoche.	PM 7:20

Qq

English	Español	Example/Ejemplo
quadrilateral a two-dimensional closed shape with exactly 4 sides and 4 angles.	**cuadrilátero** figura bidimensional cerrada que tiene exactamente 4 lados y 4 ángulos.	
quarter a coin with a value of 25 cents (25¢).	**moneda de 25¢** moneda con un valor de 25 centavos (25¢).	25 cents 25¢

Rr

English	Español	Example/Ejemplo
rectangle a quadrilateral with 4 square corners. Opposite sides of a rectangle have the same length.	**rectángulo** cuadrilátero con 4 esquinas cuadradas. Los lados opuestos de un rectángulo tienen la misma longitud.	

English	Español	Example/Ejemplo
regroup to put together or break apart ones, tens, or hundreds.	**reagrupar** unir o separar unidades, decenas, o centenas.	Regroup 10 ones as 1 ten
rhombus a quadrilateral with all sides the same length.	**rombo** cuadrilátero cuyos lados tienen todos la misma longitud.	
row a side-by-side (horizontal) line of objects or numbers, such as in an array or table.	**fila** línea horizontal de objetos o números, tal como las que aparecen en una matriz o una tabla. Los objetos o los números están uno al lado del otro.	
ruler a measuring stick that is marked in inches and centimeters. It shows 12 inches and 30 centimeters.	**regla** vara que tiene marcas que muestran pulgadas y centímetros. Muestra 12 pulgadas y 30 centímetros.	Ruler shown is not life-size.

English	Español	Example/Ejemplo
Ss		
second (s) a unit of time. There are 60 seconds in 1 minute.	**segundo (s)** unidad de tiempo. 60 segundos equivalen a 1 minuto.	60 seconds = 1 minute
shorter having a length or height that is less than that of another object.	**más bajo** que tiene una altura menor que la de otro objeto. **más corto** que tiene una longitud menor que la de otro objeto.	← shorter
side a line segment that forms part of a two-dimensional shape.	**lado** segmento de recta que forma parte de una figura bidimensional.	side
skip-count count by a number other than ones, such as count by twos, fives, tens, or hundreds.	**contar salteado** no contar de uno en uno, sino de otra forma, como de 2 en 2, de 5 en 5, de 10 en 10, y de 100 en 100.	Skip-count by twos: 2, 4, 6, 8
square a quadrilateral with 4 square corners and 4 sides of equal length.	**cuadrado** cuadrilátero que tiene 4 esquinas cuadradas y 4 lados de igual longitud.	

English	Español	Example/Ejemplo
subtract to take from, take apart, or compare to find the difference.	**restar** quitar, separar, o comparar para hallar la diferencia.	3 2 7 10 12 12 − 5 = 7
sum the result of addition.	**suma** el resultado de la suma.	34 + 25 = 59

Tt

English	Español	Example/Ejemplo
taller having a height that is greater than that of another object.	**más alto** que tiene una altura mayor que la de otro objeto.	taller
tens groups of 10 ones.	**decenas** grupos de 10 unidades.	3 tens
thirds the parts formed when a whole is divided into three equal parts.	**tercios** partes que se forman cuando se divide un entero en tres partes iguales.	3 equal parts